*"There are some people in*
*Others actually do it. Wil*
*the founder of The Salvatio*
*of two million soldiers marching to the beat of Isaiah 58). He is a visionary for the whole church. His ability to see into the future, and pull down a new thing for the rest of us to live, is the stuff of prophets and apostles. If there is a voice for our day and our time, bringing social reform and spiritual passion together in a cataclysm of Kingdom Come, it's William Booth. I recommend you listen and learn and live out all that Booth saw that is still to come."*

**– Danielle Strickland**

*"This is a glorious treasure trove of daily readings from the pen of William Booth. Stephen Poxon has created a superb anthology of devotional gems by the founder of The Salvation Army. William Booth richly deserves his twenty-first century comeback as an inspirational guide to the Scriptures."*

**– Jonathan Aitken**

*"William Booth was a cataclysmic catalyst for revolutionary change in the spiritual realm, in social welfare, and in the world of justice, always dangerously underrated and still not effectively imitated. Through the Year with William Booth will be a catalyst for revolutionary change in your life – in the spiritual realm, in social action, and in the fight for justice."*

**– Stephen Court**

*"Acknowledged as the world over a visionary social reformer, William Booth was first of all a preacher and a student of the Bible. Through a long life devoted to reaching the unconverted, William also poured his heart out in writings which today help us to understand this great man's vision. Stephen Poxon has quite brilliantly linked William's words to Scripture giving us a most worthy contribution to our personal devotions."*

**– Bramwell Booth**

# Through the Year with William Booth

Edited by
Stephen Poxon

Monarch
Books

Oxford, UK & Grand Rapids, Michigan, USA

Published by
**Lion Hudson Limited**
Wilkinson House, Jordan Hill Business Park,
Banbury Road, Oxford OX2 8DR, England
www.lionhudson.com

ISBN 978 0 85721 614 4 (hardback)
ISBN 978 0 85721 890 2 (paperback)
e-ISBN 978 0 85721 615 1

First hardback edition 2015
First paperback edition 2015

**Acknowledgments**
Scripture quotations marked ESV are from The Holy Bible, English Standard Version® (ESV®) copyright © 2001 by Crossway, a publishing ministry of Good News Publishers. All rights reserved.
Extracts marked KJV from The Authorized (King James) Version. Rights in the Authorized Version are vested in the Crown. Reproduced by permission of the Crown's patentee, Cambridge University Press.
Scripture taken from *The Message*. Copyright © by Eugene H. Peterson 1993, 1994, 1995, 1996, 2000, 2001, 2002. Used by permission of NavPress Publishing Group.
Scripture marked NASB taken from the New American Standard Bible®, Copyright © 1960, 1962, 1963, 1968, 1971, 1972, 1973, 1975, 1977, 1995 by The Lockman Foundation. Used by permission.
Scripture marked NET quoted by permission. Quotations designated (NET) are from the NET Bible® copyright ©1996–2006 by Biblical Studies Press, L.L.C. http://bible.org. All rights reserved.
Scripture quotations marked NIV taken from the Holy Bible, New International Version Anglicised. Copyright © 1979, 1984, 2011 Biblica, formerly International Bible Society. Used by permission of Hodder & Stoughton Ltd, an Hachette UK company. All rights reserved. "NIV" is a registered trademark of Biblica. UK trademark number 1448790.
Scripture quotations marked NLT are taken from the Holy Bible, New Living Translation, copyright © 1996, 2004, 2007 by Tyndale House Foundation. Used by permission of Tyndale House Publishers, Inc., Carol Stream, Illinois 60188. All rights reserved.

A catalogue record for this book is available from the British Library

Printed and bound in the USA, November 2018, LH37

*For Dad*

# Acknowledgments

I am truly indebted to the staff of Lion Hudson (Monarch) for their kind and patient guidance throughout the production of this book. My thanks are due to them for their encouragement, their gentle corrections, and their most helpful suggestions.

Likewise, I am very grateful to my good friend, the respected journalist, broadcaster, and author, Cathy Le Feuvre, who was gracious enough to recommend me for this assignment, when she could easily have added this title to her repertoire instead. Such altruism is rare.

Major Wendy Goodman, friend and fine Salvation Army officer, entrusted a number of her vintage Salvation Army books to my care, enabling crucial research to flow at a much quicker pace than it would otherwise have done. Wendy's ready willingness to lend me antique publications precious to her is by no means taken for granted.

Dawn Volz, stalwart member of the publishing department in The Salvation Army's Australia Southern Territory, was equally encouraging, voluntarily and enthusiastically sending me materials from the other side of the globe.

From the USA came ready cooperation in the form of National Salvation Army Archivist, Susan Mitchem, who responded to my transatlantic request for information with zeal and expertise. So too Ruth Macdonald, Archive Assistant at The Salvation Army's International Heritage Centre in London.

My sincere thanks are humbly extended to one and all.

Last, but definitely not least, I must also thank my wife, Heather, and my children, Jasmine and Alistair, for putting up with me while I have been busy writing, and for tolerating the loss of a kitchen table while it has been commandeered as a temporary desk.

# Introduction

William Booth – pawnbroker's assistant, Methodist minister, firebrand preacher, humanitarian, family man, devoted husband, radical reformer, advocate of women's rights, friend of the poor, hymn writer and author, outspoken critic of the idle rich, confidant of statesmen, politicians, and royalty, father of eight children, street preacher, champion of the marginalized, and Founder and first General of The Salvation Army.

Booth crammed more into his eighty-three years (1829–1912) than most people would in several lifetimes. Converted to Jesus Christ at the age of fifteen, and increasingly dissatisfied with an established Church that appeared to care little for the destitute and suffering, and which he thought all too often preached an inadequate gospel, this plain-speaking evangelist and campaigner set about his ministry with an energy and a fiery passion reminiscent of an Old Testament prophet with little time to spare.

Impressively tall, and latterly resplendent with flowing white beard, Booth unashamedly employed every natural, God-given skill at his disposal to evangelize, serve the neglected masses, and raise up what is now an international Christian movement at work in over 120 countries. He did so with flair and courage, long hours of work, superb oratory, wit, and a forthright belief in his God and the truth of the Bible. Taking on all-comers – publicans who violently opposed his ministry, influential public figures who denounced him in no uncertain terms, magazine editors who portrayed and ridiculed him as corrupt and dishonest, and leading Victorian clerics who disowned him as insanely irreverent – William Booth saw it as his mission to make the gospel relevant to people who showed little awareness of religion, and in whom the Church had appeared to lose all interest.

Far from condemning chronic drunkards, prostitutes and thieves as disgusting rejects worthy only of Hell, Booth set out to persuade them of the love of God for them personally, and of the possibility of their arrival in Heaven one day. Taking Jesus as his great example, he ignored his critics – including those who publicly decried him as the Anti-Christ – and reached out to people who considered themselves well outside the reach and concern of Almighty God and society at large. He did so with a panache rarely seen since, hiring tents and music halls for his meetings, knowing that his intended congregations would never be seen dead inside a church building. A risk-taking showman to his fingertips, Booth instinctively spotted opportunities for innovative evangelism a mile away; famously, and controversially, adapting music hall songs to Christian lyrics and endorsing the use of brass bands, all the better to reach the lost. Likewise, the gradual introduction of Salvation Army uniforms in an era when military garb was particularly grand, its wearers commanding huge respect. Prayer and practicality were the hallmarks of his burning ambition to spend his life on behalf of God and others.

General Booth's spiritual awakening and faith may well have originated in the heavenlies, but it reached him in working-class Nottingham, England, and he thereafter consistently eschewed any religious expression that did not incorporate care for people as holistic beings. He ridiculed the idea of preaching to a poor beggar while that beggar was still cold and hungry, insisting that hot sermons were better received if hot soup had first been dispensed. A man of high moral probity, he was never once afraid to be labelled the outspoken defender of street girls who would sell their infested bodies for a stale crust. An intelligent man, he would present Christ in the basic vocabulary of illiterate listeners, wooing them with a wealth of illustrative stories that made the claims of his Lord all the more fascinating and attractive to those whose lives were drab and hopeless. A man of unwavering faith in the goodness of God and the transforming efficacy of Christian teaching, he persisted against what were, often, seemingly overwhelming odds.

Booth was no lightweight theologian. He studied hard to show himself a minister who could be trusted with the word of God, painstakingly teaching himself the truths of Scripture and learning from the example of contemporary evangelists in order to develop and establish his personal theology, aided and abetted in no small way by the towering intellectual influence of his beloved wife, Catherine. His ability to effortlessly weave Bible phrases into his conversation and writing was probably unparalleled, owing much to his powers of memory and recall. In an age when appalling poverty was widespread and formalized social care lacked compassion, Booth employed every visionary power at his disposal to formulate sympathetic ideas for the betterment of his fellow human beings, and then set about skilfully persuading wealthy sympathizers to sponsor his magnificent projects. One cannot doubt a degree of persuasive charm at work, this too consecrated to God's service.

General William Booth was not by any means a plaster saint, and he knew it – so too did those around him! He was every inch a human being, with an explosive temper, an ability to permanently ostracize those who upset him, a tendency towards dark, depressive moods, and what could at times seem like a colossal insensitivity to differing viewpoints regarding the way the Church at large should go about its business. Some of his formidable strengths were also his weaknesses, just as some of his eccentricities were his bravest traits. Here was an ordinary man who one day declared that "God shall have all there is of William Booth" (faults and failings not excluded) and whose extraordinary ministry reached not only thousands upon thousands in Victorian England but whose Salvation Army today reaches out across continents and islands; in the words of one of Booth's successors as General, John Gowans, "Saving souls, growing saints, and serving suffering humanity."

Compiling this book has been an immense privilege, and nothing less than a personal spiritual adventure. I am indebted to friends who responded generously and enthusiastically to my cry for help in unearthing Booth's writings, and for lending me some of his books. His output was prolific, and what is astonishing is that only the smallest fraction of that output could rightly be deemed outdated or unsuitable for adaptation, even now. The internet has proven itself a tremendous ally in tracking down marvellous books that, despite their Victorian context, really should be lining the shelves of all good Christian bookshops. Nowadays, the General's works of encouragement, perceptive insight, and straightforward, uncomplicated "how to" are – sadly – buried treasures, and it baffles me why William Booth's name is not permanently on the lips of modern Church growth experts and people who wish to see their churches engaging robustly with their communities instead of remaining largely irrelevant. His thoughts compare well to anything produced since; this innovative, pioneering man still has a very great deal to teach us. If I have done anything at all in editing these pages, it has been to dust off inspirational teaching that should never have been allowed to become dusty in the first place. I feel as though I have handled lost gems. Without question, my own eyes have been opened, my spirit stirred, and my heart set racing as I have pored over the written thoughts and convictions of a spiritual giant. If that proves to be the experience of just one reader, then every hour of work will have been more than worth it.

William Booth laid down his sword in 1912, but who can doubt that "he being dead yet speaketh"? As many of the problems and challenges faced in his day and age continue to surface, and the fight against evil remains a live one, we who claim Christ as Lord and Saviour might wish to reflect upon the life and times of a remarkable character, and ask God to take all there is of us, that we might serve the modern age.

General William Booth – in many ways, ahead of his time, yet contemporary and, we might feel, a man for all seasons. In these pages, we glimpse the mind of a genius who viewed everything in the context of eternity. Dipping into some of his works, we sense at least a little of his passion and motivation. As we read them today, just over a century after his promotion to Glory, may they inspire us in our discipleship.

# January 1st

I am doing a new thing!

(Isaiah 43:19 *NIV)*

When this page reaches you, you will be on the threshold of New Year. New things interest us. They have done so from our cradle; they will do so to the end chapter of life. What a pleasure we derived in childhood from a new toy, a new game, or a new sweetmeat! And since then have we not found pleasure in a new house, a new friend, a new occupation, or a new country? This is according to a law of our nature. Change suits us and gratifies us. And as it has charmed us in this life so there can be little doubt that it will continue to do so through the rolling ages of the glorious future. New experiences and events will constitute some of the unfailing sources of pleasure there. We shall doubtless be continually seeing new beings, singing new songs, visiting new worlds, engaging in new adventures, experiencing new raptures, and having new revelations, not only of the character, wisdom, and works of God, but of his affection for us. Oh, what a charming, what a glorious place will the New Jerusalem be! My comrades, we must be ready for the new heavens and the new earth – new, indeed, to you and me because therein will dwell righteousness… [1]

A new thing is wanted and prized because it produces a sensation of pleasure – that is, supposing it is a pleasing thing; and another reason why a new thing is valued is because it is supposed to bring with it some new conditions of happiness, some new opportunities for obtaining the things on which the heart is set. A vain woman finds pleasure in thinking of a new dress because she thinks it will bring her admiration. A proud man finds pleasure in getting into a big house because he thinks his neighbours will think more highly of him…

I hope all we Salvationists are looking forward to, and praying for, the New Year, because it promises to afford us new opportunities of getting more of the gifts of the Holy Spirit in our own souls and spreading salvation more effectively.[2]

**Father, I praise you because you are ever-willing to bless. Open my eyes to the newness of your works, my heart to a new beat, and my soul to a new and living touch. Send a new touch of power, Lord. Amen.**

1 Revelation 21:1–2

2 From *The General's Letters.*

# January 2nd

### Zeal for your house will consume me

(John 2:17 *NIV*)

A New Year wants a new self, and it will be like the old – the same over again – unless you are new. The world outside you – here and hereafter – can only make you happy in proportion as the world inside you is a happy one. You must have new purpose; that is, a renewed one – the same as before (for I am talking now to soldiers who have already made up their minds to live holy lives, and spend all their strength for the salvation of men); but now we want a more desperate, whole-souled determination to live out, before ourselves and before God and before everybody about us, the boasted consecration of this religion. No more time-serving! No more living to please men! No more of even the very appearance of trying to serve God and Mammon![1] Inward and outward holiness of life is what we must and will have. Souls! Souls! Souls! Every day, everywhere – in season and out of season, must be our motto.[2] Onward! Reckless of consequences in the following of Christ.

There must be a new industry. Oh the lost opportunities – the unused, unimproved privileges – the unemployed hours – the wasted, more than wasted days of the past years! Oh, what hosts of sinners are damned by sheer idleness! They are too lazy to save themselves. They will not be at the trouble to pick up the gold and diamonds and coronets of Heaven that lie at their feet. They will not turn over the pages and read the documents and accept the free gifts and sign their names to the deeds of the hallelujah estates that are offered them in the heavenly Canaan. They lie down and sleep, too lazy to drink of the River of Life[3] that flows past their feet, and so perish. They are left outside the gates of gold because they are too lazy to walk in.

But if sinners perish through their own laziness, how many multitudes perish through the laziness of saints! Oh, this horrid attempt to delegate our responsibilities with regard to perishing men and women to others – to the minister, to the captain, to the sergeants – to anybody.[4]

**Father, what a privilege it is to be working alongside you! Grant me new strength at the start of this year – an energy that will make soul-winning a priority and a zeal that refuses to abdicate responsibility. Amen.**

1 Matthew 6:24
2 2 Timothy 4:2
3 Revelation 22:1
4 From *The General's Letters.*

# January 3rd

## Create in me a pure heart, O God

(Psalm 51:10 *NIV*)

You like clean clothes and clean linen, do you not? Consider the money and labour that are expended in keeping your garments clean. You like a clean home. See how the housewife scrubs and washes and brushes and dusts to keep the floor and windows and furniture clean. You like a clean city. What a laborious and costly sweeping of the streets, and carrying away of rubbish there is; and what money is spent on the fixing and cleansing of sewers to keep our towns and cities sweet and pure. We like this sort of purity, because it is pleasant to the eye and good for health. We know that dirt is hateful to the senses, breeds vermin, generates cholera, plague and diseases in general, and hurries people to the grave. So we hate it, and say, "Away with it; let us be clean!"

God loves soul purity. It is his nature to do so. I have no doubt, like us he prefers to see his children outwardly clean. He tells us, through Paul, that we are to have our bodies washed with pure water; but the washing of the heart is far more desirable to him than that of the body…[1]

Yes, God delights in holiness. Heaven, his dwelling-place, is pure. Its inhabitants are pure. Its employments, and enjoyments, and worship are all alike pure… The angels love purity. If any unholy creature could, by any means, be introduced into the Celestial City, the inhabitants would, I am sure, avoid such a creature, as we should avoid a being who had some dreadful disease…

Your happiness and your influence are all connected with your being made holy. Oh, I beseech you to kneel down here and now, and ask God to make you each and all pure, by the power of the Holy Ghost, through the blood of the Lamb.[2]

**Holy God, you always want the very best for me; your plans for me are saturated with goodwill. Thank you that your love for me includes the blessing of a pure heart. Help me to abandon anything that would hinder your good and gracious activity in my life. Amen.**

1 A reference to Hebrews 10:22, although the Pauline authorship of Hebrews is disputed.
2 From *Purity of Heart.*

# January 4th

For God so loved the world that he gave his one and only Son, that whoever believes in him shall not perish but have eternal life

(John 3:16 *NIV*)

The little town of Whitby[1] was startled… by a telegram that in a very few minutes was agitating nearly every individual in the place. The howling waves and roaring seas had kept the town pretty well awake all through the early hours… a ship had been blown on to the rocks, and her crew of six men had been compelled to take refuge in the long-boat. To reach the shore in that sea was impossible, so they had thrown out the anchor and, with the seas breaking over them, all benumbed with cold and ready to perish, they waited for either deliverance or death… Some watchers on the shore who, being unable to render help themselves, telegraphed the calamity to the men of Whitby, in the vague hope that they might be able to do something for their rescue…

Very similar telegrams to this – telegrams of a similarly heart-stirring, agitating character, and telegrams that would be productive of far more important consequences than this, if we could but get them equally credited and considered, are being handed in to us all… telegrams that tell of wrecks and of perishing crews – of fathers and mothers, and brothers and sisters, and children and friends, striking on the rocks of pride, or drink, or fashion, or Mammon, or vice, or conceit, or superstition. Telegrams which tell of men and women created and intended to live in Heaven, striking and going down straight to Hell…

Thank God, they can be helped; but oh, they must be helped at once. Already they are benumbed, frozen, all but past feeling. A little longer, and they will be gone! Oh, wire – telegraph, somebody! Will no one rush in? Is there no lifeboat for these perishing souls? Is there no eye to pity, no arm to save? Heaven and earth telegraph and entreat you to help this rescue.[2]

**You are a saving God, with a plan of salvation bearing glorious hallmarks of divine love and compassion. Thank you for sending Jesus to the rescue. Please increase my understanding of what his sacrifice means. I pray you would make Calvary real to me, that I might love you and praise you more. Amen.**

1 A coastal town and fishing port in the north-east of England.
2 From *Salvation Soldiery*.

# JANUARY 5TH

A BRUISED REED HE WILL NOT BREAK, AND A SMOULDERING WICK HE WILL NOT SNUFF OUT

(Matthew 12:20 *NIV*)

What, then, is the standard towards which we may venture to aim with some prospect of realization in our time? It is a very humble one, but if realized it would solve the worst problems of modern society. It is the standard of the London cab-horse. When in the streets of London a cab-horse, weary or careless or stupid, trips and falls and lies stretched out in the midst of the traffic, there is no question of debating how he came to stumble before we try to get him on his legs again.

The cab-horse is a very real illustration of poor broken-down humanity; he usually falls down because of overwork and underfeeding. If you put him on his feet without altering his conditions, it would only be to give him another dose of agony; but first of all you'll need to pick him up again. It may have been through overwork or underfeeding, or it may be all his own fault that he has broken his knees and smashed the shafts; but that does not matter.

If not for his own sake, then merely in order to prevent an obstruction of the traffic, all attention is concentrated upon the question of how we are to get him on his legs again. The load is taken off, the harness is unbuckled or, if need be, cut, and everything is done to help him up. Then he is put in the shafts again, and once more restored to his regular round of work…

Every cab-horse in London has three things: a shelter for the night, food for its stomach, and work allotted to it by which it can earn its corn… When he is down he is helped up, and while he lives he has food, shelter, and work. That, although a humble standard, is at present utterly unattainable by millions – literally by millions – of our fellow men and women in this country…

Can the cab-horse charter[1] be gained for human beings? I answer, "Yes." The cab-horse standard can be attained on cab-horse terms.[2]

**God of our fragile hearts, you meet us carefully and with deep understanding, when our stores of endurance are exhausted. I lift before you in prayer those who stumble or fall under the weight of life, who cannot lift themselves. Embrace them with your customary gentleness, I pray. Amen.**

1 Booth's generic term for the yardstick against which many of his social reforms were set.
2 From *In Darkest England and the Way Out*.

# January 6th

GOD WAS PLEASED TO HAVE ALL HIS FULLNESS DWELL IN HIM, AND THROUGH HIM TO RECONCILE TO HIMSELF ALL THINGS, WHETHER THINGS ON EARTH OR THINGS IN HEAVEN, BY MAKING PEACE THROUGH HIS BLOOD, SHED ON THE CROSS

(Colossians 1:19, 20 *NIV*)

What do we mean by the atonement? The word itself simply means at-one-ment, the uniting of two beings who had been separate or apart. In everyday language the word is used to signify something done by the wrongdoer to make amends for the injuries he has inflicted on others. In religion the word atonement is used to signify the sacrifice which Jesus Christ offered for our sins, by his death on the cross, by which offering the reconciliation of God and man was made possible.

Some mistaken notions are entertained with respect to the benefits flowing out of the atonement… Salvationists object to the view that Christ by his sacrifice made salvation possible or certain to a chosen portion only of the human race, leaving the remainder outside the possibility of that salvation. This doctrine is generally described by the terms "election" and "reprobation", and is more commonly known as Calvinism.[1] It sets forth the belief that one portion of mankind is elected by God to everlasting life, and the remaining portion reprobated to everlasting death. This doctrine is condemned by Salvationists…

It is in opposition to the emphatic declarations of the Bible that Christ died for all men. "For the grace of God that bringeth salvation hath appeared to all men" (Titus 2:11 *KJV*). And again: "that he by the grace of God should taste death for every man" (Hebrews 2:9 *KJV*). It is in opposition to what we know of the nature of God, as set forth in the Scriptures. He is described in the Bible as a just and benevolent Being, which this doctrine seems most emphatically to deny.

It is in opposition to our natural sense of justice. That multitudes of human beings should be appointed to suffer everlasting death, independently of any choice or action of their own, is revolting to our conceptions of right and wrong, to say nothing about our natural sympathies with suffering.[2]

**Heavenly Father, it was because of love that Jesus died, so that I could be reconciled with you. This is sometimes a love too wonderful to comprehend. I pray for an increased awareness of the glory of the atonement, so that my devotion to you increases. Amen.**

1 After the teaching of the theologian John Calvin.
2 From *The Founder Speaks Again*.

# January 7th

For the Spirit God gave us does not make us timid, but gives us power, love and self-discipline

(2 Timothy 1:7 *NIV*)

Faith in God is one of the simplest things in the world [yet] many people find it very difficult to believe. To help those who are troubled in this direction, I want to offer a few counsels, which are largely suggested by my own experience.

1. The first recommendation I make to those thus troubled is to offer themselves up without reserve to do the whole will of God, so far as that will has been made known to them. Strive after a spirit of wholehearted confidence, and do not allow any suspicions or doubts about his goodness to dwell in your hearts.

2. Get to know all you can about the character, ability, and works of God, especially those which are likely to influence your own life, interests, and doings.

3. The more you know about God, and the principles which govern his dealings with men, the better you will be able to trust him. The reason why many people find it so difficult to confide in God is because they know so little about him. How often you will hear people say, "When I first met a certain individual I thought him proud, and hard, and harsh in his character and conduct; but when I came to know him personally, and saw him benevolent in his dealings with those about him, I felt that I could leave my highest interests, nay, my life, in his hands without a misgiving or a fear."

4. Just so with God, to know him is not only to admire him, but to trust him.

5. In order to exercise faith for the blessings purchased by Jesus Christ, and promised by God in his book, you must discover as far as possible what they are.

Some… live in ignorance of the fact that God has promised to bestow them. They do not know of their existence or their value, or much less God's willingness to bestow them, or of the conditions upon which their bestowment is made to depend.[1]

**Emboldening God, you are not a distant deity, remote, unfeeling. You understand our reluctant, faltering steps. This day, please help me to receive from your hand, and to do so in faith, confident of your generosity. Amen.**

1 From *The Founder's Messages to Soldiers.*

# January 8th

**Remember your Creator in the days of your youth, before the days of trouble come**

(Ecclesiastes 12:1 *NIV*)

1. What is the supreme duty of parents with regard to their children? The duty of parents to their children is so to govern, influence, and inspire them, that they shall love, serve, and enjoy God, and in consequence grow up to be good, holy, and useful men and women. "… the father to the children shall make known thy truth."[1]

2. Can such a course of conduct be followed with children as may be reasonably expected to make them good and Christ-like?

We think so; nay, we go further. We maintain that such early training is the God-appointed and only method which can be reckoned upon with certainty to develop children into godly men and women. As surely as the child makes the man, so surely does training make both child and man.

Let the child develop and strengthen that which is mean, selfish, and devilish in him, and you will have a bad man; whereas, if you prune, subdue, and eradicate the evil, and develop, strengthen, and encourage the good, inspiring him with the love of all truth, holiness, and benevolence, he will grow up to be a good, godly, and benevolent man.

3. But do not many who have been thus trained get converted in mature life, and become both good and useful?

Yes, thank God, they do… but for every one thus saved, it is to be feared a hundred perish. Surely you don't want your children to go after "the prodigal"[2] and run such a risk of damnation. God's way for the salvation of the children of his saints is not that they are to be trained in sin and then converted, but that they are to be converted in being trained in his fear and grace. But even if you were sure that your children would be converted in mature life, after a childhood and youth of sinful indulgence, how dishonouring to God and injurious to your child and others would be such a career! Why not save your boy from so miserable an experience by moulding him in childhood for a holy life?[3]

**Great Father, I pray for parents and grandparents. Bless them as they grapple with, and enjoy, the multi-complexities and responsibilities of parenthood. May their example stand their children in good stead at home, at school, and within their friendships. Amen.**

1 Isaiah 38:19 *KJV*
2 Luke 15:11–32
3 From *The Training of Children.*

# JANUARY 9TH

IN THE LAST DAYS, GOD SAYS, I WILL POUR OUT MY SPIRIT ON ALL PEOPLE. YOUR SONS AND DAUGHTERS WILL PROPHESY, YOUR YOUNG MEN WILL SEE VISIONS, YOUR OLD MEN WILL DREAM DREAMS

(Acts 2:17 *NIV*)

I am now sixty-one years of age. The last eighteen months, during which the continual partner of all my activities for now nearly forty years has laid in the arms of unspeakable suffering, has added more than many, many former ones, to the exhaustion of my term of service.[1] I feel already something of the pressure which led the dying Emperor of Germany[2] to say, "I have no time to be weary." If I am to see the accomplishment in any considerable degree of these life-long hopes [welfare reforms], I must be enabled to embark upon the enterprise without delay, and with the worldwide burden constantly upon me in connection with the universal mission of our universal Army I cannot be expected to struggle in this matter alone.

But I trust that the upper and middle classes are at last being awakened out of their long slumber with regard to the permanent improvement of the lot of those who have hitherto been regarded as forever abandoned and hopeless. Shame indeed upon England if, with the example presented to us nowadays by the Emperor and government of Germany,[3] we simply shrug our shoulders, and pass on again to our business or our pleasure leaving these wretched multitudes in the gutters where they have lain so long. No, no, no; time is short. Let us arise in the name of God and humanity, and wipe away the sad stigma from the British banner that our horses are treated better than our labourers.

It will be seen that this scheme[4] contains many branches. It is probable that some of my readers may not be able to endorse the plan as a whole… Where this is so, we shall be glad for them to assist us in carrying out those portions of the undertaking which more especially command their sympathy and commend themselves to their judgment.

**Eternal God, my prayers today are for those distressed and disorientated by the dull agony of loss and mourning; comfort them, I pray, and help us each to labour for the Master until we too are called Home, with vision and courage. Amen.**

1 From *In Darkest England and the Way Out*, published in 1890. William Booth's wife, Catherine, was promoted to Glory in October 1890 after a lengthy illness. The book was dedicated to her memory.
2 Kaiser Wilhelm I.
3 Germany had embarked upon a system of welfare reform that was the largest and most successful in the world in its time.
4 Booth's "Darkest England" revolutionary blueprint for social reform in England.

# January 10th

The Lord added to their number daily those who were being saved

(Acts 2:47 *NIV*)

In the Riding School[1] yesterday grand meetings, but rather noisy: packed – 5,000 present – and, they say, 15,000 outside. Good collections. In the afternoon it appeared as if the devil himself was there trying to injure us. Oh, what a noise, jumping on the benches, smashing them down. Where are the police? They are of no use in a crowd. We cried unto the Lord, and he gave us the victory.

In the evening, wonderful time. We can hardly hear each other's voices, but our soldiers[2] sung in grand style; they are real "Blood-and-Fire"[3] people.

"Into the prayer meeting," said our leader. "Keep the doors of the platform open," and up came the penitent people, amid all the noise and shouting, weeping their way to the cross. In a few minutes there were over seven yards of them crying for mercy. Oh, that some door will be opened, so that we may go on. If we cannot find one, by God's help we will – we must force one. Pray for us.

Wherever we go, places packed. A congregation consisting of high people, and the lowest amongst the low. Thousands turned away, and still a place which holds 1,500 (seated) is crammed with 4,000, and the theatre, seated for 700, packed with 1,100. The masses stood outside for hours, knocked at doors and windows; took a ladder, put it against the wall, the same night, at the windows of the gallery, smashed three windows, and walked in. We had about thirty soldiers on the platform yesterday (Sunday), and when the roughs saw their old companions, and heard them confess, they were like wild people, screaming over and over again.

More and more storm now. From one meeting Lieutenant S. and I were followed to the gate of our house by a mass of people, who made an awful noise. The next night a ragged man came crying, telling us he was amongst the persecutors: he begged our pardon, and wanted salvation.[4]

**God the Holy Spirit, you speak marvellously to the hearts of men, women and children, imparting a supernatural sense of conviction followed immediately by the gracious reassurance of salvation. On this day, I pray for those involved in outreach and evangelism; strengthen their message. May many to respond to the gospel. Amen.**

1 In the early days of The Salvation Army, meetings (services) were held in all sorts of venues; tents, theatres, barns, etc.

2 Full members of The Salvation Army are known as junior or senior soldiers.

3 "Blood and Fire" is a Salvation Army motto denoting the blood of Christ and the fire of the Holy Spirit.

4 From *The Salvation War, 1883.*

# January 11th

Jacob replied, "I will not let you go unless you bless me"

**(Genesis 32:26 *NIV*)**

Be content with nothing less than the assurance that God has really and truly cleansed your soul from sin. Do not allow yourselves to rest in any pleasant feelings merely, or in any hope of a future revelation on the subject. Continue to wrestle, and pray, and believe, until you are satisfied that the work is accomplished. But do you ask again, "How can I tell whether God has cleansed my soul from sin?" I reply, "How did you find out that God had forgiven your sins? How did you come to know that precious fact?" For, assuredly, a precious fact it was when you were saved…

"How did you come to the personal assurance that you were saved?" I ask, and you reply that God spoke it to your heart. Well, the assurance of your sanctification will come in the same way.[1] The Holy Spirit will produce a delightful persuasion in your soul that all the pride and malice, and envy and selfishness, have been taken away, and that God has filled you with peace and love.

This precious persuasion will, no doubt, come in different forms to different individuals. To some it will appear as the "Rest of Faith", to others as the "Baptism of Fire", to others as the "Fullness of Love", and to others as the enthronement of Christ come to reign in their souls – supreme over an inward Kingdom, which is righteousness, peace, and joy in the Holy Ghost.[2]

But to all alike, when the work is real and complete there will be the conviction that the blood cleanses and that the heart is pure. Be content with nothing less than this, and leave to God's good pleasure the giving or withholding of more. Being satisfied that God has purified your heart, confess the fact. You must do so, if you want to retain the blessing. Many of the holiest men and women… have, under the influence of false modesty or diffidence or other motives, been hindered from avowing the wonderful things that God has done for them, and have thereby grieved the Holy Spirit[3] and lost the blessing.[4]

**Thank you for the uniquely precious gift of your indwelling Spirit, whose work is to cleanse, improve, and occupy. I pray that your Spirit will have his way in my life, until no part of me is unfit to host his presence. Holy Spirit, make a better me. Amen.**

1 Possibly, an allusion to Doctrine No. 8 of The Salvation Army: "We believe that we are justified by grace through faith in our Lord Jesus Christ and that he that believeth hath the witness in himself."

2 Romans 14:17

3 Ephesians 4:30

4 From *Purity of Heart.*

# January 12th

Jesus replied, "Foxes have dens to live in, and birds have nests, but the Son of Man has no place even to lay his head."

(Luke 9:58 *NLT*)

There are still a large number of Londoners and a considerable percentage of wanderers from the country in search of work, who find themselves at nightfall destitute. These now betake themselves to the seats under the plane trees under the [Thames] Embankment. Formerly they endeavoured to occupy all the seats, but the lynx-eyed Metropolitan Police declined to allow any such proceedings, and the dossers, knowing the invariable kindness of the City Police,[1] made tracks for that portion of the Embankment which, lying east of the Temple, comes under the control of the Civic Fathers. Here, between the Temple and Blackfriars,[2] I found the poor wretches by the score; almost every seat contained its full complement of six – some men, some women – all reclining in various postures and nearly all fast asleep. Just as Big Ben strikes two, the moon, flashing across the Thames and lighting up the stonework of the Embankment, brings into relief a pitiable spectacle. Here on the stone abutments, which afford a slight protection from the biting wind, are scores of men lying side by side, huddled together for warmth and, of course, without any other covering than their ordinary clothing, which is scanty enough at the best.

Some have laid down a few pieces of waste paper, by way of taking the chill off the stones, but the majority are too tired even for that, and the nightly toilet of most consists of first removing the hat, swathing the head in whatever old rag may be doing duty as a handkerchief, and then replacing the hat. The intelligent-looking elderly man who was just fixing himself up on a set, informed me that he frequently made this his night's abode. "You see," quoth he, "there's nowhere else so comfortable… I had no money for lodgings, couldn't earn any, try as I might. I've had one bit of bread today, nothing else whatever, and I've earned nothing today or yesterday… It's very fair out here of nights, seats rather hard, but a bit of waste paper makes it a lot softer."[3]

**God of compassion, I pray for those whose bed is the pavement, and for those who minister to them – The Salvation Army and other organizations – reaching out with faith in action. Bless their work, and comfort those they will contact this night. Amen.**

1 The Metropolitan Police Service is responsible for law enforcement in Greater London, excluding the "square mile" of the City of London, which is the responsibility of the City of London Police.

2 An area of central London, in the vicinity of Temple Church.

3 From *In Darkest England and the Way Out.*

# January 13th

THEY PICKED UP THE PIECES AND FILLED TWELVE BASKETS WITH SCRAPS LEFT BY THE PEOPLE

(John 6:13 *NLT*)

We all know the itinerant umbrella mender… that gentleman is almost the only agency by which old umbrellas can be rescued from the dust heap… We shall have a great umbrella works. The ironwork of one umbrella will be fitted to the stick of another, and even from those that are too hopelessly gone for any further use as umbrellas we shall find plenty of use for their steels and whalebone…

Bottles are a fertile source of minor domestic worry. When you buy a bottle you have to pay a penny for it; but when you have emptied it you cannot get a penny back… You throw your empty bottle either into the dust heap, or let it lie about. But if we could collect all the waste bottles of London every day, it would hardly go with us if we could not turn a very pretty penny by washing them, sorting them, and sending them out on a new lease of life. The washing of old bottles alone will keep a considerable number of people going.

I can imagine the objection which will be raised by some short-sighted people, that by giving the old, second-hand material a new lease of life it will be said that we diminish the demand for new material, and so curtail work and wages at one end while we are endeavouring to piece on something at the other. This objection reminds me of… a North Country pilot who, when speaking of the dullness in the shipbuilding industry, said that nothing would do any good but a series of heavy storms, which would send a goodly number of ocean-going steamers to the bottom, to replace which, this political economist thought, the yards would once more be filled with orders. This, however, is not the way in which work is supplied. Economy is a great auxiliary to trade, inasmuch as the money saved is expended on other products of industry.[1]

**Father, in your economy, no one is on the scrapheap. You are a God who gently recycles lives. I pray for those who are marginalized, unwanted. Reach out to them, Lord; re-design their lives. Let the pattern be divine. Amen.**

1 From *In Darkest England and the Way Out.*

# January 14th

As God's chosen people, holy and dearly loved, clothe yourselves with compassion

(Colossians 3:12 *NIV*)

"Discharged ill, and nowhere to go, are you?" said her new friend. "Well, come home to my mother's; she will lodge you, and we'll go to work together, when you are quite strong." The girl consented gladly, but found herself conducted to the very lowest part of Woolwich[1] and ushered into a brothel;… She was hoaxed, and powerless to resist. Her protestations were too late to save her, and having had her character forced from her she became hopeless…

There is no need for me to go into the details of the way in which men and women, whose whole livelihood depends upon their success in disarming the suspicions of their victims and luring them to their doom, contrive to overcome the reluctance of the young girl without parents, friends, or helpers to enter their toils.

What fraud fails to accomplish, a little force succeeds in effecting; and a girl who has been guilty of nothing but imprudence finds herself an outcast for life. The very innocence of a girl tells against her. A woman of the world, once entrapped, would have all her wits about her to extricate herself from the position in which she found herself. A perfectly virtuous girl is so often overcome with shame and horror that there seems nothing in life worth struggling for. She accepts her doom without further struggle, and treads the long and torturing pathway of "the streets" to the grave.

"Judge not, that ye be not judged" [2] is a saying that applies most appropriately of all to these unfortunates. Many of them would have escaped their evil fate had they been less innocent. They are where they are because they loved too utterly to calculate consequences, and trusted too absolutely to dare to suspect evil. And others are there because of the false education which confounds ignorance with virtue, and throws our young people into the midst of a great city, with all its excitements and all its temptations, without more preparation or warning than if they were going to live in the Garden of Eden.[3]

**God of the trapped, forgive me if I have judged anyone, and hear my prayers for those who are forced into a miserable and frightening way of life. Please mightily intervene through those agencies, such as The Salvation Army, who care enough to act. Amen.**

1 South-east London.
2 Matthew 7:1 *KJV*
3 From *In Darkest England and the Way Out.*

# January 15th

A righteous man knows the rights of the poor

(Proverbs 29:7 *ESV*)

Darkest England[1] may be described as consisting broadly of three circles, one within the other. The outer and widest circle is inhabited by the starving and the homeless, but honest, poor. The second by those who live by vice; and the third and innermost region at the centre is peopled by those who exist by crime. The whole of the three circles is sodden in drink. Darkest England has many more public houses than the Forest of Aruwimi[2] has rivers, of which Mr Stanley[3] sometimes had to cross three in half an hour.

The borders of this great lost land are not sharply defined. They are continually expanding or contracting. Whenever there is a period of depression in trade, they stretch; when prosperity returns, they contract. So far as individuals are concerned, there are none among the hundreds of thousands who live upon the outskirts of the dark forest who can truly say that they or their children are secure from being hopelessly entangled in its labyrinth. The death of the breadwinner, a long illness, a failure in the City, or any one of a thousand other causes which might be named, will bring within the first circle those who at present imagine themselves free from all danger of actual want.

The death rate in Darkest England is high… But the dead are hardly in their graves before their places are taken by others. Some escape, but the majority, their health sapped by their surroundings, become weaker and weaker, until at last they fall by the way, perishing without hope at the very doors of the palatial mansions which, maybe, some of them helped to build… A great outcry was made concerning the Housing of the Poor[4]… the disease-breeding, manhood-destroying character of many of the tenements in which the poor herd in our large cities. But there is a depth below that of the dweller in the slums. It is that of the dweller in the street, who has not even a lair in the slums which he can call his own.[5]

**Heavenly Father, you gave William Booth a heart to care for poor people. Forbid that I should worship a homeless man one day, then ignore homeless people the next. Draw close to them in their distress and discomfort. Amen.**

1 Writing *In Darkest England and the Way Out*, Booth employed the phrase "Darkest England" as descriptive of the social and moral ills prevalent in his homeland.
2 Democratic Republic of Congo.
3 The explorer, Sir Henry Morton Stanley.
4 A national debate raged in many newspapers on this complex subject.
5 From *In Darkest England and the Way Out.*

# January 16th

Since we are surrounded by such a great cloud of witnesses, let us throw off everything that hinders and the sin that so easily entangles. And let us run with perseverance the race marked out for us

(Hebrews 12:1 *NIV*)

Jesus Christ died not only to save men and women from open and deliberate sin, but to purify unto himself "a peculiar people",[1] inwardly as well as outwardly clean. Has he wrought this deliverance for you, my comrades? Or are you deterred from seeking it by doubts as to his ability to effect this purification of the heart? Let me call a few witnesses who will testify to its realization in their own experience…

1. Enoch walked with God 300 years.[2] God himself testifies that Enoch's ways were pleasing in his sight. What a blessed testimony. Who can question that Enoch had a pure heart?

2. Noah was a good man, and perfect in his generation. So far as he heard the light he lived up to it. He condemned the world and became "heir of the righteousness", that is the holiness "which is by faith".[3] He had a pure heart.

3. The Lord himself testified that Job was a perfect and an upright man. He was perfect in love, and perfect in faith. He was able to look up even in the darkest hour, and say, "Though he slay me, yet will I trust in him."[4] He loved God with all his heart, and his neighbour as himself. He had a pure heart.

4. We have a most remarkable testimony to Abraham's faith and obedience. God told him, as he tells you, to "walk before him, and be… perfect",[5] and we have the most striking evidence of Abraham's obedience to God in the offering up of his son Isaac.[6] Who can doubt that he had a pure heart?

5. Isaiah was a holy man. We read that when the prophet acknowledged his uncleanness in the Temple, God's angel touched his lips with a live coal of fire… and testified that his iniquity was taken away and his sin was purged. Whereupon Isaiah rose up and consecrated himself there and then to go out as the messenger of God.[7, 8]

**Challenged by these examples, I offer you my life afresh. Equip me to be your dedicated servant. Take my life and let it be consecrated to your service. Amen.**

1 1 Peter 2:9 *KJV*
2 Genesis 5:23
3 Hebrews 11:7 *KJV*
4 Job 13:15 *KJV*
5 Genesis 17:1 *KJV*
6 Genesis 22:6
7 Isaiah 6:7
8 From *Purity of Heart.*

# January 17th

Do not think that I have come to abolish the Law or the Prophets; I have not come to abolish them but to fulfil them. For truly, I say to you, until heaven and earth pass away, not an iota, not a dot, will pass from the Law until all is accomplished

(Matthew 5:17–18 *ESV*)

In becoming a man Jesus Christ voluntarily placed himself on the same level, in this respect, as Peter and John; that is to say, the Law required from him, as truly and really as it did from them, all the love and service which his powers enabled him to render. The extent of the Saviour's capacity determined the extent of his obligation. Having an infinite capacity he was under obligation to love and serve in an infinite degree…

Jesus Christ, by his death, offered a sacrifice for the sins of men which was of sufficient value to make amends for the damage done to the honour of the Law by man's transgression. This made it possible for God to forgive the sins of all who truly repent and believe in his Son and determine to live lives of faith and obedience. And we believe that, in virtue of this sacrifice, full forgiveness can be granted to the transgressor, without in any way diminishing, in the estimation of mankind, the honour of God, whom he has offended, the majesty of the law he has broken, or the evil of the sin he has committed. By this divine scheme God can be just, and yet be the Justifier of him that believeth in Jesus.

I want now to mention some of the reasons which are given for refusing to accept the doctrine of the atonement in any form. The first of these affirms that this doctrine is a reflection upon the justice and benevolence of God. Those who bring forward this objection say that while the Bible and our natural instincts represent God as a loving and beneficent Father, this doctrine describes him as a fierce and angry being, who cannot forgive a poor sinner without his Son coming from Heaven to suffer the shame and agony of the cross. But this is a false representation of the subject; it is not the doctrine of the Bible… the true doctrine is just the opposite.[1]

Cont/…

**Father of justice, we haven't a hope of living up to the Law. I bless you for sending Jesus, who fulfilled every requirement of the Law when we patently could not. Thank you for mercy that completely satisfies legal obligations and meets our great need. Amen.**

1 From *The Founder Speaks Again.*

# JANUARY 18TH

WE ARE INSTRUCTED TO TURN FROM GODLESS LIVING AND SINFUL PLEASURES. WE SHOULD LIVE IN THIS EVIL WORLD WITH WISDOM, RIGHTEOUSNESS, AND DEVOTION TO GOD

(Titus 2:12 *NLT*)

Cont/…

The atonement was not necessary to create compassion in the bosom of God for sin-stricken man; it was the compassion of God that generated the atonement. The sacrifice on the cross was not offered to appease the angry wrath of the Father; it was in the compassionate bosom of the Father that the sacrifice of the cross was born. Christ's sacrifice was devised to maintain the dignity of the Law man had broken, and at the same time to rescue man from the penalty he had incurred. So far, therefore, from the atonement being a reflection on the justice and benevolence of God, it is perhaps the greatest evidence we possess both of His unswerving justice and of his boundless love.

In the second place, the atonement is declared by these objectors to have been unnecessary…

The objectors deny that in man's conduct any serious offence has been committed. They affirm that nothing has been done that could correctly be described as sin – meaning by sin the transgression of the divine Law. They say that the offences [which] the Bible describes as sins are not really sins at all, but merely irregularities resulting from errors of judgment; or that they are involuntary, the working out of man's unbalanced nature; or that they are the inevitable outcome of some hereditary inclination or disposition for which the individual cannot justly be held responsible. Let us look carefully at this statement that no real sin has been committed…

God is, as we all believe, a benevolent being, and the author of our existence. Having arranged for our coming into the world, God must be desirous of our well-being. Knowing that our well-being must be largely dependent on our conduct, and knowing the kind of conduct which is likely most surely to lead to the happiest and most useful existence, it is certain that God would prefer that we should adopt that course of conduct. Those preferences and judgments with respect to the conduct of our lives God has caused to be written in the books of providence, conscience and Scripture.[1]

**Loving Father, your laws are penned in love. Forgive me for those times when I have followed my own standards and ideas, and keep me on my guard against preferring my yardsticks to yours. Amen.**

1 From *The Founder Speaks Again*.

# January 19th

I was in prison and you came to visit me

(Matthew 25:36 *NIV*)

"Monday morning, the door opened, and a complacent detective stood before me. Who can tell the feeling as the handcuffs closed round my wrists, and we started for town. As again the charge was entered, and the passing of another night in the cell; then the morning of the day arrived.

The gruff, harsh 'Come on' of the gaoler roused me, and the next moment I found myself in the prison van, gazing through the crevices of the floor, watching the stones flying as it were from beneath our feet.

"Soon the court-house was reached, and hustled into a common cell, I found myself amongst a crowd of boys and men, all bound for the 'dock.' One by one the names are called, and the crowd is gradually thinning down, when the announcement of my own name fell upon my startled ear, and I found myself stumbling up the stairs, and finding myself in daylight and the 'dock.' What a terrible ordeal it was. The ceremony was brief enough. 'Have you anything to say?' 'Don't interrupt his Worship; prisoner!' 'Give over talking.' 'A month's hard labour.'

"This is about all I heard, or at any rate realized, until a vigorous push landed me in the presence of the officer who booked the sentence, and then off I went to gaol. I need not linger over the formalities of the reception. A nightmare seemed to have settled upon me as I passed into the interior of the correctional. I resigned my name, and I seemed to die to myself for henceforth. 332B disclosed my identity to myself and others.

"Through all the weeks that followed I was like one in a dream. Meal times, resting hours, as did every other thing, came with clock-like precision. At times I thought my mind had gone – so dull, so callous, so weary appeared the organs of the brain. The harsh orders of the gaolers; the droning of the chaplain in the chapel; the enquiries of the chief warder or the governor in their periodical visits – all seemed so meaningless."[1]

**Heavenly Father, even in the depths of despair, you are there; knowing our failings and fears. Today, I lift in prayer those in prison, that your presence will accompany them. I pray for prison chaplains and those who visit prisoners. Not even prison bars can restrain your word. Amen.**

1 A prisoner's account, recorded in *In Darkest England and the Way Out.*

# January 20th

## No one can serve two masters

(Matthew 6:24 *NIV*)

As I stood by a quayside the other day, I noticed that many of the barges and ships were fastened to each other, and so when one rocked the other rocked, and if one went adrift they would all float away together; but I saw other vessels fastened to the quay, and they were all firm and immovable, as the quay itself. No matter how the others rocked, these were secure.

If you are dependent for happiness and gladness on earthly things, earthly things are always rocking, and consequently your happiness and gladness will always be rocking too; and if you are moored in part to earthly things you will be rocking and changing just to that extent.

People get into a mixed state, partly dependent on God, partly on a husband, or a wife, or children, or a shop; husbands, and wives, and shops are prone to get adrift, and then their peace gets adrift too.

If a man walks on two planks, one sound and the other rotten, it is tolerably certain the rotten one will sooner or later give way, and over he must go, and he may thank a kind providence if he gets up again. Put both feet on the sound plank, and go on your journey shouting. Depend altogether on the Lord, and your peace shall flow like a river[1] – all the changes of earth and all the malice of Hell to the contrary notwithstanding. Oh, my God, take us off from the creature to the Creator.

God only knows what he would do with a few men who cared only for him. He would save thousands and astonish the universe. O God, make us all alike – all for thee.

I was hurrying to catch an express train to London the other day, and was reckoning upon the train upon which I was travelling meeting it, but it was too late – not very late, but just late enough to let the other go and leave me behind, with a wounded leg, hurt through scrambling to catch it… God wants men and women that he can reckon on, who will be there at the very time he wants them.[2]

**Father, if I waver from full reliance upon you, graciously remind me to walk in your ways. I bless you for those traditions, and those people, that help to nurture my earthly pilgrimage, but I pray they would never usurp your supremacy in my affections or devotion; make me single-minded and single-hearted. Amen.**

1 Isaiah 66:12
2 From *Salvation Soldiery.*

# January 21st

Tell it to your children, and let your children tell it to their children, and their children to the next generation

(Joel 1:3 *NIV*)

All round you, fathers and mothers, at enormous expense, endless trouble, and tremendous sacrifices, are deliberately training their children for pursuits, occupations, and professions that they know, or might know, will curse the world and people Hell. Train yours to bless it, and people Heaven.

Look at this poor earth of ours. Get a map of it. If you do not understand maps, ask somebody to explain to you all about the countries and peoples and languages that are described on it. Count its populations, cast up the sum of its idolatries, its superstitions, its cruelties, its slavery, its wars, its vice, its misery. How it wails in its bonds! Almost the whole creation groaneth.[1] What is to be done for it?

Thank God, something has been done – something is being done. But what has been done and what is being done are as nothing compared with what is required. We want that requirement to be met. That requirement has been talked about long enough. Surely the time and the opportunity for action have come.[2] Will you do your share? Did I say the opportunity had come to help the poor world out of its sins and miseries – has not the encouragement come also? And is not that encouragement The Salvation Army?...

See what has been done by a handful of men and women, ordinary people. Just such persons as you, dear reader, whose eyes now rest upon this page. True, God has helped us, wrought by us, and through us, but he is no respecter of persons. Will you not help us? Won't you give your children to our King and train them for the war?

Make your children good. The world needs fully surrendered people – men and women who are not so much concerned about what they can get from God as about what they can do for him; who have given up their lives to save other lives. Make your children benevolent and pitiful, and send them out to seek not their own, but the things which are Jesus Christ's – to live not to please themselves, but him.[3]

**God whose love spans generations, you have taken the risk of entrusting us with the responsibility of sharing your goodness with our families. Please enable us to do so wisely and sensitively. Amen.**

1 Romans 8:22
2 John 4:35
3 From *The Training of Children.*

# January 22[nd]

### The boundary lines have fallen for me in pleasant places

(Psalm 16:6 *NIV*)

Whatever may be thought of the possibility of doing anything with the adults, it is universally admitted that there is hope for the children. "I regard the existing generation as lost," said a leading Liberal statesman[1]... "My only hope is that the children may have a better chance. Education will do much."

But unfortunately the demoralizing circumstances of the children are not being improved – are, indeed, rather, in many respects, being made worse. The deterioration of our population in large towns is one of the most undisputed facts of social economics. The country is the breeding ground of healthy citizens. But for the constant influx of countrydom, Cockneydom[2] would long ere have perished. But unfortunately the country is being depopulated. The towns, London especially, are being gorged with undigested and indigestible masses of labour and, as the result, the children still suffer grievously.

The town-bred child is at a thousand disadvantages compared with his cousin in the country. But every year there are more town-bred children and fewer cousins in the country.

To rear healthy children you want first a home; secondly, milk; thirdly, fresh air; and fourthly, exercise under the green trees and blue sky. All these things every country labourer's child possesses, or used to possess. For the shadow of the city now lies upon the fields, and even in the remotest rural district the labourer who tends the cows is often denied the milk which his children need. The regular demand of the great towns forestalls the claims of the labouring hind. Tea and slops and beer take the place of milk, and the bone and sinew of the next generation are sapped from the cradle.

But the country child, if he has nothing but skim [*sic*] milk, and only a little of that, has at least plenty of exercise in the fresh air. He has healthy human relations with his neighbours... contact with the life of the hall, the vicarage, and the farm... he is not a mere human ant, crawling on the granite pavement of a great urban ants' nest.[3]

**Christ of the human road, thank you for all that is good about where I live. I pray for those whose living conditions are unhealthy, dangerous, and depressing, and for everyone who works diligently and modestly, in ways unseen, to improve their lot: council officials, charity workers, builders, church ministers. Bless their efforts. Amen.**

1 Probably William Ewart Gladstone, Liberal prime minister of Great Britain and a contemporary of Booth's.
2 A Cockney is someone born within a certain area of London.
3 From *In Darkest England and the Way Out.*

# January 23rd

Worship and serve him with your whole heart and a willing mind. For the Lord sees every heart and knows every plan and thought

(1 Chronicles 28:9 *NLT*)

Comrades and friends, how often we complain about the little progress salvation seems to make in the world. We see commerce, wealth, pleasure, recreation, science, and other earthly pursuits growing and extending at a rapid rate, while the Kingdom of our God and his Christ advances comparatively slowly. But, after all, is it any wonder that the interests of the Kingdom of Heaven should make such slow progress, in view of the small amount of energy, time, ability, wealth, and other forces expended upon them, compared with the enormous attention that is given to earthly enterprises?

On my recent voyage to Japan,[1] as I watched so many of the passengers, some of them professed followers of Jesus Christ, spending their time in childish games, cards, fiction, and gossip, I could not help remarking what a mighty force lay buried in those people – a force which, if consecrated and sanctified, might be employed for the regeneration of the world! But are there not forces that might be employed effectively for the extension of the Kingdom of Heaven to be found nearer at home than on ships sailing over the distant seas? Are there not idle forces to be found in churches and missions and, alas, if only in a limited measure, are they not to be found in The Salvation Army?...

But wait a moment, and let me ask whether the forces already possessed are being used as fully as they might be?... Is the thinking force among you as much in active service as it might be? Is there not a certain amount of brain power lying unemployed within your borders? Might not some fresh plans be invented for more successfully attracting the people to your building, getting at them in their own homes, or button-holing[2] them in the streets or their pleasure haunts, and so compelling them to remember God and eternity? Might not something new be done to stir up... such desires, and faith as would draw the Holy Ghost down from Heaven in richer baptisms than ever enjoyed before?[3]

**Lord, the Kingdom is not a trivial pursuit, but something of the utmost importance. Please help me find and maintain the right balance of work, ministry, recreation and relaxation. Bless me with holy creativity in these ways! Amen.**

1 Booth visited Japan in 1907.

2 A Salvationist expression for one-to-one conversations with people, usually strangers, about the gospel.

3 From *The Founder's Messages to Soldiers*.

# January 24th

When the people cry to the Lord for help against those who oppress them, he will send them a savior who will rescue them

(Isaiah 19:20 *NLT*)

There is a Hell. A Hell as dark and terrible as is the description given of it by the lips of Jesus Christ, the truthful. And into that Hell men are departing hour by hour. While we write, men are going away into everlasting punishment. While we eat and drink, and sleep and work, and rest, men are going where the "worm dieth not, and [where] the fire is not quenched".[1] Can anything be done? Can they be stopped? Can drunkards, harlots, thieves, the outcasts of the Church and of society, be saved? In theory many will answer, "Yes"; but in experience they confess they have no knowledge of such things.

Look again: perhaps the more appalling aspect of mankind is its bondage. How devils and devilish habits rule it, and oh, with what an iron yoke. Ask the drunkards, blasphemers, gamblers, thieves, harlots, money getters, pleasure seekers. Ask them one and all. Ask the question, "Can the power of these habits be broken? Can these fiends be expelled? Can those do good who have been accustomed all their lives to do evil?" Speak up! Press your question – "Can these poor captives be delivered? Saved from sinning, saved into holy living, and triumphant dying? Can they be saved now?"

The desponding answer will be "Impossible!" Ask multitudes of professing Christians, and they will fear it is impossible. Ask the Salvationist, and the answer will be, from both theory and experience, that the vilest and worst can be saved to the uttermost, for "all things are possible to him that believeth".[2]

What is the use of a doctor who cannot cure, a lifeboat that cannot rescue, an overseer who cannot relieve? And what would be the value of a Saviour who was not good and gracious, and strong enough to save the vilest and worst, and to save them as far as they need? But our Redeemer is mighty to save.[3] Hold the standard high. Let us tell the world of "blood and fire". We have salvation… We believe in salvation here and now… partaking here on earth of the leaves of the tree of life.[4, 5]

**Hallelujah! What a Saviour! Deliver us from evil. Amen.**

1 Mark 9:48 *KJV*
2 Mark 9:23 *KJV*
3 Isaiah 63:1 *KJV*
4 Revelation 22:2, 14
5 From *Salvation Soldiery.*

# January 25th

I saw the Lord… Above him were seraphim, each with six wings: with two wings they covered their faces, with two they covered their feet, and with two they were flying. And they were calling to one another: "Holy, holy, holy is the Lord Almighty; the whole earth is full of his glory." At the sound of their voices the doorposts and thresholds shook and the temple was filled with smoke. "Woe to me!" I cried. "I am ruined! For I am a man of unclean lips, and I live among a people of unclean lips, and my eyes have seen the King, the Lord Almighty."

(Isaiah 6:1–5 *NIV*)

"I cannot speak, I have not courage to stand up before a congregation, or in a ring in the open air.[1] I have not nerve to speak to people about their souls, and about God, and judgment, and eternity, either in private or in public. I have not ability, I don't like, I am not called, have not the necessary gifts, am not good enough. I come and listen, and give (a little), and go out with the procession (I don't walk in the ranks), but I cannot stand up and talk. I wish I could, but I cannot."

Now, it seems to us that Isaiah felt very much after the same fashion. He could not warn the people when God wanted him, but his excuse was the correct one. He had had a vision; had seen God, and seen himself, and the result was, he perceived, and felt, and confessed the secret of his silence, and he rightly named the padlock on his lips. It was not mental or physical, or social, but spiritual inability. I am a man of unclean lips, that is, he had an unclean heart. That was the sore spot. Oh, we do love these straight, honest Bible confessions, and all the other confessions that are straight and honest, too. Out with the truth, if you know it, and if you don't, may God soon reveal it.

Oh, in what multitudes of instances have we seen just the same sort of experience as that of Isaiah. It was the vision [that] made the difference. Before the vision, all manner of excuses, such as we started with in this paper, and 10,000 more, but after there has been a vision of the divine purity and the testimony of the divine messengers, and a revealing of the divine glory, and a moving of the posts, or of those who have hitherto been as still and as stupid as posts, and a filling of the place with the smoke of the sweet precious incense of praise and glory… So the truth comes out.[2]

**Transforming God, change my reluctance into readiness. Replace my sin with sanctification. When I see you, I see your love, and I am grateful. Amen.**

1 Meetings held in the open air, a common feature of Salvation Army life and witness.
2 From *Salvation Soldiery*.

# January 26th

When we were utterly helpless, Christ came at just the right time and died for us sinners

(Romans 5:6 *NLT*)

There is a real difference between what is right and what is wrong, and this difference constitutes a gulf of infinite width and infinite depth – a gulf so wide and so deep that neither men, nor angels, nor even God himself can disregard it. For God, omnipotent and wise as he is, cannot make right wrong or wrong right. Upon this essential difference between what is right and what is wrong the whole fabric of the moral law of the universe is based. This God must be under the strongest obligation to do all that lies within his power to maintain, before all the creatures under his care, the manifest rightness of what is right and the manifest wrongness of what is wrong.

This object God seeks to accomplish by the institution of the Law – the declaration of what is right and what is wrong in human conduct, and the demand for the obedience upon all to whom the Law applies. The needed respect for the Law, and the importance of obedience to it, are guarded by the infliction of a penalty bearing some proportion to the magnitude of the transgression. And when the Law is broken the infliction of a penalty must inevitably follow.

In the case of man's sin the penalty included: everlasting condemnation as wrongdoers, and everlasting separation from God. Quite possibly, indeed probably, the same or a similar penalty applies to every transgressor of the divine Law in every part of the universe, seeing that divine Law is an expression of the divine nature and will.

It is evident that great as God is, it was morally impossible for him to remit the penalty due to sin without some sacrifice being found which would have the effect of making the Law appear as honourable, and the offence appear as awful, as would have been the case had the penalty been inflicted. Now, God's heart yearned over man in his transgressions, prompting him to desire man's deliverance from the consequences of that transgression. How was this deliverance to be effected?... Something must be done.[1]

**Perfect God, your loving desire for me is nothing less than perfection. To that end, I am entirely dependent upon Jesus, who gave his life for me – the perfect for the imperfect – and took my place. The impossible dilemma is resolved, and grace has the victory. Amen.**

1 From *The Founder Speaks Again.*

# January 27th

Let the word of Christ dwell in you richly
(Colossians 3:16 *ESV*)

Supposing we have got now a Bible correct in the letter, printed in a book, the reproduction of the mind of God so far as he has declared it to some of his people in days gone by; let us now have some equally correct reproductions of the mind of Christ – some actual flesh-and-blood translations – some living epistles inspired and empowered by the Holy Ghost, that can be read and known of all men. I mean, let us Salvationists live out before men lives on which God has written out in big heavenly words His own notions of truth and righteousness and purity and patience and love and sacrifice. Christians for generations now have been spending an enormous amount of strength upon the Bible.

They have done well in that duty; but it seems to me that with regard to the sacred book something very important still remains to be done. Christian scholars have translated it and re-translated it, and then translated it again. They have commented and printed and published it in every form, and it is hurrying on to encompass the world with its revelations in every tongue. They have explained and preached about almost every word within its covers. There seems to me only one thing left to be done with it, and that it to give us a literal and faithful and understandable translation of it in practice. Let us live it; live the real things – live the Christ-life. Such a translation, my comrades, will tell. It will be victorious. It will be triumphant.

This is possible. It does not require learned divines and scholarly men to accomplish it. Wayfaring men, though fools, can make this translation, and fifteen years' perseverance in it will, I have not the shadow of a doubt, go a long way towards bringing in the millennium.[1] In the living translation every man who bears the name of Christ says thereby, "My life is a representation of Christianity."... we must have a new translation.[2]

**Lord of the word, if my life will be the only gospel some people read, then shine through me today, I pray. May it be that friends, family and colleagues see Christ, and only Christ, in me. Amen.**

1 William Booth was convinced, as were many others in the nineteenth century, that he would bring the world to the feet of Jesus and usher in the glorious millennium. Booth believed that his Army was uniquely equipped to do so.

2 From *The Founder Speaks Again*.

# January 28th

He will turn the hearts of the parents to their children, and the hearts of the children to their parents

(Malachi 4:6 *NIV*)

If you do not want to have your declining years embittered, and your grey hairs brought with sorrow to the grave,[1] resolve that you will, in the most serious spirit, and in the strength of divine grace, set yourself to control the wills and train the hearts of your children from their earliest days in paths of righteousness and godliness. And further, if parents desire to meet their children in Heaven, let them train them for it. We have seen already how intimately the happiness of children in this life is connected with your own. Bear in mind also that this connection will be continued right away into the next. There are three leading expectations cherished by all good fathers and mothers with respect to their fullest happiness in the heavenly world.

1. There is the desire in every sanctified soul to see the King.
2. There will come the desire to see the Kingdom, the great glorified corporation, the multitude which no man can number, who have "washed their robes, and made them white in the blood of the Lamb".[2]
3. And next, there will inevitably be in every parent's breast the strong and deathless desire to see their own children there.

Heaven would be no Heaven without the King. Were it possible for us to find him absent on our arrival, we should immediately want to go where he was, wherever that might be. Heaven would be poor indeed, compared with what we anticipate it, without the glorified spirits of just men made perfect, the souls of our departed comrades. And it seems to us that Heaven would be deprived of much of its brightness and joy unless the precious children were there also, whose joys and sorrows have filled up so large a measure of our hearts on earth. Verily, verily, are they not a part of us?… He who has the arrangements for our final felicity in his hands will doubtless do what tends most perfectly to secure our everlasting joy; but surely our Heaven will be more complete with the children there.[3]

**Eternal God, bless those who have specific responsibilities for the spiritual well-being of children. Guide them as they work, teach, and encourage, that their influence may stretch from this world to the next. Amen.**

1 Genesis 42:38
2 Revelation 7:14 *KJV*
3 From *The Training of Children.*

# January 29th

He said to them, "Go into all the world and proclaim the gospel to the whole creation"

(Mark 16:15 *ESV*)

Why should not Jesus Christ have "all the world"? Has anyone got any sufficient reason? Do any of our readers know why? Is there any reason to be found in Hell why the dark stream of lost souls that rolls thitherward day by day should not be lessened and narrowed, or cut off altogether, and sent up with thundering shouts of joy to the gates of Heaven? Are there not sadly too many lost already? Can there possibly be any reason, human or theological, why God's plans of mercy should not be carried out? Oh! If Hell's fires cannot be quenched, cannot we stop the supplies?

Is there any reason to be found in Heaven? Is there room for all these millions in the city that lies foursquare?[1] Is there any angel or glorified spirit who has gone there from this or any other world, who would have any objection to all the world coming up to join their employments, share their joys, and swell their songs? Is there any reason to be found in the mind of God why his salvation should not cover the earth as completely and as plenteously as the rolling ocean covers the mighty deep?[2]

To me all the difficulties of Scripture or theology on the subject are answered by the declaration he has made of his own nature – "God is love".[3] I know of no difficulties but those existing in some of the cut-and-dried theories of men who seem to me to have had more head than heart, and not more head than other people, either; and whom I cannot to have ever understood the foundation principles of the religion of Jehovah; or in such difficulties as can easily be traced to the malice and hatred of Satan.

That there is no objection in the heart of Jesus Christ to all the world coming in with a rush – coming in now, coming in for ever – this command sufficiently proves. It seems to have been the culmination of his ministry – the completing, finishing, concentrated essence of all the pity, and love, and sympathy that dwelt in his heart.[4]

**God who is love, your grace and mercy flow deeper and wider than I can imagine. Enlarge my heart, I pray, so that I come to glimpse at least something of your magnanimity. Amen.**

1 Revelation 21:16
2 Habakkuk 2:14
3 1 John 4:8
4 From *The General's Letters.*

# January 30th

Take a census of the whole Israelite community by their clans and families, listing every man by name, one by one

(Numbers 1:2 *NIV*)

What are the dimensions of evil? How many of our fellow men dwell in this darkest England? How can we take the census of those who have fallen below the cab-horse standard to which it is our aim to elevate the most wretched of our countrymen?

The moment you attempt to answer this question, you are confronted by the fact that the Social Problem has scarcely been studied at all scientifically. Go to Mudie's[1] and ask for all the books that have been written on the subject, and you will be surprised to find out how few there are. There are probably more scientific books treating diabetes or gout than there are dealing with the great social malady which eats out the vitals of such numbers of our people.

The report of the Royal Commission on the Housing of the Poor,[2] and the Report of the Committee of the House of Lords on Sweating[3] represent an attempt at least to ascertain the facts which bear upon the condition of the people question. But, after all, more minute, patient, intelligent observation has been devoted to the study of earthworms than to the evolution, or rather the degradation, of the sunken section of our people. Here and there in the immense field, individual workers make notes, and occasionally emit a wail of despair, but where is there any attempt to take the first preliminary step of counting those who have gone under?

One book there is, and so far as I know at present, only one, which even attempts to enumerate the destitute. In his *Life and Labour in the East of London*,"[4] Mr Charles Booth[5] attempts to form some kind of an idea as to the numbers of those with whom we have to deal. With a large staff of assistants, and provided with all the facts in possession of the School Board Visitors, Mr Booth took an industrial census of East London[6]… Tower Hamlets, Shoreditch, Bethnal Green, and Hackney… less than one-fourth of the population of London.[7]

**Lord of the universe, God of the individual. Your care is detailed, and you know me by my name. Thank you. Bless those who feel anonymous. Amen.**

1 Charles Mudie's bookshop in Bloomsbury, London.
2 1884.
3 London, 1888: A report on the working conditions of those employed using pressing irons.
4 Presented to the Royal Statistical Society in 1887.
5 No relation.
6 1886.
7 From *In Darkest England and the Way Out.*

# January 31st

### Captives also enjoy their ease; they no longer hear the slave driver's shout

(Job 3:18 *NIV*)

England emancipated her [black slaves] sixty years ago,[1] at a cost of £40,000,000,[2] and has never ceased boasting about it since. But at our own doors, from "Plymouth to Peterhead", stretches this waste continent of humanity – 3 million human beings who are enslaved – some of them to taskmasters as merciless as any West Indian overseer, all of them to destitution and despair. Is anything to be done with them? Can anything be done for them? Or is this million-headed mass to be regarded as offering a problem as insoluble as that of the London sewage which, feculent and festering, swings heavily up and down the basin of the Thames with the ebb and flow of the tide?

This Submerged Tenth – is it, then, beyond the reach of the nine-tenths in the midst of whom they live, and around whose homes they rot and die? No doubt, in every large mass of human beings there will be some incurably diseased in morals and in body, some for whom nothing can be done, some of whom even the optimist must despair, and for whom he can prescribe nothing but the beneficently stern restraints of an asylum or a gaol. But is not one in ten a proportion scandalously high? The Israelites of old set apart one tribe in twelve to minister to the Lord in the service of the Temple;[3] but must we doom one in ten of "God's Englishmen" to the service of the great twin devils – destitution and despair?

According to Lord Brabazon[4] and Mr Samuel Smith,[5] "between two and three millions of our population are always pauperised and degraded". Mr Chamberlain[6] says there is a "population equal to that of the metropolis" – that is, between four and five millions – "which has remained constantly in a state of abject destitution and misery." Mr Giffen[7] is more moderate. The submerged class, according to him, comprises one in five of manual labourers, six in 100 of the population. Mr Giffen does not add the third million which is living on the border line… I am content to take 3 millions as representing the total strength of the destitute army.[8]

**Redeemer, you are angered by slavery and exploitation. I pray for those in the cruel grip of harsh, unfair employers and unscrupulous oppressors. Help them, Lord. Amen.**

1 The Slavery Abolition Act 1833.
2 An estimate of the amount of compensation paid to landowners and slave owners.
3 Deuteronomy 10:8
4 William Brabazon MP.
5 Possibly Dr Samuel Smith, factory reformer.
6 Neville Chamberlain, British prime minister.
7 Sir Robert Giffen, Scottish economist.
8 From *In Darkest England and the Way Out.*

# February 1st

But he [Jesus] said to them, "You give them something to eat"

(Luke 9:13 *ESV*)

Work, work! It is always work that they ask. The divine curse is to them the most blessed of benedictions. "In the sweat of thy brow thou shalt eat thy bread",[1] but alas for these forlorn sons of Adam, they fail to find the bread to eat, for society has no work for them to do. They have not even leave to sweat. As well as discussing how these poor wanderers should in the second Adam "all be made alive",[2] ought we not to put forth some effort to effect their restoration to that share in the heritage of labour which is theirs by right of descent from the first Adam? A considerable number walk about the streets up till the early hours of the morning to hunt up some job which will… save them from actual starvation.

I had some conversation with one such… "You see," he said, pitifully, "I don't know my way about like most of the London fellows. I'm so green, and I don't know how to pick up jobs like they do. I've been walking the streets almost day and night these two weeks and I can't get work. I've got the strength, though I shan't have it long at this rate. I only want a job. This is the third night running that I've walked the streets all night; the only money I get is by minding blacking-boys' boxes while they go into Lockhart's[3] for their dinner. I got a penny yesterday at it, and two pence for carrying a parcel, and today I've had a penny. Bought a ha'porth of bread and a ha'penny mug of tea."

Poor lad! Probably he would soon get into thieves' company, and sink into the depths, for there is no other means of living for many like him; it is to starve or steal, even for the young. There are gangs of lad thieves in the low Whitechapel[4] lodging-houses, varying in age from thirteen to fifteen, who live by thieving eatables and other easily obtained goods from shop fronts.[5]

**Merciful Father, how it must sadden you when your children are without even bread, and survival is a daily struggle. Forgive us if and when we pass judgment on the unemployed, when our only response should be one of compassion. Hear my prayer for those who can't find work, and for those who try to help them into employment. Amen.**

1 See Genesis 3:19
2 1 Corinthians 15:22 *KJV*
3 A London restaurant.
4 The area of London where the work of The Salvation Army began.
5 From *In Darkest England and the Way Out.*

# February 2nd

Turn to me and have mercy, for I am alone and in deep distress

(Psalm 25:16 *NLT*)

When a rich man cannot employ his capital he puts it out at interest, but the bank for the labour capital of the poor man has yet to be invented. Yet it might be worthwhile inventing one. A man's labour is not only his capital but his life. When it passes it returns never more. To utilize it, to prevent its wasteful squandering, to enable the poor man to bank it up for use hereafter, this surely is one of the most urgent tasks before civilization.

Of all the heart-breaking toil, the hunt for work is surely the worst. Yet at any moment let a workman lose his present situation, and he is compelled to begin anew the dreary round of fruitless calls. Here is the story of one among thousands of the nomads, taken down from his own lips, of one who was driven by sheer hunger into crime:

> *A bright spring morning found me landed from a western colony. Fourteen years had passed since I embarked from the same spot. They were fourteen years, as far as results were concerned, of non-success, and here I was again in my own land, a stranger, with a new career to carve for myself and the battle of life to fight over again. My first thought was work. Never before had I felt more eager for a downright good chance to win my way by honest toil; but where was I to find work. With firm determination I started in search. One day passed without success and another, and another, but the thought cheered me, "Better luck tomorrow."*
>
> *It has been said, "Hope springs eternal in the human breast."*[1] *In my case it was to be severely tested. Days soon ran into weeks, and still I was on the trail patiently and hopefully. Courtesy and politeness so often met me in my enquiries for employment that I often wished they would kick me out, and so vary the monotony of the sickly veneer of consideration that so thinly overlaid the indifference and the absolute unconcern they had to my need. A few cut up rough... "We don't want you. Please don't trouble us again."*[2]

**Caring Father, in your Kingdom there is a place for all, but life can include moments of exclusion and isolation. If and when depression crouches near, please draw close to those who suffer. I bring to you those who are excluded and trapped by despair. Amen.**

1 From Alexander Pope's *An Essay on Man* (1734).
2 From *In Darkest England and the Way Out.*

# February 3rd

When Jesus spoke again to the people, he said, "I am the light of the world"

(John 8:12 *NIV*)

Comrades and friends, one of the most beautiful and expressive passages in the whole Bible forms the foundation of my message… It is full of invaluable truth. I fail to see how it would be possible to crowd more important salvation doctrine into the same amount of space. You would find it in 1 John 1:7, and it reads as follows: "If we walk in the light, as he is in the light, we have fellowship one with another, and the blood of Jesus Christ his Son cleanseth us from all sin."

We will enquire, what does "walking in the light" mean? Well, it is an illustration. Can I explain the figure? Imagine for a moment that you unexpectedly found yourselves in a trackless forest, in black darkness, with wild beasts raging around you, and serpents crawling and hissing about you at every step you took, with pitfalls before and on every side of you, while darkness prevented your seeing the gloomy precipice that was only a little way ahead. And then, suppose that just as you were falling over the precipice, I came along, with a lighted lantern in my hand, knowing the way full well, and throwing the light on the path in the direction in which you were to tread, said, "If you walk in that light you will escape danger, and safely reach your journey's end" – what would you do? I think you would gladly and gratefully accept my advice by walking in the light, and so reach the desired destination.

Now, this is just what the Blessed Lord is saying to you who are here this morning: "You are in a world crowded with peril to your body, mind, and soul; peril to your family, friends, and circumstances. Devils and wicked men wait to destroy you; death and destruction are on your track. One false step may carry you over the precipice into damnation.

"You cannot by your own skill discover a path that will lead you out of these dangers and lead you to your destination. I come to be your guide. I will show you the way which will lead you to righteousness, usefulness, and Heaven."[1]

**God of our darkness and our light, you are with us every step of life's way. In your mercy, continue to shed your light upon my decisions, my plans, and all that I do. Shed the glow of your love upon those in darkness, I pray. Amen.**

1 From *The Founder's Messages to Soldiers.*

# February 4th

### Pray earnestly to the Lord of the harvest to send out labourers into his harvest

(Matthew 9:38 *ESV*)

You are saved. You say your sins are forgiven, and that you belong to the family of God. You claim the promises made to saints, and reckon when you have done with earth you are going to finish up in the same Heaven provided for them. You say the promises apply to you; why not the commands? Have one, and shirk the other? What God has joined together, no man can put asunder.[1]

Do you say you are a child and not a servant? Don't talk nonsense. How can you be a child without a child's spirit? And is it not the very essence of the child's spirit to serve his father, and seek his father's interests, and carry out his father's most sacred purposes? If you have not this, most assuredly you lack the first and most convincing evidence of your sonship, which is being willing – nay, choosing – to be a servant; having this advantage, that you are willing to do the work without the hire…

"Not called," did you say? Not heard the call, I think you should say. He has been calling loudly ever since he spoke your sins forgiven – if you are forgiven at all – entreating and beseeching you to be his ambassador. Put your ear down to the Bible, and hear him bid you go and pull poor sinners out of the fire of sin.[2] Put your ear down to the burdened, agonized heart of humanity, and listen to its pitying wail for help. Go and stand by the gates of Hell, and hear the damned entreat you to go to their brothers, and sisters, and servants, and masters…

And then look the Christ in the face, whose mercy you profess to have got, and whose words you have promised to obey, and tell him whether you will join us heart and soul and body and circumstances in this march to publish his mercy to all the world. There is no hope of any possible compliance with this command until every man who takes into his heart this hope, takes upon himself the solemn responsibility of telling all the world… the joyful news of this salvation.[3]

**International God, worldwide evangelism seems almost impossible, yet I commit myself to playing my part. Show me ways of sharing the gospel. Bless evangelists taking your word around the globe, especially those working in hostile areas. Amen.**

1 Mark 10:9
2 Zechariah 3:2
3 From *The General's Letters.*

# February 5th

If you consider me a partner, welcome him as you would welcome me
(Philemon 1:17 *NIV*)

Comrades and friends, during the first few weeks of the New Year[1] no fewer than fifty men and women declared, at the offices of our Anti-Suicide Bureau in the City of London that they had resolved to end their lives, for the simple reason that they had no friends. They had no one with whom they had any friendly association, and they felt death to be preferable to the wretched loneliness of the solitary life they were compelled to live. Is not something of this spirit, and the unhappiness which springs from it, in great or lesser proportion, to be found in society everywhere?

People walk about, eat and drink, talk and go through the ordinary duties of social life together, and yet have no real communion of spirit. Heart does not speak to heart.[2] They are, in the truest sense, largely, if not altogether, alone in the world. I am afraid that there is a good deal of this experience. We meet, sing, pray, and testify together, but heart-union is too often sadly wanting.

Yet a corps[3] ought to be, to all intents and purposes, a real spiritual family. Every soldier on its roll should regard his comrades as brothers and sisters, not only in name but in practice. Instead of this, I am afraid with some Salvationists there is a great deal of the cold, stand-off spirit, and with a great many much of that wretched indifference which is so painful to see, and more painful still to endure. This is especially so in the big cities; while the brotherhood and sisterhood so often talked about by many so-called Christian people is little more than a name. This is a great pity, and we can never tell how much we lose by it, or how much suffering it entails upon many good and faithful souls who are shy and strange. I can never forget, for example, what a disheartening and distressing effect was produced on me by this kind of spirit in the church to which I was introduced when, as a young man, I first came to London.[4, 5]

**Welcoming God, forgive us when our churches aren't as hospitable as they might be, and prompt us to offer warm friendships, especially to those visiting for the first time. Grant us the sensitivity of Christ towards those in need of conversation and a listening ear. Amen.**

1 1908.
2 The motto of Cardinal Newman (1801–90) was "Heart speaks to heart".
3 Salvation Army churches are known as corps.
4 Probably Binfield Chapel, Clapham, London.
5 From *The Founder's Messages to Soldiers.*

# February 6th

Everyone who hears these words of mine and puts them into practice is like a wise man who built his house on the rock. The rain came down, the streams rose, and the winds blew and beat against that house; yet it did not fall, because it had its foundation on the rock. But everyone who hears these words of mine and does not put them into practice is like a foolish man who built his house on sand. The rain came down, the streams rose, and the winds blew and beat against that house, and it fell with a great crash

(Matthew 7:24–27 *NIV*)

Deaths from actual hunger are more common than is generally supposed… A man, whose name was never known, was walking through St James's Park,[1] when three of our shelter men saw him suddenly stumble and fall. They thought he was drunk, but he had fainted. They carried him to the bridge and gave him to the police. They took him to St George's Hospital, where he died. It appeared that he had, according to his own tale, walked up from Liverpool, and had been without food for five days. The doctor, however, said he had gone longer than that. The jury returned a verdict of "Death from starvation". Without food five days or longer! Who that has experienced the sinking sensation that is felt when even a single meal has been sacrificed may form some idea of what kind of slow torture killed that man!

In 1888 the average daily number of unemployed in London was estimated by the Mansion House Committee[2] at 20,000. This vast reservoir of unemployed labour is the bane of all efforts to raise the scale of living, to improve the condition of labour. Men hungering to death for lack of opportunity are the materials from which "blacklegs"[3] are made, by whose aid the labourer is constantly defeated in his attempts to improve his condition. This is the problem that underlies all questions of Trades Unionism and all schemes for the improvement of the condition of the industrial army. To rear any stable edifice that will not perish when the first storm rises and the first hurricane blows, it must be built not upon sand, but upon a rock. And the worst of all existing schemes for social betterment by organization of the skilled workers and the like is that they are founded, not upon "rock" nor even upon "sand", but upon the bottomless bog of the stratum of the workless. It is here where we must begin. The regimentation of industrial workers who have got regular work is not so very difficult. This can be done, and is being done, by themselves.[4]

**God of order, I pray for those who have been let down by systems of government and social policy and whose lives are chaotic. Help them to navigate legislation. Amen.**

1 London.
2 A committee authorized to report to Parliament.
3 Possibly some kind of "loan sharks".
4 From *In Darkest England and the Way Out.*

# February 7th

Fear not, for I am with you; be not dismayed, for I am your God; I will strengthen you, I will help you, I will uphold you with my righteous right hand

(Isaiah 41:10 *ESV*)

The problem that we have to face is the regimentation, the organization, of those who have not got work, or who have only irregular work, and who from sheer pressure of absolute starvation are driven irresistibly into cut-throat competition with their better-employed brothers and sisters. "Skin for skin... all that a man hath will he give for his life";[1] much more, then, will those who experimentally know not God give all that they might hope hereafter to have – in this world or in the world to come.

There is no gainsaying the immensity of the problem. It is appalling enough to make us despair. But those who do not put their trust in man alone, but in One who is Almighty, have no right to despair. To despair is to lose faith; to despair is to forget God. Without God we can do nothing in this frightful chaos of human misery, but with God we can do all things, and in the faith that he has made in his image all the children of men, we face even this hideous wreckage of humanity with a cheerful confidence that if we are but faithful to our own high calling he will not fail to open up a way of deliverance.

I have nothing to say against those who are endeavouring to open up a way of escape without any consciousness of God's help. For them I feel only sympathy and compassion. In so far as they are endeavouring to give bread to the hungry, clothing to the naked, and above all, work to the workless, they are to that extent endeavouring to do the will of our Father which is in Heaven,[2] and woe be unto all those who say them nay!

But to be orphaned of all sense of the Fatherhood of God is surely not a secret source of strength. It is in most cases – it would be in my own – the secret of paralysis. If I did not feel my Father's hand in the darkness, and hear his voice in the silence of the night watches bidding me put my hand to this thing, I would shrink back dismayed.[3]

**Gracious Lord, you are only too willing to help us through life's difficulties, and to hold us by the hand as we find our way. When life is tough, and our problems seem to have no end, equip us to trust and obey. Amen.**

1 Job 2:4 *KJV*
2 Matthew 6:10
3 From *In Darkest England and the Way Out.*

# February 8th

You are receiving the end result of your faith, the salvation of your souls

(1 Peter 1:9 *NIV*)

There are think-so Christians, and there are hope-so Christians, and there are know-so Christians; thank God we belong to the know-so people – we know we are saved. And why not? Enoch had the testimony that he pleased God.[1] Job knew that his Redeemer lived.[2] John knew that he had passed from death unto life.[3] Paul knew that when his earthly house was destroyed he had a building in the heavens.[4] And we know in whom we have believed,[5] and the Spirit answers to our faith, and testifies in our hearts that we are the children of God.[6]

My brethren, if you have salvation you are sure of it. Not because at the corner of the street or from the stage of the theatre you have heard it preached. Not because you have read with your eyes, or heard read by others in that wonderful book, the wonderful story of the love of God to you. Not because you have seen with your eyes transformations of character wrought by the power of the Holy Ghost; changes as marvellous, as miraculous, as divine, as any that ever took place in apostolic or any other days. These things may have led up to it. But these things, wonderful as they may be, have not power to make you sure of your part and lot in the matter of salvation. Flesh and blood has not revealed this to you, but God himself, by his Spirit, has made this known…[7]

We believe in salvation, and we have salvation. We are not mere sentimentalists or theory people; we publish what we have heard and seen and handled and experienced of the word of life and the power of God. We aim at salvation. We want this and nothing short of this, and we want this right off. My brethren, my comrades, soul saving is our vocation, the great purpose and business of our lives. Let us seek first the Kingdom of God…[8] You must have the self-sacrificing, soul-seeking spirit of Jesus Christ, or you are none of his. Then you, too, must be a Salvationist.[9]

**God of eternity, I praise you because I am saved from myself and saved from Hell. Lord, reassure me in those moments when this conviction wavers; remind me of truth. I place myself at your disposal so that my life may count for the salvation of others. Amen.**

1 Hebrews 11:5
2 Job 19:25
3 1 John 3:14
4 2 Corinthians 5:1
5 2 Timothy 1:12
6 Romans 8:16
7 Matthew 16:17
8 Matthew 6:33
9 From *Salvation Soldiery.*

# February 9th

Moses said to the Lord, "Oh, my Lord, I am not eloquent, either in the past or since you have spoken to your servant, but I am slow of speech and of tongue." Then the Lord said to him, "Who has made man's mouth? Who makes him mute, or deaf, or seeing, or blind? Is it not I, the Lord? Now therefore go, and I will be with your mouth and teach you what you shall speak"

(Exodus 4:10–12 *ESV*)

Straight hitting is not common in these degenerate, maudlin days. God Almighty's ambassadors, unfortunately, are not renowned for this outspoken, unmistakable method of message bearing. And yet they ought to be. Who, like them, ought to have brows like brass, and wills like iron, and nerves like steel, and eyes like coals of fire, and words that should be verily, verily, a sharp, two-edged sword, piercing and dividing,[1] and bringing to his feet the enemies of their royal King. Oh, surely, we are the people that can afford to hold up our heads and speak the truth, and speak it out and, God helping us, we will do it. Comrades, listen!… Go straight to your post… Let there be no excusing yourself about your inability and want of voice, or courage, or time, or something else, which too often means that you are too proud or worldly, or are altogether too ashamed of Jesus Christ and his cause to be known to be on his side.

No running away in some other direction, Jonah-like, and only squaring yourself up to duty after some kind of three days' solitary confinement in the belly of some whale or other. No! No! No! Go off at once…

Oh, how God must nauseate the people who, always confessing to divine drawings and callings to duty, have to be coddled, and coaxed, and courted into discharging it… One volunteer is worth half a dozen brought in by a press-gang. Commend us to your willing, ready enthusiast before any number of weak-kneed, hesitating people, who have to be dragged into the ranks by force of arguments and persuadings and threatenings. If you have to fill a post, save a town, warn a monarch, or offer salvation to a crossing-sweeper… go to your duty straight away. Give your message in the straightest manner possible… Give it as God would have it given. Let there be no mixing up, nor diluting the strength. Give the precious souls to whom you are sent the precious truth.[2]

**Father, evangelism can be daunting; rejection is never pleasant. Yet, I trust in you to equip me, embolden me, and guide me. Make me willing to go wherever you lead, and to speak the words you would have me speak, so that souls might be saved. For Jesus' sake. Amen.**

1 Hebrews 4:12
2 From *Salvation Soldiery.*

# February 10th

## Your arrows flashed back and forth

(Psalm 77:17 *NIV*)

Men, all men, from the monarch to the beggar, are preoccupied, taken up with business, or pleasures, or glory, or joy of one kind or other. They will stare at you while you talk, and have you believe they are drinking in all you say, when all the while their thoughts are as far away as possible, and they are neither listening, nor comprehending, nor caring for a single word.

Shake them up. Startle them with apparitions of death, and judgment, and devils, and Hell. What matters taste and propriety to you? The man, the crowd you speak to are going to Hell – they are almost there already. You will hear they are dead and damned in a few days, unless something happens. So do, for their souls' sake, wake them out of sleep, and then you will have a chance of making them understand you. My comrades, make the people understand you. On this their destiny hangs. As carefully as the barrister, convinced of the innocence of the prisoner, puts his case before the jury, whose verdict is to be life or death, so carefully must you plead. The verdict you want is not from the jury, but from the criminal…

You are to make the men to whom God sends you understand that they are rebels at that moment against the Almighty Jehovah, condemned to die; in danger every moment, all the Christmas time, while they eat and drink and sit at the pantomime, and shout, and dance, and play, and at all other times, in danger of being damned, and that God wants them to submit, so that he may save them there and then. Oh, make them understand.

Oh, write in big, unerasable characters, guilt and heaven, and judgment and damnation, and Calvary, upon their memories. Be sure you are plain. Go it over and over and over again, till you can see in their eyes, and tears, and hear in their cries that they understand. Feather your arrows… with illustrations and facts, and then send them home, straight home, and as far home as you possibly can.[1]

**Almighty God, these words speak of a solemn duty. This style of forthright evangelism probably came more naturally to William Booth than it does to many of us, but still I pray for courage and opportunities to share words in season, firing gospel arrows. Help me to do this sensitively and under your guidance, so that some may be saved. Amen.**

1 From *Salvation Soldiery.*

# February 11th

SUPPOSE A MAN COMES INTO YOUR MEETING WEARING A GOLD RING AND FINE CLOTHES, AND A POOR MAN IN FILTHY OLD CLOTHES ALSO COMES IN. IF YOU SHOW SPECIAL ATTENTION TO THE MAN WEARING FINE CLOTHES AND SAY, "HERE'S A GOOD SEAT FOR YOU," BUT SAY TO THE POOR MAN, "YOU STAND THERE" OR "SIT ON THE FLOOR BY MY FEET," HAVE YOU NOT DISCRIMINATED AMONG YOURSELVES AND BECOME JUDGES WITH EVIL THOUGHTS?

(James 2:2–4 *NIV*)

A hue and cry will be made about excitement, and emotional religion, and fanaticism, and forcing religion down people's throats, and there may be hysterics, and fits, and swoons, and prostrations, and persecutions, and hatreds, and all manner of opposition, and imitations, and counterfeits; but these things must not turn you aside. You hold on, giving the truth of God out in the straightest manner…

Don't be led off or hindered by any notion of the respectability of the people God sends you to warn… don't prostitute and disgrace the faith of our Lord Jesus by having respect to the clothes, or gold chains, or position, or money of anybody. For, if there comes into your hall a prosperous shopkeeper, with a gold ring and a black coat and a white waistcoat, and a soul all unsaved, don't put him, on account of his respectability, in a respectable seat and soften your speech, and modify your message to please him; but bring him up to the front, close to the penitent form, where your soldiers are praying and believing all the time; then turn on him your heaviest guns, and do your best to get him saved.

Oh! You must not do as the Gentiles do, and be troubling yourself about a man whom God has sent you to save from Hell being better educated than other people, or having money, or being offended or coming no more. Oh, no! pleased or displeased, give his money or keep it, come again or stay away, your work is not to please but to profit, not to comfort but to convict, not to salve but to save! So think about their poor souls, and give them the truth, which can only profit, and convict, and convert, and save, and give it them in the straightest manner possible… If ever there was a time, this is the time for straight dealing. God has set before you an open door. You have the ear of the million. The people are in multitudes of instances prepared to receive the word at your lips.[1]

**Father of all, it is so easy to look on some people more favourably than others. Please forgive me if I have done that. We are all seeking the same Saviour, lowly and exalted alike. Thank you, Lord, that the ground at the foot of the cross is level. Amen.**

1 From *Salvation Soldiery.*

# FEBRUARY 12TH

ESAU LOOKED UP AND SAW THE WOMEN AND CHILDREN. "WHO ARE THESE WITH YOU?" HE ASKED. JACOB ANSWERED, "THEY ARE THE CHILDREN GOD HAS GRACIOUSLY GIVEN YOUR SERVANT"

(Genesis 33:5 *NIV*)

**You say that a godly parentage is the first condition of that training which will be successful in making the children true servants and good soldiers of Jesus Christ. Will you explain what you mean?** We mean that the parents should both be converted and wholly devoted to God before the birth of the children, in which case there is little doubt that the children will come into the world with tendencies in favour of goodness. Just as we see children inherit the bad tendencies and passions of bad parents, so the children of godly parents must inherit dispositions, tempers and appetites favourable to lives of goodness and self-sacrifice. There is nothing with which we are more familiar than the transmission from parent to child of physical qualities, such as peculiarity of features, tones of voice, colour of hair, eyes, and the like; also physical appetites, such as tastes for particular kinds of food, for strong drink, unnatural tendencies to uncleanness, and a hundred other things. We are also familiar with the fact that mental qualities descend from parents to children. For instance, clever parents will be likely to have children, not only clever, but gifted in the same direction as themselves. We also know that parents transmit their peculiar temperaments to their children. Thus you will find them sanguine, nervous, bilious, or melancholy, after the fashion of father or mother, or both conjoined. And it is equally certain that moral qualities are transmitted – such as tendencies to truth or falsehood, generosity or selfishness, honesty or dishonesty, and the like.

**Does not this notion contradict the doctrine of inbred depravity, or the indwelling sinfulness of children?** Certainly not. The children of godly parents, in common with the children of wicked parents, notwithstanding all the advantages of the former over the latter to which we have referred, are nevertheless born into the world with tendencies which, if left to themselves, will invariably lead them into a life of selfishness and rebellion against God. Nevertheless, in the degree of evil inclination with which children come into existence, there is manifestly a very great difference. The children of holy parents must have a far better chance in the race for the heavenly goal.[1, 2]

**I pray for children – some born into love, others born into neglect. Bless those known to me personally, whatever their start in life. Amen.**

1 2 Timothy 4:7
2 From *The Training of Children.*

## February 13th

Remember your leaders, who spoke the word of God to you

(Hebrews 13:7 *NIV*)

My dear Brigadier and Mrs Deleri Singh,[1] I am sending this Xmas time[2] the assurance of my good wishes and prayers to my commissioners and TCs[3] throughout the world. Of all men, what a chance you have to do something that will help the Army to make a name for God and Christianity.

Sir John Hewitt[4]... called to see me at headquarters when [he] was in London, and the way in which he spoke of the effective methods we practise for reaching the criminal tribes, and the tone of respect with which he referred to our people generally cheered me immensely. But greater things have happened since then and are going to happen, but it is the salvation work in which you are more particularly concerned on which I place my good reliance.

We are the only people who have taken our stand to the extent we have on conversion and the benefits that flow out of it and we must keep this great feature that is salvation to the front. God bless you and your dear wife and make you both more than ever a great blessing to India. And now, I find that I shall not be able to go any further with my own pen,[5] but there are several things of very considerable importance, not only to you, but to other Territorial Commanders, that I should like to say as I consider some of the essential measures that must be taken, in order to make our work the triumph that we all desire. I am, therefore, going to dictate them to a confidential secretary, and send them to you and to others who occupy similar positions. I shall trust to your reading them, reflecting on them, and considering wherein and to what extent they apply to your own responsibility, and the manner in which you are dealing with it. You will admit that it is likely that I should know something of the measures necessary for effective work, and the manner in which that work should be discharged. It would be a shame if after sixty-six years' experience I did not.[6]

**Lord of the Church, you have appointed leaders to direct your work. Theirs is sometimes a difficult task; with the privilege of high office comes great responsibility. Sustain your leaders with grace, and fill them with the joy of ministry, that the body of Christ may serve your Kingdom purposes. Amen.**

1 Brigadier and Mrs James Melling, here addressed by their adopted Indian names.
2 Written on Christmas Day 1911.
3 A commissioner is a senior leader within The Salvation Army – a rank given to many Territorial Commanders (TCs).
4 Chief Administrator for the British government, United Provinces of India.
5 Probably due to failing eyesight.
6 From *Essential Measures*, a letter circulated to Territorial Commanders worldwide.

# February 14th

My strength fails me, and the light of my eyes – it also has gone from me

(Psalm 38:10 *ESV*)

Without any boasting I think I know what course a Territorial Commander should follow in order to reach the goal on which his eye is fixed, and secure the success which is expected of him. I will strive to lay these down in as brief a manner as is possible, and with the recollection of my years, the honour God has put upon me, the effective work I have done, the fact that you are my selection for the position you occupy and, I may say also, the love you bear me, I have ground for expecting you will not disappoint me. Before, however, I come to the main topic of my letter, I think you will expect that I should say something with regard to the present condition of my health and the prospects [I] entertain for its restoration.

On this, although I cannot report a complete recovery, I think I am gradually approaching it, and the doctors whom I have consulted, some of them the most eminent men in their profession, assure me that there is good ground for hoping that the operation on my eye[1] will restore my vision, and that with care and a reasonable limitation of my labours, I may calculate on staying with you for some years to come.

And now, to the main object of my letter… to lay down some of the principles that are essential to success and:

1. I remark that the first and foremost of these is the absolute necessity for spiritual life. Without life there can neither be affection, beauty, useful labour or any other good thing, but, on the contrary, everything that is powerless, repugnant and injurious. Even the woman who has thought for so long that husband or children were necessary to her existence says, when death intervenes, "Give me a piece of land that I may bury my dead out of my sight."[2] And if you are to have life, with all its advantages in your command as a whole, you must have it in individuals.[3]

Cont/…

**Great Physician, bless those for whom ill health is frightening, painful or distressing. During long days of discomfort, embrace them and those who care for them. Amen.**

1 Booth's eyesight had been failing for some time, and in 1909 he was diagnosed blind in his right eye, despite cataract surgery.

2 See Genesis 23:4

3 From *Essential Measures.*

# February 15th

I have come that they may have life, and have it to the full
(John 10:10 *NIV*)

Cont/...

If you want life, it will not help you to have a large number of dead people. The quantity will not produce the quality. You must have men and women who have life individually. When dealing with officers, soldiers[1] or professors of religion of any description, the first question should be: "Is this man really a regenerated man? Is he converted?"

2. The next essential to successful fighting is right Salvation Army training, and training that takes in the detail of every important class of work to be discharged. One of the drawbacks in the way of training is that those who are trained are not always made to understand the detail of the duties they will have to discharge. It is impossible to set the value of thoroughness in training too high. I am supposing that you have got the hearts of your young officers in your hands and, as you know, neither men nor women, whatever their abilities may be, will be of lasting service in the Salvation Army unless their hearts are right with it.[2]

And now, having got the hearts of your people, what you want to do is to secure and instruct their brains. You must take them to the sort of ground they will have to occupy in the future and place before their eyes the sort of work they will have to do. You must point out their shortcomings, applaud their budding abilities, and not let them go out of your hands until they have not only the desire but the ability to do the work for which they are designed.

3. The third essential... is faithful oversight... Beware of hearsay, gossip, the belittlement born of envy, the slander that comes out of that bitterness which ever wants to pull down anyone who is, or gives the promise of being, better or more useful than those who entertain it are themselves.

When you hear an evil report... get to know what proof there is... follow it down and you will often save a wrecked reputation and a broken heart.[3]

**Lord of life, these points were made to Salvation Army leaders, but they apply to every follower of Christ. Thank you that he came to give us abundant life. Help me to dispense with hindrances, in order to devote myself to you fully. Amen.**

1 Salvation Army officers are full-time ministers. Soldiers are full members (laity).
2 Salvation Army officers engage in a period of residential training, as cadets.
3 From *Essential Measures*.

# FEBRUARY 16TH

THE LORD THUNDERS AT THE HEAD OF HIS ARMY; HIS FORCES ARE BEYOND NUMBER, AND MIGHTY IS THE ARMY THAT OBEYS HIS COMMAND

(Joel 2:11 *NIV*)

The Salvation Army. What a strange name! What does it mean? Just what it says – a number of people joined together after the fashion of an army, and therefore it is an army, and an army for the purpose of carrying salvation through the land. It is neither more nor less than that. If it be wise and lawful and desirable for men to be banded together and organized after the best method possible to liberate an enslaved nation, establish it in liberty, and overcome its foes, then surely it must be wise and lawful and desirable for the people of God to join themselves together after the fashion most effective and forcible to liberate a captive world, and to overcome the enemies of God and man.

When Jehovah finished the work of creation, he turned from the new earth to the new Adam,[1] and gave him the commission to multiply and increase and subdue and govern it, so that it should become a happy home for him and his posterity, and bring honour and glory to its Creator. Adam failed in his mission, and instead of Adam subduing the earth the earth subdued Adam, and he and all his family went off into diabolical rebellion. But God still claimed his own, and a second time appeared, this time to redeem by sacrifice the world he had before created; and when he had finished the work, he turned to his disciples the spiritual Adam, and gave him a commission similar to that given to the first Adam, to go and disciple all nations, baptizing them "in the name of the Father, and of the Son, and of the Holy Ghost".[2]

Again it is, as at the first, to overcome, conquer, subdue, not merely teach, but persuade, compel all nations, that is, all men to become the disciples of the Son of God.

So at least it is understood by The Salvation Army. This is the idea which originated and developed and fashioned it in the past, and which dominates it and propels it today.[3]

**Warrior God, grace enlists us into the army of salvation, but fighting for the King comes more naturally to some than others. I pray for your equipping, that I might fight my corner for Jesus, whatever that involves. Amen.**

1 Romans 5:12–21
2 Matthew 28:19
3 From *Salvation Soldiery*.

# February 17th

It is for freedom that Christ has set us free. Stand firm, then, and do not let yourselves be burdened again by a yoke of slavery

(Galatians 5:1 *NIV*)

The world, this very world, including this very England, which never ceases boasting of its freedom, is sold under sin, held in slavery by Satan, who has usurped the place and power and revenues of Jehovah, and who is indeed its lord and master,[1] and to deliver it and fulfil it to the very letter [of] the Master's command, an army of deliverance, or redemption, of emancipation is wanted.

In the name of the great Three in One the standard has been raised, and recruits are flowing in. Drilling, skirmishing, fighting, advancing are going on. Some territory has been won, some captives have been liberated, some shouts of victory have been raised, together with plenty of misfortunes and losses and disasters and mistakes, and all of that which might naturally have been expected in such a war, unless men had suddenly mended of their depravity, and devils had miraculously ceased to be devils; but with it all there has been growth and increase continually. Every day it is becoming more fierce and determined and courageous and confident, and every day more and more a Salvation Army.

Does all this sound strange, my brother – not sacred, not ecclesiastical, not according to the traditions of the elders, and after the pattern of existing things and institutions? Is it something new? It may be so, and yet it may be none the less true and scriptural, and none the less of divine origin, and made after some heavenly pattern for all that. Let us look at it. What is this work we have in hand? To subdue a rebellious world to God. And what is the question to which many anxiously desire an answer? How is it most likely to be accomplished? Now, there are some things on which we may reckon all to be agreed:

That if ever the world, or any part of it, is subdued, it will be by the instrumentality of man. By holy men – saved, spiritual, divine men. By men using substantially the same means as were used by the first apostles, that is, preaching, praying, believing etc. That all that is effected will be by the cooperation and power of the Holy Ghost.[2]

**Liberating God, Christ has won my freedom by taking captivity captive. Help me therefore to live as a beneficiary of that freedom, and to share Christ with others; the Lion of Judah, whose power breaks every chain. Amen.**

1 John 12:31
2 From *Salvation Soldiery*.

# FEBRUARY 18TH

A PERSON STANDING ALONE CAN BE ATTACKED AND DEFEATED, BUT TWO CAN STAND BACK-TO-BACK AND CONQUER. THREE ARE EVEN BETTER, FOR A TRIPLE-BRAIDED CORD IS NOT EASILY BROKEN

(Ecclesiastes 4:12 *NLT*)

How could a number of the Lord's disciples conduct themselves in order the most effectually to succeed in the direction of discipling all nations, subduing the world to God? Supposing 5,000 godly men and women of varying ages and conditions presented themselves to St Paul's Cathedral tomorrow, saying, "We are so deeply impressed with the awful spiritual condition and peril of the world that we cannot rest; the word of the Lord is as a fire in our bones, and the love of souls is such a constraining power in our hearts that it will not let us remain idle,[1] and we want to join in a holy crusade for the redemption of mankind. Take us and all we have, and use us in the way most likely to accomplish this end." What in such a case could best be done? How could these 5,000 burning hearts be used with the greatest force and likelihood of success? Let us see…

The 5,000 must work in the most complete and perfect combination possible. To separate and scatter them, leaving them to work out varying plans, would surely be unwise. No, no. Two working in combination will accomplish more than two in separation. Let them be one and the same force, though acting in varying divisions and scattered to the ends of the earth. Mould and weld and keep them together. Let them be one army, and make them feel that they are working out one plan. Shoulder to shoulder. Brethren, sisters, comrades, division is weakness, unity is strength? Why?

Combination gives the strength which flows from sympathy. The knowledge that if one is sore pressed, wounded, a thousand hearts feel with him, that if he falls they will shout victory o'er his grave, follow him in imagination to "the river", and anticipate meeting him again before the Throne will be stimulus unutterable, will make him willing to face enemies, loss, death, and devils. Combination gives confidence. There is a wonderful power in the consciousness that a multitude are shouldering the same weapons, engaged in the same conflict, for the destruction of the common foe.[2]

**Lord of unity, you call your Church to work as a body. A united work and witness is a powerful tactic. Dissolve division and disharmony, for the Kingdom's sake. Amen.**

1 Jeremiah 20:9
2 From *Salvation Soldiery.*

# February 19th

God delivered the Hagrites and all their allies into their hands, because they cried out to him during the battle. He answered their prayers, because they trusted in him

(1 Chronicles 5:20 *NIV*)

Confidence makes men into heroes. Hold together, close together, and there will be giants again even in our own days… With a system of combination which is a reality, the strong will bear the infirmities of the weak. In a real war, no matter how carefully the forces are distributed, there will be weak places that will need strengthening when the conflict rages all along the line. There will be positions against which the enemy will hurl his most powerful battalions, which positions must be reinforced or all will be lost. How glorious for the fresh troops to come pouring in. What would have become of Lucknow had there been no Havelock,[1] and but for Blücher[2] England would never have been so proud to tell the story of Waterloo…

We know now how the battle will go, and no wing or detachment must be without its supports, and all must be so arranged that the power and force of the whole can be directed to strengthen and sustain the weakest part. Combination gives the power which comes from example. Man imitates. The deeds of daring and self-denial and sacrifice done here will be talked about, and printed, and written about and imitated there. Men emulate. In every company there will be spirits more courageous and daring than others… These will lead and the rest will follow.

But such combination of oneness of action will only be possible with oneness of direction. If all are to act together all must act on one plan, and therefore all must act under one head. Twenty different heads, according to the nature and experience and history of heads, will produce twenty different plans with twenty different methods for their accomplishment, clashing and hindering each other more or less. Then what next? Difference of opinion, of feeling, of following, of action. Disagreement, confusion, separation, destruction. I am of Paul and I am of Apollos[3] soon leads, so far as the actuality of things is concerned, to being of nothing save wrangling and the devil.[4]

**God of harmony, it can seem strange to think about outreach and evangelism in terms of military strategy, yet the value of combination and cooperation cannot be underestimated. Use me to strengthen and encourage those caught in the heat of battle, so that we all fight to the best of our ability, supporting one another. Amen.**

1 British soldier Major General Henry Havelock, who led forces liberating the Indian town of Lucknow.
2 Prussian Field Marshal Gebhard Leberecht von Blücher, an ally of the Duke of Wellington at the Battle of Waterloo.
3 1 Corinthians 3:4
4 From *Salvation Soldiery*.

# February 20th

### With God we shall do valiantly
(Psalm 60:12 *ESV*)

Bring in your earthly usages. How do men ordinarily act? Do you want to tunnel a mountain, bridge a river, manage a railway, or conquer a nation? Is it committeed? Did a committee build the ark, emancipate the Israelites, or ever command, or judge, or govern them after they were emancipated? Is it not an axiom everywhere accepted, in time of war, at least, and we are speaking of times of war, that one bad general is preferable to two good ones?...

Is this direction of one mind all the direction needed? By no means. Subordinate leadership there must be in all manner of directions; all the talent in this direction possessed... must be called into play; but one controlling, directing will must be acknowledged, accepted, and followed, if you are to keep the unity... and make the most of it for God and man.

Then of course you will train... An army without training, without drill, would simply be a loose, helpless mob, a source of weakness and danger impossible to hold together... though every one of them may now have hearts full of zeal for God and love to man; so we must train them, and that to the uttermost. We must teach them how to fight, how to fight together, and how to fight in the very best way. Train them in the industrious, practical, and self-sacrificing discharge of their duties. They will improve. They are only babes now, they will grow up to be men, some of them to be head and shoulder above their fellows; think what they will become when trained and taught, and developed, and inured to hardship and accustomed to war. Don't despise the gift that is in any; you will very often find the last to be first, and the first to be last.[1] Let everyone have a chance; God is no respecter of persons[2] nor sex, neither must you be. Every gift you need is here, and only wants calling forth and cultivating, and you will be fully provided for the war.[3]

**Victorious God, in your strength, we are made strong. You graciously lend us your power so that we can take part in the war against evil, even when our strength is exhausted. Embolden me to go – today – in the strength of the Lord, to work you have called me to do. Amen.**

1 Matthew 20:16
2 Acts 10:34
3 From *Salvation Soldiery*.

# February 21st

If you know that he is righteous, you may be sure that everyone who practises righteousness has been born of him

(1 John 2:29 *ESV*)

Comrades and friends, I have been thinking recently of the happy condition of the righteous. The Bible, as you know, contains many references to their blessedness. It is to be well with the righteous man living, well with him dying, and well with him for ever. Here are a few of the many allusions to the righteous:

"The righteous shall flourish like the palm tree; they shall… bring forth fruit in old age";[1] "the righteous [shall] have hope in his death";[2] "[they] shall be [held] in everlasting remembrance";[3] and the Master himself said, the righteous shall go "into life eternal".[4] No matter, then, what tribulation or persecution they may be called on to endure in this world; the righteous have the best of it in the long run. I need not say, therefore, that it is most important that we should be able to justify the claim, the possession of the character that entitles us to be numbered amongst the righteous. The assurance that we can do so must be very welcome. The knowledge that we belong to the class whom God regards as righteous will be a strength to us amid all the storms of life, comfort us in the valley of the shadow of death,[5] and enable us to stand without fear before the Great White Throne.[6]

It will be quite clear to all that several things are required to constitute this confidence… There must be the conscious possession of a religious character; that is, you must be right, and know that you are right. Any effort to persuade yourself that you are righteous when you know that you are not will be labour spent in vain. Some people are always putting the best possible construction on their own actions, and magnifying their own virtues; although all the time they are tormented with the horrid reflection that something is wrong in their lives. They do not belong to the righteous. The character of the righteous cannot be separate from righteousness. No man has a right to claim the character of the righteous whose life does not harmonize with the righteousness described in the Bible.[7]

**Holy God, I myself would holy be; to be like Jesus. Amen.**

1 Psalm 92:12, 14 *KJV*
2 Proverbs 14:32 *KJV*
3 Psalm 112:6 *KJV*
4 Matthew 25:46 *KJV*
5 Psalm 23:4
6 Revelation 20:11
7 From *The Founder's Messages to Soldiers.*

# FEBRUARY 22ND

"YOU SHALL LOVE THE LORD YOUR GOD WITH ALL YOUR HEART AND WITH ALL YOUR SOUL AND WITH ALL YOUR MIND"

(Matthew 22:37 *ESV*)

You Salvationists say you are followers of Jesus Christ, and that the Spirit of God dwells in you. You say that you love the world as the Father did; which means that you love the ignorant, unkind, and bad people around you. Now is this so in reality, or is it only so much talk? God gave unmistakable proof of his love for you. What proof have you given to the world of your love for him? What proof are you giving today? For example: How much of your thought does the world's sad condition really receive? Do you ponder over the sins and miseries, and dangers and coming doom of those around you? Do you ever meditate on these things?

I have no doubt that you have many other important matters that claim your attention; but, surely, the honour of God and the needs of the perishing souls around you demand a little of your time and thoughts. Suppose you were to set apart a few minutes every night and morning to think about the sins and sorrows of men, and of the great sacrifice God has made on their account. A quarter of an hour every day would not be thrown away, I think, in considering how far your responsibility extends with respect to them, and what additional efforts you can make on their behalf. How much of your sympathy and compassion do you give? Does your heart ever ache, and do your eyes ever weep, when you see men and women forgetting the love of the Father, and trampling on the blood of His Son? Does your soul ever groan as you watch them giving themselves up to wickedness, and running down the broad, dark road that leads to destruction?[1] How many compassionate tears does this perishing world get from you?

Then, further: How much real labour do you devote to the business of the world's salvation? I daresay many of you work very hard at your daily callings. But if you were to come home some evening and find your neighbour's house on fire, you would forget the toils and fatigues of the day and rush to the rescue of those in danger.[2]

**Father, it is sometimes difficult to comprehend the fact that you are totally committed to me, and yet, you are. I ask you to work in my heart so that my love for you becomes some kind of reflection of your love for me, and for the world. Amen.**

1 Matthew 7:13
2 From *The Founder Speaks.*

# February 23rd

Now all has been heard; here is the conclusion of the matter: fear God and keep his commandments, for this is the duty of all mankind

(Ecclesiastes 12:13 *NIV*)

No matter how hard you may have to toil in other ways, you ought to spend a little strength on the work of pulling the poor sinners out of the fire.[1] Really pulling them out of the fires of sin, devilry and ruin, I say. Pulling them out in the open-airs – in the hall – in the drinking dens – in their homes. Whether young or old, in season or out of season, pulling them out of the fire. The Father gave his Son for this. Have you given any of your sons and daughters to help him in this task? If God counted it a joy to give his Son, what about your children? Perhaps you say you have no big boys or girls to send to the Training Garrison.[2] Well, what about the little ones, or what about some other dear one you could give? Have you consecrated them for the salvation of the world, and are you training them with that object in view?

How much money do you give to help to carry on the soul-saving work? If it were all added together, what would it amount to? If you were called up to Heaven today, and the account of your actual givings to God was read out before the angels, would the record make you blush for shame, or would the offerings of your generous heart make you rejoice with true joy? Oh, my comrades, God gave his Son to live and toil and die to save a perishing world. What have you given? What are you giving today?

God expects the Salvationist to do his duty; your General,[3] your officers, your comrades, and even the wicked world around you, expect it of you. By doing your duty I mean doing what you know you ought to do – to yourselves, to your fellow men, and to the God above you. Now, the consciousness that you are doing your duty is to be much admired. To eat and drink, to move about the world, to go in and out of your home conscious all the time that you are doing your duty, must be a very desirable experience.[4]

**My spiritual duty is simple and straightforward, Father; to love you and to love others. Yet, it can seem the hardest thing in the world to fulfil, and to do so consistently. That being the case, I rest in your provision of all that I require, day in and day out, as your servant. Amen.**

1 Zechariah 3:2
2 Built in 1900 for the purpose of training Salvation Army officers.
3 The world leader of The Salvation Army.
4 From *The Founder Speaks*.

# February 24th

Do not be negligent now, for the Lord has chosen you to stand before him and serve him

(2 Chronicles 29:11 *NIV*)

"There is therefore now no condemnation to them which are in Christ Jesus, who walk not after the flesh, but after the Spirit";[1] that is, those who are so united to Jesus Christ by their faith and his power that they are able to live not to please themselves, but to please God.

True peace is impossible to any man who wilfully neglects his duty. Whether that neglect concerns small or greater matters does not affect the question. The things done, or left undone, may be of the most trifling importance in themselves; but if it is a neglect of duty it becomes immensely important, because it is destructive of all confidence, and is in reality a defiance of all authority. Any form of religion, therefore, that allows a man to keep a hope of Heaven while living in the conscious neglect of duty, is a hypocrisy and, perhaps, the most dangerous form of hypocrisy ever invented either on earth or in Hell.

Consider your opportunities, your abilities, your circumstances, and find out what you can do to please your God and to bless your fellows. That work will be your duty. Having settled what your duty is, give yourselves up to the doing of it, without regard to any cost or consequences. If it really is your duty, that is, if God has called you to the task, you can rely upon his furnishing you with the means you require for its discharge. I have trusted him myself, again and again, for the means and power to carry me through with the discharge of my duty when the task has appeared all but impossible; and, glory to his name! He loves Salvationists who are prepared to struggle with difficulties in the discharge of their duty.

Then you must put away all that would be calculated to hinder you doing your duty. Come out from those pursuits and associations that are likely to make the discharge of your duty difficult, if not impossible. How foolish some Salvationists are in rushing into conditions which make their faithfulness to Christ and their spiritual warfare almost impossible.[2]

**Father, great God of detail, I pray today for your gracious help in attending to every detail of my walk with you, that I might not be negligent or careless. Keep my heart alert to opportunities, and also to dangers. Amen.**

1 Romans 8:1 *KJV*
2 From *The Founder Speaks.*

# FEBRUARY 25TH

MY GRACE IS SUFFICIENT FOR YOU, FOR MY POWER IS MADE PERFECT IN WEAKNESS

(2 Corinthians 12:9 *NIV*)

You must cast yourselves on the living God for strength to do your duty. He will enable you to grapple with any work he may have called you to do. He has promised that his grace shall be sufficient for you…

You must persevere. Do not be afraid of either circumstances, men, or devils. Satisfy yourselves on the rightness of the path on which you are travelling, and then let the cry be "Forward!" By this kind of perseverance you can look forward with confidence to the joy of receiving the crown of righteousness, which the Lord, the righteous Judge, will in the Last Great Day give to all those who have done their duty.[1] Oh, for a brave year! We shall have one! You will fight and drive the foe, rescue the prey, and enter the multitudes saved, sanctified, and safely landed in Glory!

We believe in salvation! We believe in the old-fashioned salvation. We have not developed and improved into Universalism, Unitarianism, or Nothingarianism, or any other form of infidelity, and we don't expect to. Ours is just the same salvation taught in the Bible, proclaimed by the prophets and apostles, preached by Luther and Wesley, and Whitefield, sealed by the blood of martyrs – the very same salvation which was purchased by the sufferings and agony and blood of the Son of God. We believe the world needs it, and that this and this alone will set it right. We want no other nostrum – nothing new. We are on the track of the old apostles.

You don't need to mix up any other ingredients with the heavenly remedy. Wound and kill with the old sword, and pour in the old balsam, and you will see the old result – SALVATION. The world needs it. The worst man that ever walked will go to Heaven if he obtains it, and the best man that ever lived will go to Hell if he misses it. Oh! Publish it abroad!…

To break them in pieces before the Lord, and bring them humbled in the dust at his footstool, is just what you want.[2]

**Victorious God, you have provided the ultimate remedy for the world's ills and woes. These are stark truths about eternal destiny; while they may sound old-fashioned, I pray that you will use me in my generation to lead people to the Lord Jesus, who died for them. Amen.**

1 2 Timothy 4:8
2 From *The Founder Speaks.*

# February 26th

This is what you must do: Tell the truth to each other
(Zechariah 8:16 *NLT*)

Pricking them [the people to whom God sends you] in the skin is worse than useless; you want them pricked in the heart. Never mind how they wince and cry out. Go over and over again with the truth that pierces and moves…

If ever there was a time, this is the time for straight dealing. God has set before you an open door.[1] You have the ear of the million. The people are in multitudes of instances prepared to receive the word at your lips. Surely you are the candle set in a candlestick;[2] you are the city set on a hill[3] – the eyes and ears of the multitude who are as sheep without a shepherd[4] turn to you – they hunger, they famish of hunger; they are dying, and being damned of hunger; will you give them pretty polished stones, flowers, flourishes, amusements, pacifications, or will you give them bread, plenty of bread, sufficient bread, the Bread of Heaven?[5] There is bread in your Father's house, and to spare. Hand it out, officers, hand it out, privates, men and women, hand it out seven days a week – Sundays and weekdays. Hand it out, that the people he has bought with his blood perish not.[6]

If you have any care for yourself, you must deal straight with the people; if you do not they will perish, and then you will hear of it again. An account of your stewardship will have to be rendered. Those eyes you look into now will confront you again, and those lips that now are silent while you speak will have an opportunity of speaking to you then. Oh, they shall reproach you with the bitter, never-to-be-forgotten reproach of not having dealt faithfully with them, not having told them the truth, all the truth, and told it them in such an earnest, plain, straight manner that they were made to hear and understand and feel the peril in which they stood, and the open way of escape provided for them… Make up your mind to speak about God's will.[7]

**Saving God, you have provided such a great means of salvation in Jesus Christ. Thank you! Sharing the gospel – speaking the truth – can seem daunting. Grant me courage. I pray for those within my circles of influence who do not believe, that your Holy Spirit will graciously soften their hearts. Amen.**

1 Revelation 3:8
2 Mark 4:21
3 Matthew 5:14
4 Matthew 9:36
5 John 6:32
6 2 Peter 3:9
7 From *The Founder Speaks.*

# February 27th

Preach the word; be prepared in season and out of season; correct, rebuke and encourage – with great patience and careful instruction

(2 Timothy 4:2 *NIV*)

Do not think it absolutely necessary to decide beforehand what you shall say. The Holy Spirit will supply you with words, and bless you in speaking[1] – keep a sharp look-out for opportunities as they arise. Again, I say, God will guide you. But wherever there is a chance, strive to make the most of it. Oh, how often these chances come and go unimproved! Do we not often reproach ourselves for having let such opportunities slip? "Why did I not speak about his soul to that man with whom I had the chat?" or "Why did I not drop a word to that woman whom I spoke to on some other matter?" Sometimes those to whom God has given us the chance of speaking are suddenly stricken down, and pass away. Then in bitterness of heart we say: "Oh, why did I not utter a word of warning when the chance was mine? Now they are gone beyond my reach for ever!" Perhaps God, on the Judgment Day, will echo that question, "Why?" Therefore, be watchful.

In speaking to strangers, be careful not to give needless offence. Speak kindly and gently, and with all due courtesy and respect, and you will be surprised how far you can go without creating ill-feeling. Should anyone ever be offended, you must apologize. Be sure and deal faithfully when you do speak. In many cases you can create interest by relating something of your own experience. Testimony is a wonderful thing and, when given modestly, with faith in God, generally moves the hearts of those who hear it.

Reckon on the conscience of every individual to whom you speak being on your side. For, however worldly they may appear, or with whatever scorn or indifference they may at first receive your words, everyone has a conscience, although perhaps dormant, but which may be quickened by the Holy Spirit using some word you may say. With a heart full of love, practice will bring the chief qualification for this kind of work: and that is courage. Be sure every time, and all the time, to cast yourselves on God for his blessing on what you say, remembering that he is with you.[2]

**Loving Father God, give me opportunities to speak of your love. Make me quick to recognize them. I trust you to provide me with the words I will need. Thank you. Amen.**

1 Matthew 10:19
2 From *The Founder Speaks.*

# February 28th

LET NO CORRUPTING TALK COME OUT OF YOUR MOUTHS, BUT ONLY SUCH AS IS GOOD FOR BUILDING UP, AS FITS THE OCCASION, THAT IT MAY GIVE GRACE TO THOSE WHO HEAR

(Ephesians 4:29 *ESV*)

Do not be discouraged if your words are rejected, or received with scorn or, it may even be, cast back in your teeth with sneers or curses. You can remember that this was the experience of your Lord, and that it is no proof that you have not said the right thing, and that it may not have the desired effect. It is not you who do the work, but the truth you speak. Unknown to you, the leaven you have imparted may be working in the heart you have approached, and the seed you have sown may be destined to bring forth precious fruit…

Conversation, in one form or another is, we can readily imagine, a privilege common to all living creatures. We know that the great Father in Heaven holds some sort of high intercourse with the holy beings by whom he is surrounded; and we have reason to believe that he does this through the medium of some celestial language. The archangels and angels, the Seraphim and Cherubim, and other of the inhabitants of Heaven, we are expressly informed, bow before his face, and cry, "Holy, holy, holy, is the Lord God Almighty."[1]

The Bible contains the record of many conversations that have taken place between God and his people on the earth in the past. Indeed, the sacred book is full of messages from Jehovah to men, commencing with "Thus saith the Lord", and of prayers and thanksgivings addressed back to God. All such communication is of the nature of conversation – God speaking to man, and man speaking to God…

The profit and pleasure proceeding from useful conversation can scarcely be overstated. Only count up the number of hours spent in a single year in company with kindred, friends, or strangers, which afford us the chance of profitable talk, and you will be surprised at the total. Instead of wasting all this precious time in useless gossip, think how large a portion of it could be agreeably employed in doing good to the peoples around you by profitable talk.[2]

**Lord of my speech, as I trust you for opportunities to share your love through my conversations, I pray too for wisdom to use those conversations well. Thank you for the numerous chances you give to share words that are influential, encouraging, and edifying. Please help me to maximize every opportunity.**

**Amen.**

1 See Isaiah 6:3
2 From *The Founder Speaks.*

# March 1st

**By the Holy Spirit who dwells within us, guard the good deposit entrusted to you**

**(2 Timothy 1:14 *ESV*)**

It is... gloriously true. God wants to live with you, not only in your home, but in your very heart. Poor and ignorant as you may be among men, and little noticed, nay, even despised, by the great and rich people of the world, yet God – the great God, whom the "heaven of heavens cannot contain"[1] – wants to come and live in your heart, and that not as a visitor only, but as an abiding guest. An old writer[2] curiously says, "God is like the rich people in one respect. He has two houses, a town house and a country house. His town house is in the celestial city, but his country house is in the hearts of his people." Hear what he says himself: "For thus saith the high and lofty One that inhabiteth eternity, whose name is Holy; I dwell in the high and holy place" and "with him also that is of a contrite and humble spirit" in order to "revive the spirit of the humble, and to revive the heart of the contrite ones".[3]

Brother, sister, can you not hear him saying, "Behold, I stand at the door, and knock: if any man hear my voice, and open the door, I will come in to him"?[4]... Will you not say, "Amen, come in, Lord Jesus, and come quickly"? Will you not let all go that would prevent him enter? Will you not fling the gates of your soul wide open, and let him come in? If you will, go down before him just now and bid him welcome. I have much more to say to you on this precious subject, but it must wait until another time. Meanwhile, wait no longer for a full salvation.

*O joyful sound of gospel grace!*
*Christ shall in me appear;*
*I, even, I, shall see his face;*
*I shall be holy here.*

*This heart shall be his constant home;*
*I hear his Spirit's cry;*
*"Surely," he saith, "I quickly come";*
*He saith, who cannot lie.*[5, 6]

**Living God, make my poor heart your dwelling. What a privilege it is to host the presence of deity. Amen.**

1 1 Kings 8:27 *KJV* and other verses
2 Unknown.
3 Isaiah 57:15 *KJV*
4 Revelation 3:20 *KJV*
5 Charles Wesley, 1707–88, "O Joyful Sound of Gospel Grace".
6 From *Purity of Heart*.

# March 2nd

Now may the Lord of peace himself give you peace

(2 Thessalonians 3:16 *NIV*)

A pure heart will give you peace. It is a condition for peace. You cannot have peace without it. I am always saying to you, in one form or another, that you must not expect a life of uninterrupted gladness in this world. It cannot be. Our imperfect bodies, with all their pains and weaknesses; the temptations of the devil, and the miseries of a world in rebellion against God prevent anything like a life of unmixed rejoicing for you and me.

But peace, the peace of God, the peace that "passeth all understanding",[1] is your birthright and, with a pure heart, the treasure shall be yours. I say again, that while you are here you must have certain strife. You cannot help it. You will have strife with the devil. War to the knife with Hell. You will have strife with wicked men. They will fight you because you are for righteousness and God, and for the deliverance of men. But, hallelujah! In the heart that is purified by the Holy Spirit, and sprinkled with the blood of the Lamb, the strife with God has ceased, the war with conscience is ended, the fear of death and Hell is over. The soul possessed of a pure heart has entered the rest that remaineth to the people of God.[2]

Do you enjoy this rest, my comrades? Is the inward strife over? Oh, make haste and let the blessed Spirit, who waits to sanctify you wholly, cast out the enemies of your soul!

It is not your poverties, nor your persecutions, nor your afflictions, nor your ignorance, nor ever so many things all put together, that prevent your perfect peace. Sin is the enemy; and when malice and indolence, and ambition and unbelief and every other evil thing has been cast out, your "peace shall flow as a river, and your righteousness shall abound as the waves of the sea".[3]

Purity of heart is the condition on which God will enter and dwell in your soul. Now listen, my comrades, and cry to God for an increase of faith.[4]

**Prince of Peace, my thoughts and prayers go to those who have no peace today – those who are troubled and whose thoughts give them no rest. Please, Lord, visit them, embrace them, and fill them with your peaceful Spirit. Amen.**

1 Philippians 4:7
2 See Hebrews 4:9
3 See Isaiah 48:18
4 From *Purity of Heart.*

# March 3rd

For as many of you as were baptized into Christ have put on Christ

(Galatians 3:27 *ESV*)

My dear comrades, has anything I have said set anyone among you longing after the possession of the precious, the inestimable, blessing of a pure heart?... It is those who "hunger and thirst after righteousness"[1] that are to be "filled". If this desire has been created, in any degree, I am delighted. Let me try and increase that longing, by holding up before your eyes some of the advantages that flow out of the possession of the blessing. And the first thing I mention that seems calculated to create this desire is [the] fact that:

A pure heart will ensure a holy life... What do I mean by a holy life? I answer that it is a life that meets the requirements, and ensures the fulfilment of the promises of this holy book; a life fashioned after the life of the Lord Jesus Christ. It will, at the best, be very imperfect, have many weaknesses about it, and be subjected to many mistakes; but still, according to the light possessed, it will be a holy life.

Is not such a life desirable, my comrades? Is not a man who is able to live out his religion before his family, before his workmates, and before the world, highly privileged? Will he not be a means of blessing to those around him, whichever way he turns? Look at him.

He is true to his promises and engagements. His word is his bond. You can trust him either in or out of sight. He has a true heart. He is industrious. He neither shirks his duty, nor wastes his time, nor scamps his work. He has an industrious heart. He is kind. He is loving to his wife, tender to his children, faithful to his comrades, considerate for his servants, gentle to the weak, sympathetic to the sick. He has a kind heart. He is compassionate. He pities the poor, yearns over the backslider, fights for the salvation of sinners in public, and cries to God for their deliverance in private; He has a soul-loving heart.[2]

**May the beauty of Jesus be seen in me. Amen.**

1 Matthew 5:6 *KJV*
2 From *Purity of Heart.*

# March 4th

## Unless I wash you, you have no part with me
(John 13:8 *NIV*)

"Then I will sprinkle clean water upon you, and ye shall be clean: from all your filthiness, and from all your idols, will I cleanse you. A new heart also will I give you, and a new spirit will I put within you; and I will take away the stony heart out of your flesh, and I will give you a heart of flesh. And I will put my spirit within you, and cause you to walk in my statutes, and you shall keep my judgments, and do them."[1] "… all things are possible to him that believeth."[2]

[Regarding sanctification] in the first stage the soul is under sin. In the second stage the soul is over sin. In the third stage the soul is without sin. In which stage are you, my comrades? Settle it for yourselves. Have you got a pure heart? Examine yourselves. What is your reply?

Some of you describing your experience can adopt the words of the apostle, with a little variation, and say: the very God of peace has sanctified me wholly; and he preserves my whole spirit and soul and body blameless, and he will continue to do so unto the coming of our Lord Jesus Christ. Faithful is he that has called me to this experience of purity, who also will do it.[3]

All glory to God, my comrades. Give him all the praise. Be careful to "walk in the light, as he is in the light", then shall you have fellowship with him and with other sanctified souls, and the blood of Jesus Christ his Son shall keep you cleansed from all sin.[4] In which case he will use you to promote his glory, make you useful, and show you still greater things.[5]

To those who know that they do not possess a pure heart, I put the question, will you have one now? God is waiting to cleanse you. What doth hinder your receiving the purifying baptism? "… now is the accepted time".[6, 7]

**The promise of a divine exchange is attractive: a clean heart for a stained one. As I pray, I offer you my heart, that no trace of sin may remain. Wash me, Lord, till every part be clean. Thank you. Amen.**

1 Ezekiel 36:25–27 *KJV*
2 Mark 9:23 *KJV*
3 1 Thessalonians 5:23–24 and Doctrine No. 10 of The Salvation Army: "We believe it is the privilege of all believers to be wholly sanctified, and that their whole spirit and soul and body may be preserved blameless unto the coming of our Lord Jesus Christ."
4 1 John 1:7 *KJV*
5 John 14:12
6 2 Corinthians 6:2
7 From *Purity of Heart.*

# March 5th

I will not be mastered by anything

(1 Corinthians 6:12 *NIV*)

In some people the governing evil may be something that is looked upon by the world as vulgar, such as drunkenness, or lust, or dishonesty, or gambling, or some other evil passion that has got hold of the sinner, and from which he cannot get away, and for which every precious thing on earth and in Heaven is sacrificed. In other cases it may be some sin that is not so much despised by what is called the respectable part of the community, such as pride, ambition, selfishness, secret infidelity, or the like. But, in some form or other, sin rules in the heart of every ungodly man. He is mastered by sin.

When [a man] is saved, not only does he receive the pardon of sin, but deliverance from its bondage. The yoke is broken, the fetters are snapped, the prison doors are opened: he is free! Instead of sin being his master, he is the master of sin. Instead of drink, or temper, or money-worship, or worldly pleasure, or some other devilish thing driving him down the broad way to destruction, against his judgment, against his own wishes, against the strivings of the Spirit, he is made free to do the will of God and climb the narrow way to Heaven. But, great and glorious as is the change wrought in the heart at conversion, maybe deliverance is not complete. The power of sin is broken, but there are still certain tendencies left in the soul. There are what the apostle terms "the roots of bitterness".[1] These evils ordinarily grow and increase in power, involving the soul in constant conflict, and as the time goes by often gain the mastery, and as the result there is much sinning and repenting…

Tired of this conflict, hating these internal evils, weeping over the pride and malice, and envy and selfishness that the soul still finds within, it rises up, and cries out… "Must I always have sin dwell within?" [2, 3]

**Father of liberty, to be trapped in sin is a terrible thing, but you have great and unique power to liberate all who come to you. My prayers reach out to those who are battling demons of all kinds, that you will visit them with a powerful touch, and bring release. Amen.**

1 See Hebrews 12:15
2 *The Song Book of The Salvation Army*, No. 459.
3 From *Purity of Heart.*

# March 6th

The life I now live in the flesh I live by faith in the Son of God, who loved me and gave himself for me

(Galatians 2:20 *ESV*)

I may be asked the question, "Does not God bestow... deliverance from sin on the soul at conversion? Does he not sanctify and make it good and holy at the same time that he pardons its sins?"

No, I reply; although a great work is done for the soul at conversion, its deliverance from sin at that time is not complete. It is true that he does a great deal for a man when he makes that remarkable change. He destroys the bondage in which sin holds the transgressor; but the destruction of sin out of the heart and out of the life is not entire...

Before a man or woman is converted, some particular sin is the master of the soul. That is, some unlawful appetite or selfish passion always rules the individual, and makes him act as it dictates.

What do I mean by sin being the master? I answer that the unconverted soul is held by it in a bondage from which it cannot get away. It has no choice. It is under its power. It must sin. The soul may have light to see its evil and ruinous character. It may hate it, struggle against it, make resolutions never to do it again. But it is driven by its own nature to do the things that it does not want to do; and is prevented from doing the things it wishes to do, often, as the apostle Paul describes, crying out in bitterness of spirit as it struggles and fights with it, "O wretched man that I am! Who shall deliver me from this wretched condition of slavery that is worse than death?"[1]

This is the experience of every unsaved man and woman; at least of everyone who has light to see what an evil thing sin is. It is true that the character of the mastering sin will differ in different persons.[2]

**Faithful God, however many times I get things wrong, and however I might struggle against one particular sin or another, I know that you will never give up on me. Your power to assist is always available. Your grace outweighs my weaknesses. Let that truth be my strength today. Amen.**

1 See Romans 7:24
2 From *Purity of Heart*.

# March 7th

For what I received I passed on to you as of first importance

**(1 Corinthians 15:3 *NIV*)**

My dear comrades, I hope that I shall not weary you by returning again to the question of a pure heart. The subject is so important to the whole Christian Church, to the entire Salvation Army, nay, to the wide, wide world, that it must be lifted up. Holiness has been so great a blessing to us in the past, and will, I am sure, be so much greater a blessing to us in the future, that I feel that it must be brought to the front. You must see its value, and understand its meaning.

If you are not living in the enjoyment of the peace, power, and gladness of holiness, it is, possibly, because you entertain some mistaken notions respecting it. The ability of the devil to lead people astray on this, as on many other questions, is largely in proportion to his power to deceive them. Can I better make you understand what is meant by purity of heart?…

By a pure heart we did not mean a heart that could not, or would not, be tempted, or that could not, or would not, be called to suffer; nor that the soldier out of whose heart all impurity had been expelled could not sin, or would have reached such a state of experience beyond which he would not be able to grow in faith, and hope, and charity, and in all the graces of the Holy Spirit.

Alas! Alas! We have the unspeakable sorrow of too frequently seeing saints and soldiers fall from holiness into sin. Some of the many miserable backsliders around us once walked closely with God.

What, then, is a pure heart? I reply that a pure heart is a heart that has been cleansed by the Holy Spirit from all sin, and enabled to please God in all it does; to love him with all its powers, and its neighbour as itself. Where this experience is enjoyed by anyone it may be said that God has made the heart pure, even as he is pure.[1]

**Dear Lord, prompt me to prioritize in a way that pleases you. Open the eyes of my heart to what is important and what is less important, in your opinion. Order all my days according to your will. Amen.**

1 From *Purity of Heart.*

# March 8th

Satan might not outwit us. For we are not unaware of his schemes

**(2 Corinthians 2:11 *NIV*)**

A pure heart is not a heart that cannot suffer. Beyond question, Jesus Christ had a pure heart; he was holy and undefiled, and yet he was "The Man of Sorrows".[1] [Peter] tells us that although he exercised himself to have always a conscience void of offence towards God and towards man, yet was he not saved from being, at times, "in heaviness through manifold temptations".[2] By a pure heart we do not mean a heart that cannot sin…

However pure you may become, it will be possible for you to sin. Though you wash your garments white, and for a season walk with God in holy communion, and have faith so that you can remove mountains and save multitudes, you must remember that while you are in this life it is possible for you to fall from grace. Nay, you must remember that unless you take heed to yourselves, and watch and pray, the probabilities are that you will be overtaken by some besetting sin and, after having saved others, become yourself a castaway. Therefore, "let him that thinkest he standeth take heed lest he fall".[3]

By a pure heart, we do not mean any experience of purity, however blessed it may be, that cannot increase in enjoyment, usefulness, and power. Pull the weeds out of your garden, and the flowers and plants and trees will grow faster, flourish more abundantly, and become more fruitful.

Just so, at this very moment, let Jesus Christ purge the garden of your souls of envy and pride, and remove the poisonous plants of malice and selfishness and every other evil thing, and faith and peace, and hope and love, and humility and courage, and all the other beautiful flowers of Paradise will flourish in more charming beauty and more abundant fruitfulness.

Oh, will you not go down now before God and give yourselves fully over into the hands of your precious Saviour? He is waiting to sanctify you. Cast overboard all that hinders. It is God that purifies the heart. Will you let him do the work?[4]

**Gracious Lord, I am safest when I keep close to you, despite every wily trick of my enemy. Hold me today, I pray, and keep me well within the boundary of your love. This is to your glory. Amen.**

1 See Isaiah 53:3
2 1 Peter 1:6 *KJV*
3 1 Corinthians 10:12 *KJV*
4 From *Purity of Heart.*

# March 9th

Conduct yourselves in a manner worthy of the gospel of Christ
(Philippians 1:27 *NIV*)

I want to tell you some good news. I've got a letter from Captain Windy, and it's a real beauty. He says that the Provincial Commander[1] has been made up to his division, and that they have a great Congress,[2] and all the officers have got a mighty blessing for this winter's campaign; and that he believes God has cleansed his soul from all desire to cut it fine on the platform, and all that sort of thing; and that he went home and burnt all his flowery sermons. He says now that the heavenly gales are blowing in his heart all the time, and that at every meeting he holds the soldiers are being revived, and sinners are getting saved.

The letter has "set me up on a rock",[3] and our Sarah as well, because Captain Windy was a bit of a favourite with her, and she says that she always believed that he would come out all right some day, and that she's put that letter away in the same drawer where she keeps the letters that Jack sends from America. And she says that she is going to get Captain Windy to pray for Jack, which is what she always does with anybody whom she thinks has got any extra blessing.

That news about Captain Windy has greatly cheered me, and I shall try and persuade our captain to have him over to our corps this Christmas-time. I was talking about it to Sarah over breakfast this morning, and she said she would like it very much; and, if he came, she would put him up with pleasure. Now, I was glad to hear that, because she has refused to have anybody here since Captain Makebelieve stayed with us last Easter twelve months... Sarah didn't like the captain... what she did not approve of was that the captain never did any religion in the family. He never read the Bible, nor prayed, nor said anything to the children about being officers; and she has fairly set her heart on that.[4]

**Heavenly Father, I pray for grace so that in public and in private, I may live in a way that brings credit to the name of Christ. Whether I preach from a pulpit or witness within my family circle, fill me with your Spirit so that my life is seen as authentic, bringing glory to you. Amen.**

1 A rank now obsolete.
2 A national (territorial) or local (divisional) gathering of Salvationists.
3 See Psalm 27:5
4 From *Sergeant-Major Do-Your-Best.*

# March 10[TH]

Be fervent in spirit, serve the Lord

(Romans 12:11 *ESV*)

Jim Wobbleton… has lots of persecution, poor fellow, and not overmuch backbone to stand up against it. He has been in and out of the corps I don't know how many times; and, in fact, he has never gone straight so long, and seemed so firm, as he has done since this captain came on the scene; and I really believe that if our captain could stop here for ever that Jim would never backslide again. Well, I do like to see Jim looking bright and happy…

And, then, although I'm sergeant-major of this corps, and have a good wife as always helps me along, and a situation at twenty-five shillings a week all the year round, only as when there is something happens such as a strike – which I'm sorry to say they're talking about now. But, if they pull it off, as two or three of them say they're going to, I've made up my mind to have a regular go at the people in every house of the town about their souls, and trust in God to find the family a bit of bread and butter till the thing is over.

I mentioned the scheme to Sarah last night, after we got in bed, and she says to me: "Steve, you're a good man, and you've got more faith than I have, and the Divisional Officer says you're the best sergeant-major in the division, but you haven't got the responsibility on you for feeding these children, as I have; but," says she, "the captain says as how the Lord will provide, so we'll trust him, and go to sleep."

Still, as I was saying, I have my trials, and I like to forget 'em all, and have my soul set on fire, and our captain is just the man to make such a meeting as does that for you. Then, there is another reason why I like our captain; and that is, because he gets souls saved… I do like to see people come to the penitent form… and our captain is the boy to do it.[1]

**Lord, inspire me with a selfless love for souls. Amen.**

1 From *Sergeant-Major Do-Your-Best.*

# March 11th

"But what about you?" he asked. "Who do you say I am?" Simon Peter answered, "You are the Messiah."

(Mark 8:29 *NIV*)

[An objection] to the necessity of the atonement declares: "If the offence of man was the serious evil that you assert, and if God could not forgive that offence without being some remarkable intervention on the part of some great being who should become a wonderful example of freedom from sin, and yet of suffering for it – then are we not justified in believing that the holy life of Jesus Christ and the death he endured were sufficient to impress humanity with the required sense of the value of the Law, and the evil of the offence that had been committed against it, without our being called upon to regard him as a divine being? That is – could he not have made the needed sacrifice without being more than man?"

No! We do not think he could. If he had been nothing more than man he must himself have been a transgressor of the Law, seeing that "all have sinned, and come short of the glory of God" (Romans 3:23 *KJV*), and in that case he would have required a sacrifice for his own sins. Even if that difficulty were surmounted, but Jesus Christ had been only a human being, it would have been impossible for him to furnish sufficient merit to meet the needs of a world of sinners. Again, in whatever meritorious work Jesus Christ performed, or whatever sufferings he endured, if he had been merely human, instead of being the Saviour of the world, as he is presented to be, he would have been only one of the saviours of the world.

If he were not more than man, the Christian world has been deceived for 2,000 years as to the value of the blood he shed, the intercession he has made and the worship that has been rendered him. If his work for me were nothing more than human wisdom devised, and human passion compelled, and human nature endured, then I can accept it or reject it as I think fit, without condemnation from anyone. If Jesus Christ were not a divine person there would be nothing more to make me condemn myself for not accepting him as my Saviour, than in my refusing to believe in some other human benefactor.[1]

**Lord Jesus, I acknowledge you as God. I worship you as my Saviour. You are Messiah and Lord. Yours is the name high over all. Amen.**

1 From *The Founder Speaks Again.*

# MARCH 12TH

LET YOUR SPEECH ALWAYS BE GRACIOUS, SEASONED WITH SALT, SO THAT YOU MAY KNOW HOW YOU OUGHT TO ANSWER EACH PERSON

**(Colossians 4:6 *ESV*)**

Poor Yorkey took quite a fancy to the Army, attending its meetings and purchasing an Army medal, though without the least idea that he would ever take his place in the ranks. One Sunday afternoon, when in his drunken desperation he had actually resolved to murder his wife, what he heard so affected him that the captain's wife coming round from seat to seat to seek the lost ones, found this strong man in tears. "Oh!" said he, when she spoke to him. "It is no use talking to me; you would not speak to me if you knew what a bad man I am. There could not have been a worse than me anywhere." Of course, this avowal only brought upon him the more kindly pressure, and the redoubtable fighting man was soon completely subdued, and pleading for mercy with others at the penitent form, where his Saviour speedily lifted the load of guilt from his heart.

When he rose up to speak, someone suggested that he now put on his medal,[1] which he immediately did, and he went out from that hall to be from that time invariably and everywhere a bold witness for Christ. Who will ever forget seeing the active little man as he stood on the platform at Exeter Hall, and before other great audiences, to show how great things God had done for him? So far from having any inclination to boast of past ill deeds, he would almost always burst into tears when he came to speak of the dark deeds of the past, and especially of his ill-treatment of his wife.

He said, in Exeter Hall: "I'm thankful to say I'm saved. I wasn't seven months ago; I was following the devil's forces, but now, thank God, I'm following the Lord above. I was very pleased when I got to know I was coming up to my old quarters in London. I have done many bad deeds in this part of the country, and I'm going to do many good 'uns now… I've gone to chapels and churches, but they could never do anything wi' me, but, thank God… the Army did the thing for me – they plucked me out of the gutter."[2]

**Father, the captain's wife in this story took the time to speak words of love and grace to someone in great need of your love. She was not deterred, or easily discouraged. Bless me, I pray, and all your witnesses, with similar compassion and tenacity. Amen.**

1 Possibly, a local award of some kind – maybe an award for temperance.
2 From *The Salvation War, 1883.*

# MARCH 13TH

WHEN YOU MAKE A VOW TO GOD, DO NOT DELAY TO FULFIL IT

(Ecclesiastes 5:4 *NIV*)

Do not all professedly Christian parents desire that their children shall be really religious? They say so when first their babe is placed into their arms. You would think so as you hear them pray when kneeling by its little cot; they declare it at the baptismal font, and elsewhere, when in the most solemn manner they promise to train it for God, and on its behalf renounce the world and all its pomps, and the devil and all his works.

Parents do a great deal of sentimental talking and praying about their dear children being nurtured for the Lord, but we fear that in the hearts of very few is there any definite purpose that their sons and daughters shall be trained to follow the Lord Jesus Christ, in such hardships and persecutions, self-denial, and toil as the following of Christ really signifies. Alas! How few professedly Christian fathers and mothers plan anything higher for their children than that they should be so educated and brought up as to secure comfortable earthly positions! Is not this made only too evident by their being just as anxious as the rest of the world that their children shall be comfortable or rich, or learned, or famous? And do not these purposes determine, in the main, the training and education that they give them?...

If anyone were to prophesy to them that these children would grow up godless, and at last die in their sins, and go to Hell, and also propose that they should train their children for this end, they would be very much shocked, and indignantly refuse to educate them after such an inhuman manner. But the poor children would have a far better chance of finding out the truth were they to do so; for as it is, while praying and talking about their anxiety that their children should be Christians, they are all the time training them as closely as possible for a life of worldliness and selfishness. All the blessing such parents want from the Lord is that the children may have success down here, and that when living on earth any longer is impossible, they may be taken to Heaven.[1]

**Promise-keeping God, it is so easy to make vows and take part in ceremonies without always realizing their solemnity. My prayer is that you will touch and bless the lives of all those who offer their children for baptism or dedication, that your Spirit would impress upon them the truth of the words they speak. May I be a good example of honesty and faithfulness. Amen.**

1 From *The Training of Children.*

# March 14th

LIKE ARROWS IN THE HANDS OF A WARRIOR ARE CHILDREN BORN IN ONE'S YOUTH

(Psalm 127:4 *NIV*)

There shall be on the part of the parents a clear idea of the nature and value of the godly life desired for their children, of the training to secure it, and of their own responsibility for imparting it… Because children are entrusted to them for the very purpose – this is the parents' special duty. They are stewards before God, responsible to him for the discharge of it. Every father and mother ought to look upon their child as a sacred trust from Jehovah, as much so as though sent to their arms by an angel direct from Heaven, with the similar command which Pharaoh's daughter gave with the infant Moses, when she placed him in the charge of his mother, "Take this child away, and nurse it for me, and I will give thee thy wages." – Exodus [2:]9 (*KJV*).

Indeed, this is exactly what the King of kings has done. He has entrusted you with that boy or girl in order that you may lead it to the Saviour, train it in holy living, instruct it as to the nature of the foul rebellion raging against his authority, and inspire it with undying devotion to His cause. In other words, you may mould and shape it into a holy, loving saint, fit for the worship of God and the companionship of angels in Heaven, and into a courageous, self-sacrificing, skilful warrior, able to war a good warfare on his behalf on earth.

By many – even professing Christians – children seem to be regarded as a necessary evil, to be avoided, if possible, as being in the way of their comfort and ease, and involving a great deal of trouble and expense. By others children are looked upon simply as a means of selfish gratification, welcomed and regarded with no higher feelings than those with which the animals regard their offspring. Parents calculate about their children with favour or disfavour just as they seem likely to minister to their own pleasure, gratify their family pride… or help them in carrying out some ambitious aims.

How will you deal with your trust?…[1]

**Father, help me always to regard children as a great gift and a blessing, and in doing so, to treat them kindly. Today, I pray for children in my neighbourhood who appear to have no Christian influence at home. Please use my church, and the churches nearby, to reach them for Christ. Inspire our outreach and planning. Amen.**

1 From *The Training of Children.*

# March 15th

SAUL WAS UTTERING THREATS WITH EVERY BREATH AND WAS EAGER TO KILL

(Acts 9:1 *NLT*)

When those who have been discussing the good and bad of The Salvation Army, and when some of its true friends read or hear how men and women, remarkable for everything that is most irreligious and horrible, have been changed into bold witnesses for Christ, it is very natural that the question should be asked – Will they (the converts) stand? Do they stand? Can they stand? One of the many answers which we could delight to point to upon this question comes to us in the saddened form of funeral notes sent up from time to time, as someone who has done noble service in the ranks is called away to take his eternal place above.[1]

The year just closing [1883] has been remarkably rich in these records, or rather would have been remarkably rich in them, but for the fact that so few of our officers or soldiers being skilled writers, we get but scanty accounts of most of those who in life have been most serviceable, and who in death leave behind the brightest testimony.

Last year, a man who had been pre-eminent for wickedness, even amongst the worst, came to our services in the Albert Hall in Sheffield. Wasting his earnings in drunkenness and vice for many years past, he had had his home sold up eleven times, had lived in thirty-eight different houses, and had fought scores of times for money. An old companion of his worst days once wrote to one of our officers, about him: "Captain, I am very pleased you have got one of the worst characters that ever walked about England. I am pleased to say he has turned a different man. He has stripped and fought many a battle, and has never been beaten to my knowledge. He fought seven battles in our part in twelve months. The last battle he fought was with me… Our sporting men will be surprised to hear that he has joined The Salvation Army… He has done everything but murder, and we don't know whether he has done that or not."[2]

**Gracious Father, when I read that Saul was transformed from someone with murder in mind to arguably the greatest evangelist of all time, I marvel at your power to change lives. Bless your Church with faith to believe wholeheartedly in that transforming grace, that even the vilest offender might be saved. Amen.**

1 Announcements and tributes in Salvation Army publications.
2 From *The Salvation War, 1883.*

# March 16th

I HAVE TOLD THE GLAD NEWS OF DELIVERANCE IN THE GREAT CONGREGATION

(Psalm 40:9 *ESV*)

If our captain is not much to look at, what there is of him is good stuff, and I always forget his looks once he gets going. No, he is not a great Bible man either, although he has got some pieces out of the old book that he can put [to] you in such a way as makes your flesh creep, or softens you down till you cry like a child. And then, all that he does say, when he gets into the Spirit, sounds like Bible to me.

But, anyhow, there is one thing he can do, if I am any judge – and I reckon I am, at least I ought to be, or I should not be fit to be sergeant-major of this corps; and the Divisional Officer said, when he met our soldiers three months ago, that I was one of the best local officers[1] in the division, which our Sarah will never forget, and is always calling to mind when anybody says anything that reflects on me. I don't think the dear little woman will forget that speech of the Divisional Officer's as long as she lives – God bless her! Well, what I was saying was, that our captain can make a proper Salvation Army meeting. What do I mean by a proper meeting? Well, I reckon that a good meeting should cheer the soldiers up – and some of my comrades have a great deal to put up with, I can tell you.

There's Harry Hardtimes, poor fellow, he is not very strong, and has the rheumatics, and can only do odd jobs now and then, and he has a sick wife and five youngsters. I expect the devil gets at him pretty strong now and then, and I like to see him forget his troubles and get real happy.

Then, there is Mary Holdfast, with her drunken husband who, our Sarah says, knocks her about awfully in his mad fits. I feel sure she don't get enough to eat, and I made Sarah fetch her into dinner the other Sunday; and my didn't she eat ravenous.[2]

**Father, the privilege of Christian fellowship is so easily taken for granted. Thank you for my friends at church. Use me to make people feel welcome, and to practise hospitality towards those who might appreciate a handshake or a meal. Bless my fellowship with your continued presence. Amen.**

1 Local officers are The Salvation Army's equivalent of church elders; given certain responsibilities on a voluntary basis.

2 From *Sergeant-Major Do-Your-Best.*

# March 17th

I will be with you as you speak, and I will instruct you in what to say

(Exodus 4:12 *NLT*)

When we opened barracks after barracks[1] eighteen months ago, people asked me where I should get my preachers from. I replied, "From the tap-rooms."[2] That this answer was a correct one, The Salvation Army itself is an unanswerable affirmation. Alas! Alas! These kindred institutions seem still to form inexhaustible sources of supply of the same sort of people – close to us, at our doors. There they are; young men and young women, exactly the kind we want – the right age, the right height, the right strength, with just such strength, with just such gifts, and go, and enterprise, and daring we need.

They can sing and march and pray just after the fashion we need. All that is wanting is that they shall have another spirit in them – a right spirit, a good spirit – the Spirit of holiness, the Spirit of love, the Spirit of Christ; that, instead of being filled with the devil, they should be filled with God. Then they will talk the right talk, sing the right songs, march in the right direction. Instead of living for themselves, they will live for others. Instead of taking men by their influence, gifts and songs, and enthusiasm down to Hell, they will, by their influence, gifts, songs, and enthusiasm take them with them up to Heaven.

Now, my comrades, here is the plan. You see what I want. You see what the world needs. You see what the Army requires. Here is the demand, and there is the supply.

A man in a country, the woods of which abounded with game, and the rivers of which were filled with fish – to all of which he was welcome if only he had the nous and the ability to capture them – would have little excuse for starving, and little pity for being in want. Let him take his gun and go into the woods, and his lines and go to the river; and just so, my comrades, there are the streets and the alleys and the lanes and the houses swarming with exactly the sort of men and women we want.[3]

**Lord of the word, those charged with the responsibility of preaching the gospel have a great privilege. I give thanks for those you call and equip, praying your rich blessing on evangelists, teachers, and all who speak in the name of Jesus. Bless, too, those involved in training and nurturing preachers and ministers. Amen.**

1 Salvation Army halls and training bases were known as barracks.
2 Public house saloons.
3 From *The General's Letters.*

# March 18th

The Spirit of the Lord is on me, because he has anointed me

(Luke 4:18 *NIV*)

Dear comrades, I… found some encouragement… in the consideration that a host of young people were being trained up by Salvation mothers and fathers in different parts of the world to come boldly forward and bear their burdens in the coming campaigns. But it has occurred to me that this is rather a chilly consolation, seeing that the coming of this host to the rescue is in the distance. What is to be done in the present generation? Before the rising one is reared, and sanctified, and trained, this generation will largely have passed off the stage, and gone to its reward. Cannot something definite and desperate be done to meet the definite and desperate demands of the moments?

We must have officers. The people are perishing. We want men and women filled with this idea, and filled with the idea of the grand remedy that is provided, and filled with the resistless power of the Holy Ghost, who will go and force these same ideas upon the world about them. Surely there should not be any difficulty in finding a multitude of such.

God speed the rising race! Let everybody help God to speed it! Mothers and fathers, captains and lieutenants, sergeants and soldiers, help the little ones! Put them on the altar. Spend time and money and strength in teaching and training them. Nurse them for God. Fill them with the war spirit. When they fall, pick them up again. When they are discouraged, cheer their little hearts. Get them saved. Get them into uniform. Write their names on the roll.

When they are carried away by their childish impulses from the straight paths of truth and righteousness, fetch them back again; get them washed and forgiven, and encourage them for another start. March them in the procession. Possess their minds with the truth. Fill their mouths with your songs. Teach them your music, and hurry them on in every possible way to get ready for the fight.[1]

**God of all ages, this day I pray for those called to vocations, that your good hand would guide them and steer them. For those you call as children, I ask your shield of protection around them, that nothing would hinder their calling, that you would nurture their destiny. Amen.**

1 From *The General's Letters.*

# March 19th

Stand up and praise the Lord your God
(Nehemiah 9:5 *NIV*)

Another good reason why I like our captain is because he makes good meetings. We always have a good time when he's at the hall. Is he always there? Why, no, I should think he isn't. Where is he? Well, he has got two outposts,[1] which he works with all his might. Why, ours is as good as a Circle Corps,[2] and some of our soldiers don't altogether like it, because he often goes off and leaves his lieutenant and your humble servant to do our own concern as best we can; and some of them say… if they pay the salary of a captain, they ought to have all his services; which seems to me very selfish, and I don't like it. But, then, the captain thinks the outpost's all right, and that's enough for me.

But, I was saying, when you interrupted me, that we always have good times when he's at the hall. I don't know how it is, either, for he's not what you would call a great preacher. He can't keep at it a long time, and say lots of fine things you can't understand, and he never uses hard words that you don't know what they mean. He is nowhere in the running alongside of Captain Spin-it-out in these matters; but what he does say goes into your stomach, and fetches the water out of your eyes, and makes you feel ashamed of the bit of religion you've got, and resolve you'll get more before the day is out.

And then he can't come up to Captain Melodian at singing a solo, no how; but, still, my word, he makes everybody else sing. Why, there's my poor old mother – God bless her! She's been a dear old soul to me as was a deal of trouble to her before I was saved – Granny, the children call her, for she is getting on in years now, and it takes two sticks and a quarter of an hour to get her into the hall; but the captain makes mother sing, I can tell you![3]

**Lord God, you are worthy of all the praise and worship I can offer, though even that is humble and inadequate. Know that I love you, and receive my homage, whether that is in word, music, song, or action. Give me a melody in my heart today. Amen.**

1 Church plants, or "daughter" corps.

2 A corps where the officers lived and primarily worked, with outposts or other corps within a radius of eight or ten miles.

3 From *Sergeant-Major Do-Your-Best*.

# March 20th

## Be shepherds of the church of God

(Acts 20:28 *NIV*)

Our captain… is so kind. You can see his love for you in his very face, and hear it in his talk; and, best of all, it comes out in such a many little ways in his life. He's not proud, nor uppish, nor above anybody. The roughs in the street speak to him as if he belonged to them – which he always reckons he does. They say: "Good morning, Captain; how are yer today? Keep yer pecker up!" and he always answers them back with a kind word.

And then he's always ready to help anybody about the place, and does lots of things that some people don't reckon to be in the regular work of a captain. You should see how he visits the soldiers, and anybody else that's sick; and how kind he is to the old folks, and how he pats the children on the head, and speaks to them just as if they were his own relations. And I believe he drags miles every week to visit poor old cripples that can't get to the citadel at all. And then he thinks nothing of helping anybody with their work. Why, I've known him carry an old woman's bundle to the station, and wheel an old man's barrow up the hill. And isn't he just at home advising people on their troubles. He has such a kind way about it that our poor soldiers go and tell him when they're stuck fast as would not get up courage to go and talk to many captains.

He is what I call regler kind, and you can't help but love him – at least, I can't; and, if I was a captain, I would try and do just that sort of thing myself, because I know that it makes people pray for you, and work in the meetings, and sell "Crys",[1] and do something in the Harvest Festivals, and put something into the box at the collection, and all that kind of thing. He's not grand enough for some folks that I know of, but he is just my sort. Three cheers for our captain![2]

**Thank you, Lord, for good ministers and leaders. Bless them, Lord, as they go about their business. Strengthen them if they face criticism or tough times. Refresh them when they are weary. Use me to support and encourage my minister in prayer and practical ways. Amen.**

1 *The War Cry*, sold in public houses and on the streets as a way of sharing the gospel and raising funds.
2 From *Sergeant-Major Do-Your-Best.*

# March 21st

### Whatever you do, work heartily, as for the Lord

(Colossians 3:23 *ESV*)

We had Captain Gentleton here last year, and he was a very good man, I believe. The Divisional Officer said he was, when he introduced him. But, then, he wasn't strong. And his wife wasn't strong, and his children wasn't strong either, and the poor fellow always had to be taking care of himself, or nursing the family, or doing it for them, so that people somehow got the notion that he took things a little easy – which I never believed, because I make it a part of my religion not to think evil things about our officers. But the roughs never shout after our captain, as they did after Captain Gentleton, "Go and work!" which used to hurt his feelings very much, and made me very sorry for him; besides, it was a kind of reflection on the corps. I hope he is in better health now, wherever he is, although I think as how he was having a furlough somewhere the last time I heard about him…

Our captain works; and I do think myself, sometimes, that he goes rather too far for his strength; because, as our Sarah puts it, he's not strong; and she's a knowing little woman; although she's not so little either, as she tells me sometimes. "Steve," she says, "what good should I have been to tug after thee and thy nine children, if I'd been little?" But then, you know, it is only a way I have of talking about her.

Well, Sarah says that the captain's wife told her the other day, when she was trying to get Sarah to persuade the captain to have a furlough, "Yes, I do think," she said, "that John goes to extremes, for he works all through the day as hard as he can, and he never turns in at night while he can sit up any longer; and I say to him sometimes: 'Do you want to leave me a widow, and the three children, the eldest of whom is only five years, all [alone] in the world?' But he answers nothing, except it is that he must do his duty."[1]

**Lord of my labours, I thank you for the privilege of employment, and I ask you to bless my endeavours today. Keep me mindful of a healthy balance between work and recreation, for my sake, and for the sake of others. Equip me for every task that is mine this day. Amen.**

1 From *Sergeant-Major Do-Your-Best.*

# March 22nd

This is how we know what love is: Jesus Christ laid down his life for us

(1 John 3:16 *NIV*)

Think, only think, what it would mean if the Saviour were to change. So that he could no longer make his sun rise and his rain to fall on the evil and on the good;[1] if he could no longer bestow his convincing, guiding, comforting Spirit; if he were to grow weary of interceding at the Father's right hand;[2] if he could no longer forgive repentant sinners or perform other works of mercy. Can you realize how calamitous that change would be? But, 10,000 hallelujahs! There is a friend who changes not! His name is Jesus!… He is the same yesterday, and today, and for ever.[3] That means:

He loves us as much today as he did the hour he came down from Heaven to save us. Oh, how he must have loved you, my comrades, on that day – even you, who are listening to this letter – to face for you the humiliation, hardship, scorn, and suffering that he endured! And I want you to see and feel that he loves you just as much today.

He knew all about your unworthiness; he foresaw your unfaithfulness; he realized the poor return you would make for his love; but these things did not deter him from coming. He has not altered. He has not given you up. You have not worn out his compassion. He still has the same pitying love for you. He is just the same today. He loves you the same as he did at that solemn moment when he died for you. Job says: "all that a man hath will he give for his life."[4] Jesus gave up his life for you. What a love that must have been!

You may have friends who would be willing to give their money, or their time, or their country, to save you from suffering or death, but very few who would give up their lives.[5] But Jesus gave up his life for you. What a love that must have been! And he loves you as well today as he did when he broke his mighty heart for you on the cross.[6]

**Lord Jesus, the thought of you changing is unimaginable. So much – everything – rests upon your love, power and presence. Your faithfulness towards me is humbling. Thank you for dying for me, unchanging Saviour! Amen.**

1 Matthew 5:45
2 Romans 8:34
3 Hebrews 13:8
4 Job 2:4 *KJV*
5 Romans 5:7
6 From *The Founder's Messages to Soldiers*.

# March 23[RD]

For all the promises of God find their Yes in him

**(2 Corinthians 1:20 *ESV*)**

There are some changes which cannot be considered either profitable or desirable. For instance: There is backsliding. Going back on your pledges; breaking your vows to the Lord; deserting the flag;[1] leaving your comrades to struggle as best they can; throwing up your hope of Heaven, and crucifying your Saviour afresh. That is a shameful and distressing change. If anyone listening to this message has been guilty of such conduct, and has not repented and turned to his Lord, let me implore him to make the change from the miserable condition of the prodigal in the far country to the gladness and plenty of the Father's heart and arms.[2] Before this meeting closes, let him come home. Some personal changes are deplorable. For two hearts and lives once joined together in close affection, like David's and Jonathan's,[3] to be separated in spirit and action, must be a distressing change indeed, no matter how the severance may have been brought about. But when those hearts belong to members of the same family, the change is more painful still.

The love of the Chinese and Japanese peoples for their kindred, and especially the honour and reverence with which they regard their parents, and even their long-departed ancestors, greatly endeared them to me, when instances of this affection were brought before my notice during my recent Japanese Campaign.[4] When, on account of sickness, or old age, or for any other cause, children get tired of their parents, count them a burden, throw off their guidance, and leave them to their fate, they neglect one of their most sacred duties, and displease him who says, "Honour thy father and thy mother, that thy days may be long in the land which the Lord thy God giveth thee."[5]

What a calamity it must be when a husband's affection for his wife, or a daughter's love for her mother, changes into indifference, hatred, or something more dreadful still! It seems to me that there is only one change which could cause more pain to a human heart, and that would be if the Saviour were to change.[6]

**You are a God who heals, restores, and forgives. Today, I bring to you those who are struggling with change; for whom it is traumatic. Gently minister your love. Amen.**

1 Salvationists are sworn into membership underneath a Salvation Army flag.
2 Luke 15:11–32
3 See 1 Samuel 20 ff.
4 Booth visited Japan in 1907.
5 Exodus 20:12 *KJV*
6 From *The Founder's Messages to Soldiers*.

# March 24th

I HAVE STORED UP YOUR WORD IN MY HEART

(Psalm 119:11 *ESV*)

The Bible is a valuable book, because from it we learn all that we know about the birth and life and suffering and death and resurrection of our Lord and Saviour, Jesus Christ. Except for one or two passing remarks in one other very ancient book, we should all be in ignorance of the career of our Lord but for the Bible. Then we have the wonderful story of his earthly journeyings, his marvellous miracles, his wonderful addresses; his glorious death and resurrection; and oh, what a fascinating story it is!

The Bible tells us all we know with certainty about the future state. We should be in utter ignorance of what happens after death if it were not for the Bible. It is the Bible that tells us of the resurrection of the dead, the Great White Throne,[1] the Heaven of delight, and the Hell of misery. But for the Bible we should be in complete darkness concerning these important things. It is the Bible that tells us of the merits of the precious blood of our dear Saviour, the possibilities of the forgiveness of sins, the purification of our hearts, the protection of God, and the triumphs of a dying hour. Of these blessed possibilities mankind would know nothing without the Bible.

The truths written down and explained in the Bible have done wonders for Salvationists. But for the free salvation set forth in the Bible, many of you would have been in the grave, and your souls cast into outer darkness, while others would have been on their way there. Oh, precious book! What a priceless blessing…

Now, my comrades, what ought you to do with the Bible? Ought you to neglect it – pass it over for the newspaper, the storybook, or other rubbish? By no means. That is how the godless world around you deals with the precious treasure. What, then, ought you to do?… Read a few verses at a time; read them on your knees; read them as you walk the streets; while you take your midday meal, when you rise in the morning, when you retire at night; and read the blessed book in your spare moments.[2]

**Thank you for your uniquely powerful word, for its depth of riches and its marvellous quality as spiritual nourishment. As I read the Bible, please shine your light on its pages, so that I may correctly understand your ways and feast on your love. Bless those of your children who are denied access to your word. Amen.**

1 Revelation 20:11

2 From *The Founder Speaks.*

# March 25th

## I the Lord do not change

(Malachi 3:6 *NIV*)

I want to talk to you a little this morning about our unchangeable Saviour, and have chosen as a text that beautiful passage in Hebrews 13:8, which reads: "Jesus Christ the same yesterday, and to day, and for ever" (*KJV*).

Now this world is a world of change from the very beginning of life to the end. Many of its changes are useful and profitable and, therefore, interesting and desirable. For instance: There are the seasons. Winter changes into spring, then comes summer, which is followed by autumn, and then we have winter again. What interest, profit, and pleasure these changes impart to our lives! Again, there is the weather. We are always complaining of its fickleness; at least, some of us are; but only think of the benefits the changes about which we grumble too heartily often bring to us. We should not like it to be always hot or always cold, however much we may prefer at times to have a long spell of either one or the other.

Then, there are the changes from poverty to riches, from riches to poverty, from bondage to liberty and, again, from liberty to bondage, which we often hear about. All these have their advantages…

Then, there are the changes of comradeship and command which we, as Salvationists, are constantly experiencing. The coming and going of the officers of the corps, or of the division, or even of those in higher positions still, make things not only more useful, but more lively.[1]

And, then, the changes which belong to our passing from childhood to youth, and from youth to maturity, are also of great interest. What a different thing life would have been had we all come into the world full-grown men and women! And yet I do not think that such an arrangement would have been as good for us, or that we should have liked it so well as the present one. Then, there is the change that comes last of all – the passing out of time into eternity. Death is, at best, a mournful event, but none of us who have a good hope of the change from earth to Heaven[2] would wish to continue in this world.[3]

**Your faithfulness is truly great, God my Father. Cause me to be mindful of that when doubts or changing circumstances might challenge my faith. Amen.**

1 Salvation Army officer personnel are frequently moved from one appointment to another.
2 Colossians 1:5
3 From *The Founder's Messages to Soldiers.*

# March 26th

## Shepherd the flock of God that is among you

(1 Peter 5:2 *ESV*)

Faithful oversight will include direction as to duty and all that concerns it. It almost amounts to cruelty to put officers down without careful guidance to the discharge of their duties, which priests and bishops, who have spent years studying and practising, would stagger at.

You must help them in their talking; help them in their praying; help them in their singing; help them in the management of their soldiers; help those who are engaged in office or other work behind the scenes, and see that they get a share of work on the public battlefield; help them all as far as you can to do their work, and do it well, and you shall share in their reward.

Faithful oversight will include the exercise of impartial discipline. You must be a disciplinarian or you will be a failure – but you must be an affectionate one, and if your discipline is based on these qualities it will not only be accepted, but those who are disciplined will "kiss the hand that gave the blow". And, if your discipline has the core of affection running through it, it will show itself after the fashion of the child who said, "Whip me father, but don't cry."

I very seldom give a man a difficult task to perform or make a difficult requirement, but I ask myself how far I am acting in the spirit of self-denial and sacrifice which I expect from him…

Encouragement. I have seldom, if ever, known either officer or soldier who has not been subject to strange visitations of depression, often bordering on despair. Sometimes these visitations are to be accounted for, and sometimes, on the other hand, they are a perfect mystery, and unless a superior officer is prepared to make allowance for such trials in the treatment of his people he is not fit to have the control of the lives and labours of men and women.[1]

**Heavenly Father, you call some to lead your Church. Those people carry responsibilities that often have to be kept confidential and carried in loneliness. I pray that they will turn to you as their Counsellor, so that the pressures and demands of leadership are borne lightly. Bless them, I pray, with wisdom, strength, and guidance. Amen.**

1 From *Essential Measures.*

# March 27th

You gave your good Spirit to instruct them
(Nehemiah 9:20 *ESV*)

They [the righteous] think of the rightness of others, and ask how they can promote it. They have pity for those who are wrong in their temporal conditions; they have mercy on those who have been carried away with wrongdoing; they weep over the backslidings[1] of God's people, and they strive and fight for the honour of their Lord and the salvation of others. Neither do they allow themselves to hear or read anything calculated to injure them in body, mind, or soul.

Do you, my brother or sister, feel that you have just ground for concluding that you belong to the righteous? If so, rejoice and be exceeding glad. Let me give you a word of counsel:

Beware of trusting in your own righteousness as the ground of your acceptance with God, and as being sufficient reason for expecting your deliverance at the Last Great Day. Salvation then and for ever will be through the blood of the Lamb.[2] Beware of supposing that because you have reached your present happy experience you can dispense with any of the means of grace by which you attained it. You must believe, and pray, and deny yourselves, and take up your cross daily,[3] and fight for the salvation of those about you as you did in the days of your first love.

Beware of thinking that you can maintain a righteous character without increasing your knowledge of divine things, your realization of the divine character, your love for souls, and your faith that conquers men, devils, and sin. Beware of judging others, especially the ignorant, the poor, and the degraded, by the standard which the Holy Ghost has allowed you to set up for yourselves, and to which you have been so graciously brought. Much has been given to you, and through the loving kindness of your Lord, you have been able to make a glad and happy return.

Beware of neglecting to subscribe all honour, and praise, and glory to the Holy Ghost, to whose aid you owe all that is good, pure, and Christ-like within you.[4]

**God the Holy Spirit, I thank you for your gracious presence in my life. Your infilling is my hope of righteousness, and I praise you for your constant willingness to help and bless. Spirit of God, fall afresh on me. Amen.**

1 "Backsliders" are Salvationists who have fallen away from their profession of faith.
2 Revelation 12:11
3 Luke 9:23
4 From *The Founder's Messages to Soldiers.*

# March 28th

Above all else, guard your heart, for everything you do flows from it

(Proverbs 4:23 *NIV*)

Purity commanded...

I want to say something on the subject in its practical application to yourselves. What did our dear Lord mean when he spoke of the "pure in heart" and pronounced them blessed?[1] What is it to have a pure heart? To answer that question, I must begin by asking another: what is meant by the heart? To which question I answer, we do not mean that organ which you can feel beating in your breast, and which is the central force of the bodily system. That is a very important part of man, and the keeping of it in good condition is most essential. But it is not the heart in your body to which Jesus Christ referred in this passage, and about which I want to talk to you; but that power which, being the central force of your soul, may be used to answer to it. As the heart which palpitates in your bosom is the great driving force of the natural man, so the heart we are talking about is the great driving force of the spiritual man.

In this sense it is your heart that feels joy or sorrow. When you say, "That poor woman died of a broken heart on account of the ill-treatment of her husband", you mean it was the bitter anguish of her soul which killed her. It is the heart that chooses between right and wrong. When you say, "My brother's heart is on the side of God, and goodness, and truth", you mean that these things are the supreme choice of his soul. It is the heart that decides on the particular line of conduct to be pursued. When you say, "This young man went to the mercy seat and gave his heart to God", you mean that he decided, in his inmost soul, to accept salvation and become a soldier of Christ.

It is the heart that loves righteousness and hates iniquity. When God says, "My son, give me thine heart",[2] he means, "Come along, young man or woman, and love me and holiness, and souls."[3]

**Lord of my heart, you desire that my spiritual heart should be in good condition. Thank you that, by grace, it can be. I invite you to perform heart surgery on me whenever you notice it is required. I completely entrust my heart to you. Amen.**

1 Matthew 5:8
2 Proverbs 23:26 *KJV*
3 From *Purity of Heart.*

# March 29th

### To the pure, all things are pure
(Titus 1:15 *NIV*)

There must be the conscious possession of a righteous character; that is, you must be right, and know that you are right. Any effort to persuade yourselves that you are righteous when you know that you are not will be labour spent in vain. Some people are always putting the best possible construction on their own actions, and magnifying their own virtues; although all the time they are tormented with the horrid reflection that something is wrong in their lives. They do not belong to the righteous. The character of a righteous man cannot be separated from righteousness. No man has a right to claim the character of the righteous whose life does not harmonize with the righteousness described in the Bible.

Righteousness is not a matter of profession, but of practice. For example, a man may say, "I greatly desire to be right. I know I ought to be right; I have known it all my life; I very often pray to be made right. I am a student of the Bible; I am joined in fellowship with the church, or the Army," and ever so much more of the same kind, and yet not have just grounds for believing that God regards him as a righteous man.

If a man is right, his thoughts will be right. He will not allow foolish or unclean imaginations to dwell in his mind. If a man is right, his affections will be right – he will love right things and hate evil things. If a man is right, his actions will be right. He will act rightly towards God, his own interests, his parents, his wife, his family, his master, or his servant, and his supreme desire will be to make other people right. In a word, the righteous do nothing, wear nothing, eat nothing, visit no place, join in no partnership, form no companionship, engage in no labour, which is not in keeping with what they believe to be true and right. The men and women who have a just claim to be counted righteous, neither touch, taste, nor handle the things that they know to be wrong.[1]

**Holy God, this definition of righteousness is challenging and encouraging. As I come to prayer today, I thank you that you impart righteousness as a gift. Help me to live as you would want me to, revealing to me anything you would like to change or improve. Amen.**

1 From *The Founder's Messages to Soldiers.*

# March 30th

You, dear children, are from God and have overcome them, because the one who is in you is greater than the one who is in the world

(1 John 4:4 *NIV*)

Hate the devil and sin, with all the powers you possess. It is the heart that moulds the character, guides the choice, and masters all the course and conduct of a man's life. The heart is the captain of the ship. It determines whether a man shall accept mercy, follow God, follow righteousness, live for the salvation of his fellows, and finally enter the heavenly harbour in triumph, or whether he shall live a life of rebellion, die in his sins and finish up a wreck on the rocks of everlasting despair.

How important it is to each one of us that we should have a good – a right – a pure heart.

Now, seeing that the heart is so thoroughly master of the man, nothing can be much plainer, can it, my comrades, than the necessity for the heart being pure? But what is a pure heart? What is it to have a heart that has been cleaned by the power of the Holy Spirit through the blood of Jesus Christ?[1] This is a very important enquiry, and I do hope that my dear soldiers will give me their careful attention when I strive to answer it…

A pure heart is not a heart that is never tempted to do evil. Possibly there is no such thing in this world, nor ever has been, as a non-tempted heart, that is, a man or a woman who has never been exposed to temptation to commit sin of one kind or the other. Not only was our blessed Lord tempted by the devil in the wilderness, but he was beset with evil attractions all the way through his life. The apostle Paul expressly tells us that our Saviour was in all points tempted… as we are but hallelujah! he effectually resisted the world, the flesh and the devil, and came through the trying ordeal without a stain. He triumphed over all, for the apostle exultingly assures us that he was "without sin".[2]

You will be tempted, my comrades, all through your earthly journey, even to the very gates of Heaven.[3]

**Father God, I thank you that I need not feel guilty if I am tempted; your power at work within me is greater than any power of temptation. Remind me to call upon that power in moments of vulnerability, knowing that each victory will help me another to win. Amen.**

1 Hebrews 10:22 *NLT*
2 Hebrews 4:15 *KJV*, although the Pauline authorship is disputed.
3 From *Purity of Heart*.

# MARCH 31ST

HER CHILDREN RISE UP AND CALL HER BLESSED

(Proverbs 31:28 *ESV*)

I want you to realize... that Christ has planned a happy, holy, useful life for your children, and provided the means by which they can reach that life, and to maintain it when they have reached it. And I want you to see and feel that upon your shoulders he has placed the obligation of making his plans a success. He will intercede for them. He will mention their names to his Father. His Spirit will strive with them, and his providence will work in harmony with his purpose. But I want you specially to realize that the fulfilment of your Saviour's wish depends upon your earnestly taking your part in the work of their salvation. That is:

You must pour the necessary light into their minds. You must shield them, as far as you can, from temptations likely to lead them astray. You must present to their youthful eyes, in your own conduct, an example of what you want them to be. You must hold them to lives of purity, love, and duty with all the force you can command. You must never rest until you are convinced that they are really and truly converted.

In a remarkable meeting I held in one of the large cities of Japan, during my visit to that country,[1] a dear woman came to the mercy seat. She found forgiveness for herself, and went straight from the Registration Room to the place where she had been sitting, brought her two children to the penitent form and, kneeling between them, pointed them to the Saviour, whom she had just found. While engaged in this work, a Salvationist came along, and thinking she would be better able to lead the children into the Kingdom, offered her assistance; but, gently pushing her aside, the mother said: "Leave them to me; I am their mother."

In this, the mother was perfectly right. The first obligation for the discharge of that duty was upon the mother's heart, and she was qualified for its discharge before every other individual. Oh, that every mother and every father would accept this obligation for themselves![2]

**God of families, your plan for us to live within the warm security of loving homes has yet to be improved upon. Thank you for parents whose godly influence is lasting. Please bless Christian parents striving to lead their children to Jesus. Amen.**

1 1907.
2 From *The Founder Speaks*.

# April 1st

## The Lord supports the afflicted

(Psalm 147:6 *NASB*)

To attempt to save the lost, we must accept no limitations to human brotherhood. If the scheme which I set forth in these pages is not applicable to the thief, the harlot, the drunkard, and the sluggard, it may as well be dismissed without ceremony. As Christ came to call not the saints but sinners to repentance,[1] so the new message of temporal salvation, of salvation from pinching poverty, from rags and misery, must be offered to all. They may reject it, of course. But we who call ourselves by the name of Christ are not worthy to profess to be his disciples until we have set an open door before the least and worst of these who are now apparently imprisoned for life in a horrible dungeon of misery and despair. The responsibility for its rejection must be theirs, not ours. We all know the prayer, "Give me neither poverty nor riches; feed me with food convenient for me"[2] – and for every child of man on this planet, thank God for the prayer of Agur, the son of Jakeh, may be fulfilled.

At present how far it is from being realized may be seen by anyone who will take the trouble to go down to the docks and see the struggle for work. Here is a sketch of what was found there this summer:

London Docks, 7:25 a.m. The three pairs of huge wooden doors are closed. Leaning against them, and standing about, there are perhaps a couple of hundred men. The public house opposite is full, doing a heavy trade. All along the road are groups of men, and from each direction a steady stream increases the crowd at the gate.

7:30 [a.m.] Doors open; there is a general rush to the interior. Everybody marches about 100 yards along to the interior – a temporary chair affair, guarded by the dock police. Those men who have previously (i.e. night before) been engaged, show their ticket and pass through, about 600. The rest – some 500 – stand behind the barrier, patiently waiting for the chance of a job, but less than twenty of these get engaged.[3]

**God of the poor, God of the rich, your love and compassion is for those in high positions and to those of lowly status, equally. Today I pray for those whose lives are hard; those for whom each day is a struggle; use your Church to step in with practical mercy. Amen.**

1 Luke 5:32
2 Proverbs 30:8 *KJV*
3 From *In Darkest England and the Way Out.*

# April 2nd

## You are precious and honoured in my sight

(Isaiah 43:4 *NIV*)

Look at the crowds of brave men and women who, when children, had no better chance than your children and those around you, but who, with the blessing of God, are today possessed of the Spirit of Jesus Christ, and fighting the evil forces of earth and Hell. Look at some of the officers and soldiers in our ranks, who are lessening the sorrows that oppress human hearts, delivering the victims of sin, and pressing forward to hear the "Well done" of their Lord,[1] and to receive the "crown of glory that fadeth not away".[2] Why, oh, why, should not your children join this God-inspired, blood-washed multitude? It was my supreme ambition when I first looked on the faces of my children that this should be their portion. Does not that ambition possess and control your hearts as fully as it did mine? It ought to be so.

In order to encourage you in seeking with all your hearts the salvation of the children, I want you to realize several things: I want you to believe that Jesus Christ is really anxious for their salvation. He says: "Let the children come unto me.[3] I am their friend. I want to be their Saviour." If he wants them, won't you help them, with all your hearts, to get to him?

I want you to realize that the children are his property. They belong to him. He has bought and paid for them with his precious blood.[4] They are not given to you to be your playthings, or to feed your vanity, or to add to your income, or to render some personal service merely, regardless of the Kingdom of God. Your children are the property of Jesus Christ. They are intended to follow in his footsteps, and to be lovers of souls and saviours of men.

I want you to realize that Jesus Christ loves your children. When he said, "Suffer little children to come unto me" [*KJV*] – and he is saying it still – he meant your children. He loves them. They were included in the compassion that brought him from Heaven to earth, and carried him to the cross.[5]

**Lord Jesus, anyone who places their trust in you will be saved. In my prayers today, I lay before you every precious child I know – family, loved ones, friends, children who belong to my church – and pray that you will bless, guide, and protect them. Amen.**

1 Matthew 25:21
2 1 Peter 5:4 *KJV*
3 See Luke 18:16
4 1 Corinthians 6:20
5 From *The Founder Speaks*.

# April 3rd

### Even if my father and mother abandon me, the Lord will hold me close

(Psalm 27:10 *NLT*)

Ask the men and they will tell you something like the following story, which gives the simple experiences of a dock labourer.

R.P. said – "I was in regular work at the South West India Dock[1] before the strike.[2] We got 5d[3] an hour. Start work 8 a.m. summer and 9 a.m. winter. Often there would be 500 go, and only twenty get taken on (that is besides those engaged the night previous). The foreman stood in his box, and called out the men he wanted. He would know quite 500 by name. It was a regular fight to get work, I have known 900 to be taken on, but there's always hundreds turned away.

You see, they get to know when ships come in, and when they're consequently likely to be wanted, and turn up then in greater numbers. I would earn 30s[4] a week sometimes and then perhaps nothing for a fortnight. That's what makes it so hard. You get nothing to eat for a week scarcely, and then when you get taken on, you are so weak that you can't do it properly. I've stood in the crowd at the gate and had to go away without work, hundreds of times. Still I should go at it again if I could. I got tired of the little work and went away into the country to get work on a farm, but couldn't get it, so I'm without the 10s that it costs to join the Dockers' Union.[5] I'm going to the country again in a day or two to try again. Expect to get 3s a day perhaps. Shall come back to the docks again. There is a chance of getting regular dock work, and that is, to lounge about the pubs where the foremen go, and treat them. Then they will very likely take you on next day."

They wait until eight o'clock strikes… the barrier is taken down and all those hundreds of men, wearily disperse to "find a job". Five hundred applicants, twenty acceptances!… A few hang about until midday on the slender chance of getting taken on then for half a day.[6]

**Inclusive God, the sadness of rejection can be overwhelming. From the child in the schoolyard who is not included, to those who are experiencing isolation at the hands of their parents, to those unable to take their place in the world of employment – Father, fill my heart with sensitivity and concern. Amen.**

1 Isle of Dogs, London.
2 The Great Dock Strike, 1889.
3 5d (from the Latin denarii), roughly equivalent to 2p in modern money.
4 Thirty pre-decimal shillings, roughly equivalent to £1.50.
5 The National Union of Dock Labourers.
6 From *In Darkest England and the Way Out.*

# April 4th

When I was a child, I talked like a child, I thought like a child, I reasoned like a child. When I became a man, I put the ways of childhood behind me

(1 Corinthians 13:11 *NIV*)

The children are about us every way we turn. We cannot get away from them if we would; and we would not, if we could. Full of life and energy, readily amused, and easily influenced for good or evil, they are always interesting. What shall we do with them? Well, first I would say, consider the possibilities of happiness or misery that lie before them. To help you do this, look for a moment at the men and women around you. Glance at them in their haunts of pleasure and recreation, in the drinking saloons, and gambling hells, in the houses of shame, and the prison cells, laughing, dancing, toiling, weeping, cursing their way to the left hand of the Throne,[1] and the Hell of everlasting woe.

Once these wretched men and women were just such boys and girls as your children are. Just as innocent, affectionate, and promising, and just as easily influenced in favour of honesty, truth, and goodness as the merry little creatures who are now playing in the fields or amusing themselves in your homes. Why should some of your children be immune from becoming thieves, drunkards, or blasphemers, and from being led away to lives of sin, or from becoming partners of some human wastrels, or the willing occupants of some black hole of infamy?

But should you, however, reject the possibility of any of your dear ones becoming the slaves of these open vices, or of their being led into the commission of any of these disgraceful crimes, is there not a terrible danger of their growing up into habits of indifference and unbelief, living godless lives, and dying with hearts hardened in selfishness on hopeless beds of despair, and finishing up in the sorrow and darkness of Hell? What is to hinder such a future? It is constantly coming to other people's children. Why should it not come to yours?

Now, if you can bring yourselves to realize this awful possibility, it will help you to deal more earnestly with every boy or girl who comes within your influence.[2]

**Father, hear my prayer today for all who have any influence in the lives of children; schoolteachers, church teachers, club leaders, and so on; that they will set good foundations, so that children who are loved and cared for may in turn become loving, caring adults. Amen.**

1 Matthew 25:41
2 From *The Founder Speaks*.

# April 5th

For the word of God will never fail

(Luke 1:37 *NLT*)

It is not only at the dock gates that you come upon these unfortunates who spend their lives in the vain hunt for work. Here is the story of another man whose case has only too many parallels. C is a fine built man, standing nearly six feet. He has been in the Royal Artillery for eight years and held very good situations whilst in it. It seems that he was thrifty and consequently steady. He bought his discharge, and being an excellent cook opened a refreshment house, but at the end of five months he was compelled to close his shop on account of slackness in trade, which was brought about by the closing of a large factory in the locality.

After having worked in Scotland and Newcastle [up]on Tyne for a few years, and through ill health having to give up his situation, he came to London with the hope that he might get something to do in his native town. He has had no regular employment for the past eight months. His wife and family are in a state of destitution, and he remarked, "We only had 1lb of bread between us yesterday." He is six weeks in arrears of rent, and is afraid that he will be ejected. The furniture which is in his home is not worth 3s and the clothes of each member of his family are in a tattered state and hardly fit for the rag bag. He assured us he had tried everywhere to get employment and would be willing to take anything. His characters are very good indeed.

Now, it may seem a preposterous dream that any arrangements can be devised by which it may be possible, under all circumstances, to provide food, clothes, and shelter for these Out-of-Works without any loss of self-respect; but I am convinced that it can be done; providing only that they are willing to work and, God helping me, if the means are forthcoming. I mean to try to do it… So long as a man or woman is willing to submit to the discipline indispensable in every campaign against a formidable foe, there appears to me nothing impossible about this ideal.[1]

**Lord of the breakthrough, thank you for the brave and resilient example of William Booth, who was undaunted in the face of problems. May that inspire me to lean on you when my challenges appear overwhelming, or obstacles seem endless. Teach my heart to remember that with you, nothing is impossible. Amen.**

1 From *In Darkest England and the Way Out.*

# April 6th

I KNOW THAT THIS MAN WHO OFTEN COMES OUR WAY IS A HOLY MAN OF GOD

(2 Kings 4:9 *NIV*)

You can always believe what he [the captain] says. You can't think of him doing "the big" about his relations, or his superior bringing up, and such things, like Captain Swellum used to do, bless him! And he had many good points, had Captain Swellum; but he used to come it a little too much about what he had given up to come into the work. When our captain says, "A spade's a spade" you can reckon on it being so: you can't think of him deceiving you about anything. If he says that he will meet you for visiting the pubs, or selling *The War Crys*,[1] or going to see anybody that is sick and dying, you can reckon that if so be as he's alive and able to crawl, he'll be there.

Yes, our captain's a good man. I consider him a real holy man. You can feel it when you are with him. The influence kind o' comes out of him, not only when he gives his experience in the Free and Easy,[2] but all the time. He seems to live in prayer, and love to God and the poor sinners.

When he tells us, in the Holiness Meeting,[3] that he has got "the blessing" and loves God with all his heart, and his neighbour as himself, it all seems so natural that you feel it is true; and I always feel like getting up, and saying: "Yes, Captain, I believe you; I have never seen anything that contradicts that bit you have just been saying." No, he seems to live in prayer and love…

Then there is another thing about our captain that I like, and that is, he works. My word, doesn't he tug at it! Summer and winter he's the same. He's never in bed after seven in the morning, and he trots about the town after everybody that he can do any good to, all through the day.[4]

**Thank you, Lord, for those whose example serves as an inspiration. I ask for your grace, that my life may make a positive impact on those I meet; reflecting Christ. Amen.**

1 The Salvation Army's evangelical weekly newspaper.
2 Time allocated in Salvation Army meetings for personal testimonies.
3 Traditionally, The Salvation Army would hold holiness meetings for teaching and instruction, and salvation meetings, for outreach and the proclamation of the gospel.
4 From *Sergeant-Major Do-Your-Best*.

# April 7th

## Now be pleased to bless the house of your servant

(2 Samuel 7:29 *NIV*)

There is, unfortunately, no need for me to attempt to set out, however imperfectly, any statement of the evil case of the sufferers that we wish to help. For years past the press has been filled with echoes of the "Bitter Cry of Outcast London", with pictures of "Horrible Glasgow", and the like. We have several volumes describing "How the Poor Live" and I may therefore assume that all my readers are more or less cognizant of the main outlines of "Darkest England".

My slum officers[1] are living in the midst of it. Their reports are before me, and one day I may publish some more detailed account of the actual facts of the social condition of the sunken millions. But not now. All that must be taken as read. I only glance at the subject in order to bring into clear relief the salient points of the new enterprise.

I have spoken of the houseless poor. Each of these represents a point in the scale of human suffering below that of those who have still contrived to keep a shelter over their heads. A home is a home, be it ever so low; and the desperate tenacity with which the poor will cling to the last wretched semblance of one is very touching. There are vile dens, fever-haunted and stenchful crowded courts, where the return of summer is dreaded because it means the unloosing of myriads of vermin which render night unbearable which, nevertheless, are regarded at this moment as havens of rest by their hard-working occupants.

They can scarcely be said to be furnished. A chair, a mattress, and a few miserable sticks constitute all the furniture of the single room in which they have to sleep, and breed, and die; but they cling to it as a drowning man to a half-submerged raft.

Every week they contrive by pinching and scheming to raise the rent, for with them it is pay or go and they struggle to meet the collector as the sailor nerves himself to avoid being sucked under by the foaming wave.[2]

**Father God, thank you for a roof over my head. Amen.**

1 Salvation Army officers who lived and worked amongst the most poor and wretched, nursing the sick, caring for the dying, and holding meetings.

2 From *In Darkest England and the Way Out.*

# April 8th

Choose a good reputation over great riches; being held in high esteem is better than silver or gold

(Proverbs 22:1 *NLT*)

I've known every blessed captain that we've had, and very good ones they've been. But you know as how... some must be better than others; though I always stand by our officers, whether they come up to my mark or whether they don't; because, as I tells my comrades, if some of 'em aren't exactly what we would like 'em to be, it won't make 'em any better by pulling 'em to pieces.

This captain we have now is more to my fancy than any of the lot, and no disrespect to any of 'em. He's a real beauty, without any paint. God bless him, body and soul – that's what I've got to say. Why do I fancy him? you ask. Well, I think I can tell you; and to put it plain, there are several things that lifts him up in my opinion. I won't "enlarge" upon them, as Captain Windy used to say about his last point, when he had been going on for three-quarters of an hour, and Jim Snorehard had woke up, and was getting his hat ready to rush off; and I know some of them as are good talkers, but poor listeners. They'd like you to hear them for ever, but when you get talking a bit yourself, they are soon on to you with "Amen, Amen!" like Captain Windy, who, whenever I was giving him a bit of my mind, always used to say, "Cut it short, Sergeant-Major, for you know what the song says, 'Time is earnest, passing by.'"[1]

But you must have patience with me if I am going to make things plain to you, or else I can't do it. And here goes; and what I have got to say is, that the reason why I like our captain is:

Because he is a good man. I don't exactly know how it's made up; but I always feel when I come alongside of him, whether it is in the open-air [meeting] or in the hall, or whether it['s] when we're having a fight to get some poor sinner into the fountain, or whether it's when we are reckoning up the money, or doing business together, that he is a downright, good-hearted fellow.[2]

**Lord, a good name is something precious, all the more so if it leads other people to think of you. Help me this day to represent Christ well, wherever I am. I would that others may see something of Jesus in me. Amen.**

1 A line from a hymn by Sydney Dyer (1814–98), an American Baptist minister.
2 From *Sergeant-Major Do-Your-Best.*

# April 9th

Bear one another's burdens, and so fulfil the law of Christ
(Galatians 6:2 *ESV*)

It is bad for a single man to have to confront the struggle for life in the streets and Casual Wards. But how much more terrible must it be for the married man with his wife and children to be turned out into the streets. So long as the family has a lair into which it can creep at night, he keeps his footing; but when he loses that solitary foothold then arrives the time if there be such a thing as Christian compassion, for the helping hand to be held out to save him from the vortex that sucks him downward…

"The heart knoweth its own bitterness and the stranger inter-meddleth not therewith."[1] But now and then out of the depths there sounds a bitter wail as of some strong swimmer in his agony as he is drawn under by the current. A short time ago a respectable man, a chemist in Holloway,[2] fifty years of age, driven hard to the wall, tried to end it all by cutting his throat. His wife also cut her throat, and at the same time they gave strychnine to their only child. Their effort failed, and they were placed on trial for attempted murder. In the court a letter was read which the poor wretch had written before attempting his life:

> *Twelve months have I now passed of a most miserable and struggling existence, and I really cannot stand it any more. I am completely worn out, and relations who could assist me won't do any more… I can face poverty and degradation no longer, and would sooner die than go to the workhouse… We have, God forgive us, taken our darling Arty with us out of pure love and affection, so that the darling should never be cuffed about, or reminded or taunted with his heartbroken parents' crime… May God Almighty forgive us for this heinous sin, and have mercy on our sinful souls, is the prayer of your miserable, broken-hearted, but loving brother, Arthur. We have now done everything that we can possibly think of to avert this wicked proceeding, but can discover no ray of hope.*[3]

**God of compassion, I pray for those who carry heavy burdens, that you would reach out to them. Help me, Lord, to be sensitive to everyone I meet, so that my friendship might encourage conversation when talking might alleviate secret despair. Be with, Lord, those who have no one else to turn to. Amen.**

1 See Proverbs 14:10
2 In the London borough of Islington.
3 From *In Darkest England and the Way Out.*

# April 10th

WINE IS A MOCKER, STRONG DRINK A BRAWLER, AND WHOEVER IS LED ASTRAY BY IT IS NOT WISE

(Proverbs 20:1 *ESV*)

Now, you see, it is a fact, and there is no mistake about it, that I do really like our captain, and I shall be downright sorry when the time comes for him to move off.[1]

I have been in this corps ever since I was converted, which is just six years come next November. I can remember the time exactly, because our Jack, my eldest boy, went to America a week before, and I got so excited that I had a week's spree over it, and on the Sunday afternoon the Salvationists – God bless 'em! – picked me up, half boozed, just as I was coming out of "The Swan with Two Necks", and dragged me to the hall in the procession,[2] whether I would or not; and there they put it into me so hot about the fool I was making of myself in throwing my soul away, that I couldn't help feeling as though I was hearing my dear old father talking to me again as he used to do. He has been dead and gone these twenty years. I was a bad lad, but he was a good man – God bless him!

I went straight home that afternoon, and had a cup of tea and a wash-up, and then I said to Sarah – that's my missis, and a good wife she's been to me – "Sarah," says I. "Well, what are you on with now?" says she. "Well," I says, "I'm going to The Salvation Army." And she says: "I don't believe you; but it's time you went somewhere. Haven't you been spending the bit of money we had laid up for the funerals, and such things, and wasting your time and making me miserable long enough?" "Well, "I says, "will you come with me?" And she says: "That I will, if you are going to them people."

And away we went, and that very night we knelt at the penitent form together,[3] and I really believe we both got properly saved; and I chucked up the drink and the devil at a go, and came over on to the Lord's side, which was a fine job for the missis and the youngsters.[4]

**Victorious God, you have wonder-working power to change lives, and to release your children from all kinds of addictions. I bring before you today those whose circumstances are dismal and loaded with despair. Draw them towards your love, I pray. Break chains, Lord. Amen.**

1 Salvation Army officers are moved from appointment to appointment at the Army's disposal.
2 Salvationists would "raid" public houses to drag drunkards into gospel meetings.
3 A mercy seat or penitent form – a place of prayer in Salvation Army halls and meeting places.
4 From *Sergeant-Major Do-Your-Best*.

# April 11th

Do not merely listen to the word, and so deceive yourselves. Do what it says

(James 1:22 *NIV*)

Mr T, Margaret Place, Gascoign Place, Bethnal Green,[1] is a boot-maker by trade. [He] is a good hand, and has earned three shillings and sixpence to four shillings and sixpence a day. He was taken ill last Christmas, and went to the London Hospital; was there three months. A week after he had gone Mrs T had rheumatic fever, and was taken to Bethnal Green Infirmary, where she remained about three months. Directly after they were taken ill, their furniture was seized for the three weeks' rent which was owing. Consequently, on becoming convalescent, they were homeless.

They came out about the same time. He then had two pence, and she had sixpence, which a nurse had given her. They went to a lodging-house together, but the society there was dreadful. Next day he had a day's work, and got two shillings and sixpence, and on the strength of this they took a furnished room at ten pence per day (payable nightly). His work lasted a few weeks, when he was again taken ill, lost his job, and spent all their money. Pawned a shirt and an apron for a shilling; spent that, too. At last pawned their tools for three shillings, which got them a few days' food and lodging. He is now minus tools and cannot work at his own job, and does anything he can. Spent their last two pence on a pen'orth[2] each of tea and sugar. In two days they had a slice of bread and butter each, that's all. They are both very weak through want of food.

"Let things alone" the laws of supply and demand, and all the rest of the excuses by which those who now stand on firm ground salve their consciences when they leave their brother to sink; how do they look when we apply them to the actual loss of life at sea? Does "Let things alone" man the lifeboat? Will the inexorable laws of political economy save the shipwrecked sailor from the boiling surf? They often enough are responsible for his disaster… no law of supply and demand actuates the volunteers who risk their lives to bring the shipwrecked to shore.[3]

**Father, you are a practical God, and you call your people to minister in practical ways, and not merely theorize. In the face of human anguish, help me to put your word into practice, serving you with actions, rather than words. Amen.**

1 East London.
2 One penny worth.
3 From *In Darkest England and the Way Out.*

# April 12th

At just the right time, when we were still powerless, Christ died for the ungodly

(Romans 5:6 *NIV*)

We must hold on to the doctrine of the atonement because of the fullness of the Holy Spirit's influence which it makes possible to men. "I will pray the Father, and he shall give you another Comforter, that he may abide with you for ever; Even the Spirit of truth" (John 14:16, 17 *KJV*). We must hold on the doctrine of the atonement because of the preparation for Heaven it makes certain for those who accept it. Think of the multitude which no man can number, already assembling on the heavenly plains, who have washed their robes and made them white in the blood of the Lamb,[1] and the multitudes more who have availed themselves of the same preparation and are coming on.

We must hold on to the doctrine of the atonement because of the verification it affords of the prophecies, promises and general statements of the Bible. To take the atonement out of the Bible would not only rob the sacred volume of its chief, if not its entire interest, but largely destroy its power to bless the souls of its readers. In fact, without the atonement the Bible would cease to be one of the lights of the world, and would speedily vanish from the earth in the gloom that would surround it. We must hold on to the doctrine of the atonement because its loss would rob multitudes of the holiest men and women of the most powerful motive to purity of heart and life.

We must hold on to the doctrine of the atonement because it constitutes our most powerful weapon in the fight with the godless crowds. Whether in the churches, the market-places, the theatres, the music halls, the brothels, their own homes or elsewhere, the death of Jesus Christ is our battle cry of victory. Christ weeping, suffering, dying for them, and waiting to wash their sins in his blood, constitutes the most powerful motive to submit themselves immediately to God, accept his mercy and commence a new life calculated to please him, promote their own happiness and ultimately lead them to Heaven.[2]

**God of my salvation, the message of the gospel has great power to touch human hearts. Thank you for the day it touched mine. I pray for those who will be confronted with the claims of Christ today; may they respond to your love. Bless those engaged in sharing the good news of eternal life. Amen.**

1 Revelation 7:14
2 From *The Founder Speaks Again.*

# April 13th

## You, O children of Jacob, are not consumed

(Malachi 3:6 *ESV*)

We want a Social Lifeboat Institution, a Social Lifeboat Brigade, to snatch from the abyss those who, if left to themselves, will perish as miserably as the crew of a ship that founders in mid-ocean. The moment we take in hand this work we shall be compelled to turn our attention seriously to the question [of] whether prevention is not better than cure. It is easier and cheaper, and in every way better, to prevent the loss of home than to have to recreate that home. It is better to keep a man out of the mire than to let him fall in first and then risk the chance of plucking him out. Any scheme, therefore, that attempts to deal with the reclamation of the lost must tend to develop into an endless variety of ameliorative measures, of some of which I shall have somewhat to say hereafter.

I only mention the subject here in order that no one may say I am blind to the necessity of going further and adopting wider plans of operation than those which I have put forward in this book. The renovation of our social system is a work so vast that no one of us, nor all of us put together, can define all the measures that will have to be taken before we attain even the cab-horse ideal of existence for our children and our children's children. All that we can do is to attack, in a serious, practical spirit, the worst and most pressing evils, knowing that if we do our duty we obey the voice of God. He is captain of our salvation.[1] If we but follow where he leads we shall not want for marching orders, nor need we imagine that he will narrow the field of operations.

I am labouring under no delusions as to the possibility of inaugurating the millennium by any social specific. In the struggle of life, the weakest will go to the wall, and there are so many weak. The fittest, in tooth and claw, will survive. All that we can do is to soften the lot of the unfit and make their suffering less horrible than it is at present.[2]

**God of victory, if the cry is to "attack", then fill my heart with courage. Protect me, I pray, from thoughts of despair or discouragement if and when it seems my contribution is only small. Remind me that I can make a difference. Fire my imagination. Amen.**

1 Hebrews 2:10
2 From *In Darkest England and the Way Out.*

# April 14th

The Lord is not slow in keeping his promise, as some understand slowness. Instead he is patient with you, not wanting anyone to perish, but everyone to come to repentance

(2 Peter 3:9 *NIV*)

Millions have entered the gates that lead to the celestial city with the sentiments in their hearts which we Salvationists express by our song, "His blood can make the foulest clean".[1] Millions upon millions more will reach the golden pavement who have never heard his precious name before they gained the heavenly shores. There can be no question that sincere souls who, by living up to the light they possess, prove that if they had had the opportunity they would have laid themselves at the Saviour's feet, will not have to suffer banishment on account of their ignorance. You will remember Paul says, "In every nation he that feareth him, and worketh righteousness, is accepted with him" (Acts 10:35 *KJV*). This shows that God is going to deal with people according to their sincerity. If they are obedient to what they hear, there will be salvation for them; and if they have never heard but would have been obedient if they had heard, they will not be rejected.

We must hold on to the doctrine of the atonement because it justifies us in believing in the transference to the heavenly shores of multitudes of young children who have never heard his name below. More than half the human race dies in infancy and, in view of the holy examples set before them by the heavenly host, grow into celestial maturity in the heavenly Canaan.

We must hold on to the doctrine of the atonement because of the example the Saviour himself furnishes for imitation. Nowhere in the history of the human race, from Adam down to the present hour, have we any being, until we come to Jesus Christ, to whom we can point with confidence, and say, "Take not only the precepts of his mouth as your guide, but the example of his life and death." We must hold on to the doctrine of the atonement because of the material, mental, moral, and spiritual blessings which stream from it out into our dark and desolate world. We must hold on to the doctrine of the atonement because of the fire of compassion and love for the sinning, suffering bodies and souls of men, which it kindles in the hearts of those who yield themselves to its influence.[2]

**Heavenly Father, your mercy is wider than I can realize. Keep me searching for you with a teachable mind, a humble heart, and a spirit ready to embrace your will and ways. Amen.**

1 Charles Wesley, 1707–88, "O For a Thousand Tongues to Sing".
2 From *The Founder Speaks Again*.

# April 15th

**People will come from east and west and north and south, and will take their places at the feast in the kingdom of God**

(Luke 13:29 *NIV*)

One officer went to India last week,[1] but they want eight, and are fully expecting that four are on the sea. Ten are all but ready to sail, to be divided between Canada, California, the United States, Sweden, South Africa, and Switzerland; but what are these among so many? But what are we to do? Officers cannot be despatched without two things. First – one which is very important to us just now – money for their outfit and passage; the second, the officers themselves.

Supposing we get over the first by contrivance and importunity, we cannot get over the second so easily. Therefore we must have more men and women for the business whose hearts God has touched, whose tongues the Holy Ghost has fired, and whose lives are consecrated to the highest possible ends to which any being, human or divine, can be offered up – the helping of Christ to save the world.

No spot on the wide field in which the Army is operating demands and deserves more help at the present moment than India. I suppose you have read the reports that have appeared from time to time in these columns;[2] I suppose you have stopped to take in their mighty meaning – that a door of access to this nation of nearly 300 millions of people now stands wide open: that in the province of Gujarat and the island of Ceylon, taken alone, there are thousands of natives literally waiting and wanting to receive The Salvation Army. But to win them, and keep them when won – as with poor fallen humanity everywhere else – requires love and patience and skill; in fact men and women whose every energy is consecrated to the redeeming task – men and women who will literally lay themselves on the altar, strip themselves of all encumbrances that would hinder them in the war, adopt the salvation of India as their life-work, go forth to practise just as much self-denial, and endure just as much suffering as may be found necessary and helpful in learning the language, conforming to the customs, becoming all things lawful and expedient to the people…[3,4]

**Dear Lord, I pray for the great nation of India, with all its complexities and its mixture of religious faiths. Father, as people search for spiritual meaning there, I pray that you will reveal Jesus to them, by your Spirit. Bless those who serve you in that vast land. Amen.**

1 Written in 1884. Salvation Army work in India commenced in 1882.
2 Originally published in *The War Cry.*
3 1 Corinthians 9:22
4 From *The General's Letters.*

# April 16th

I will praise you, Lord, among the nations
(Psalm 18:49 *NIV*)

Going means leaving. You can't go to all the world without leaving something – something that flesh and blood would like to keep, something that perhaps, apart from saving the world, flesh and blood would have a right to keep; but which flesh and blood gladly gives up. And so for you to go means leaving some father and mother, or sweetheart, or someone who objects, who will count you a fool and a madman.

Where are you to go? Everywhere. Commence with the house where you live, the shop where you work, the town in which you are known. Then join with others in filling the land. Go to the drunkard at public house corners; follow them home. Go to anybody – you can't go wrong. Go to thieves, harlots, publicans. Get a barracks at every corner of every street. Hoist the colours in every port, city and village. March, sing, play, testify, make a noise. Fill the world with the sound of salvation.

Begin with Europe. Here doors are already opened. How they listen in Sweden! How they flock to the barns in the South of France, listen in secret in Switzerland! Yes, Switzerland, by all means. Go there, as there is a real chance of winning a martyr's crown as well as a labourer's hire, in that land of boasted freedom. Never mind. Go to America. Think of Chicago, with its 600,000 inhabitants; thirteen theatres in full swing on Sunday nights; as many drinking saloons as there are lamp-posts, and never a Salvation Army officer in it. Go to Asia. Think of the 500 millions in the two empires of India and China who will not only hear, but welcome you. Go to Africa, with its… multitudes, among whom our simplicity and sympathy and adapted methods would make conquest certain. Go to Australia, where 100 officers are pleaded for at this moment.

Don't answer with difficulties and excuses. "Married a wife," do you say? Take her with you. "Bought a piece of land," have you? Sell it again, and pay someone's passage to India, or give us a share of the rent, at least.[1]

**King of the world, I place myself at your disposal, as your subject. If I am called to my neighbourhood, or overseas, use me to bless someone. For Jesus' sake. Amen.**

1 From *The General's Letters.*

# April 17th

Jabez cried out to the God of Israel, "Oh, that you would bless me and enlarge my territory!"

(1 Chronicles 4:10 *NIV*)

Several very considerable improvements in our future government and operations were laid before the council,[1] which met with unanimous approval. One of these was that the divisions into which the United Kingdom is at present cut up were to be divided into sections, each section to be under charge of an officer who should act as sub-major.[2] This sub-major is to be held responsible for the maintenance and extension of the war in his particular section, reporting to the chief major, and referring to him on all matters of extension, property, and finance. The present major will still be responsible to headquarters for the entire division. The title of the sub-major has not yet been decided.

By this alteration it is hoped to secure for every corps the advantages of that personal oversight and sympathy, for even the smallest of them, which has been impossible from majors who have had from forty to eighty corps under their charges. The business arising out of the extension and changes of officers and acquisition of property... has been sufficient to occupy the attention of the majors during the present arrangements, leaving them very little time to see to the spiritual interests of their people. Now, there will be the opportunity for every corps being visited, every officer being personally cared for, and new departures made in every direction. God bless the Divisional Officers! Let us pray for them more than we have ever done before. When they visit you receive them with open arms, and they will help you, and you will help them, to roll the old chariot along.

The claims of the foreign work continue to increase, and to be more pressing and important day by day.[3] By the by, I don't like the word "foreign", and only use it to signify the work outside of Great Britain; for with the Army no land is "foreign", and no people are aliens. However, the claims of other countries are being urged upon us continually. From every country where the flag is flying requests for officers come by every mail.[4]

**God of the globe, you like strategy; you are the answer to chaos. Give your peace to those whose lives are chaotic, all across your world. Amen.**

1 A council of Salvation Army leaders responsible for implementing strategy, held in London.
2 Salvation Army work is organized into geographical divisions, each led by a Divisional Commander. The designation "sub-major" is now obsolete.
3 The Salvation Army first ventured overseas in 1880.
4 From *The General's Letters*.

# April 18th

Surely you need guidance to wage war, and victory is won through many advisors

(Proverbs 24:6 *NIV*)

Dear comrades, nothing was more earnestly or frequently insisted upon at the recent council than the undeniable fact that our strength and wisdom for the war must be more than ever in the future that, and that only, which comes directly from God, creating a deep, unchanging sympathy of man with man. As was expressed more than once during the meetings, it must be more than ever heart-to-heart work. That no rules, regulations, inspections, hunting up defaulters from duty, or any other human arrangement could be put in the place of this; that to trust in anything like a government of returns and red-tape would be to insure failure in every respect.

Still, the process of laying down rules for a better oversight and direction of the movement was steadily continued. Rules, laws, and regulations – what are they? Surely they are nothing more or less than the simple statement in words understood by everybody, of those plans and methods of doing things which are found, after thought and experience, and, we hope, divine revelation, to be most useful and successful.

We say "divine revelation", for why should not God reveal his mind to us? Are we not doing his business – the business that, so far as we know, or so far as we can judge, lies the nearest to his heart of any of the stupendous affairs he has on hand? And if so near his heart, and so important, having to do with the undying destinies of millions of souls whom he thought of sufficient importan[ce] to send his Son to the humiliation and agony of Calvary to redeem, why should he not give his own Holy Spirit according to his own special promise to show us the best and easiest methods for carrying out his wishes and gaining his ends? In other words, why should he not direct us in carrying on the war?

However, you know this is one of the ways we look at salvation work. Several very considerable improvements in our future government and operations were laid before the council, which met with unanimous approval.[1]

**Thank you for those upon whom I can rely for good counsel, honest advice and caring guidance. May I be someone who is approachable and trustworthy. Amen.**

1 From *The General's Letters.*

# April 19th

### He will render to each one according to his works
(Romans 2:6 *ESV*)

Many of my soldiers are not quite satisfied with the character of their earthly business. In some cases they had no hand in choosing it; it was selected for them by their parents. In other cases it was their own selection before they were converted; whilst in others, again, it was decided by circumstances over which they had no control. Now, although a change may seem desirable, it is not always possible to effect it. But, even in this respect, if they walk with God, and aim at his glory, a way may be opened for them to find some employment more in harmony with their present preferences, and presenting greater opportunities for usefulness.

Whatever your work may be, if you would imitate your Heavenly Father, you must seek to do it to the best of your ability. Whether you work in the field or the factory, the shop or the office, at home or abroad, you must ever strive to produce the best work you can. Whether you tend the baby, wash the clothes, dig the garden, serve the customers, or discharge some other task which the providence of God has assigned you, do it in the best manner possible. This applies equally to your work in the corps. What I have said about doing good work for man applies specially to that work which more directly concerns the Kingdom of God, particularly when that work bears directly on the salvation of souls.

I am afraid there are some Salvationists who, although they are very particular about the character of the work they turn out for themselves or for their earthly employers, are not over careful in the discharge of the duties they owe to their Heavenly Father.

With respect to their earthly business they say: "I must be sharp to time; I must keep my tools in order; I must work close to my pattern; I must observe the rule, or I shall make those over me angry, and so run the risk of losing my situation." But when it comes to their work for Christ and immortal souls, they say in action, if not in words: "Oh, anything will do here."[1]

**Father, sometimes it's easy to give priority to being diligent at work, which is temporal, yet less diligent in matters of the Kingdom, which are eternal. Forgive me, I pray, and show me those areas in which I may work for you efficiently and to the best of my ability for the furtherance of your Kingdom. Amen.**

1 From *The Founder's Messages to Soldiers.*

# April 20th

## God's word is not chained

(2 Timothy 2:9 *NIV*)

Read it [the Bible] in your families. Impress its precious truths to your children, if you are parents. Explain them to the ignorant – make them understand. Use the *Soldier's Guide*.[1] If you read a chapter of that book every morning and one every night, you will go through the Bible in a year.

See to it that you experience in your own hearts the blessings the Bible offers you. Remember, it will be little better than a curse to you if you only know the word, and do not possess and live in the spirit of it. If you only believe it with your head, and do not enjoy the things that it describes, and accept the mercy, wash in the fountain, receive the Holy Ghost, and live and die in the light and joy of its good tidings, it will only add to your condemnation and guilt.

Fulfil the duties it commands. It is the doers of the word who are blessed.[2] Make it the guide of your life; at home, abroad, in your corps, in sickness and in health, in joy and sorrow, everywhere and all the time. Publish the salvation of the Bible wherever you go – in the streets, in the barracks, in your home, at your work – everywhere tell the glad tidings. Oh, my comrades, do not let the Bible rise up in judgment against you, as it surely will if you either neglect it, or if, reading and knowing about the salvation and victory of which it tells you, you do not enjoy that salvation and experience that victory.

The Salvation Army believes that the Scriptures (both of the Old and the New Testament) were given by the inspiration of God, and that they, and they only, constitute the divine rule of Christian faith and practice.[3] The Bible, in spite of all criticism – much of it absurd – still stands forth impregnable as the inspired word of God to man and the revelation of his only begotten Son, our Saviour and Lord, Jesus Christ… the Bible does what scientists and the rest of the philosophers cannot do. It speaks to the spirit of man.[4]

**Father, the Bible is a living word, not just a collection of dusty pages full of empty words. It is life-giving and life-enhancing. As I read my Bible, let it be to me as soul-nourishment that feeds my mind and penetrates my heart. Grant me understanding. Amen.**

1 A pocket book of daily readings issued to Salvationists, with readings for morning, afternoon, and evening.
2 James 1:22
3 Doctrine No. 1 of The Salvation Army.
4 From *The Founder Speaks*.

# April 21st

Work hard so you can present yourself to God and receive his approval. Be a good worker

(2 Timothy 2:15 *NLT*)

Comrades and friends, in the story of the creation, as related in the book of Genesis, we read that after having made the world, God saw everything that he had made, and pronounced it "very good".[1] Now it seems to me that we ought, as far as possible, to imitate God in our labours: and, like him, strive to produce good work. To begin with:

I need not say that men of all classes and in all places ought to be engaged in some form of labour. Men were made to work: therefore every man ought to have some task for which he is responsible; that is, he ought to do something to promote his own welfare, and the welfare of those about him. Neither wealth, nor position, nor power, will exempt him from it. It is a mistake to suppose that work is a disgrace to anyone; on the contrary, good work gives dignity and confers honour upon those engaged in it. Work is necessary to health. Man is so constituted that unless he employs his powers of body and mind and heart, they deteriorate and perish. Work is necessary to happiness. Idleness means misery. Even in the weakness and anguish of disease, employment in some profitable task relieves the monotony of existence, and creates a measure of satisfaction if not of enjoyment to the worker.

But not only ought we to work, we ought to strive to do good work. In this, as in other respects, we are called to be imitators of God, and his work is always good.

I should have liked to see the world on the glad morning of its creation. I have no doubt that it appeared to be a perfect exhibition of what the wisdom of God could produce: beautiful beyond the power of tongue to describe. That privilege was, however, denied me. Still, I am hoping to see the new Heaven and the new earth, wherein righteousness shall dwell, and into which neither sin nor Satan will ever enter. Now, my comrades, you must imitate God, and not only work, but above all, you must ever strive to do work which on examination will be found to be good.[2]

**God of my labours, I consecrate my daily work and routine into your hands, whether that be paid employment, work around the house, or errands done for others. I commend it all to you. Amen.**

1 Genesis 1:31 *KJV*
2 From *The Founder's Messages to Soldiers.*

# April 22nd

### They were all with one accord in one place
(Acts 2:1 *KJV*)

Why are only ones and twos saved? Not because of any decree to save ones and twos only, but because only ones or twos go out to save them. A crowd that understands its business, and knows how to take hold of God, and how to deal with men, will catch a crowd. Individual effort has been extolled, and that not at all too highly. Let every man learn the art of personal attack and self-defence, and God give all our soldiers wisdom and courage to stand up alone, and to stand to the very death; but after all, in spiritual armies, as a great captain said with respect to killing armies, victory is on the side of the big battalions.[1] True! God can and does deliver by the few as well as by the many, and he greatly prefers the true-hearted few to the double-minded many. But how much more he prefers to use the true-hearted multitude, we need not wait to argue – it is self-evident; it is supported by the Holy Scriptures, and by ungainsayable facts.

Think of the wonderful results that would follow the united, skilful, persistent attacks of a spiritual force, say only 1,000 strong, upon any town, howsoever large that town might be. A thousand men and women who alike knew how to plead with God and man, who had faith to pull down holy fire from Heaven, and to set on fire the consciences of sinners with the fear of death, and judgment and damnation, and who could do this just in such a manner, at such times, and in such different places as should best be adapted to arouse and trouble and harass the enemy into submission to their rightful Sovereign.

In other words, think what might be accomplished by 1,000 saints familiar with the use of the weapons of their warfare, and able to act singly and in combined force against a common enemy. We say, think of the results, of the night and day, and week by week, and year by year, attacks and bombardments, and surprises and all... other kinds of unsettlements and miseries which such a force would produce.[2]

**Lord of the Church, my prayer is for Christians to unite in worship, work, and witness. Draw us together by your Spirit; help us to respect diversity and teach us to learn from different traditions with respect and humility. Bless and use your Church as a strong force for good. Amen.**

1 Attributed to Napoleon.
2 From *The Founder Speaks.*

# April 23rd

For the life of a creature is in the blood, and I have given it to you to make atonement for yourselves on the altar; it is the blood that makes atonement for one's life

(Leviticus 17:11 *NIV*)

[An] objection to the doctrine of the atonement affirms that the benefits flowing out of the sacrifice are not equivalent to the amount of humiliation and sacrifice that Jesus Christ endured. In answer to this objection, let us consider some of the blessings flowing out of the atonement, and show that they constitute incontrovertible reasons why we Salvationists should hold to the doctrine with all our might.

We must hold on to the doctrine of the atonement because of the marvellous revelation it affords of the love of God to man. You have the revelation of that love in the creation, the provision made for man's health and happiness. You have a revelation of that love in providence. All things work together for our good.[1] That we do not understand why things that appear opposed to our welfare come to us does not disprove the fact.

You have a revelation of that love in the Bible. Who would ever have dreamed of many of the things we know about God if they had not been there revealed? You have a revelation of that love in grace. Grace is the sign of the infinite compassion, love, and beauty of God in the conversion, sanctification, preservation, and utilization of his people, and in their final triumph over death and Hell. But in Christ – in his hanging, dying on the cross – we have a manifestation of the heart of love which made all this possible, and which, in importance, far transcends it all.

We must hold on to the doctrine of the atonement because it forms a strong incentive for us to love God in return… I kneel before his bleeding form, and remember who he was, and why he came there… We must hold on to the doctrine of the atonement because of the picture it presents of the majesty of the divine law, and the importance of its maintenance. As I look upon the suffering Christ, not only am I compelled to think of the high estimate God sets upon the law that keeps the universe in order, but my heart bounds to render obedience to that law.[2]

**Father, when I ponder the sacrifice of Jesus Christ, I realize afresh that the only fit response I can make is to offer my soul, my life, my all. I do so here and now. Thank you for your law of love. Amen.**

1 Romans 8:28
2 From *The Founder Speaks Again*.

# April 24th

No soldier gets entangled in civilian pursuits, since his aim is to please the one who enlisted him

(2 Timothy 2:4 *ESV*)

The lives of sinners would become unendurable in the presence of... warriors who were always, both in season and out of season,[1] bringing them face to face with God, and the coming consequence of their ways, and they would be constrained to remove to some other town, to emigrate, even to wish for death, to get away from this harassing warfare or, and oh, hallelujah! the more probable result would be that the rebels in large numbers would submit and be forgiven and become themselves soldiers in the army of the King.

Look at these 14 hundred millions of our fellow men, mostly in the arms and power of the foul usurper of Hell, who has largely his own way with them, making this possible Paradise into blackest and most hellish perdition here, and dragging multitudes down to the deeper depths of all possible woe hereafter. What do Jesus and all the angels say of professed soldiers of Jehovah who look on, and sing, and speak, and read and understand all about the actual condition of things and are so very contented with the same looking on, and speaking, and reading, and understanding all about the ruin and desolation, and do so little fighting to prevent and hinder and deliver?

Oh, what can we say of the professed followers of Jesus Christ who don't fight: fight when they are wanted, fight always, fight their way through the darkness and the devils to the salvation of a redeemed world? What can we say? That they are orthodox, learned, theological, ornamental? Say anything and everything, but don't call them soldiers for, without excuses and self-consideration of health, or limb, or life, true soldiers live to fight, love to fight, love the thickest of the fight, and die in the midst of it. Another mark of a good soldier is that he endures hardness. I suppose the worst possible form of soldiers would be men who from their appearance and capacity and antecedents led their officers to rely upon them for the discharge of difficult and important duties, but who in the hour of difficulty gave way.[2]

**Father, you have graciously enlisted me to fight for the King. Bless me with the ability to realize that every word spoken as a witness for Jesus, and every good deed done in his name, is like a bullet fired or a victory won, in Kingdom terms. May this be my encouragement today. Amen.**

1 2 Timothy 4:2
2 From *The Founder Speaks.*

# April 25[th]

I URGE YOU, BROTHERS AND SISTERS, IN VIEW OF GOD'S MERCY, TO OFFER YOUR BODIES AS A LIVING SACRIFICE, HOLY AND PLEASING TO GOD – THIS IS YOUR TRUE AND PROPER WORSHIP

(Romans 12:1 *NIV*)

It is argued... that it is an unjust arrangement for one being to be sacrificed in the interests of another, as in the case of the atonement. It seems to me to be most curious that such an objection should be raised in a world that is so full of sacrifice at every turn you take it in. When we look round us it seems as though in this life sacrifice were a law of existence...

The material world is full of sacrifice. Matter is sacrificed to propagate and support every sort of vegetable, as well as animal life. Coal has to be burned in order to create warmth, prepare food and supply the means of motion. The vegetable world is sacrificed to sustain animal life. And the animal world is sacrificed, with a vengeance, for the maintenance of human life.[1] Husbands sacrifice themselves for their wives, or ought to do so. Wives are sacrificed for their husbands. Parents are sacrificed for their children. Patriots are sacrificed for their country. And in some Eastern lands, one human being is accepted as a sacrifice for another.

One the one hand, the highest admiration of men of all stations is given to those who sacrifice their interests or even themselves for the good of others. On the other hand, selfishness – taking care of yourself, and allowing other people to suffer or perish, sometimes through your unwillingness to suffer on their account – is everywhere despised; although, alas, largely practised by those who hold it in such contempt.

And when we come to the religious world, we find sacrifice everywhere taught. No religion has a powerful hold upon the people that has not sacrifice as a principle of its action, if not a main reason for its existence. Without sacrifice, religion would not be religion at all. Why then should it be counted as unreasonable or unjust for the Son of God to inhabit a human body for a season, in order the he might be a man of sorrows and die a suffering death, to make a sacrifice for our sins and leave behind him an example for us to imitate?[2]

**Lord of my life, I offer all that I am to your service. I have not much to give you, but all I have is yours. Amen.**

1 Booth was vegetarian.
2 From *The Founder Speaks Again.*

# April 26th

How can I give you up, Ephraim? How can I hand you over, Israel?... My heart is changed within me; all my compassion is aroused

(Hosea 11:8 *NIV*)

There are many vices and seven deadly sins. But of late years many of the seven have contrived to pass themselves off as virtues. Avarice, for instance; and pride, when re-baptized thrift and self-respect, have become the guardian angels of Christian civilization; and as for envy, it is the cornerstone upon which much of our competitive system is founded. There are still two vices which are fortunate, or unfortunate, enough to remain undisguised, not even concealing from themselves the fact that they are vices and not virtues. One is drunkenness; the other fornication. The viciousness of these vices is so little disguised, even from those who habitually practise them, that there will be a protest against merely describing them by the right biblical name. Why not say prostitution? For this reason: prostitution is a word applied to only one half of the vice, and that the most pitiable. Fornication hits both sinners alike. Prostitution applies only to the woman.

When, however, we cease to regard this vice from the point of view of morality and religion, and look at it solely as a factor in the social problem, the word "prostitution" is less objectionable. For the social burden of this vice is borne almost entirely by women. The male sinner does not, by the mere fact of his sin, find himself in a worse position in obtaining employment, in finding a home, or even in securing a wife. His wrongdoing only hits him in his purse or, perhaps, in his health.

His incontinence, excepting so far as it relates to the woman whose degradation it necessitates, does not add to the number of those for whom society has to provide. It is an immense addition to the infamy of this vice in man that its consequences have to be borne almost exclusively by woman.

The difficulty of dealing with drunkards and harlots is almost insurmountable. Were it not that I utterly repudiate as a fundamental denial of the essential principle of the Christian religion the popular pseudo-scientific doctrine that any man or woman is past saving by the grace of God and the power of the Holy Spirit, I would sometimes be disposed to despair.[1]

**Truthful God, you call us to acknowledge sin for what it is. Set against that, you offer tremendous saving grace; no one is beyond your reach. Thanks to your mercy, we do not despair. Amen.**

1 From *In Darkest England and the Way Out.*

# April 27th

I KNOW THE PLANS I HAVE FOR YOU, DECLARES THE LORD

(Jeremiah 29:11 *ESV*)

I always pray when our captain does; whether it's long or short (he can't come near to Captain Wrestler at long prayers); and, curious like, I always want to go on when he leaves off. Then, he is not much to look at. He made me think of David and Goliath[1] when I saw him the other day standing alongside Major Pull-the-house-down, who was here booming the Grace-before-meat boxes.[2] But, then, the major has got uncommonly stout lately. My! He is a weight. He broke our bit of rail down a-leaning on it, and I was glad the old platform didn't go as well. Our Sarah says she's sure he ought to have more exercise, or he'll have a happoplektic fit, or something of that kind, some day.

But, never mind, if our captain is not much to look at, what there is of him is good stuff, and I always forget his looks once he gets going… and, then, all that he does say, when he gets into the Spirit, sounds like Bible to me…

Then, there is another reason why I like our captain; and that is, because he gets souls saved. Now, I can't tell you how it is; perhaps it is because of the superior education I have had in the Army – for, you see, I couldn't read a letter in the Book when I was converted, and now I can read my Bible and the dear old [*War*] *Cry* beautifully. Or, perhaps it is the feeling that came from the blessed Lord straight away into my heart when I was converted.

Or, perhaps, it may be with thinking so much about the dreadful Judgment Day[3] that is coming on, and what will follow after; I can't tell what it is, but howsoever it may be, I do like to see people come to the penitent form. I never reckon it a good meeting on a Sunday night if we haven't had somebody out – anyway, unless there has been a good fight made for it; and our captain is the boy to do it.[4]

**Lord, you have made each of us as an individual. You are not a bland God who copies, but a God who delights in remarkable creativity. Help me always to be the "me" that you created me to be, and to resist the temptation of comparing myself with anyone but Jesus. Amen.**

1 1 Samuel 17

2 In 1893, a Commissioner Coombes instituted the Grace-before-meat scheme whereby Salvationists would forgo a meal or part of a meal and make a donation to Salvation Army social work instead. ("Booming" is the Army phrase used for publicizing an activity or selling something to raise funds; as in "pub booming" when literature is sold in public houses. Agents were appointed to distribute Grace-before-meat collecting boxes to homes.)

3 Matthew 12:36

4 From *Sergeant-Major Do-Your-Best.*

# April 28th

### I know your deeds, that you are neither cold nor hot
(Revelation 3:15 *NIV*)

I have been visiting the Salvationists of Switzerland, Italy, and France.[1] Everywhere I find vast openings for The Salvation Army. Everywhere I have met with dear comrades longing to make the most of their opportunities; and everywhere, it has seemed to me, that more red-hot religion would make these comrades equal to the splendid chances of usefulness that lie right before them. But is it not the same in Great Britain, America, Australia,[2] and every other part of the world to which these letters will come? Is it not so in your corps? Nay, is it not so with every individual soldier?...

By red-hot religion I mean hearts made hot with love for God, for comrades, for perishing souls, for noble work, and for every other good thing possible to men and women on earth or in Heaven. I mean hearts made hot with holy love, such love as will compel us to toil and sacrifice for the welfare of the object cared for. Such love as will make its possessor the servant of those beloved, and exercise a self-denying mastery over the heart that experiences it. Such love will be like our Master's...

Look at the mother's love. Does it not make her sacrifice time, comfort, and health for her child? Look at the patriot's love. Does it not compel him to turn his back on home, family, business, to fight and die for his country? And so hot love in the Salvationist will make him lay health, time, goods, and all he possesses at the feet of his Lord, and there use all in blessing and saving the souls of men. Now it is this spirit of love which makes this blessed heat in the souls of men and women. As the devil lights and feeds the fires of malice, ambition, selfishness, pride, lust, and the other evils that encourage and strengthen souls in their warfare with God... so the fierce heat of pure love, created and maintained by the Holy Spirit, makes the Salvationist watch and pray, toil and talk and suffer.[3]

**My prayer this day is that the fire of the Holy Spirit may rest upon me, inhabit me, enable me, and energize me, for Jesus' sake. Amen.**

1 In 1882, a few Salvationists entered Switzerland from France, but were expelled. In 1886, the Army was accepted in Switzerland as a religious organization, but banned again in 1890. Booth visited Switzerland in 1892, where the work is now part of the Switzerland, Austria and Hungary Territory. The Salvation Army commenced operations in Italy in 1887, but withdrew. Work was re-established in 1893. Salvation Army ministry in France began in 1881, led by "La Maréchale", William Booth's eldest daughter.

2 The first meeting held by The Salvation Army in Australia took place in 1879. The Army opened fire in America in 1885, and in Australia in 1880.

3 From *Purity of Heart*.

# April 29th

## Set your minds on things above
(Colossians 3:2 *NIV*)

Parents have no more right to train their children for the gratification of their own selfish interests and fancies than a steward has to use his master's property for his own personal advantage, or a nurse to train the children entrusted to her care to advance her own particular views or interests. Let every parent carefully consider this, and be prepared to give account [of] how he deals with this precious trust…

The superior information which the parent possesses concerning the child's welfare shows him to be positively cruel if he refuses to impart it. What would be thought of a parent who, seeing the dangers, difficulties, and enemies scattered through the coming life of his child, should refuse to warn, counsel, and strengthen it to the utmost of his ability as to the best way to meet, resist, and overcome them; or, who, seeing the happiness and usefulness possible to his child, should fail to do all in his power to instruct, guide, and inspire it to attain to them?…

The natural instincts which lead the parent, mother or father, to yearn with indescribable and irrepressible desire for the supreme good of the child, show that the parent is responsible for the employment of every possible method for promoting the present and future welfare. However far the parents themselves may be from righteousness, there are instincts in them which lead them to desire – and that very strongly – that their children should be good and happy. Do not all parents, at times at least, feel how easy it would be for them to make any sacrifice for the real well-being of their children? It would not be difficult – nay, it would be easy – for them to die to save them from any terrible woe, or to secure for them any great good.

Why did God implant these instincts if not to lead parents to do all that is possible for the good of their children? A bear will die to save her cubs from death; and the parental instinct was implanted for a more glorious salvation than that of the body only.[1]

**Father, touch my heart afresh with an eternal perspective, so that my dealings in this life have a bearing on the next. For Heaven's sake, make me useful on earth. Amen.**

1 From *The Training of Children.*

# April 30th

## Let your conversation be always full of grace

(Colossians 4:6 *NIV*)

Men are known by their conversation, as well as by the company they keep. Their chief interests are revealed the moment we have conversation with them. It is not too much to state that assuming we give anyone an opportunity to converse with us, we shall soon discover not only his mentality and spirituality, but that which constitutes his chief basis, his aim, his calling in life. Here is a matter meriting the most earnest attention of all children of God, of Salvationists in particular, and even more especially (if we may say so) of officers and local officers or others who have influence in the direction of helping any of our dear people.

Conversation in the home – conversation in the office – conversation in the mine – conversation in the band room – conversation in the hall. How does it stand? Does it commend us and our profession to the One whose ear is always open and who registers, as the scientists have declared, in the ether about us every sound we ever breathed? In the divine library of heavenly "phonographic record" there is stored every curse we ever breathed, every prayer we ever made, every song we ever sung, every bit of scandal we ever purveyed, every piece of foolishness that has passed our lips. God holds the key! One day he will release it all – this vast accumulation of spoken words. It is little wonder the Bible affirms the startling truth that for every idle word we shall be brought into judgment.[1]

Conversation, in one form or another is, we can readily imagine, a privilege common to all living creatures. We know that the great Father in Heaven holds some sort of high intercourse with the holy beings by which he is surrounded; and we have reason to believe that he does this through the medium of some celestial language. The archangels and angels, the seraphim and cherubim, and other of the inhabitants of Heaven, we are expressly informed, bow before his face, and cry, 'Holy, holy, holy, is the Lord [God] Almighty".[2] The Bible contains the record of many conversations that have taken place between God and his people on the earth.[3]

**Lord, when I consider the thousands of millions of words that spill from my lips every day, every month, and every year, I realize my need of your guidance. Guard my mouth, Lord. Grant me your wisdom to speak words that help and heal. Amen.**

1 Matthew 12:36
2 Isaiah 6:3 *TLB*
3 From *The Founder Speaks.*

# May 1st

There are different kinds of gifts, but the same Spirit distributes them

(1 Corinthians 12:4 *NIV*)

Is there not a certain amount of brain power lying unemployed within your borders? Might not some fresh plans be invented for more successfully attracting the people to your building, getting at them in their own homes, or button-holing them in the streets or their pleasure haunts, and so compelling them to remember God and eternity? Might not something new be done to stir up your soldiers to such desires, resolutions, and faith as would draw the Holy Ghost down from Heaven in richer baptisms than ever enjoyed before, so setting their hearts on fire with overcoming love?

Might not a little extra thought make your meetings more interesting and spiritual, and therefore more useful? When I was in the United States[1] I heard that a prosperous firm had a letter-box fixed in their premises in which any employee could deposit any suggestion for doing any part of the business of the establishment in a more rapid or economical manner, a reward being offered for valuable suggestions. Could there not be something of that sort in your corps, my comrades? Anyhow, wake up your sleeping brains, and think, and study how you can faster roll the old chariot along.

Again, let me ask, is there not a large amount of talent lying buried in your corps? Supposing you have only forty or fifty soldiers, may there not be some valuable slumbering gift that has not yet been brought into active service? It is quite probable that the commanding officer has no knowledge of the treasure; that the sergeant-major has not seen anything of it, and that even the possessors themselves have no idea of its existence. For example, is it not quite possible you have some soldier on your roll who could effectively sing a solo, but who as yet has never had the chance of doing so? What do you say, my comrades? Is it not quite probable that there is some soldier in your ranks who could pray in public with unction and power, but who as yet has never poured forth his soul before the people? What do you say, my comrades?[2]

**Gifting God, if there is any latent passion lying dormant within me, please stir it into flame; nothing would I withhold. Likewise, help me to make a point of encouraging others in the use of their gifts and abilities, for Jesus' sake. Amen.**

1 Possibly 1895.

2 From *The Founder's Messages to Soldiers.*

# May 2nd

So I took the heads of your tribes, wise and experienced men, and set them as heads over you, commanders of thousands, commanders of hundreds, commanders of fifties, commanders of tens, and officers, throughout your tribes

(Deuteronomy 1:15 *ESV*)

My dear comrades, I was not able to say all I wanted on the subject of… the supply of officers to carry on the war… I alluded to the expectations that I cherish in the little soldiers [young people] coming in shoals to the help of the Lord; but feeling that there must needs be some time before this supply would be available, I turned to the crowds of unsaved young men and women waiting to be pressed into the Army, and capable of being almost immediately trained for the service. And then my eye fell upon a multitude more, already saved, enrolled, and one might almost say, to a very large extent, trained and ready for the fight. I allude to the soldiers in our own ranks whom God is wanting to lead forth his sanctified hosts to the battle.

In this letter let me speak to these. If you are qualified for this business, I want you to set your affairs in order. Bid farewell to your loved ones. Separate yourself from all worldly pursuits. Come out and place yourselves, with every power you possess for doing or suffering, at the Master's feet. Why should the war suffer? Why should the enemy triumph? Why should the battle languish for want of leaders when you are the very people – possess the very gifts – have been saved for the very purpose of carrying it on? We need not wait for the little ones growing up, nor for the wicked ones to be converted; you are grown up, and you are converted, and you are to hand. We cannot, must not, will not wait.

"Be patient," do you say? "Wait the Lord's time"? This is the Lord's time; why should I wait? There is a sanctified anger because it is just, and there is a sanctified impatience because it is born of benevolence. How can we wait and see the people die, and see the generation sweep off before our eyes into eternal woe, that might be rescued – that might be saved?[1]

**Captain of the host, my prayer today is that you would speak, loud and clear, to those called to spiritual leadership and ministry. May their applications be successful. Place your hand upon them and open every door along the way. Amen.**

1 From *The General's Letters.*

# May 3rd

## Whoso trusteth in the Lord, happy is he

(Proverbs 16:20 *KJV*)

How far can I be saved? This is a question of thrilling interest to every really converted soul. Hunger and thirst after all inward and outward rightness with God and before him is natural to the spiritual man. And the possibility of complete deliverance must, whatever be his opinion, interest him and deserve his most careful attention.

Can I be saved from sinning and from sin here? I know, you know, we all know, that we shall have deliverance there, in the new heavens and the new earth.[1] But what about this very earth in which we are compelled to live for the present? Can I love God with all my heart here in this town, in this house? Aye, in this poor body, with all its aches, pains and infirmities, with devils tempting me and men opposing me, and the mighty work of winning souls to Jesus on my hands? Is it my Father's good pleasure to give me now that inner hidden kingdom of righteousness, peace, and joy in the Holy Ghost?[2] That is the question; and that is a question of surpassing importance to every redeemed soul whose eyes shall rest on this paper.

It means happiness! Sin is the great evil of your existence. Perhaps you have thought otherwise. The devil's great interest is to delude you by making you feel that your happiness is dependent on your circumstances. You used to think so in an unsaved state. You said then, if you could only secure some form or other of earthly treasure you would be blessed. And now, you say, with Christ and something else you will be happy. Give me this or that and Jesus, and it will be all right.

But it was not so then, and it is not so now. God is your great good. You were made to enjoy him. He, and he only, can fill and satisfy your soul. Sin separated you from God before conversion, and now sin dulls your senses and clouds your vision, and prevents God manifesting himself in all his glorious power within you.[3]

**Thank you, Lord, for this clear definition of happiness; all my lasting joys are found in Jesus. Please teach me more about it, so that my happiness is found in you and your happiness is found in me. Amen.**

1 Revelation 21:1
2 Romans 14:17
3 From *The Founder Speaks Again.*

# May 4th

Jesus answered him, "Truly I tell you, today you will be with me in paradise"

(Luke 23:43 *NIV*)

We seem remarkably to realize the meaning of the expression, "snatched from the burning"[1] as we remember case after case in which notorious sinners have been laid hold of, and brought to Christ, very shortly before their death. Ben Ive, a barber of Otley,[2] and one of the most notable drunkards in the town, came to Chris, and showed an excellent example of devotion to his cause, whilst he was spared, wearing his shield at work as well as at the meetings; but he had only three weeks of this happy life when sudden illness struck him down. The night he died, he remarked to the secretary of the corps that he thought he should have died that morning. "But," added he, "it would have been all right, I should have gone to Glory" – and who could doubt that was really the case?

Thank God, it is not only to those who have the strength, and are able to take front places in the fight, that the preciousness of salvation has been fully proved, in health and sickness, and in the hour of death. A sister who had been amongst us for two and a half years in Sunderland,[3] and whose happy appearance, notwithstanding much weakness and family care, had been very striking, remained the same contented, happy woman throughout an illness of more than six months and, on the evening before her death, when asked, "How is it with your soul now?" answered, "Praise the Lord, I am going home to Glory. I am trusting in Jesus. He is with me."

A sister in Cheltenham,[4] who had nursed another, who died in 1882, through a serious illness, caught from her the same serious disease and, after three weeks' illness, went to Heaven. This sister, who had been converted seventeen years ago at one of our East End services,[5] had ever since steadfastly kept on her way, so that it was not necessary she should say much at the last. Her voice was almost entirely gone, but she managed to say, "Hallelujah! I am coming, I am coming," repeatedly, before she passed away from us to her heavenly home.[6]

**Saving God, your mercy is quite overwhelming, that you offer the gift of salvation even to "the last minute". I praise you because you persist until the very end, so great is your love. Amen.**

1 See Amos 4:11
2 Yorkshire, England.
3 North-east England.
4 Gloucestershire, England.
5 The East End of London, where the Army's work began.
6 From *The Salvation War, 1883*

# May 5th

Show yourself in all respects to be a model of good works
(Titus 2:7 *ESV*)

If it had not been for his [Captain Makebelieve's] uniform, you would not have known that he was an officer, and all his talk was about politics, and running down his brother officers, and his sergeant-major; and Sarah says she never thinks any better of any captain who speaks against his sergeant-major, because she says her husband always supports his captain; and so she thinks every captain ought to support his sergeant-major… And ever since that time, when our captain has asked her to billet an officer… she always says: "No, Captain, I respect you, and if ever you come back to this corps when you have left it, which I hope will not be for a long time to come, you must always come here; but I don't want any more Captain Makebelieves in my house; and I won't have them, if I can help it."…

Now, I was talking… about our captain, and I must just have another word on him. I promised that I would finish up my account this time, and I want to keep my word; although, when I've done, it will, I am afraid, be like what the captain told us the other night was the opinion that the Queen of Sheba had of Solomon when she went over from Buluwayo[1] to see him. She said the half of Solomon's wonders had not been told her. It will be just like that with our captain when I've done with him… he is good at visitation. And yet it isn't that he does so much more of it than many officers we've had; that is, he doesn't put in many more hours than Captain Gossipton… Captain Gossipton would sit down in the kitchen with the servants, and talk for an hour until the girls were ashamed for being kept from their work so long, or he would talk to the shoemaker while he hammered the shoes… What did he talk about? Ah! That is the question.[2]

**Father, help me to remember that I am your ambassador, and that people will notice the things I talk about. By the same token, help me to remember when it is time to stop talking. May my lips be filled with messages from Heaven. Amen.**

1 1 Kings 10
2 From *Sergeant-Major Do-Your-Best.*

# May 6th

## Whoredom and wine and new wine take away the heart

(Hosea 4:11 *KJV*)

The doctrine of heredity and the suggestion of irresponsibility come perilously near re-establishing, on scientific bases, the awful dogma of reprobation which has cast so terrible a shadow over the Christian Church. For thousands upon thousands of these poor wretches are, as Bishop South truly said, "not so much born into this world as damned into it". The bastard of a harlot, born in a brothel, suckled on gin, and familiar from earliest infancy with all the bestialities of debauch, violated before she is twelve, and driven out into the streets by her mother a year or two later, what chance is there for a girl in this world – I say nothing about the next?

Yet such a case is not exceptional. There are many such differing in detail, but in essentials the same. And with boys it is almost as bad. There are thousands who were begotten when both parents were besotted with drink, whose mothers saturated themselves with alcohol every day of their pregnancy, who may be said to have sucked in a taste for strong drink with their mothers' milk, and who were surrounded from childhood with opportunities and incitements to drink. How can we marvel that the constitution thus disposed to intemperance finds the stimulus of drink indispensable? Even if they make a stand against it, the increasing pressure of exhaustion and of scanty food drives them back to the cup. Of these poor wretches, born slaves of the bottle, predestined to drunkenness from their mother's womb, there are – who can say how many?

Yet they are all men; all with what the Russian peasants call "a spark of God" in them, which can never be wholly obscured and destroyed while life exists, and if any social scheme is to be comprehensive and practical it must deal with these men. It must provide for the drunkard and the harlot as it provides for the improvident and the Out-of-Work… the drink difficulty lies at the root of everything. Nine-tenths of our poverty, squalor, vice, and crime spring from this poisonous taproot. Many of our social evils… would dwindle away and die if they were not constantly watered with strong drink.[1]

**Lord God, how it must sadden you to see lives wrecked and ruined, and some like that from childhood. My prayer this day is for those who work to rehabilitate such lives; those who staff adult rehabilitation centres, experts in recovery, and churches that host detox programmes. Use them to bring freedom. Amen.**

1 From *In Darkest England and the Way Out.*

# May 7th

For we are to God the pleasing aroma of Christ

**(2 Corinthians 2:15 *NIV*)**

The Holy Spirit only dwells, in all his mastering power and burning zeal, in souls that have been cleansed from evil; so that if you are resolved to spend your life in blessing and saving men, and fighting for your Lord, you must have a pure heart. A pure heart will make you a blessing to those around you, and that not merely as a result of what you do, but from the fact of what you are. People, will, no doubt, be drawn to love Christ, and seek salvation, and fight for the Army by what you say and sing. Your appeals and your prayers will all affect them; but if, in addition, you possess this treasure, they will also be led to God and holiness and Heaven by what they see you are.

A pure heart, as we have seen, makes a good life. Goodness is attractive; men respect it, and are drawn to it, for what it is in itself. Even if they are themselves the slaves of what is bad and devilish, they cannot help admiring what is holy and divine. And if this is the case with the slaves of sin and vice, it will be a thousand times more so with those around you who have already been captivated by the charms of holiness. To such hearts, your life, if governed and inspired by pure love, will be a constant source of light, and strength, and consolation.

This is what we call influence. It is something that is always going on. It is like the fragrance of a rose. You take the flower and place it in the middle of a room, and day and night it will send forth a sweet smell to all around. You have not to [do] anything to it, or with it. You need not wave it about, or pass it from one to another. It will spread abroad its pleasant perfume quite apart from any movement. So it is with the soldier who enjoys purity of heart, and lives in harmony with the experience. A holy influence will be going out from him all the time, not only from what he says and does, but from what he is himself.[1]

**Father God, preserve me from any kind of holiness that is forced. Holy Spirit, dwell within me so that the fragrance of Christ emanates without any effort on my part, save that of praying for your reign in my heart. Amen.**

1 From *Purity of Heart*.

# May 8th

Jesus said unto her, I am the resurrection, and the life: he that believeth in me, though he were dead, yet shall he live

(John 11:25 *KJV*)

A little fellow, who died at Exeter early in the year, deserves to rank among our veterans, although he was only nine years old at the time of his death. He had been converted almost immediately after the establishment of the work in the city, and had marched with the rest continually, even in the stormiest of times, having been down on the ground during the Skeleton[1] attacks more than once; but having always been happy and ready for duty outdoors or in, playing his violin in the meetings inside. At his death he had only saved half-a-crown, and that he gave to the Army.

In one week our Chippenham Corps lost two soldiers – one a sister, only sixteen years of age, who suffered very great agony in her last hours, and who died, nevertheless, with a happy smile upon her face, after asking everyone in the room to meet her in Heaven. The other was a woman, seventy-two years of age, who had been converted about a year previously, and had marched in almost every procession during the year. Her daughter asked her to "fix bayonets"[2] as she died if she felt happy and was unable to speak, and she did so – a remarkable specimen of a thorough soldier, made such in her old age. Our people being continually employed in all manner of callings where they are daily exposed to danger, it is remarkable that we should not oftener have to mourn over the loss of them by accident. To the general rule of their preservation from these dangers there have been some sad exceptions during the last twelve months. What a blessing that amidst all the discussions about the Army, so many thousands daily exposed to danger are getting a real salvation, which fits them in a moment to go triumphantly away from the regions of doubt and discussion to the rest and joy of Heaven.

Although thousands of our soldiers are miners, we do not know that we have lost more than one of them by accident in the course of the year – Matthew Wood, of Tamworth,[3] who was injured, and who died on the following day, peacefully and calmly.[4]

**Lord of life and death, to die in Christ is safe. Thank you for that wonderful reassurance. Draw alongside those of your people who are dying today; may your peace gently escort them from earth to eternity. Amen.**

1 The "Skeleton Army" was an army of thugs violently opposed to Salvation Army mission. Their flag carried a skull and crossbones image.
2 To raise one's right hand in response to a statement of faith either spoken or sung.
3 Staffordshire, England.
4 From *The Salvation War, 1883.*

# May 9th

**Be careful; you must not drink wine or any other alcoholic drink**

**(Judges 13:4 *NLT*)**

The agreement as to the evils of intemperance is almost as universal as the conviction that politicians will do nothing to interfere with them. In Ireland, Mr Justice Fitzgerald[1] says that intemperance leads to nineteen-twentieths of the crime in that country, but no one proposes a Coercion Act to deal with that evil. In England, the judges all say the same thing. Of course it is a mistake to assume that a murder, for instance, would never be committed by sober men, because murderers in most cases prime themselves for their deadly work by a glass of Dutch courage. But the facility of securing a reinforcement of passion undoubtedly tends to render always dangerous, and sometimes irresistible, the temptation to violate the laws of God and man.

More lectures against the evil habit are, however, of no avail. We have to recognize that the gin palace, like many other evils, although a poisonous, is still a natural outgrowth of our social conditions. The tap-room in many cases is the poor man's only parlour. Many a man takes to beer, not from the love of beer, but from a natural craving for the light, warmth, company, and comfort which is thrown in along with the beer, and which he cannot get except by buying beer. Reformers will never get rid of the drink shop until they can outbid it in the subsidiary attractions which it offers to its customers.

Then again, let us never forget that the temptation to drink is strongest when want is sharpest and misery the most acute. A well-fed man is not driven to drink by the craving that torments the hungry; and the comfortable do not crave for the boon of forgetfulness. Gin is the only Lethe[2] of the miserable. The foul and poisoned air of the dens in which thousands live predisposes to a longing for stimulant. Fresh air, with its oxygen and its ozone, being lacking, a man supplies the want with spirit. After a time the longing for drink becomes a mania. Life seems as insupportable without alcohol as without food. It is a disease often inherited, always developed by indulgence, but clearly a disease.[3]

**Father, these strong words are laced with compassion. May they reflect my approach to those trapped by an addiction to alcohol; that I may remember mercy and always consider underlying factors. Amen.**

1 A prominent Irish judge.
2 In Greek mythology, the stream of oblivion.
3 From *In Darkest England and the Way Out.*

# May 10th

We escaped like a bird from a hunter's trap. The trap is broken, and we are free!

(Psalm 124:7 *NLT*)

How many are there who are, more or less, under the dominion of strong drink? Statistics abound, but they seldom tell us what we want to know. We know how many public houses there are in the land, and how many arrests for drunkenness the police make in a year; but beyond that we know little. Everyone knows that for one man who is arrested for drunkenness there are at least ten and often twenty who go home intoxicated. In London, for instance, there are 14,000 drink shops, and every year 20,000 persons are arrested for drunkenness. But who can for a moment believe that there are only 20,000, more or less, habitual drunkards in London? By habitual drunkard I do not mean one who is always drunk, but one who is so much under the dominion of the evil habit that he cannot be depended upon not to get drink whenever the opportunity offers.

In the United Kingdom there are 190,000 public houses, and every year there are 200,000 arrests for drunkenness. Of course, several of these arrests refer to the same person, who is locked up again and again. Were this not so, if we allowed six drunkards to each house as an average, or five habitual drunkards for one arrested for drunkenness, we should arrive at a total of a million adults who are more or less prisoners of the publican – as a matter of fact, Isaac Hoyle[1] gives one in twelve of the adult population. This may be an excessive estimate but, if we take half a million, we shall not be accused of exaggeration. Of these some are in the last stage of confirmed dipsomania; others are but [on] the verge; but the procession tends ever downwards.

All this should predispose us to charity and sympathy. While recognizing that the primary responsibility must always rest upon the individual, we may fairly insist that society which, by its habits, its customs, and its laws, has greased the slop down which these poor creatures slide to perdition, shall seriously take in hand their salvation.[2]

**Father, give me a heart of compassion. Move me to play my part in society. I might only be able to help one or two people in my lifetime, but I pray for the millions who are enslaved. I call upon your great power to intervene and deliver freedom. Amen.**

1 British mill owner and Liberal politician.
2 From *In Darkest England and the Way Out.*

# May 11th

It is not for kings to drink wine, not for rulers to crave beer

(Proverbs 31:4 *NIV*)

The loss which the maintenance of this huge standing army of a half of a million of men who are more or less always besotted men whose intemperance impairs their working power, consumes their earnings, and renders their homes wretched, has long been a familiar theme of the platform. But what can be done for them? Total abstinence is no doubt admirable, but how are you to get them to be totally abstinent? When a man is drowning in mid-ocean the one thing that is needful, no doubt, is that he should plant his feet firmly on terra firma. But how is he to get there? It is just what he cannot do.

And so it is with the drunkards. If they are to be rescued there must be something more done for them than at present is attempted; unless, of course, we decide definitely to allow the iron laws of nature to work themselves out in their destruction. In that case it might be more merciful to facilitate the slow workings of natural law. There is no need of establishing a lethal chamber for drunkards like that into which the lost dogs of London are driven, to die in peaceful sleep under the influence of carbonic oxide. The State would only need to go a little further than it goes at present in the way of supplying poison to the community. If, in addition to planting a flaming gin palace at each corner, free to all who enter, it were to supply free gin to all who have attained a certain recognized standard of inebriety, delirium tremens would soon reduce our drunken population to manageable proportions.

I can imagine a cynical millionaire of the scientific philanthropic school making a clearance of all the drunkards in a district by the simple expedient of an unlimited allowance of alcohol. But that for us is out of the question. The problem of what to do with our half of a million drunkards remains to be solved, and few more difficult questions confront the social reformer.[1]

**Father God, the State must accept its share of responsibility for licensing laws that might be irresponsible, and for legislation that can encourage behaviour that is ruinous. I pray for politicians, councillors, and law-makers, that you would fill them with wisdom and courage in their decision-making. Amen.**

1 From *In Darkest England and the Way Out.*

# May 12th

## Seek the Kingdom of God above all else

(Matthew 6:33 *NLT*)

Within the last few weeks, in addition to the countries we already occupy, we have had earnest entreaties to send officers to Spain and Germany and China and Norway and Assam and St Helena and Egypt and Singapore, and I know not where else; and, as I said before, one of the main hindrances in complying with these Macedonian cries is the vast want of men to send.[1]

But this is a very important question. Are all to become officers? Yes, all who are adapted for it. We go on the lines of adaptation. If you are cut out for being an officer, an officer you must be, and an officer you will be, or it will be so much the worse for you both here and hereafter. And here let me remark that it is a very serious matter – as thousands can testify – for any man or woman to allow any consideration of gain or pleasure or friendship to turn them aside from treading that track of labour which God gives them to understand in their hearts as being most likely to glorify him and save men. If God sets before you an open door through which you know there is an entrance to a career of usefulness, enter it; though in doing so you turn your back on fame and friends and fortune. I would not like to be in any man's shoes – or any woman's either – who, when the two courses lay before them, chose that which led to worldly ease and enjoyment in preference to the suffering track which if followed meant the salvation of men.

"But what is to become of business?" said a lady at the breakfast table when I expressed the wish that I could have her five sons for officers. "The business of the world, you mean, I presume. Oh, let the business of the world take care of itself," I replied. "My business is to get the world saved; if this involves the standing still of the looms and the shutting up of the factories, and the staying of the sailing of the ships, let them all stand still."[2]

**Lord, your call is to one of surrender. This day, please guide me through my priorities; I give you my permission to realign them as you prefer. Please let me know if anything is out of place. All to Jesus I surrender. Amen.**

1 Acts 16:9
2 From *The General's Letters.*

# May 13th

LIGHT SHINES ON THE GODLY, AND JOY ON THOSE WHOSE HEARTS ARE RIGHT

(Psalm 97:11 *NLT*)

God is your great good. You were made to enjoy him. He, and he only, can fill and satisfy your soul. Sin separated you from God before conversion, and now sin dulls your senses and clouds your vision, and prevents God manifesting himself in all his glorious power within you.

Peter told the Jews that God, having raised up his Son Jesus, had sent him to bless them.[1] But how? By destroying the Roman yoke and making them a great, free, powerful nation? No! By the completion of their beautiful Temple, and the revival, in all its pomp and magnificence, of that Temple's ritual and service? No! By sending them trade, commerce, plenty, health, friendships, and all the desired relationships of family life? No! How then? Oh, hallelujah! By turning every one of them away from his iniquities. That was the Lord's plan for making the Jews blessed. But they would not have it; they rejected it and him who brought it, and the great bulk of them clung to their iniquity, although it was the deadly poison which destroyed their life's joy and shut out from them the great healer and Saviour and joy-giver. They died and were damned in it.

And so with you. God has sent Jesus to you on the same heavenly, benevolent errand. He comes to your heart to bless and gladden and satisfy; but he comes to do it in this very way. He cannot do it in any other, and that is by turning you away from your iniquities. They are the asps whose venom poisons the springs of gladness in your soul. He has come to "destroy the works of the devil"[2] – all of them, big and little; and the little – if any of them with propriety can be so called – no less than the big; to destroy them root and branch, fruit and flower, and leaves and branches – the whole upas tree[3] must go! His mission to you – his mission of mercy and blood and sacrifice – is to make an end, a complete end, of sin in your soul. So shall ye have peace and abiding joy, and in no other way.[4]

**God of joy, you alone are the source of my happiness. Keep me, I pray, in fellowship with you day by day, through all kinds of circumstances, so that my base-line of spiritual joy thrives and develops. Amen.**

1 Acts 2
2 1 John 3:8
3 An African tree that yields a poison.
4 From *The Founder Speaks Again*.

# May 14th

These three remain: faith, hope and love. But the greatest of these is love

(1 Corinthians 13:13 *NIV*)

Is it not possible that there is some soldier amongst you who could testify to his own salvation, and exhort the people to seek the mercy he has found, whose mouth has not as yet been opened to do anything in that direction? What do you say, my comrades? Then, is it not possible that there may be some comrade, young or old, who in the days gone by has made some public effort and failed in its discharge, and who in his despair resolved never to try again? Ought not such a one to be encouraged to make another effort? What do you say, my comrades? Here then, in your corps, we have buried forces, whose success, if they can only be aroused and set to work, will be a wonder to themselves, and a blessing to the world.

Is there not a large amount of affection buried among you? I am not sure whether I have visited your corps, or whether I know your commanding officer, or whether I have ever spoken in your neighbourhood; but there is one thing of which I am quite sure, and that is, that a baptism of love to God, to one another, and to the poor sinners around you would help you forward immensely. Love is a precious commodity; an active force for good. Love works miracles, and every soldier on your roll has a heart that can love. Oh, stir yourselves up, my comrades, stir yourselves up to the exercise of this power, and let it no longer be a buried, and therefore a useless, force.

Perhaps there are graves about here in which the first love of some of those to whom I am speaking lies buried. Do you not remember the days when some of you could hardly work by day, or sleep by night, for the hot, burning love in your hearts for Jesus and your comrades and the man and women dying around you? Oh, go in for a resurrection! Fetch out the precious affection from its hiding place. It is just the thing your corps requires. Love will meet your every need. Love will prove the conqueror.[1]

**God of love, all that you do is founded in love. Make my heart, Lord, a copy of yours, so that I see this world through your eyes and love others with your perspective. Rekindle the glow of your Spirit's life within me. Amen.**

1 From *The Founder's Messages to Soldiers.*

# May 15th

## Do not withhold good

(Proverbs 3:27 *NIV*)

The psalmist was right when he said, "Truly God is good to Israel, even to such as are of a clean heart."[1] The very word rendered "God" in our language means "good". God is not only good, but he is "The Good". Not only is he good himself, but he is the author of all good. "Every good gift and every perfect gift is from above".[2] He is the source of all blessedness. Bless his holy name! He is the stream of loving kindness that never runs dry. He is the fountain of mercy that never fails. The world in which we live was good when it came from his holy hand. Its mountains and valleys, oceans and rivers, and every living thing, including our first parents, Adam and Eve, were good, when he first called them into existence.[3]

What a glorious world it was! And what a still more glorious world it would have become had man continued good! But, alas, as with so many hearts since then which God, by his grace, has made like Paradise, the devil entered Eden with his temptations; deceived its inhabitants, induced them to cast away their confidence, and so brought in the misery that has followed.

But God, in the overflowing benevolence of his heart, arranged for the bad work of Satan to be counteracted and overcome. To effect this desirable end he sent his Son Jesus Christ to live and suffer, in order that man, who had so cruelly rebelled against him, might be pardoned, and that the law he had broken and disgraced might be honoured. By this plan the way was opened for the race to find again the goodness it has lost. Every true Salvationist has been made good through that precious gift. Do you possess a good heart? Are you leading a good life? Are you doing good work? Are you trying to make people good? Is this your aim with your husband or wife, your father and mother, your sons and daughters, your brothers and sisters, your friends and workmates? Are you trying to make them good?… Oh, if God has made you good, you must delight in the God-like task of making other people good![4]

**God, you are good. That is beyond doubt. It follows that you desire goodness in your children, in order that goodness might be shared. I offer you my heart and my life, and I pray that you will do what it takes to make me good. Amen.**

1 Psalm 73:1 *KJV*
2 James 1:17 *KJV*
3 Genesis 2:3 – 3:24
4 From *The Founder Speaks*.

# May 16th

You are heirs of the prophets and of the covenant God made with your fathers. He said to Abraham, "Through your offspring all peoples on earth will be blessed"

(Acts 3:25 *NIV*)

Do parents sometimes admit their responsibility for… training their children for God?

Parents confess it in the little religious teaching they give their children. They show it in the prayers they offer for them; in the hymns they teach them to sing themselves, and the hymns they sing about them. Also in their anxiety about them if they die young, and in all their imaginings concerning them after death. If any of their children die, they always approve of their being very religious, of their serving God with all their strength, and being fully consecrated in the next world. They are quite willing for them to be as holy as possible in Heaven. They can wear uniform, and play music, and march about in procession through the golden streets of the New Jerusalem,[1] weekdays and Sundays, to any extent – nay, they like the idea of their doing so. They would be disgusted at the thought of their departed darlings growing up to live selfish, unruly, proud, vain, conceited lives in the Holy City.[2] They would be ashamed of them setting up their interests against those of Christ in a second Paradise. Indeed, they would condemn the very thought of the children who have gone away to Heaven living just such lives in spirit and in manner there, as they are quite content for the children whom God has not taken, to live down here.

All of which goes to show not only that in their own consciences parents ordinarily recognize the justness of God's claims to the wholehearted service of their children, but at the same time bears testimony to their responsibility for securing it. The solemn religious dedicatory vows taken upon them in multitudes of instances, bind them in the most sacred manner to give their children the best possible training with a view to making them good, holy, and Christ-like. The fact that large numbers of parents stand up with their children in dedicatory, baptismal, and other religious ceremonies and declare their desire that their children should truly serve God… shows in the consciences of the parents a recognition of this solemn obligation.[3]

**Father of all, parenthood is a privilege, yet a challenging responsibility. I pray for Christian parents, that in the midst of every other demand upon their time, you will help them to include spiritual instruction and influence. Be with them, and with their children. Amen.**

1 Revelation 21:2
2 Revelation 21:2
3 From *The Training of Children*.

# May 17th

Blessings will come on you and accompany you if you obey the Lord your God

(Deuteronomy 28:2 *NIV*)

There is another inducement which should lead you to seek a pure heart, and that is because it will bring you into the possession of a good hope.[1] This is a precious treasure. To feel that whatever clouds may darken the sky, or whatever sorrows may sweep over your soul, there is good ground for anticipating peace, and joy and victory in the future, must be a precious and desirable thing.

A soldier who knows that he sincerely loves God, and that he is living in obedience to him, has an inward assurance that God will care for him, whatever troubles may arise. Whereas one who feels that he has malice, hatred, pride, love of the world, and other wrongs hidden away in his secret soul, and who knows that he is daily neglecting his duty to his family or himself, to his corps, or the poor sinners around him, can no more have a bright hope that God is going to make him a happy future than the sinners can expect that they are going to have Heaven at the end of a sinful life. He may hope for it, but it will be like the hope of a hypocrite, certain to be destroyed.

But when the soul has the witness of the Spirit and of a consistent life, to the possession of inward purity, it can look forward with confidence to victory over every foe, deliverance out of every [sorrow] and, in the end, glory and honour, immortality and eternal life.

Have these blessed experiences any charm for you, my comrades? There is the holy life that will be the outcome of a pure heart... There is the peace of God that "passeth all understanding",[2] which is ever associated with inward holiness... There is the presence and indwelling of God as a flame of holy love... There is the useful life and the holy example that flows from a pure heart... There is a blooming hope of the future and the brightness of your own in eternity... These are only some of the inestimable blessings that flow out of this eternal spring.[3]

**Heavenly Father, you are a generous God; this is quite some list, and it seems baffling why anyone should desire anything else. I praise you for your willingness to bless. Please open my hands to receive from you. Amen.**

1 Titus 2:13
2 Philippians 4:7 *KJV*
3 From *Purity of Heart.*

# May 18th

### This very night your life will be demanded from you
(Luke 12:20 *NIV*)

It will be remembered that, early in the year, some factory girls were burnt to death in Belfast. Amongst them was Maggie Johnstone, one of the brightest soldiers in our 2nd Belfast corps who, for the seven months since her conversion, had always been ready to do anything she could to help in the work. Speaking in her usual earnest way to a large congregation, the night before her death, she concluded by saying, "Friends, thank God, I am ready should he call me!" Little did anyone think, however, that before noon on the following day she was to be taken from us. Thank God, she was ready!

Another accidental case was that of Johnny Davies of Merthyr Tydfil, who met his death while at work cleaning out a big engine boiler. It is supposed that he had been overpowered by gas, and had fallen into the boiler, which was half full. He was converted at Dowlais[1] two years previously, and great had been the change in him from that time forward to the last. Everybody loved Johnny, whose smiling face and cheery voice was sadly missed by his comrades, and by all who had been around him. The night before his death, he and a workmate, being overcome with foul air in the engine house, the man proposed to Johnny that they should have some beer together. "No," said Johnny. "I am going in for some coffee." "Coffee is no good, man; nothing but beer will clear this off," replied the other. "Then," said Johnny, "rather than take beer I would die first." Johnny kept a Bible in the window near his bedside in which he always read before he went to work, and he had two little testaments – one in his working clothes and one in his best – always ready to his hand. His favourite verse was:

*Our lamps are trimmed and burning,*
*Our hearts are white and clean;*
*We're ready for the Bridegroom,*
*Oh, may we enter in.*[2]

Well, indeed was it for him that his "lamp was trimmed and burning" when the call so suddenly came.[3]

**Father, thank you so much that by your grace, I am ready to die. Thank you for sending Jesus to pay the price of sin. My times are in your hands, my God. Amen.**

1 Merthyr Tydfil and Dowlais are both in Wales.
2 Probably based on George Frederic Root (1820–95), "Behold the Bridegroom Cometh". See Matthew 5:7
3 From *The Salvation War, 1883.*

# May 19th

All Scripture is breathed out by God and profitable for teaching, for reproof, for correction, and for training in righteousness

(2 Timothy 3:16 *ESV*)

You want to be of some service to the Master and to your brethren and to poor perishing sinners. Very good! This… is a never-absent instinct of a divine nature. You want to win souls for Christ, and to nurse and strengthen them when they are won, to be a saviour of men. Hallelujah! You are such in some measure already. You have his Spirit and are ever and anon about his business. But you are feeble and inconstant. The fire burns low and often seems ready to expire. It takes you almost all your time to keep yourself saved. Well, you want a higher-up religion. You need to be holy, because holiness means strength and faithfulness and power. It removes doubts by bringing in assurance of personal salvation and doubts, you know, mean always weakness. It also removes the hindrances to the perpetual indwelling of Jehovah. As sin goes out, God comes in; and with Christ fully dwelling in the vessel, in the Temple, in the body, you will be fully equipped and qualified for every good work.[1]

Holiness, then, means usefulness. Come, let us pursue this interesting and important enquiry. How far can God save from sin here? The question can be satisfactorily answered only by hearing what the Lord says on the subject and, having listened to the Scriptures, you may then with propriety and advantage listen to the testimony of those who boldly profess to have an experience on the subject.

What says the word of the Lord? What people say – whether they be learned or unlearned, official or unofficial, or anything else – if they speak not in harmony with the direct and plain teaching of the word of God, they speak not the truth on this subject, whatever they may do on any other. And as the opinions of other men are not our standard, neither are their lives. If A and B say I cannot be saved from sinning – if they say I must go on in unbelief and unfaithfulness and evil tempers unto the end of my earthly days, if they say I cannot love God with all my heart and be loyal with simple obedience to my heavenly King – I ask A and B for their authority.[2]

**God of the word, I take the Bible as my authority for truth and righteousness. Thank you that your word teaches me how to be useful; how to lead a useful life. Amen.**

1 Hebrews 13:21
2 From *The Founder Speaks Again.*

# May 20th

THE LOVE OF MONEY IS A ROOT OF ALL KINDS OF EVIL

(1 Timothy 6:10 *NIV*)

The question of the harlots is... insoluble by the ordinary methods. For those unfortunates no one who looks below the surface can fail to have the deepest sympathy. Some there are, no doubt, perhaps many, who – whether from inherited passion or from evil education – have deliberately embarked upon a life of vice, but with the majority it is not so. Even those who deliberately and of free choice adopt the profession of a prostitute, do so under stress of temptations which few moralists seem to realize.

Terrible as the fact is, there is no doubt it is a fact that there is no industrial career in which for a short time a beautiful girl can make as much money with as little trouble as the profession of a courtesan. The case recently tried at Lewes assizes,[1] in which the wife of an officer in the army admitted that while living as a kept mistress she had received as much as £4,000 a year, was no doubt very exceptional. Even the most successful adventuresses seldom make the income of a cabinet minister. But take women in professions and in business all round, and the number of young women who have received £500 in one year for the sale of their person is larger than the number of women of all ages who make a similar sum by honest industry. It is only the very few who draw these gilded prizes, and they only do it for a very short time. But it is the few prizes in every profession which allure the multitude, who think little of the many blanks. And speaking broadly, vice offers to every good-looking girl during the first bloom of her youth and beauty more money than she can earn in any field of industry open to her sex. The penalty exacted afterwards is disease, degradation, and death, but these things at first are hidden from her sight.

The profession of a prostitute is the only career in which the maximum income is paid to the newest apprentice. It is the one calling in which at the beginning the only exertion is that of self-indulgence; all the prizes are at the commencement.[2]

**Gracious Father, forbid that I should ever judge. In your mercy, for pity's sake, reach out to prostitutes with your safe embrace. By your Spirit's loving power, touch their lives for good. Amen.**

1 East Sussex, England.
2 From *In Darkest England and the Way Out.*

# MAY 21ST

### IF THE SON SETS YOU FREE, YOU WILL BE FREE INDEED
(John 8:36 *NIV*)

It [prostitution] is the ever-new embodiment of the old fable of the sale of the soul to the devil. The tempter offers wealth, comfort, excitement, but in return the victim must sell her soul, nor does the other party forget to exact his due to the uttermost farthing.[1] Human nature, however, is short-sighted. Giddy girls, chafing against the restraints of uncongenial history, see the glittering bait continually before them. They are told that if they will but "do as others do" they will make more in a night, if they are lucky, than they can make in a week at their sewing; and who can wonder that in many cases the irrevocable step is taken before they realize that it is irrevocable, and that they have bartered away the future of their lives for the paltry chance of a year's ill-gotten gains?

Of the severity of the punishment there can be no question. If the premium is high at the beginning, the penalty is terrible at the close. And this penalty is exacted equally from those who have deliberately said, "Evil, be my good" and for those who have been decoyed, snared, trapped into the life which is a living death. When you see a girl on the street you can never say without enquiry whether she is one of the most-to-be-condemned, or the most-to-be-pitied of her sex. Many of them find themselves where they are because of a too trusting disposition, confidence born of innocence being often the unsuspecting ally of the procuress and seducer. Others are as much the innocent victims of crime as if they had been stabbed or maimed by the dagger of the assassin.

The records of our Rescue Homes abound with life-stories, some of which we have been able to verify to the letter – which prove only too conclusively the existence of numbers of innocent victims whose entry upon this dismal life can in no way be attributed to any act of their own will. Many are orphans or the children of depraved mothers, whose one idea of a daughter is to make money out of her prostitution.[2]

**Heavenly Father, we are all susceptible, in one way or another, to the dazzling sights and tempting sounds of this world. Only by your grace is there deliverance, and the chance of a better way to live. Pour out your love towards all those trapped by temptation's relentless power. Bless those who have a ministry to those working in the sex industry. Amen.**

1 Pre-decimal English coin, worth one quarter of a penny.
2 From *In Darkest England and the Way Out.*

# May 22[ND]

**Nothing in all creation will ever be able to separate us from the love of God that is revealed in Christ Jesus our Lord**

(Roman 8:39 *NLT*)

A girl in her teens lived with her mother in the "Dusthole", the lowest part of Woolwich.[1] This woman forced her out upon the streets, and profited by her prostitution up to the very night of her confinement. The mother had all the time been the receiver of her gains. "E", neither father nor mother, was taken care of by a grandmother till, at an early age, accounted old enough. Married a soldier, but shortly before the birth of her first child, found that her deceiver had a wife and family in a distant part of the country, and she was soon left friendless and alone. She sought an asylum in the workhouse for a few weeks, after which she vainly tried to get honest employment. Failing that, and being on the very verge of starvation, she entered a lodging-house in Westminster and "did as the other girls". Here our lieutenant found and persuaded her to leave and enter one of our homes, where she soon gave abundant proof of her conversion by a thoroughly changed life…

The following 100 cases are taken as they come from our Rescue Register. The statements are those of the girls themselves. They are certainly frank, and it will be noticed that only two out of the 100 allege that they took to the life out of poverty:

CAUSE OF FALL: Drink: 14. Seduction: 33. Wilful choice: 24. Bad company: 27. Poverty: 2.

CONDITION WHEN APPLYING: Rags: 25. Destitution: 27. Decently dressed: 48.

Out of these girls, twenty-three have been in prison. The girls suffer so much that the shortness of their miserable life is the only redeeming feature. Whether we look at the wretchedness of the life itself; their perpetual intoxication; the cruel treatment to which they are subject by their taskmasters and mistresses or bullies; the hopelessness, suffering, and despair induced by their circumstances and surroundings; the depths of misery, degradation, and poverty to which they eventually descend; or their treatment in sickness, their friendlessness and loneliness in death, it must be admitted that a more dismal lot seldom falls to the fate of a human being.[2]

**Father, how it must hurt you when your children fall, whatever the reason. Thank you for Booth's compassion. Help me to see everyone I meet today as a child of yours, and to look beyond circumstances, to see the person. In your great love, reach those who live in misery and despair. Amen.**

1 South-east London.
2 From *In Darkest England and the Way Out.*

# May 23rd

Surely he has borne our griefs and carried our sorrows

(Isaiah 53:4 *ESV*)

Probably the primary cause of the fall of numberless girls of the lower class, is their great aspiration to the dignity of wifehood – they are never "somebody" until they are married, and will link themselves to any creature, no matter how debased, in the hope of being ultimately married by him. This consideration, in addition to their helpless condition when once character has gone, makes them suffer cruelties which they would never otherwise endure from the men with whom large numbers of them live.

One case in illustration of this is that of a girl who was once a respectable servant, the daughter of a police sergeant. She was ruined, and shame led her to leave home. At length she drifted to Woolwich, where she came across a man who persuaded her to live with him, and for a considerable length of time she kept him, although his conduct to her was brutal in the extreme. The girl living in the next room to her has frequently heard him knock her head against the wall, and pound it, when he was out of temper, through her gains of prostitution being less than usual. He lavished upon her every sort of cruelty and abuse, and at length she grew so wretched, and was reduced to so dreadful a plight, that she ceased to attract. At this he became furious, and pawned all her clothing but one thin garment of rags. The week before her first confinement he kicked her black and blue from neck to knees, and she was carried to the police station in a pool of blood, but she was so loyal to the wretch that she refused to appear against him.

She was going to drown herself in desperation, when our Rescue Officers spoke to her, wrapped her own shawl around her shivering shoulders, took her home with them, and cared for her. The baby was born dead – a tiny, shapeless mass. This state of things is all too common… The state of hopelessness and despair in which these girls live continually, makes them reckless of consequences, and large numbers commit suicide who are never heard of.[1]

**Father, how desperate some must be to tolerate cruelty and sheer misery in place of love and affection. How bleak life must be, when suicide looks like the only option. Bless those who suffer in silent privacy, Father; their hurts known only to you. Guide and reward the efforts of those who seek to protect and shelter. Amen.**

1 From *In Darkest England and the Way Out.*

# May 24th

Let us not love in word or talk but in deed and in truth

(1 John 3:18 *ESV*)

[Our captain] is a busy man, and nobody expects that he can stop to hear small talk, and so they never think of offering it to him; and then, second, they know he is after their souls, and they expect that he will go for them as soon as the first words are out of his lips. This makes it easy for him to talk religion, and they all expect, if there's a chance at all, that he'll want to pray; and that makes it seem the right thing for him to get on to his knees, and to be off again as soon as he gets up… the captain is full of sympathy with all the troubles and anxieties of his soldiers. That is what makes our Sarah like him so much. He never comes along here but he wants to know when she heard from Jack last, and how the boy's coming on, whether there's any signs of his getting converted, and no matter how short his prayer is, there is always something in it for Jack.

Then, there's the children. He knows their names, and all about them; and when they are ailing, with such things as the chicken pock, or with the baby cutting his teeth, or that sort of thing, and he's always got some good advice. Why, Sarah says, "He's as good as a doctor about sickness" and, if she was in any trouble, she would rather go to him than anybody she knows.

Then, you see, he visits the unconverted folks, as well as the soldiers. Why, he has a list of all the people who come to our hall, and has a run-in regularly to see them, and everybody else. There's Mrs Peck-o'-troubles, who lives just opposite. He generally pops in there when he comes to see Sarah. "Ah," he says. "Mrs Peck-o'-troubles, I was making a call at the sergeant-major's, and so I thought I would look in and see how you are today. How's the guv'nor, and the children, and yourself?" And then he is on to her soul, so kind and natural like, that she cannot take it amiss.[1]

**Thank you, Lord, for those who take a kindly, selfless interest in others. Make me one of them. Amen.**

1 From *Sergeant-Major Do-Your-Best.*

# May 25th

The steps of a good man are ordered by the Lord
(Psalm 37:23 *KJV*)

I want you to stand up more boldly and firmly than you ever have done for the great object for which God made you Salvation Army officers. You know what that object is. You know that it is not merely the doing of certain duties, the maintenance of particular beliefs, or the conducting of special meetings, important as those may be, but that it consists in an intelligent, practical partnership with God in the great business of saving the world. This you may take to be: 1) the putting down of the rebellion of men against the divine government. 2) The expulsion of all wrongdoing from the earth. 3) The dethronement of the devils that now occupy the hearts of men. 4) The universal acceptance by men of Jesus Christ as their Sovereign Lord. 5) The bringing about of the reign of righteousness, and the obedience of the entire race to the law of love.

There can be no possible room for doubt in your minds as to this object being the divinely appointed end at which, as Salvation Army officers, you are to aim. You can read it written on every page of your Bibles. You will gather it from the example of every true Salvationist. It will be urged by the instincts of the nature that you received at conversion; and if you will only listen, you will hear it whispered by the Spirit of the living God in your own heart. This is the object God has been seeking after from the beginning. This is the object for which Jesus Christ came into the world. This is the end for which, day by day, the Holy Ghost wrestles with the souls of men. This is the object in accomplishing which God invites you to join hands with him. This is the object to which you are already pledged before Heaven and earth and Hell.

Are you clear that you are aiming for it, and that with all your might? To be not doing so is to come very near to being a sounding brass or a tinkling cymbal.[1, 2]

**Thank you, Lord, for a clear sense of vocation, whatever that might be. Those you call, you also equip. I pray that you would sharpen my vision and re-call me today, so that my days are filled with purpose. Amen.**

1 1 Corinthians 13:1
2 An eightieth birthday letter from *The Founder Speaks Again*.

# May 26th

## You are the salt of the earth

(Matthew 5:13 *NIV*)

There are always, especially in young people, times when Satan or some natural weakness suggests to the officer that it is no use – he has misused his vocation – he will never make anything out – he has made a fool of himself, and he is tempted to write to his friends, if he has friends, and tell them he is going to give up. Now, it is worth a king's ransom in these moments of darkness for an officer who has influence to come in and find out the good qualities of the downcast soul, spread them before him, cheer him up, and send him forward with a new life.

I know how valuable such words of cheer have been to me in the years gone by, and I know also the fact that some of the finest writers, and speakers, and governors of men that the world has ever known have been subject to such times of depression. When you deal faithfully as to the sins and shortcomings of those under your command, cheer up the people who deserve it, my comrade – cheer them up again, and again, and again.

Another quality essential to suitable leadership is the discovery of suitable work for those under your direction and making them do it. No man, woman, or child can keep the grace of God alive in the soul without making some constant effort for the spiritual welfare of others. The profession of a man who claims to be a Christian when he does not possess the Spirit of Jesus Christ is a positive contradiction, and it is impossible to possess the Spirit of Jesus Christ without making it manifest in such efforts as Jesus Christ himself would make, were he in the same circumstances…

Show the people around you what they must be. Show it to them, and show it them by your own life, your own activity, your own zeal, your own manner, your own work, and your own faith in God in times of difficulty and storm. This is the only way you can make men and women understand many things that are essential to their happiness and success.[1]

**Lord, it is a sobering thought to remember that my lifestyle has a direct influence on others. This day, I pray that your Holy Spirit would work in me to such an extent that my conduct may help someone else to draw closer to you. I don't need to know how; it is sufficient that you bless others in some way, to your glory. Amen.**

1 From *Essential Measures.*

# May 27th

### They all alike began to make excuses

(Luke 14:18 *NIV*)

If a nation be thoroughly roused to any tremendous struggle, fighting for its own existence, part of its inhabitants will go forth to the field, part nurse and care for the wounded, part make the ammunition and the weapons, and the remainder till the fields to support the whole. When God's people wake up to the importance of this great war, and go forth to engage in it after this fashion, the millennium will not be very far away...

Officers I am after, and I want those soldiers whose names are already on our rolls, who are qualified for the task, to look themselves up, and if qualified, to send in their names at once. But at this point a soldier asks, "How am I to know whether I am qualified, and whether God wants me for this position?" Go down before God, and tell him that you are willing to go; then you shall have these words verified in your experience, "If any man will do [my] will, he shall know of the doctrine".[1] Consecration honestly made to go if wanted, will bring the answer back from Heaven into your own heart.

"Can't do it"? "Have not the gifts"? "Wanting in courage and power of speech, and ever so many other kinds of power"? How do you know? Have you tried? Give yourself a chance. Go on to Outpost duty. Do something in your own streets. Shake the napkin. You do not know what talents you possess. If you have not got courage to shake it yourself, go to your captain and tell him he can do what he likes with you. You can only find out what your gifts really are in the actual war, and so settle the matter for ever beyond controversy; and do not go to the end of your days thinking that you may have missed your calling. "Afraid of the consequences"? Ah! We are coming to it now; perhaps you cannot face a life of poverty, persecution, or hardship in general. Could do anything in your own town, but could not leave father or mother![2]

**Lord, I know you don't like it when people shirk their responsibilities, so please turn me into a soldier fit for royal duties. Help me not to count the cost, but simply to obey daily orders. Amen.**

1 John 7:17 *KJV*
2 From *The General's Letters.*

# May 28th

Repent and believe the good news!

(Mark 1:15 *NIV*)

It is important that we should understand repentance, seeing that it is a condition on which God bestows his mercy upon wrongdoers. We have all sinned, and exposed ourselves to the penalty that follows the law we have broken.[1] Without repentance there is no salvation. What Jesus Christ said is true… "except ye repent, ye shall all likewise perish".[2] When men and women come to their senses about the folly of wrongdoing, repentance is usually their first thought. They feel that it is the right thing; nay, the only thing they can do that will bring peace to their consciences, and satisfaction to those whom they have injured.

There is no story in the Bible more tender and effective… than that which describes the broken-hearted repentance of the prodigal son, followed by his return home and his welcome there. Whenever we hear that parable we feel he did the right thing, and it is a satisfaction to us to see him weep over his sins, and offer himself for any form of obedience that his father might choose…[3]

There are different kinds of repentance. There is the repentance that is like the morning cloud and the early dew. It soon passes away, leaving little or no trace behind. This was too often the character of the repentance of the Israelites of old. They acknowledged their sins, sorrowed on account of them, and promised never to do the like again; but very quickly they relapsed, and became as bad or worse than they were before. We are all of us only too familiar with instances of this class of repentance in our own circles. We have frequently met with them in our halls, and we may count ourselves very fortunate if we do not find some in our own experience.

Then there is the repentance of despair. That was the repentance of Judas… The devil tempted him to believe that there could be no mercy for such a sinner as he was. And, then, instead of going to the feet of the Saviour… he threw himself headlong into the abyss from which there was no deliverance.[4], [5]

**Gracious God, you receive our repentance; thank you that you do not treat us as our sins deserve. Amen.**

1 Romans 3:23
2 Luke 13:5 *KJV*
3 Luke 15:11–32
4 Matthew 27:5
5 From *The Founder's Messages to Soldiers*.

# May 29th

## Jesus… went around doing good

(Acts 10:38 *NIV*)

I cannot bring myself to believe that you have a good nature, a good religion, a good hope, unless this [goodness] is your aim, your delight, your everyday practice. Does not the apostle Paul tell us that if any man have not the Spirit of Christ, then he is none of his?[1] And we all know that the Spirit of Christ was the Spirit of goodness, and that it was this Spirit that brought him from Heaven, not only to save a world of sinners from Hell, but to make them good; that is, useful and holy and fit for Heaven. The Bible tells us that without holiness – that is, without true goodness – "no man shall see the Lord".[2]

If you are not good, in temper and disposition, in conversation and employment; in fact, in everything connected with your heart and life, you must seek to be made good right away. Go to God. He, and he alone, can make you good. Kneel down, here and now, in submission before him, and:

1. Tell him that you give up everything in your heart and life which you have reason to believe is bad and wrong and opposed to his glory and the well-being of those about you; that you turn away from it for ever.
2. Tell him that you will be a lover and friend of all and everything that is good; in yourselves, your homes, your corps, your work, your pleasures.
3. Tell him that you not only believe that he can, but that through the sacrifice of Jesus Christ, he does, here and now, make you good. That is, he forgives your sins, adopts you into his family. And enlists you as soldiers of the cross.
4. Go right on, in the spirit of this surrender, wherever you may be, and whatever may happen, until, without a doubt, and without a fear, you realize in your inmost souls that God has made you good.

My comrades, it is a beautiful thing to be good – beautiful in the sight of God and beautiful in the sight of good people around you.[3]

**Lord, preserve us from do-gooders, and from self-righteousness. Fill my heart with authentic, attractive, Spirit-filled goodness. Amen.**

1 Romans 8:9
2 Hebrews 12:14 *KJV*
3 From *The Founder Speaks.*

# May 30th

Who can say, "I have kept my heart pure; I am clean and without sin"?

(Proverbs 20:9 *NIV*)

Both during the late storm and since it has passed away, there has been a great hue and cry in the country about the filthy condition of the streets.[1] There has been questioning in Parliament, writing to the newspapers, discussions innumerable in the corporations and councils and committees, as to the getting rid of the filth. And we don't wonder at it either, nor think it out of place that some should raise their voices against an obstruction at once so offensive and disagreeable, and so practically brought home to every door. Filth of any kind is an unpleasant and disgusting thing. Whether piled up in heaps, or spread about ankle deep, or deeper, it is unpleasant to eyes and nostrils, and unpleasant for poor, wet, sodden feet to stand in or wade through, splashing or sprinkling ourselves and everybody about us; and the more completely and speedily it can be got rid of the better. Away with it!

But there is another kind of filth, a kind more objectionable and disgusting still to all rightly adjusted eyes and nostrils, whether they belong to this or to any other world. Moral filth, we mean – the filth that lies about and lodges in men's hearts, and is thence poured forth in ceaseless streams in market-places and streets, and shops and, we venture to say, almost everywhere else. O God! Is it not enough to drive the very pitying angels to despair, as they wing to and fro in this redeemed world, that they find it so generally polluted and cursed, and obstructed by this filth?

Look at the selfish filth of drunkenness, which devours up the very life-blood of wives and little children for its mean satisfaction. Look at the filth of blasphemy poured forth from the throats of young and old. Walk the streets and hear the dirty, obscene blackguardism which garnishes almost every sentence. Look at the filth of mean, ungrateful infidelity, which revels in the denial of all the natural impulses of goodness and the instinctive yearnings for the divine and the eternal. Look at the 30,000 thieves who walk about this one city alone.[2]

**Holy God, you are the divine washer. You call us to shower our hearts and our lives in your goodness and cleansing love. There is no stain that your grace cannot remove. Thank you. Amen.**

1 "The Great Stink" of 1858, when London's sewage system proved inadequate.
2 From *Salvation Soldiery*.

# May 31st

## Greet all your leaders and all the Lord's people

(Hebrews 13:24 *NIV*)

A great opportunity lies before the Army, and before you as representatives of the Army. You have looked at that opportunity; you have wondered about it and, if you are men and women of God, which I believe you are, your souls are stirred with gratitude at the thought that God has honoured you by any association with a movement that has been the means of so greatly glorifying him, and so largely blessing the world. The use that is made of this mighty opportunity for promoting the happiness of mankind, and the glory of the God of Heaven, very largely depends upon the field officers of The Salvation Army.[1]

Officers make the character of the armies they lead. This is true of military armies – Napoleon not only led his army, but made it. This is true of commercial armies. The great financiers and traders mould the business world. The same may be said of political armies. This is equally true, if not more so, of Salvation Armies. On you, then, this responsibility rests. The field officer fashions the force he controls, chiefly in three ways: by his mind, character, and methods. In short, he constitutes the mould in which those whom he commands will be cast. The shape you give the men and women under your command today will go down to the third, the fourth, and the fifth generations. You are making the kind of Salvationists who will be walking about here 500 years hence, if the world lasts so long.

If the officer is a coward, those whom he commands will be cowards. If he is holy, they will be holy. If he is a man of resistless courage and daring, they will be like him. Our responsibility for success or failure is therefore enormous. Where we are successful we are not only gaining victories today, but making the conquerors of the future. Let us remember – we shall have to give an account of our stewardship; we are passing over, one by one, to that great Tribunal… the words, "Behold, I come quickly"[2] are ever sounding in my ears.[3]

**I pray for those who lead, Lord, that you would bless them as they plan ahead; fill them with every quality required for successful, visionary leadership. May your Spirit rest upon them. Amen.**

1 Field officers are responsible for corps and outposts, as opposed to being stationed at headquarters.
2 Revelation 22:7 *KJV*
3 From *The Seven Spirits or "What I Teach My Officers"*.

# June 1st

We must quickly carry out the tasks assigned us by the one who sent us. The night is coming, and then no one can work

(John 9:4 *NLT*)

[Look at] the thousands of professional harlots: what the number of the non-professional, and the multiplied number of the manufacturers and supporters of both professional and non-professional are, the Great God only knows. Look at the gambling, and the lying, and the cheating, and the trickery, and the hypocrisy, and the grinding of the faces and the bowels of the poor and the widow… which day and night sends up a ceaseless stench into the nostrils of the Almighty. This filth, which he hates, however men may tolerate, and which, however men may bless, he curses, and intends sooner or later to sweep into Hell, to the great satisfaction of all true beings who have the welfare of this great universe at heart.

There it is, you don't see it? Blind, are you? Incapable of discerning good from evil? More the pity, and all the worse for you unless you get those blind eyes speedily opened. Not so loathsome, is it, as described? Hidden, is it? Covered over? Painted and gilded and christened as goodness? And yet, painted and gilded and christened as it may be, its nature is not changed; and it will burst up some day and burst you up with it, unless you wake up. "God is not mocked".[1] The mask will be torn away, the loathsomeness made manifest, for you may "be sure your sin will find you out"![2]

Now, what is to be done with all this filth? How can it be got rid of? We must do something. There are some puzzling problems than can be left for future deliberation. If you don't exactly see what to do with them, let them drift. They may rectify themselves. The snow obstruction, and the filthy condition of things which came out of it, has done so. The soft wind has helped us. But we cannot leave this filth to the chapter of accidents, and sit down and wait for something to turn up – at least this won't by any means be a safe course to take.[3]

**Holy Spirit, nudge me, whatever the issue or concern, to act promptly, and not to procrastinate. Remind me of this prayer the next time I am tempted to leave important things undone, lest one day it is too late. Amen.**

1 Galatians 6:7 *KJV*
2 Numbers 32:23 *KJV*
3 From *Salvation Soldiery.*

# June 2[ND]

You have heard me teach things that have been confirmed by many reliable witnesses. Now teach these truths to other trustworthy people who will be able to pass them on to others

(2 Timothy 2:2 *NLT*)

What kind of officers are required?…

I think I possess some ability for pointing out the qualities needed for satisfactorily answering this question. I have read my Bible and pondered over the great responsibilities which lie at the very foundation of an officer's duties. I hope I have not read that book in vain. I have listened to the voice of the Spirit of God within me. He has shown me something of what an officer should be and do, in order that he may efficiently fulfil the mission to which he has been called. I have studied the hearts and circumstances of the men you are sent to save. Human nature is, as we very often say, much the same in all ages and in all places. What I have seen of the failings, the prejudices, and the sins of men with regard to religion during my life should be of service in helping and guiding you in your warfare.

I have profited by the experience of other warriors on the field: from those of the prophets down to the last Army captain who has any reputation for bringing men to God. In the days of old, men walked over land, and sailed over water, thousands of miles, penetrating the depths of barren wildernesses and tractless forests, in order to gaze upon some skeleton hermit who had acquired a special reputation for holiness, or who had gained a more intimate knowledge than his fellows of the dealings of God with men. Something like this has been my custom ever since I was a youth, fifteen years of age. To hear of anyone possessing any extra skill in soul-saving has been enough to excite my curiosity, lead me to seek a knowledge of their doings, and carry me to their feet. Surely, I must have learned something from these worthies. What I have learned I want to tell you.

I have studied the needs of the world around me. A large part of my life has been spent in considering and mourning over the sins and sorrows of men, and in making plans for their deliverance.[1]

**Father, if I have any skills or experience that you might think worth passing on, then lead me to the people who would benefit most, so that I can encourage them. Likewise, lead me to people who can teach me more about you and your ways. Amen.**

1 From *The Seven Spirits.*

# June 3[rd]

So we keep on praying for you, asking our God to enable you to live a life worthy of his call. May he give you the power to accomplish all the good things your faith prompts you to do

(2 Thessalonians 1:11 *NLT*)

God only knows what he would do with a few men who cared only for him. He would save thousands and astonish the universe. God wants men and women that he can reckon upon, who will be there at the very time he wants them, and do the very work he wants doing, whatever may stand in the way. For still, as of old, "his eyes run to and fro throughout the whole earth that he may show himself strong on behalf of those whose hearts are perfect towards him".[1] And we can be made such by the Holy Ghost.

Always acknowledge what God does by and for you. I think we do ourselves harm, and greatly grieve the Holy Spirit, by not acknowledging what he does for us. We forget, if we don't actually deny, his cooperation, and then we get downcast and grumble. I don't say, because I don't for a moment think, that there is any danger of our not acknowledging what we do. The devil is always ready to prompt us to say, "I did this, and I did that, and I did it well", and others are always ready to speak of what we do. But we do err, I am sure, by not sufficiently acknowledging and glorifying the cooperating work of the Holy Ghost. Why not say, "the Holy Ghost was at work this afternoon. We have had a hard night, but the Holy Spirit has done his work. Blessed Spirit, I thank thee"?

Before we go on our knees to receive the Baptism of Fire, let me beg of you to see to it that your souls are in harmony with the will and purpose of the Holy Spirit whom you seek. See to it that the channel of communication by which the baptism must be received is open. I heard of some people the other day who could not get any water. They turned the tap repeatedly, but no water came. They sent to the office of the company, who sent a man to examine the connexions and fittings, but all was right… at last they pulled up the pipe, and found a mouse in it.[2]

**Father, as I pray today, and seek a fresh infilling for the day that lies ahead, I invite you to show me anything in my soul that would block or hinder your life within me. Help me to check honestly for that which would stem the flow of your power at work in my life. Amen.**

1 See 2 Chronicles 16:9
2 From *The Founder Speaks*.

# June 4[TH]

### He shall do according to all that proceeds out of his mouth

(Numbers 30:2 *ESV*)

The dying thief… attended no Bible class; heard no sermon; knew very little about theology; partook of no sacraments; and yet his was the repentance of the heart. The Master declared it to be genuine. It landed him in Heaven.[1]

Perhaps some of you here today have never really repented of your sin, or have never seen its evil. You have never been truly sorry for it – you have never renounced it, and so you have never found forgiveness for it. What a pity! Perhaps there is a backslider here who will not repent. Ah! That is a greater pity still! There is a text in the Revelation that always impresses me very powerfully when I read it. It applies with force to such impenitent souls as those of whom I am speaking: "I gave her space [for repentance] and she repented not".[2] Is that to be said of you when the opportunity for repentance is for ever gone?

But, then, there are those here, thank God, who have repented, and whose repentance has been sincere, and that repentance has brought great blessing into their lives. Now to you, I should like to propose an important question. Have you been true to the repentance you professed? You remember when you came to God, and knelt at the mercy seat, and you remember what you said and did there. You said you hated the falsehoods of the past, and that you would never be guilty of them again. Have you been true to that declaration? You confessed the uncleannesses and lusts and abominable practices of the past, and promised that you would renounce the companions and the follies that led to them. Have you been true to that promise? You confessed with shame and regret to your neglect of prayer, and of your Bible, and your rejections of mercy; and you promised to live a new life, and to do what you can to help Jesus Christ and his people in their struggle with the godless world. Have you been true to those pledges? Those promises were a part of your repentance.[3]

**Oh, Jesus, I have promised to serve you. Strengthen me, I pray, to be a promise-keeper. As I stand on your promises, make me someone you can rely upon to keep mine. Amen.**

1 Luke 23:39–43
2 Revelation 2:21 *KJV*
3 From *The Founder's Messages to Soldiers.*

# June 5th

Jesus said: "A man was going down from Jerusalem to Jericho, when he was attacked by robbers. They stripped him of his clothes, beat him and went away, leaving him half-dead. A priest happened to be going down the same road, and when he saw the man, he passed by on the other side. So too, a Levite, when he came to the place and saw him, passed by on the other side"

(Luke 10:30–32 *NIV*)

If we go to the government, neither the ministry nor the opposition nor Private Members can help us. They can do nothing to stem the rising tide of blasphemy or obscene-ness and atheism and whoredom and harlotry and godlessness. Not their province. Judges and magistrates and police are helpless. They can condemn and punish and confine for a season the doers and abettors thereof, but alas! This is not getting rid of the filth – it is only a moving of it into another place for a season, to return, with all possible speed, to its own place to be more filthy still.

If we turn to churches and chapels, and ministers and deacons and officers connected with the same, and say, "Here, this is surely your business. Let us go to St Giles,[1] let us go to the East End, let us go to all the dark dens of infamy – let us move the filth. Let us unite together. This festering condition of things is a disgrace to us, and an evil that day and night cries out to God for vengeance with a voice millions of times louder than did the blood of Abel[2] or the loathsome sins of Sodom and Gomorrah."[3] "Come along," they will say. "The cares and christenings, and marriages and funerals, and joys and sorrows of their flocks, absorb and employ all their talents and time and substance, and that there must be societies and officers who shall be scavengers by business, who shall find a special employment in dealing with this filth." Oh, disappointment supreme. We thought, ye learned and wealthy and ordained brethren, that it was to this end ye had been taught, and to this end ye had consecrated your good, and to this end, above all others, ye had been ordained, that ye might follow in the Master's steps, to seek and save that which was lost.[4] What must be done? Something must be done, and done at once. The filth has been discussed, and lectured, and scolded, and coaxed, and coddled, and prayed about, but there it is – far blacker and more loathsome than ever. Not let us move it.[5]

**Father, never let me walk away from my Christian duty when it is tough or difficult or unsavoury. Show me, instead, how to get stuck in for Jesus. Amen.**

1 St Giles's Roundhouse, London, was a prison used to hold suspected criminals.
2 Genesis 4:10
3 Genesis 19
4 Luke 19:10
5 From *Salvation Soldiery.*

# June 6th

### The Son of Man did not come to be served, but to serve

(Matthew 20:28 *NIV*)

Off with coat and gloves. Doff your finery. This is not to be done by proxy. You have tried a subscription of half-a-guinea a year[1] to support a sort of isolated sweeper. But this has not done much. Come and sweep yourself. Set up a broom and come along. Set up a broom, did we say? What nonsense we are writing. You must be the broom; put yourself into God's hands, and he will do some sweeping by you. "A dirty job", do you say? Granted, and so, I suppose, is digging silver, and gold, and diamonds; but men reckon that it pays. Anyhow, this soul-scavenging trade pays; will pay a hundredfold in this life and a millionfold in the life everlasting.

There is, we say, no other way to move this burden of iniquity but by going to it yourselves. It won't come to you. Who moves it? Anybody; The Salvation Army, and anybody else who has a heart for the task. Come along. You may spread it yourselves out in church, chapel, hall, or elsewhere, and say – "Come here, o ye poor, burdened, filthy souls, and we will help you." As well, and with quite as much prospect of success, might the Lord Mayor and the Corporation have invited the dirt to depart out of their streets, or come to them at the mouth of the common sewer in order to be swallowed up, and disposed of there. No, that would have failed.

There is only this way; you must go to it with your scraper, and broom, and cart, and any other contrivances; and so with this vast accumulation of moral filth, we must go and deal directly with it, if it is to be moved. A good lot of people must go. We saw a lot of scavengers the other day all in a row, quite a procession of them; and they put broom to broom, and then they marched and swept the tide of black slush, and dirt, and snow before them right away to the grating of the sewer, and there another man brushed it in, and off it went, to be seen no more.[2]

**Lord Jesus, you wonderfully exemplified servanthood. Let me count it a high privilege to be used as a "broom" in your hands, in the service of the Kingdom. Grant me the contentment of knowing that I do your will. Amen.**

1 Roughly eleven shillings.
2 From *Salvation Soldiery.*

# June 7th

### You may be filled to the measure of all the fullness of God
(Ephesians 3:19 *NIV*)

It is nearly sixty years now since I made my first attempt to influence men in favour of salvation. Could I tell the number of individuals whom during that time I have seen kneeling at the mercy seat it would sound like a fiction. Perhaps I have been as highly privileged in this respect as any man that ever lived. God has indeed endorsed my work with his blessing. I think I know you, my comrades, and have some idea of what you are able to do, and the circumstances in which you are called to labour, and I am sure my heart will not allow me to ask you what is beyond your ability to give. Nothing can be gained by seeking impossibilities.

I propose to tell you frankly what I think is the kind of officer called for at this juncture of our history; and, among other things, I think he should answer to the following description:

He should be possessed of the Spirit of divine life. Dead things will be of no use here. He should be possessed of the Spirit of holiness. Sanctified men are the world's great need. He should be possessed of the Spirit of supreme devotion to the object of the Army. Given up without any secret reservations. He should be possessed of the Spirit of light. Making men know themselves, and know the things of God. He should be possessed of the Spirit of war. With fighting officers the Army can conquer the world. He should be possessed of the Spirit of faith. "... all things are possible to him that believeth."[1] He should be possessed of the Spirit of burning love. Love never faileth.[2] Love shall be the conqueror.

You may take the possession of these qualifications as being the will of God concerning every one of you. You may take them as commandments coming directly from God himself. In the book of Revelation, John speaks of the seven Spirits of God[3] which are before his Throne, and which go out into all the earth to make men what is the mind of God respecting them. These seven Spirits are still travelling to and fro on their heavenly mission.[4]

**Spirit of the living God, I offer you full and complete access to every area of my life, that I may know your blessed will concerning me. Come, great Spirit, come. Amen.**

1 Mark 9:23 *KJV*
2 1 Corinthians 13:8
3 Revelation 1:4
4 From *The Seven Spirits*.

# June 8th

To this you were called, because Christ suffered for you, leaving you an example, that you should follow in his steps

(1 Peter 2:21 *NIV*)

[Your example]... is the only way you can show them [others] the value of a satisfying assurance of a personal salvation. It is the only way of making men and women see and feel the charm of holiness, the gladness of salvation, and the many other things which a Salvationist ought to possess. It is the only way you can create in them a restless love for souls, and make them realize the joy that comes with the saving of them. It is the only way in which you can inspire them with courage.

When they see you dare, they will dare. When they see you go through floods, fires, persecutions and devils to gain your end, they will want to do the same. This is the only way in which you can create in them that loving and enduring zeal which is, as it were, the life-blood of The Salvation Army, and without which it would languish and shrivel up, lose its beauty and become a byword instead of blessing to the world.

It is good to possess this spirit of zeal, the spirit that can flame out and stir up everybody within your reach. It is good for you to go about commending and approving lives of risk and daring for the sake of souls and the sake of your command; but it is better still to show it them in your own life. You can tell a man that he should be holy, tell him that he should be on fire, tell him that he should fight, tell him these things over and over again, but he will say, "How am I to do it?" But when he sees you do it before him he will be likely to try himself, and if he tries and keeps on trying he will succeed. "Do as I say and not as I do" is felt to be as impotent, if not as ridiculous, as ever it was; it stamps the man who demands it with inconsistency, nay, with insincerity, and ensures failure in the long run.[1]

**Lord Jesus, you have set the greatest, most inspiring example of all. The last thing I want is for my example to result in failure. I pray today for a right spirit that will burn through my life and blaze for the Kingdom. Amen.**

1 From *Essential Measures.*

# JUNE 9TH

## YOU OFFER FORGIVENESS

(Psalm 130:4 *NLT*)

I can very well imagine that some of my soldiers, after reading what I have been saying about a pure heart, will be asking the question: "Is it possible for me to obtain this treasure?"

I am aware that many people outside our borders openly assert that such an experience is impossible. They declare that no man or woman can live in this world without committing sin. They say that no matter how we hate our sins, or weep over them, or pray to be delivered from them, or trust in Jesus Christ for victory over them, we must be beaten in the strife and go on sinning or, at the best, keep on sinning and repenting, right down to the River of Death. Now, with regard to this objection, I maintain with the apostle John that not only is God willing and able to forgive us our sins – which no one who believes the Bible will deny – but that he is equally willing and able to cleanse us from all unrighteousness.[1]

But before we go further, let us have another word of explanation. We must understand one another. What is it that I am saying? I reply, I am declaring to you who hear these words nothing less than the scriptural doctrine that God can keep you from committing sin. Perhaps some of you will ask, "What is sin?" I reply that the same apostle… answers that question in such a simple manner that anyone can understand him. He says in his epistle that "All unrighteousness is sin".[2] That is, whatsoever thing a man does, or consents to being done, in his thoughts, desires or actions, which he knows to be wrong, that is sin.

Now I affirm, on the authority of the Bible, that Jesus Christ your Saviour is able and willing to keep you from doing wrong. His name was called Jesus, that is, Saviour, because he should "save his people from their sins"[3]… He has saved you from many sins already. Evil habits and passions that used to reign over you have been mastered; nay, some of them have been destroyed. Why, then, should not your prayer be answered?[4]

**Merciful God, you not only save, but you keep, and you persist with your children; you are indeed faithful. Grant me faith to believe that no work is too difficult for you, and that not one of my sins is beyond your cleansing reach or ability. Amen.**

1 1 John 1:9
2 1 John 5:17 *KJV*
3 Matthew 1:21 *KJV*
4 From *Purity of Heart.*

# June 10th

My heart's desire and prayer to God for the Israelites is that they may be saved

(Romans 10:1 *NIV*)

There is [a type of] repentance on which I would like to have a word – and that is, repentance on behalf of other people. If the people who sin will not themselves repent of their evil doings and their ill-treatment of Jesus Christ, then it is our duty to repent for them. Was not this the repentance which Jesus Christ himself practised? Did he not repent for Jerusalem when he wept over it?[1]

I daresay you may remember the story I tell sometimes of the little girl, in Salvation Army uniform, who came to the penitent form, weeping bitterly. The sergeant knelt by her side, and said, "My dear, what is the matter? Have you been led into telling a story?" "No, Sergeant," she replied. "Have you lost your temper, or been using bad words?" "No," said the child. "What, then, have you come here for, my dear?" "Oh," said the child, sobbing, "I have come here for my mother. She won't come to the penitent form herself, so I have to come for her." The sergeant comforted the child, and the feeling came into her heart that God would save her mother. So, running home and leaping on her mother's lap, and throwing her arms around her neck, she burst out: "O mother, mother, I've been to the penitent form for you. Now you must go there yourself! I am sure Jesus will save you." The mother did go to the mercy seat for herself, and found that salvation which all find who go there in sincerity.

Do you ever practise this kind of repentance? You sometimes condemn and scold the sinners; but do you ever weep over them? You are angry with the backsliders that hinder your meetings, but do you ever repent for them? Perhaps you have a wife or a husband, or a boy or a girl, or someone else under your roof who is trampling underfoot the blood of Christ, and counting it an unholy thing.[2] If there be no one inside your home belonging to that class, there are sadly too many outside. Does their sin or their danger ever cause you grief?[3]

**Gracious God, my prayer right now is for family, friends and loved ones who do not know of your love, and show little interest in finding out. Would you hear my prayers for them and bless them? Amen.**

1 Luke 19:41–44
2 Hebrews 10:29
3 From *The Founder's Messages to Soldiers.*

# June 11th

For you know the grace of our Lord Jesus Christ, that though he was rich, yet for your sake he became poor, so that you through his poverty might become rich

(2 Corinthians 8:9 *NIV*)

Want to make the best of life, do you? Have a good opening for business? A good prospect for getting comfortably settled? A track to fortune? Do you say you have your foot on the first round of the ladder leading to fame and fortune, otherwise you would follow him? I might reply to you with his words, "If any will be my disciple, let him deny himself, take up his cross, and follow me".[1] But I will argue with you for a moment on your own grounds. You are in for doing the best you can for yourself. I will take you on these lines; hear me. Is it riches you want? See here, my brother or sister, you can have thousands of souls; there is a value for your labour. Weigh them over against your gold and your silver and your precious stones. Tell me, what are sovereigns to souls? You need not stop till you are dying, or till you face the Throne; you have light and knowledge enough now. Go into your inner chamber and settle it which way the riches lie.

Are you carried away with ambition, the admiration of your fellows? Go in for the admiration of yourself. Face and force a career that will win for you your own everlasting respect and, if that is not enough, aim at having said of you what was said of John, "He was great in the sight of the Lord."[2]

Pleasure? A life of pleasure? As the fire-escape man, if he ever has any thrill of delight equal to that he is privileged to have now and then when he fights his way through the blinding smoke and rescues the people ready to perish and carries them in his arms safely down the ladder and hands them over to their waiting, shivering friends at his foot. Risks, partings, separations, hardships, possibilities of being rejected, sent home, wounded, killed. Well, I won't say a word to lessen them…

Do not go to the end of your days thinking that you may have missed your calling.[3]

**Father, your Kingdom has its own priorities, and its own definitions of what is important, and what constitutes real wealth and success. Implant those Kingdom values deep into my DNA, until they become my values too. Amen.**

1 See Luke 9:23
2 See Luke 1:15
3 From *The General's Letters.*

# June 12th

"I know the plans I have for you," declares the Lord
(Jeremiah 29:11 *NIV*)

Throw open the doors of your souls to the spirit of compassion which, by night and by day, in season and out of season, shall, in a more restless and resistless manner, lead you out to be saviours of men, and Christs in that particular world in which the providence of God calls you to live and labour.

O my comrades, do not seek to excuse yourselves on the ground of the humbleness of your position, or the apparent insignificance of your talents, your strength, or your past accomplishments. Do not forget that God has from the beginning chosen the "things which are not, to bring to nought things that are".[1] Gideon, a deliverer of Israel, was only a farmer's son;[2] Saul, a mighty king before his backsliding, was of common degree;[3] David, who built up that mighty kingdom, was a shepherd boy;[4] Elisha, the miracle-working prophet was, probably, a village ploughman;[5] the apostles were mostly plain working men; the earthly calling which Jesus Christ himself condescended to follow was that of a humble carpenter.

When that lad of fifteen walked out unsolicited and unnoticed to the mercy seat, and made a full consecration of his little all to the service of his King, who would have thought that God had such a wonderful future in store for him? That boy certainly at that time entertained no higher notions of his own powers and possibilities than to have the privilege of leading a cottage prayer meeting, or singing "His blood can make the foulest clean"[6] in the slums of his native town. And yet, see the honour that God has conferred upon him by making him the General of The Salvation Army! O my comrades, let your souls embrace this glorious object that God has set before you, and give yourselves, at all costs and consequences, to its attainment, and mightier things will come to pass than you have yet dreamed of… I want you not only to see more clearly the vastness and desirability of this object, but to give yourselves up to its realization with more passionate earnestness than you have yet done.[7]

**Enlarge my imagination, Lord, for holy ambitions, and give me faith to match. Amen.**

1 1 Corinthians 1:28 *KJV*
2 Judges 6–7
3 1 Samuel
4 1 Samuel 16
5 1 Kings 19:21
6 Charles Wesley, 1707–88, "O For a Thousand Tongues to Sing".
7 An eightieth birthday letter from *The Founder Speaks Again*.

# June 13th

As for me and my household, we will serve the Lord

(Joshua 24:15 *NIV*)

The actual, everyday lives of parents should be formed after the pattern and in the spirit of the Lord Jesus Christ. He is the great model whom they wish their children to imitate, and how can they with any hope of success press their children to walk as he walked, and make their whole lives on the model of his, unless they do the same? For a parent to set a good example before his children, therefore, involves –

Consistency. Everything must be in keeping with the profession made, the whole force of the example depending upon its being truthful. If the children once get the idea into their little heads that the religiousness of their parents is a cloak or a pretence only, no good impression will be possible on their hearts until that idea is removed. If they see one spirit at the breakfast table, and another at family prayers; one spirit in everyday affairs, and another in the barracks or the church; if the religious exercises are not the natural outcome of what is in the parents' hearts, they will put the whole affair down, with their quick and merciless instincts, as a mere performance, and the example will, of course, lose all its weight.

But if, on the other hand, they are made to feel – however imperfect the prayer and other religious utterances may be – that the ruling purpose of the soul of father and mother is to please God, keep his commandments, and shape their daily life according to the good pleasure of his will, such example cannot but have the most blessed effect upon the children.

To be the most effective, the example set before the children should be that of the whole family. Father, mother, and servants (if servants are kept), and everybody about, should all speak, act, and move under the influence of one spirit. If the whole working, and eating, and dressing of everybody in the house are shaped and fashioned by this one spirit, and that is the spirit of love to God and man, the influence of such an example will be almost overwhelming.[1]

**Lord, today I lift to you in prayer Christian families, that there may be unity, harmony and a spirit of faith within their homes. Bless, I pray, Christian parents who strive to exemplify Jesus to their children. Help and support those families where the love of God is not experienced by everyone living under the same roof. Amen.**

1 From *The Training of Children.*

# June 14th

I URGE YOU, BROTHERS AND SISTERS, IN VIEW OF GOD'S MERCY, TO OFFER YOUR BODIES AS A LIVING SACRIFICE, HOLY AND PLEASING TO GOD – THIS IS YOUR TRUE AND PROPER WORSHIP

(Romans 12:1 *NIV*)

Men and women who will die at their posts are the very sort in demand just now in The Salvation Army and elsewhere. They are what the world needs; what we are praying for, and what God wants.

We are constantly being told that we make the service of God and the obtaining and retaining of his favour too important and serious a thing. That we demand too much when we say that there must be no compromise, no holding anything back, no denying him in little matters – that his disciples are to come out and be separate, and neither touch, taste, nor handle whatever God Almighty is against.

When, in the name of our Master and the Bible and the very nature of things, we make these demands, men reply to us with weeping and wailing, how can these things be so? The price is too high; the sacrifice is too great. They say plainly that husband and wife, and father and mother, and brothers and sisters, and houses and lands, and friendly circles, and business, and money, and politics, and health, and big idols and little idols, bar the way, and they cannot suffer what it would cost them to come and stand forth before the heavens, having dared to leave all and offer all up for the sake of him who left and offered all for the sake of them.

Oh, friends, what about the heroic martyrs of old whose faces look at you through blinding smoke and devouring flames? Are there, then, two standards of service, one high and Christ-like for them, and one much lower, made to meet the case of little, lean, and cowardly souls? Nay, are there three ways for the feet of those who travel towards eternity? One wide and broad for the wicked, another straight and narrow for martyrs and martyr spirits,[1] and the other a middle middling, some sort of silver slipper path, for those who would have the pearl without the price, the crown without the cross. No! No! No!... Come along! No more reckoning up of what an out-and-out life for Jehovah down here among men will cost.[2]

**How can I withhold anything, when Jesus gave his all?**

1 Matthew 7:13
2 From *The Founder Speaks.*

# June 15th

## Sins cannot be hidden from you

(Psalm 69:5 *NLT*)

I sent you a message a short time ago on the subject of repentance. Many of you, I have no doubt, regarded the topic as very important; and important the topic is, seeing that by sincere repentance a man is enabled to obtain the forgiveness of his sins and make a friend of his Maker. Everyone, in his senses, who realizes the possibility of his sinning against God or wronging his fellows, must know that regret for his transgression is a right and necessary feeling.

When John the Baptist showed the Jewish people the evil character and destructive consequences of their sins, and preached the doctrine of repentance and the blessings following it, they replied to the prophet that they had already repented. John answered: "Perhaps you have, but at present I only have your word for it. Prove to me the genuineness of your assertion by conduct corresponding with it." In other words, "Bring forth… fruits meet for repentance."[1] Doubtless, many of those who listened to my previous message considered that they had repented. Indeed, I am afraid that a great many people in our day think that they never do any wrong without being genuinely sorry for it.

I go to Berlin every year, or nearly so, on a day specially set apart by the German nation, and which they call Repentance Day. It is intended, I believe, that on this day the whole nation should confess and repent of its sin. That is a wise custom, not only for Germany, but for every nation, and it might be followed to good purpose, wherever this message is read. Anyway, I think we Salvationists might set aside one day in the year upon which the entire Army could be called upon to repent, not only for the sins of its own people, or their families, but for the sins of the whole world… Can you not set apart one particular Sunday for Repentance Day at your corps? And could you not on such an occasion go down before God, weep and agonize over… the awful sins and terrible dangers of your unsaved neighbours?[2]

**Father, I know very little about the sins of the whole world, but you know all about them; you know how they grieve you and offend you. Have mercy, Lord. Amen.**

1 Matthew 3:8 *KJV*
2 From *The Founder's Messages to Soldiers.*

# June 16th

They grope through the streets… No one dares to touch their garments

(Lamentations 4:14 *NIV*)

There is scarcely a lower class of girls to be found than the girls of the Woolwich "Dusthole"[1] – where one of our Rescue Slum Homes is established. The women living and following their dreadful business in this neighbourhood are so degraded that even abandoned men will refuse to accompany them home. Soldiers are forbidden to enter the place, or to go down the street, on pain of twenty-five days' imprisonment; pickets are stationed at either end to prevent this. The streets are much cleaner than many of the rooms we have seen. One public house there is shut up three or four times in a day sometimes for fear of losing the licence through the terrible brawls which take place within. A policeman never goes down this street alone at night – one having died not long ago from injuries received there – but our two lasses go unharmed and loved at all hours, spending every other night always upon the streets.

The girls sink to the "Dusthole" after coming down several grades. There is but one on record who came there with beautiful clothes, and this poor girl, when last seen by the officers, was a pauper in the workhouse infirmary in a wretched condition. The lowest class of all is the girls who stand at the pier-head – these sell themselves literally for a bare crust of bread, and sleep in the streets. Filth and vermin abound to an extent to which no one who has not seen it can have any idea. The "Dusthole" is only one, alas, of many similar districts in this highly civilized land…

In hospitals it is a known fact that these girls are not treated at all like other cases; they inspire disgust, and are most frequently discharged before being really cured. Scorned by their relations, and ashamed to make their case known even to those who would help them, unable longer to struggle out on the streets to earn the bread of shame, there are girls lying in many a dark hole in this big city positively rotting away, and maintained by their old companions on the streets.[2]

**Father, a century after Booth wrote these words, women still weep, and streets across the world remain filled with their cries. Have mercy, Lord, and bless the work of those who labour in squalid situations where humanity continues to suffer. Amen.**

1 The "Dusthole" was a riverside area of Woolwich, London, where wharves sprung up, many unloading coal. It grew in notoriety in the mid-to-late Victorian era.

2 From *In Darkest England and the Way Out.*

# JUNE 17TH

WHOEVER DOES NOT OBEY THE LAW OF YOUR GOD AND THE LAW OF THE KING MUST SURELY BE PUNISHED BY... IMPRISONMENT

(Ezra 7:26 *NIV*)

One very important section of the denizens of darkest England are the criminals and semi-criminals. They are more or less predatory, and are at present shepherded by the police and punished by the gaoler. Their numbers cannot be ascertained with very great precision, but the following figures are taken from the prison returns of 1889: The criminal classes of Great Britain, in round figures, sum up a total of no less than 90,000 persons, made up as follows: Convict prisons contain 11,660 persons.[1] Local prisons contain 20,883. Reformatories for children convicted of crime 1,270. Industrial schools for vagrant and refractory children 21,413. Criminal lunatics under restraint 910. Known thieves at large 14,747. Known receivers of stolen goods 1,121. Suspected persons 17,042. Total 89,046.

The above does not include the great army of known prostitutes, nor the keepers and owners of brothels and disorderly houses, as to whose numbers government is rigidly silent. These figures are, however, misleading. They only represent the criminals actually in gaol on a given day. The average gaol population in England and Wales, excluding the convict establishments, was, in 1889, 15,119 but the total number actually sentenced and imprisoned in local prisons was 153,000, of whom 25,000 only came on first term sentences; 76,300 of them had been convicted at least ten times. But even if we suppose that the criminal class numbers no more than 90,000, of whom only 35,000 persons are at large, it is still a large enough section of humanity to compel attention.

90,000 criminals represents a wreckage whose cost to the community is very imperfectly estimated when we add up the cost of the prisons, even if we add to them the whole cost of the police. The police have so many other duties besides the shepherding of criminals that it is unfair to saddle the latter with the whole cost of the constabulary. The cost of prosecution and maintenance of criminals, and the expense of the police, involves an annual outlay of £4,437,000. This, however, is small compared with the tax and toll which this predatory horde inflicts upon the community on which it is quartered.[2]

**Father, guide those responsible for managing systems of law and order; the police, lawyers, judges, and prison officers. Grant them mercy and compassion. Amen.**

1 Convict prisons were operated by the government and held prisoners who were sentenced to longer periods of imprisonment.

2 From *In Darkest England and the Way Out.*

# June 18th

I SANK BENEATH THE WAVES, AND THE WATERS CLOSED OVER ME

(Jonah 2:5 *NLT*)

Every year, in the Metropolitan district alone, 66,100 persons are arrested, of whom 444 are arrested for trying to commit suicide – life having become too unbearable a burden. This immense population is partially, no doubt, bred to prison, the same as other people are bred to the army and to the bar. The hereditary criminal is by no means confined to India, although it is only in that country that they have the engaging simplicity to describe themselves frankly in the census returns.[1] But it is recruited constantly from the outside. In many cases this is due to sheer starvation. Fathers of the Church have laid down the law that a man who is in peril of death from hunger is entitled to take bread wherever he can find it to keep body and soul together. That proposition is not embodied in our jurisprudence. Absolute despair drives many a man into the ranks of the criminal class, who would never have fallen into the category of criminal convicts if adequate provision had been made for the rescue of those drifting to doom.

When once he has fallen, circumstances seem to combine to keep him there. As wounded and sickly stags are gored to death by their fellows, so the unfortunate who bears the prison brand is hunted from pillar to post, until he despairs of ever regaining his position, and oscillates between one prison and another for the rest of his days…

A man, after trying in vain to get work, fell before the temptation to steal in order to escape starvation… "To get away from the scene required very little ingenuity, but the getting away from one suffering brought another. A straight look from a stranger; a quick step behind me, sent a chill through every nerve. The cravings of hunger had been satisfied, but it was the cravings of conscience that were clamorous now. It was easy to get away from the earthly consequences of sin, but from the fact – never. And yet it was the compulsion of circumstances that made me a criminal."[2]

**Loving God, how unbearable it must be to feel haunted at every step; bring your peace today to those who are scared, to those who suffer the torment of paranoia, and to those whose days and nights are loaded with fear. Amen.**

1 Particular tribes whose livelihood was criminal activity.
2 From *In Darkest England and the Way Out.*

# June 19th

From the lips of children and infants you have ordained praise

(Psalm 8:2 *NIV 1984*)

Now, there is one more thing about our captain which I like, and I won't say any more after that, lest you should think I am partial, and have favourites, which I haven't, except it is for those who come up to my notions, which I have told you what they are, so that you can judge for yourself.

But there is one thing I do like our captain for, and that is, he is the boy for the Juniors.[1] Now, perhaps it is through Sarah drilling it into me at home that it's the children that makes the men and women soldiers of a few years to come; and perhaps it is through thinking that I might have been a captain myself, or perhaps a Divisional Officer, if there had been anybody to make me a junior soldier; or, perhaps, it is through having seen the children of so many of my neighbours, and some of our soldiers, grow up to be drunkards and ne'er-do-wells, for want of being taken hold of when they were young, I don't know, but I do believe in the Juniors, and I do want to see them done well for.

Then, perhaps it is because our Junior Corps[2] has been so shamefully neglected for some years past by some of our officers, that has made me think so much more of what our captain has done for it.

There was Captain Highflyer. He told me himself that he was not going to spend his precious time and his God-given abilities on a lot of ignorant children. He had something more important to do. His mission was to their fathers and mothers: he would get them saved, and they must look after the children. Then, there was Captain Mary Tall-Talk. Why, the first week she was here she met the Junior locals, and addressed them for three-quarters of an hour about the importance of the children being saved, and about the way the thing should be done, and a great deal more, but she never lifted her little finger towards doing it.[3]

**Thank you, Lord, for every child in my church. Thank you for their innocence, their harmlessness, their joy, and all that they have to teach me about Kingdom values. I pray for churches that do not have children as part of their fellowship; bless them with that specific increase. Amen.**

1 The children and young people of a Salvation Army corps.
2 Salvation Army corps were, traditionally, divided into Junior Corps and Senior Corps, with appropriate activities and meetings.
3 From *Sergeant-Major Do-Your-Best*.

# June 20th

So they took Jeremiah and put him into the cistern… which was in the courtyard of the guard. They lowered Jeremiah by ropes into the cistern; it had no water in it, only mud.

(Jeremiah 38:6 *NIV*)

Jeremiah; or, putting down the Salvationists… Now, then, seize the bold prophet, with his words of ill omen. We hate the message of destruction – seize him, the king consents; at least, he does not dissent. Seize him, bind him – tighter: never mind his flesh. Now then, swing him over the pit. Steady there: hold hard; now let go – lower – lower. Let him try his doleful alarms on the crawling things down there; lower, still lower; until his eyes say farewell to the light, and his feet touch and sink in the mire. There, let go now, for good; pull up your ropes, shut down the doors, and leave the old man to both meditation and starvation. He would not hold his peace; he will be quiet enough now, and we shall be done with him – done with him for ever!

Now, whatever was all this about? It was just here. The city of Jerusalem had become a Sodom[1] of such iniquity that God had doomed it to destruction; but willing to save whoever in it would obey him by leaving it, he sent Jeremiah with a message to this effect. A large number of the leading men of the city neither believed God nor were willing to leave Jerusalem; and because Jeremiah would not cease persuading the people, they tried to shut his mouth by shutting him up in this dungeon. Alas that a similar necessity for such messages still exists!

But do not all the ungodly live in a doomed Jerusalem? Has God not sentenced to destruction every city of ease and sinful indulgence, and worldly pomp, and fashion, and devilish iniquity in which the millions around us live? Has he not declared that there is no peace, and never shall be; but rather wasting, and mildew, and wrath, and perdition for ever, to those who abide there?[2] This is an awful condition of things but, thank God, with it there comes direct from the mouth of the same Jehovah the message that if men will rise, and depart, and flee out of their Sodom of iniquity, they shall have salvation.[3]

**Jehovah God, you are merciful even in the face of provocation, and you do not treat us as our sins deserve. May your Church be like Jeremiah and, in a world of shifting values, declare that there are standards that remain. Amen.**

1 Genesis 19
2 Jeremiah 6:14
3 From *Salvation Soldiery.*

# June 21st

## Whoever has the Son has life

(1 John 5:12 *NIV*)

Spiritual life is the essential root of every other qualification required by a Salvation Army officer. With it he will be of unspeakable interest. He will be a pleasure to himself. There is an unspeakable joy in having healthy, exuberant life. He will be of interest to those about him. Who cares about dead things? Dead flowers – throw them out. Dead animals – eat them. Dead men – bury them. Dead and dying officers – take them away. Give them another corps. If he is living he will be of interest to all about him. Men with humble abilities, if full of this spiritual life, will be a charm and a blessing wherever they go. Look at the lives and writings of such humble men as Billy Bray,[1] Carvosso,[2] and Hodgson Casson.[3] Their memory is an ointment poured forth today after long years have passed away. Without this life an officer will be of no manner of use. No matter how he may be educated or talented, without life is to be without love; and to be without love, the apostle tells us, is to be only as a "sounding brass"…[4]

The first thing life does for its possessor is to lead him to look after its own protection. When the principle of life is strong, you will have health and longevity. When it is weak, you will have disease. When it is extinct, you have decay and rottenness. Only vigorous spiritual life will enable a Salvation Army officer to effectually discharge the duties connected with his position. Life is favourable to activity. It is so with all life. Go into the tropical forests, and see the exuberant growth of everything there. Look at the foliage, the blossom, the fruit. Look at the reptiles crawling at your feet, and take care they do not sting you. Look at the birds chattering and fluttering on the trees, and they will charm you. Look at the animals roving through the woods, and take care they do not devour you. Contrast all this movement with the empty, barren, silent polar regions or the dreary, treeless sand of the African desert.[5]

**Giver of life in all its fullness, I pray for your exuberance to flow through me this day, so that those I contact may find it infectious. In a world that is slowly dying, use me to speak of eternal life. Amen.**

1 An uneducated preacher and evangelist (1794–1868).
2 William Carvosso, Wesleyan preacher (1750–1834).
3 Wesleyan minister (1788–1851) and writer of Song No. 360 in *The Song Book of The Salvation Army* (1986): "My Saviour Suffered on the Tree."
4 1 Corinthians 13:1 *KJV*
5 From *The Seven Spirits*.

# June 22nd

## Always learning but never able to come to a knowledge of the truth

(2 Timothy 3:7 *NIV*)

It will be said the child of today has the inestimable advantage of education. No; he has not. Educated the children are not. They are pressed through "standards", which exact a certain acquaintance with ABC and pothooks[1] and figures, but educated they are not in the sense of the development of their duties in life. The new generation can read, no doubt. Otherwise, where would be the sale of "Sixteen String Jack",[2] "Dick Turpin", and the like? But take the girls. Who can pretend that the girls whom our schools are now turning out are half as well educated for the work of life as their grandmothers were at the same age? How many of all these mothers of the future know how to bake a loaf or wash their clothes? Except minding the baby – a task that cannot be evaded – what domestic training have they received to qualify them for being in the future the mothers of babies themselves?

And even the schooling, such as it is, at what an expense is it often imparted? The rakings of the human cesspool are brought into the same schoolroom and mixed up with your children. Your little ones, who never heard a foul word and who are not only innocent, but ignorant, of all the horrors of vice and sin, sit for hours side by side with little ones whose parents are habitually drunk, and play with others whose ideas of merriment are gained from the familiar spectacle of the nightly debauch by which their mothers earn the family bread.

It is good, no doubt, to learn the ABC, but it is not so good that in acquiring these indispensable rudiments, your children should also acquire the vocabulary of the harlot and the corner boy. I speak only of what I know, and of that which has been brought home to me as a matter of repeated complaint by my officers, when I say that the obscenity of the talk of many of the children of some of our public schools could hardly be outdone even in Sodom and Gomorrah.[3, 4]

**Father, how often we muddle our priorities, thinking that some matters are important while regarding crucial issues as secondary! Help me afresh to assess what really matters in life. I pray for those who suffer and experience hurt when standards clash, and when decency collides with indecency; help all concerned to aim for a better way of life. Amen.**

1 An "S"-shaped hook used for hanging pots over an open fire.
2 John "Sixteen String Jack" Rann, an English highwayman in the mid-eighteenth century. He wore colourful silk strands (strings) on his breeches.
3 Genesis 19
4 From *In Darkest England and the Way Out.*

# June 23rd

THERE ARE SIX DAYS WHEN YOU MAY WORK, BUT THE SEVENTH DAY IS A DAY OF SABBATH REST

(Leviticus 23:3 *NIV*)

Childish innocence is very beautiful; but the bloom is soon destroyed, and it is a cruel awakening for a mother to discover that her tenderly nurtured boy, or her carefully guarded daughter, has been initiated by a companion into the mysteries of abomination that are concealed in the phrase – a house of ill-fame.

The home is largely destroyed when the mother follows the father into the factory, and where the hours of labour are so long that they have no time to see their children. The omnibus drivers of London, for instance, what time have they for discharging the daily duties of parentage to their little ones? How can a man who is on his omnibus from fourteen to sixteen hours a day have time to be a father to his children in any sense of the word? He has hardly a chance to see them except when they are asleep. Even the Sabbath, that blessed institution which is one of the sheet anchors of human existence, is encroached upon. Many of the new industries which have started or developed since I was a boy ignore man's need of one day's rest in seven.

The railway, the post office, the tramway all compel some of their employees to be content with less than the divinely appointed minimum of leisure. In the country, darkness restores the labouring father to his little ones. In the town, gas and electric light enables the employer to rob the children of the whole of their father's waking hours, and in some cases he takes the mother's also. Under some of the conditions of modern industry, children are not so much born into a home as they are spawned into the world like fish, with the results which we see. The decline of natural affection follows inevitably from the substitution of the fish relationship for that of the human.

A father who never dandles his child on his knee cannot have a very keen sense of the responsibilities of paternity. In the rush and pressure of our competitive city life, thousands of men have not time to be fathers. Sires, yes; fathers, no.[1]

**Father, forgive me when I think I know best, and I succumb to the tyranny of busy-ness. Help me, Lord, in what can sometimes be a frantic world, to follow your instruction to ease up; for my health's sake, for the sake of my friendships and relationships, and because you know my limitations. Amen.**

1 From *In Darkest England and the Way Out.*

# June 24th

### Ye are our epistle written in our hearts, known and read of all men

**(2 Corinthians 3:2 *KJV*)**

I contend that if you are to train children to be good and godly, and to meet you at last at the right hand of the Throne, you must not only have the form, but the spirit in the form: "the letter killeth, but the spirit giveth life" – 2 Corinthians 3:6 (*KJV*)… A holy parental example is of inestimable value, because example explains more directly and clearly to the child what religion is, than any other method that can be employed. Men and women learn more from what they see than by what is taught them. Example with them is more instructive than precept. This is infinitely more so with children. It requires a cultivated intellect to be able to form a correct judgment of things from mere verbal instruction.

Who among us, if we had never seen a locomotive engine, would have as good an idea of what it was by reading a volume or hearing a course of lectures, as we should have by seeing it at work, especially if the exhibition were accompanied by a spoken explanation on the spot? Just so, father and mother, if you want your children to understand what practical godliness is, let them see it exemplified and illustrated in your own life and in your own home.

I do not object to your lecturing the children… I do say, however, that no amount of talking, reading, or sermon-hearing, will make them understand the nature and value of religion as clearly as they will if you yourselves are living epistles, descriptive of the same. Nay, it will be very difficult, if not impossible, for them to comprehend it in any other way. Did you ever stop to consider what those words of Paul's, "living epistles" (see 2 Corinthians 3:3), signified? They meant that he, the apostle, expected the lives of the saints to whom he wrote to be as a written communication, expressing the wishes and feelings of God towards men about their lives and work and warfare. Your children are young, and perhaps cannot read their Bibles at present; but now… they ought to be able to read the will of God expressed in your life.[1]

**Help me, Lord, to be well read. Amen.**

1 From *The Training of Children.*

# June 25th

He who did not spare his own Son, but gave him up for us all – how will he not also, along with him, graciously give us all things?

(Romans 8:32 *NIV*)

If God is able to make and keep you pure, you cannot question his willingness to do it. This must be equally plain to you, and yet it will bear looking at. It is very important indeed, that you should see – yes, and feel as well – that Jesus Christ is not only able, but perfectly willing – nay, waiting, even while this is being read to you – to take away from your hearts the evil things that have been the plague of your lives, for ever to keep them from coming back to harass, and wound, and torment you again.

The very nature of God proves his willingness to make you holy. All beings everywhere act out their nature. You see illustrations of this around you every day – wicked people delight in the wickedness of their neighbours. Good people find pleasure in their goodness. God is holy. He tells us so, again and again; and being holy and hating iniquity, he must abhor wickedness in men and women, and find the great delight of his heart in making them pure and good like himself. I am sure that nothing would gratify him more, my comrades, than to take everything that is unclean out of your hearts and lives. Will you let him do it?

God tells us, in plain language, in the Bible, that he wants to make you holy. Listen to some of his words: "Put on the new man," he says, "which after God is created in righteousness and true holiness... Be ye therefore perfect, even as your Father which is in heaven is perfect... For God hath not called us unto uncleanness, but unto holiness... this is the will of God, even your sanctification".[1] Jesus Christ came into the world, and lived and suffered and died that you might be made holy. This was the main object of his life and death and resurrection. "For this purpose the Son of God was manifested, that he might destroy the works of the devil."[2, 3]

**Gracious Lord, how often I mistakenly assume that I must overcome your unwillingness to assist me – please forgive me. I praise you, not only for your great power, but for being unendingly willing to help, strengthen, and bless. Amen.**

1 Ephesians 4:24, Matthew 5:48, 1 Thessalonians 4:7, 1 Thessalonians 4:3

2 1 John 3:8

3 From *Purity of Heart.*

# June 26th

### Born by the power of the Spirit

(Galatians 4:29 *NIV*)

Spiritual life is divine in its origin. It is a creation of the Holy Spirit. I need not dwell on this truth. Jesus Christ was at great trouble to teach it: "That which is born of the flesh is flesh; and that which is born of the Spirit is spirit. Marvel not that I said unto thee, Ye must be born again."[1] You have gone through this experience yourselves. You must insist on it in your people. Spiritual life proceeds from God. It can be obtained no other way. Spiritual life not only proceeds from God, but partakes of the nature of God. We see this principle, that the life imparted partakes of the nature of the author of being that imparts it, illustrated around us in every direction. The tree partakes of the [maturity] of the tree from which it is derived. The animal partakes of the nature of the creature that begets it. The child partakes of the nature of its parents. So the soul, born of God, will possess the nature of its Author. Its life will be divine.

This is a mystery. We cannot understand it, but the apostle distinctly affirms it when he refers to the promises "that… ye might be partakers of the divine nature".[2] Spiritual life, like all other life, carries with it the particular powers belonging to its own nature. Every kind of life has its own particular powers – senses, instincts, or whatever they may be called. Vegetable life has its powers, enabling it to draw nutrition out of the ground. Fish life has power adapting it to an existence in the water. Animal life has power of senses suitable to its sphere of existence, such as seeing, hearing, tasting, and the like. Human life has faculties, emotions, loves, and hatreds, suitable to its manner of existence. And it has its own peculiar destiny. It goes back to God, to be judged as to its conduct when its earthly career terminates. The spiritual life of which we are speaking has powers or faculties necessary to the maintenance of its existence and to the discharge of the duties appropriate to the sphere in which it moves.[3]

**Father, thank you that I am born of the Spirit with life from above. Thank you that I am born into your family, and adopted! It is a mystery indeed, but one which I am grateful to accept and embrace. Amen.**

1 John 3:6–7 *KJV*
2 2 Peter 1:4 *KJV*
3 From *The Founder Speaks Again.*

# June 27th

As a dog returns to its vomit, so fools repeat their folly
(Proverbs 26:11 *NIV*)

My dear comrades, my mind has been a good deal exercised the last few days on the subject of backsliders. By a backslider, I mean one who has known the forgiveness of sins, felt the power of the Holy Ghost in the changing of his heart and life, rejoiced in the prospect of Heaven, and gone about doing good; but who has, by disobedience and unbelief, fallen again under the power of sin, and gone back like the sow that was washed to be pleased and occupied with the amusements, pleasures, works, and anxieties of the world.[1]

It is a common charge brought against the Army that a large number of those who profess to be saved in our meetings become backsliders, and I suppose there is some truth in it. If so, it is only in accordance with what we see in the natural world around us. Every spring shows us a large amount of blossom that never comes to fruit. A great number of children are born into the world who never reach maturity. And there are no doubt among us a multitude of souls in whom the beginnings of divine life are implanted, who are filled with holy purpose and spiritual longings and solemn submission and sincere repentance, and who, through the blood of the Lord Jesus, enter into the divine favour, who yet, for various reasons, go back from following the Master when the hour of adversity comes, when the cup of anguish is put to their lips, when the baptism of tears and blood is about to descend upon them.

The good seed is sown in their hearts; it takes root, bursts into life, and springs up; but from various causes it dies away again. The soil of poverty and difficulty is too poor, or the sun of prosperity shines too hotly, or the tares of worldly relationships are sown too thickly, or the wild blasts of persecution beat on them too fiercely, so that they do not grow at all; or growing, they are soon terrified by tribulation, or choked with prosperity.[2, 3]

**Hold me tight this day, Father, especially in moments of struggle or temptation. I need your saving power moment by moment. Amen.**

1 2 Peter 2:22
2 Luke 8:5
3 From *The General's Letters.*

# June 28th

TAKE UP THE SHIELD OF FAITH, WITH WHICH YOU CAN EXTINGUISH ALL THE FLAMING ARROWS OF THE EVIL ONE

(Ephesians 6:16 *NIV*)

[A] proof of genuine repentance is the forgiveness of those who may have injured you. Especially when a confession of the evil has been made, and regret expressed for its commission. How can either God or man believe that you honestly regret the injuries you have inflicted on others, if you will not forgive those who may have injured you? "But if ye [do not] forgive… neither will your Father… forgive your trespasses."[1] Do you understand? Another fruit of genuine repentance is the use of such means as are likely to prevent a repetition of the sin repented of. "The burnt child dreads the fire" is an old saying. That is, having once suffered the pain caused by the burning, the child is likely to keep at a respectful distance from the fire.

Now, those whose sins have been in the direction of strong drink, novel-reading, worldly fashion, grudge-bearing, or other similar evils will, if their repentance is genuine, not only renounce such evils with all their heart, but carefully guard against anything calculated to lead them again into the power of the enemy. One step on the sinful ground, one look at the sinful thing, one glass of the ruinous liquor, one trifling touch of the accursed object may be sufficient to carry the soul over the borderline to the demon from whose clutches they have just been rescued. Do you understand?

Another proof of repentance is separation from the company and conditions that have in the past led the wrongdoer astray. While the penitent who is wisely guided will go to his or her old companions at the first opportunity, tell them of the change that has come about, and invite them to join with him on the way to Heaven, at the same time he will make it quite plain that he cannot and will not travel any farther with them on the road to destruction. Do you understand? Another sign of sincere repentance will be the immediate alliance of the penitent with the people whose society and influence are most likely to keep his feet in the way of righteousness.[2]

**Grant me wisdom today, Father. Guide my steps by your Spirit. Please, Lord, surround those who are struggling with the fiery darts of seductive temptations. Draw close and shield them, I pray, for their sake, and for your glory. Amen.**

1 Mark 11:26 *KJV*
2 From *The Founder's Messages to Soldiers.*

# June 29th

Defend the cause of the weak and fatherless; maintain the rights of the poor and oppressed. Rescue the weak and needy

(Psalm 82:3–4 *NIV 1984*)

The degradation and helpless misery of the poor stockingers of my native town,[1] wandering gaunt and hunger-stricken through the streets… or toiling like galley slaves on relief works for a bare subsistence kindled in my heart yearnings to help the poor which have continued to this day and which have had a powerful influence on my whole life. At last I may be going to see my longings to help the workless realized. I think I am.

The commiseration then awakened by the misery of this class has been an impelling force which has never ceased to make itself felt during forty years of active service in the salvation of men.

During this time I am thankful that I have been able, by the good hand of God upon me, to do something in mitigation of the miseries of this class, and to bring not only heavenly hopes and earthly gladness to the hearts of multitudes of these wretched crowds, but also many material blessings, including such commonplace things as food, raiment, home, and work, the parent of so many other temporal benefits. And thus many poor creatures have proved godliness to be "profitable unto all things, having promise of the life that now is, [as well as of] that which is to come".[2]

These results have been mainly attained by spiritual means. I have boldly asserted that whatever his peculiar circumstances might be, if the prodigal would come home to his Heavenly Father, he would find enough and to spare in the Father's house to supply all his need both in this world and the next; and I have known thousands, nay, I can say tens of thousands, who have literally proved this to be true, having, with little or no temporal assistance, come out of the darkest depths of destitution, vice and crime, to be happy and honest citizens and true sons and servants of God.[3]

**Caring Father, I pray that "the good hand of God" may rest upon me too. I commit myself this year, in the name of Jesus, to care for the fragile, intervene on behalf of the vulnerable, and give to those in need. Use me in the service of suffering humanity. Amen.**

1 Booth was born and bred in Nottingham, England, where many of his contemporaries left school to work in stocking factories, working fourteen hours a day in stifling heat.

2 1 Timothy 4:8 *KJV*

3 From *In Darkest England and the Way Out.*

# June 30th

Blessed are the pure in heart, for they will see God

(Matthew 5:8 *NIV*)

My subject is "Purity of Heart". I want to explain what we mean by a pure heart; to show you how you may obtain the precious treasure, if you are not possessed of it already; and how you may keep the blessing when attained…

We all know what is meant by being pure. When we talk about the purity of things around us, we mean that they are clean and unadulterated. That is, that they are not only without dirt or filthiness, but have no inferior substance mixed with them. When we say a man is pure, in the religious sense, we mean that he is right and honest and true inside and out; that he not only professes, but practises the things that have to do with his duty to God and man. Sin is spoken of in the Bible as filthiness or defilement of the body, mind, or spirit. Purity in religion must mean, therefore, the absence of such filthy things as drunkenness, gluttony, dishonesty, cheating, falsehood, pride, malice, bad tempers, selfishness, unbelief, disobedience, or the like…

In short, to be pure in soul signifies deliverance from all and everything which the Lord shows you to be opposed to his holy will. It means that you not only possess the ability to live the kind of life that he desires, but that you actually do live it…

We all like material purity; for instance, I am sure that everyone reading this letter[1] prefers to have a clean body. When you rise in the morning, you are not comfortable until you have washed yourselves. When the miners come from the pit, or the farmers from the field, or the girls from the factory, their first demand is for water with which to clean themselves…

All right-minded beings admire the purity of the soul far more than they do the purity of the body, or the clothes, the home, or anything else; because that is so much more important.

**Gracious God, you are more than willing to help me to live the life you have planned for me; this enabling is your loving gift. Thank you, Lord, for offering and then facilitating spiritual satisfaction. Enter right into my heart, Lord. Amen.**

1 From *Purity of Heart.*

# July 1st

THE FIGHTING GREW FIERCE

(1 Samuel 31:3 *NIV*)

Our Divisional Officer, Major Never-Rest, was at our corps last night, telling us all about a great Staff Council that they've been having in London, where the General – God bless him! – has been laying down the law, that everybody has to rouse himself up, and go for the drink, and the sinners, and the devil in dead earnest all through the country – I'm not sure whether he didn't say all through the world; and the major says that this means our corps among the rest; and he says there must be a general shaking up of ourselves, and a desperate lot of fighting with the enemy, or else we shall be left behind.

Oh, my, didn't the major go it strong! And I quite agree with every word he said. It made me feel just like the old days, when we couldn't rest without doing something fresh continually, and when we were mobbed in the market-place, and had every window broken in the hall, and the captain was locked up for a fortnight. Don't I remember that time? I should think I do! My face was so covered with sticking plaster, through the stones and scratchings of the roughs, that Sarah, my wife – God bless her! – could hardly find a clear spot for a kiss, and she declared that I looked more to her liking with all them patches on than I ever did before. She's a plucky little woman is our Sarah!

Yes, the General's all right. The dear old Army was made for fighting; and it's my honest opinion that it's the fighting what has made us Salvationists what we are. I don't know a single corps that has gone down which has kept up the fighting; while I know a few, I'm sorry to say, that hasn't done much good since the fighting slackened. And, to make a clean breast of it – which I might as well do while I'm about it – I think this very corps of ours has settled down a good deal on the comfortable line. Sarah says straight out that we're all stagnated, and that I'm stagnated myself – which is an awful thing to say about a sergeant-major![1]

**Lord, sometimes, in the fight, we grow weary, and settling for becoming comfortable creeps in as an attractive option. Wake us up, Lord! Re-arm us for the battle. Amen.**

1 From *Sergeant-Major Do-Your-Best.*

# July 2nd

God will bless you in all your work

(Deuteronomy 15:10 *NIV*)

The first topic to which I shall call your attention is your daily employment; and by that, I mean the method by which you earn your livelihood. Or, supposing that having some independent means of support, you are not compelled to labour for your daily bread; then I shall point out that special form of work, the doing of which providence has plainly made to be your duty. Because it is difficult to conceive of any Salvationist who has not some regular employment, for which he holds himself responsible to God.

Work is a good thing, my comrades. To be unemployed is generally counted an evil – anyway, it is so in the case of a poor man; but, it seems to me, that the obligation to be engaged in some honourable and useful kind of labour is as truly devolved upon the rich as upon the poor, perhaps more so. Work is necessary to the well-being of men and women of every class, everywhere. To be voluntarily idle, in any rank or condition of life, is to be a curse to others and to be accursed yourself. Everything in God's creation works. The stars travel round and round in space, the ocean rises, falls and dashes itself about in storms and tempests, the winds career to and fro in the heavens, the clouds are ever receiving and pouring forth their life-giving waters. All the forces of nature are ever active, in order to fulfil the bountiful purposes of their Maker.

Everything that can be said to have life, works. The plants, the trees, struggle into being, pushing their way upwards through all sorts of opposition, and then fighting the very elements, in order to maintain their existence and bring forth their fruits. All the living creatures on the earth, or in the waters, work. They have to hunt for their food; in many cases to construct their homes; and, in every case, to defend themselves against their enemies…

God works. He is the greatest worker in the universe. No being toils with the ceaseless activity, with the unerring wisdom, the gigantic energy, the beneficent purpose of Jehovah.[1]

**Father, I commit my work to you this day, that it may be of blessing in some way, and may serve your purposes. I thank you for it. Amen.**

1 From *Letters to Salvationists on Religion for Every Day.*

# July 3rd

Don't let anyone look down on you because you are young, but set an example for the believers in speech, in conduct, in love, in faith and in purity

(1 Timothy 4:12 *NIV*)

I hardly see how we are going to do anything very powerful in a hurry, fixed as we are. Our new officers have just come in, and they're only two lads. Why, bless me, I don't think the captain is much older than our Jack, and how he's going to manage a corps like Darkington, with all these steady-going soldiers and old-fashioned locals in it, I can't see for the life of me. But I must say the captain is rather a promising-looking young fellow. I reckoned him up at the first meeting, and I says to Sarah, as soon as I got home: "Sarah," says I, "the captain's the right sort. I felt it in my bones the first time when I heard him pray; but I'm afraid he'll find Darkington a difficult job,"

But before I could get any further with what I was going to say, Sarah stopped me. "Sergeant-Major," says she – Sarah is very proud of my rank, and she always gives me my title when she addresses me, either at home or anywhere else – "Sergeant-Major, you'll have to stand by that captain. It's true as he is a young man, but that's not a fault, is it? Isn't it the young officers who are so cheerful, and always willing to venture into something, and who are so attractive to other young folks, and so easily led? Cannot a sergeant-major of your abilities do as you like with a young officer when he wants to do the right thing, when some of them old cut-and-dried people won't listen to a local officer at all?

"But, you see," says she, "perhaps it's the thought about my own children who are just gone out from the Training Home – both being so young – that makes me feel as though I want to mother all the young officers that come along; and now, mind, Sergeant-Major Do-Your-Best, I hope you are going to stand by this young captain and do by him as you hope the sergeant-major is going to do by your own son, Jack, who is just gone into his new corps."[1]

**Father, give me a heart that respects and encourages leaders who are young. May I learn from them, and support them. Bless those who are inexperienced in ministry. Amen.**

1 From *Sergeant-Major Do-Your-Best.*

# July 4th

I devoted myself to the work

(Nehemiah 5:16 *NIV*)

All the best, greatest and most useful men and women who have ever lived in this world have been untiring workers. They would not have been eminent in character, position, or achievement without unceasing toil. They have risen early, sat up late, redeemed the moments, begrudged the time necessary for sleep and food and the ordinary demands of life.

Work is a good thing, my comrades. I have ever found it to be so in my own experience. And specially has it proved itself to be a blessing in these, the latter days of my life. It has been a means of grace to my soul, an unfailing recreation to my mind, and a perennial source of satisfaction and comfort to my heart. The more I do, the more I want to do; and the more I am able to do, the more I see needs to be done. Now, I want every Salvationist to join with me in regarding some kind of honest work as his bounden duty – a duty from which no circumstances of wealth, position, or ability can relieve him. Nay, I want him to see that it is a privilege which he cannot forgo without entailing loss and damage upon himself and those about him. If he would [have] health of body and mind and soul for himself, he must be an industrious worker. For I verily believe that idleness is the fruitful parent of disease, insanity, and sin. And the divinely ordained plan by which he can benefit his family, his friends, and his neighbours is to work for them.

Whosoever, therefore, would prosper in every respect for this world and the next, must give themselves up to the doing of some kind of profitable work, and that with their might.[1] I should also like to say that, in my judgment, every Salvationist should not only accept his secular employment as of divine appointment, but that in the condition of life in which he finds himself placed, he is called upon to be a worker together with God for the salvation of his fellow men…[2]

**Lord, I thank you for giving me this perspective on my work. Keep this uppermost in my mind, I pray, that I may, first and foremost, work for you. Amen.**

1 Ecclesiastes 9:10
2 From *Religion for Every Day.*

# July 5th

### The sinful nation is as good as dead

(Isaiah 1:4 *NET*)

What a valley of dry bones the world appears to the man whose eyes have been opened to see the truth of things.[1] Verily, verily, it is one great cemetery crowded with men, women, and children dead in trespasses and sin. Look for a moment at this graveyard, in which the men around you may be said to lie with their hearts all dead and cold to Christ, and all that concerns their salvation. Look at it. The men and women and children in your town are buried there. The men and women in your city, in your street. Nay, the very people who come to your hall to hear you talk on a Sunday night are there. There they lie. Let us read the inscriptions on some of their tombs.

Here lies Tom Jones. He had a beautiful nature, and a young virtuous wife, and some beautiful children. All starved and wretched through their father's selfish ways. He can't help himself. He says so. He has proved it. He is dead in drunkenness. Here lies Harry-Please-Yourself. Mad on footballing, theatres, music halls, dances, and the like. Nothing else morning, noon, or night seems to interest him. There he is, dead in pleasure. Here lies James Haughtiness. Full of high notions about his abilities, or his knowledge, or his family, or his house, or his fortune, or his business, or his dogs, or something. There he is, dead in pride. Here lies Jane Featherhead. Absorbed in her hats, and gowns, and ribbons, and companions, and attainments. There she is, dead in vanity. Here lies Miser Graspall. Taken up with his money – sovereigns, dollars, frans [*sic*], kroner, much or little. "Let me have some more" is his dream, and his cry, and his aim, by night and day. There he is, dead in covetousness. Here lies Sceptical Doubtall. Hunting through the world of nature, and revolution, and providence, and specially through the dirty world of his own dark little heart, for arguments against Christ, and God, and Heaven. There he is, dead in infidelity.[2]

**God of life, how tragic to be dead and not even realize it. Only your Spirit can open dead eyes and impart life. My prayer today is for those known to me who need your merciful awakening. As I name them before you now, please speak to them. Amen.**

1 Ezekiel 37

2 From *The Seven Spirits.*

# July 6th

## Whoever welcomes a prophet as a prophet will receive a prophet's reward

(Matthew 10:41 *NIV*)

The words of our Lord have a terrible meaning: "… they that take the sword shall perish [with] the sword."[1] There is a public house still pointed out in Staffordshire[2] where, at a drunken frolic, some man, to show his hatred and contempt of Christianity, literally hung a Bible on a spit, and roasted it before the fire, basting it as he would have done a joint of meat, until it fell to pieces. So far, we suppose, it was a good lark, real fun; the story, however, does not end here, but goes on to say that soon after, the man was smitten with a peculiar disease, his flesh rotting and falling off his bones, and his death being one of awful and terrible despair.

History is full of the records of men and women who having, in some form or other, "roasted" the prophets of the Lord, have met with a fearful retributive fate, even in this life. The method of dealing with the Lord's prophets is, therefore, a long way from being a satisfactory one; and we say to those who are tempted in this direction, "Touch not [the Lord's] anointed, and do [his] prophets no harm"…[3]

The blood of the martyrs has been said to be the seed of the Church. It was no uncommon thing, in the days when burning and crucifying and pulling to pieces by wild beasts the soldiers of the cross was common, for men and women to leave the ranks of the persecutors and take their places alongside the sufferers, convinced and won over by the peace and consolation which they possessed. Cruelty creates pity, and pity leads to enquiry, which enquiry leads to salvation. Publicity means success. Whenever men suffer for Christ's sake, not only does God draw near to bless, but men draw near to enquire. It must be so. Therefore, if the putting down of one [prophet] means the making of several others, is it not the wisest course for those who are opposed to the multiplication of salvation soldiers or prophets to let them alone?[4]

**Father, I pray for a heart that will embrace the prophetic, and for wisdom to discern that which is true and authentic, and that which is false and empty. Raise up prophets to speak your words into contemporary society. Amen.**

1 Matthew 26:52 *KJV*
2 West Midlands, England.
3 Psalm 105:15 *KJV*
4 From *Salvation Soldiery*.

# July 7th

## When he saw the crowds, he had compassion

(Matthew 9:36 *NIV*)

While it is quite true that there are many who are out of work, and not less true that there are many who sleep on the Embankment and elsewhere, the law has provided a remedy, or if not a remedy, at least a method, of dealing with these sufferers which is sufficient: The secretary of the Charity Organization Society[1] assured one of my officers, who went to enquire for his opinion on the subject, "that no further machinery was necessary. All that was needed in this direction they already had in working order, and to create any further machinery would do more harm than good".

Now, what is the existing machinery by which society, whether through the organization of the state, or by individual endeavour, attempts to deal with the submerged residuum?… The first place must naturally be given to the administration of the Poor Law.[2] Legally the state accepts the responsibility of providing food and shelter for every man, woman, or child who is utterly destitute… As to the method of Poor Law administration in dealing with inmates of workhouses or in the distribution of outdoor relief, I say nothing… All that I need to indicate is the limitations – it may be necessary limitations – under which the Poor Law operates. No Englishman can come upon the rates so long as he has anything whatever left to call his own.

When long-continued destitution has been carried on to the bitter end, when piece by piece every article of domestic furniture has been sold or pawned, when all efforts to procure employment have failed, and when you have nothing left except the clothes in which you stand, then you can present yourself before the relieving officer and secure your lodgings in the workhouse, the administration of which varies infinitely according to the disposition of the Board of Guardians under whose control it happens to be.[3]

**Lord, I pray for those who face destitution or eviction, with the fear and panic that accompanies their plight. Lead them to kind and helpful people. Amen.**

1 Charity Organization Societies were founded in England in 1869, seeking to restrict the distribution of outdoor relief. Societies were formed with the intention of restricting relief to the elderly, ill, or "non-able bodied" and to force them to accept the workhouse test.

2 The Poor Law stated that each parish had to look after its own poor. If someone was unable to work, they were given some money. However, the cost of the Poor Law was increasing every year; by 1830 it cost about £7 million and criticism of the law was mounting.

3 From *In Darkest England and The Way Out.*

# July 8th

The kingdom of heaven may be compared to a king who gave a wedding feast for his son, and sent his servants to call those who were invited to the wedding feast, but they would not come… they paid no attention and went off

(Matthew 22:2–5 *ESV*)

Now, I want to tell you what has happened lately. What with our captain going away, and another coming in, we didn't have a Soldiers' Meeting on Tuesday, and so the captain got one on Friday, and a remarkable meeting it was, I can tell you. First of all, we sang the song, "Send the Fire!" and then the lieutenant prayed. And then the captain got up, and made a little speech. "My dear comrades," he said. I liked the way he started off. He stood straight up like a man that knew what he was after, looked us all fairly in the face, spoke out strong, although in nice, easy words, so that everybody could understand him; and we all felt at once that while he was of the humble sort, he was not without a will of his own. He didn't say much, but what he did say was to the point.

"Comrades," says he, "I've not been with you very long; but I've been on the ground long enough to see the hall, a few of the soldiers, to look through the roll, to shake hands with the local officers, and to praise God for having raised up such a fighting force in this town of Darkington! Then," says he, "comrades, I've also had a stroll or two through the place; I've looked at the crowded pubs and the theatre, and I've been inside that devilish low concert hall just round the corner; and I've seen the crowds of young people all rushing, giggling, and laughing, down the broad road.[1]

"And, then, comrades," says he, "I've compared these thousands who are for sin, and the devil, and Hell, with the handful at our corps who are for salvation, and God, and Heaven, and the thought has made my heart ache. Comrades," says he, "we must have a revival; we must have something done. I'm here on purpose for it. These poor deluded slaves of sin and the devil have ears, and we must make them hear about Calvary; they have eyes, and we must show them a few Salvationists in dead earnest."[2]

**Lord, I pray for those who live without so much as a thought for their souls or anything more than having a good time. Speak to them and ask them gently if they have any time for Jesus. Embrace them in your love, Father, wherever they might be just now. Amen.**

1 Matthew 7:13
2 From *Sergeant-Major Do-Your-Best.*

# July 9th

### We may share his holiness

(Hebrews 12:10 *ESV*)

I come now to the task of showing, as far as I am able, what the plan of life is which God has formed for a Salvation Army officer. What must an officer be and do who wants to satisfactorily… fill up the plan God has formed for him? Of course, there will in some respects be certain striking differences in that plan. But in the main there will be remarkable resemblances. The first thing that God asks is that the officer shall possess the character he approves. You might say the character that he admires. The very essence of that character is expressed in one word – holiness.

In the list of qualifications for effective leadership in this warfare, The Salvation Army has ever placed holiness in the first rank. The Army has said, and says today, that no other qualities or abilities can take its place. No learning, no knowledge, or talking, or singing, or scheming, or any other gift will make up for the absence of this. You must be good if you are to be a successful officer of The Salvation Army.

Let us suppose that a comrade was to present himself before us… and say, "I am a Salvationist, I want to be an officer amongst you, and I want to be an officer after God's own heart; but I am ignorant of the qualifications needed." If I were to ask you what I should say to this brother, I know what your answer would be; you would say, with one voice, "Tell him that, before all else, he must be a holy man." Suppose, further, that I appeared before you myself for the first time… and were to say to you: "My comrades, I have come to be your leader. What is the first, the foundation, quality I require for your leadership?" I know the answer you would give me. You would say, "O General, you must be a holy man."… Holiness must be in the first rank… Holiness comes first.[1]

**Help me today, Lord, to take time to be holy. Amen.**

1 From *The Seven Spirits.*

# July 10th

Do what is fair and just to your neighbor, be compassionate

(Micah 6:8 *The Message*)

The treatment of the women is as follows: Each Casual has to stay in the Casual Wards[1] for two nights and one day, during which time they have to pick 2lb of oakum[2] or go to the wash-tub and work out the time there. While at the wash-tub they are allowed to wash their own clothes, but not otherwise. If seen more than once in the same Casual Ward, they are detained three days by order of the inspector each time seen, or if sleeping twice in the same month the master of the ward has power to detain them three days. There are four inspectors who visit different Casual Wards; and if the Casual is seen by any of the inspectors (who in turn visit all the Casual Wards) at any of the wards they have previously visited they are detained three days in each one.

The inspector, who is a male person, visits the wards at all unexpected hours, even visiting while the females are in bed. The beds are in some wards composed of straw and two rugs, in others coconut fibre and two rugs. The Casuals rise at 5:45 a.m. and go to bed by 7 p.m. If they do not finish picking up their oakum before 7 p.m., they stay up till they do. If a Casual does not come to the ward before 12:30, midnight, they keep them one day extra...

J. C. knows Casual Wards... They vary a little in detail, but as a rule the doors open at six; you walk in; they tell you what the work is, and that if you fail to do it, you will be liable to imprisonment. Then you bathe. Some places the water is dirty. At Whitechapel (been there three times) it has always been dirty... You then tie your clothes up in a bundle, and they give you a nightshirt. At most places they serve supper to the men, who have to go to bed and eat it there. Some beds are in cells; some in large rooms. You get up at 6 a.m. and do the task.[3]

**Lord of mercy, these working conditions are barbaric, yet nothing has changed in some places; where young children work in dangerous, back-breaking conditions in brick factories, where people are treated as slaves, picking cocoa and tea, or when sweatshop workers are exploited. Please move in power to bring justice. Amen.**

1 Casual Wards were part of a workhouse complex, housing non-locals (Casuals) who were expected to move on after a short time.

2 Picking oakum was a particularly difficult form of forced labour. Old ropes (sometimes tarred) had to be unpicked by hand, and the individual threads then rolled.

3 From *In Darkest England and the Way Out.*

# July 11th

THERE IS NOTHING BETTER FOR A PERSON THAN THAT HE SHOULD... FIND ENJOYMENT IN HIS TOIL

(Ecclesiastes 2:24 *ESV*)

A man who works ten hours a day, six days a week, for forty years, spends upwards of 124,000 hours of his life at his daily toil. It surely cannot be unimportant to him as to what kind of work it is that occupies so large a portion of his life. Only think of the energies of body and mind put forth by him, during that long round of toil; and think also of the influence of the work of all those years, for good or for evil, upon himself and upon those around him. That influence, you will see, I am sure, ought to be made to tell, as far as possible, in favour of the honour of God, the goodness and happiness of himself, and the well-being of his fellow men; but that can only be the case when good and useful work is done...

It is very probable that many who read this letter will be already employed in some kind of labour that does not answer to this description. For instance, your work may be far from being agreeable, either to your taste or your judgment. It is not what you like. It does not seem calculated, so far as you can judge, to bring either glory to God or benefit to man.

But then you say, what am I to do? I had no choice in the matter of my trade or my calling. It was fixed up for me by my parents, or I selected it when my head was full of foolish notions, or I came into it by accident, and now, however much I may desire to do so, I cannot get away from it... That is very much where I found myself, my comrades, when as a youth, I came to see life and its responsibilities...

I put myself and my destiny into God's hands. I told him that I was just willing to be and do with my daily work what he desired, and I waited to know his will.[1]

**Father, hear my prayer for those who feel trapped in mundane work that provides little scope for personal fulfilment. Would you please open up doors for them, and provide better opportunities? Help them to know that all their work is for the Master, and that you are perfectly capable of creating good avenues of service. Amen.**

1 From *Religion for Every Day.*

# July 12th

The God of peace will soon crush Satan under your feet

(Romans 16:20 *ESV*)

When the devil took our Master up into a high mountain, and showed him all the kingdoms of the world, and said unto him, "All this power I will give thee and the glory of them, for that is delivered unto me, and to whomsoever I will give it, if thou wilt worship me all shall be thine",[1] it is ordinarily supposed to have been a vain and boastful assertion. And yet, how much there is of the past recorded on the page of history, and how much we see in the present, turn which way we will, to justify the assertion of Satan that he is really and truly in possession of the bodies and souls of men and of the very world they dwell in.

Look at the savage nations with their superstitions, and vices, and their bloody wars. Look at the professedly religious nations with their superstitions, and vices, and their bloody wars, all quite as ruinous, or more so and, anyway, more unreasonable and inexcusable, and all alike soul-destroying in the long run, and we have the most striking justification of the assertion that Satan is really and truly now, as then, in an awfully solemn sense, the god of this world.[2]

Whether to dislodge and drive the usurper out and rescue the whole world from his diabolical grip may, or may not, be in the divine purpose, we care not now to enquire, but there can be no question that it is of God that those who are on the Lord's side should aim at this great and God-like purpose, and direct and devote all their energies to its accomplishment. But what a formidable task. True. Formidable because it is not one rebel only, although he be so mighty, but because he has incited to rebellion so many millions of other beings. Indeed, the whole world is entrenched in dire enmity against God. But though the task be so formidable, thank God, it is possible, for is not even this, the biggest impossibility of which we have any conception, possible to God?[3]

**Almighty God, I would be foolish to imagine my enemy is anything but powerful. I therefore pray for your protection. Having said that, you are much more powerful. Help your people to remember that as we go about our business for the Kingdom. Let us not entertain thoughts of intimidation or defeat. Amen.**

1 See Matthew 4:1–11
2 2 Corinthians 4:4
3 From *Salvation Soldiery.*

## Quench not the Spirit

**(1 Thessalonians 5:19 *KJV*)**

He [our captain] stopped a bit, and the tears came into his eyes, and he said: "Comrades, I've made up my mind to have a crowd of these poor sinners saved, or I'll die in the attempt, and you shall bury me in your cemetery." And when he said those last words, it all seemed so real earnest-like, that I felt all tender, and I turned to look at Sarah, and she was crying like a child; and she said to me in a whisper: "Sergeant-Major," says she, "you're going to help that young man, or I'll leave you and go and live with Jack; for I feel I must go somewhere where sinners are coming to Jesus, or I shall die as well."

Well, now, after this, the captain, he says: "Comrades, as to what is to be done, I don't exactly see at the minute. I've had a talk with the sergeant-major and with his wife" – which he had, and I'm glad he mentioned Sarah – "and I've had a word with the treasurer; but I am going to think and pray about it, for I'm determined," he says, "to do something desperate; and I think we'll begin with a half-night [of prayer] next Tuesday, and have a meeting in the fair that they say is coming off on Wednesday. I find that I can hire a tent right in the middle of the ground, and we'll have a meeting on Sunday morning at half-past twelve opposite the 'Blue Boy'; and we'll all pray every day for the down-coming of the Holy Ghost on this town… "

And when he said at the finish, "Let's all go down, and cry to God," my heart was fairly bursting; and before that bit of prayer was over there was a shaking among the dry bones of Darkington Corps, I can tell you. Still, there wasn't many "Amens". Some of the old-stagers, especially, were a little stiff. The meeting wasn't a very large one either, and altogether I could see the captain was a little disappointed.[1]

**Father, I pray today for those whose enthusiasm is sometimes met with apathy. Please draw alongside them with encouragement, and help them not to quit. Bless creativity with courage. Amen.**

1 From *Sergeant-Major Do-Your-Best.*

# July 14th

## Soldiers prepared for battle

(1 Chronicles 12:33 *NIV*)

We cannot bow, or notice, or persuade the devil out of his favourite citadel and stronghold. If polite requests, and eloquent persuasions, and logical arguments addressed to his majesty would have done it, he would have departed long ago. Nay, if indolent or even fervent prayers to the Divine Spirit to drive him out would have effected this purpose, we should have had our Eden back again a long time ago. But, no, there is only one way – a way, alas, most unpalatable to indolent and selfish humanity, and that is to drive him out by actual persevering, self-sacrificing warfare. There is nothing for it but to fight, and to fight to the death. Who is willing for this?

If, then, there is to be fighting, and such fierce and terrible fighting as will overcome this great enemy, there must of necessity be soldiers, and they must be good soldiers, too; and I propose here briefly to describe what appears to me to be a good soldier of Jesus Christ.[1] A good soldier is a good man or a good woman. In this war both men and women are equally eligible, but whether man or woman, goodness is indispensable. In other armies this is not a particular desideratum. The recruiting sergeant does not enquire if the recruit has been converted, if he prays without ceasing,[2] or has a clean heart. Very bad men have, I suppose, been reckoned in the killing armies very good soldiers; but in the Army of salvation – the Army whose object is to destroy sin, defeat the devil, and deliver souls from going down to Hell – we must have good men.

God Almighty wants veterans who have been themselves delivered from the power of the foe, and washed in the blood of the Lamb,[3] and who will follow him whithersoever he leadeth. This is the only metal out of which God can make spiritual "ironsides", "invincibles", "more than conquerors".[4] A good soldier makes war his business. He may do something in other lines of duty; he may be a farrier, a tailor, a shoemaker, a servant, or what-not, but after all, fighting is his trade.[5]

**Lord of the battle, today I pray that you will use me as a good soldier. Please keep me alert in the fight, so that I quickly recognize opportunities to promote the name of Jesus. Show me my battlefield. Amen.**

1 2 Timothy 2:3
2 1 Thessalonians 5:17
3 Revelation 7:14
4 Romans 8:37
5 From *Salvation Soldiery.*

# July 15th

### Establish the work of our hands

(Psalm 90:17 *NIV*)

In trying to discover how God wants him to employ himself while he is on the earth, there are certain things the Salvationist will not be likely to do, and certain things that I think he will be likely to do… In making a choice as to the various methods of labour possible to him, I do not think he will be influenced by the question of wages. I am sure he will not, if he understands his principles and is true to them. He would most strongly object to a master standing him up on a block in the market-place and selling him for the sake of his labour to the highest bidder. And to embark in any trade or profession regardless of its character, merely because it will produce the most money, amounts to very much the same thing. Yet, I am afraid, nothing loftier in the way of motive influences many people in the selection of their daily toil.

Instead of asking, "How can I spend my time and energies to the best advantage for my Lord, and to the most profit for my fellows?" The question is simply, "In what way can I earn the most money?" We admire Paul when he says, "I determined not to know any thing among you, save Jesus Christ, and him crucified."[1] If he had said, "I determined not to know anything among you but how to make money, and the soonest get a big balance to my credit at the Savings Bank," we should have despised him. Do not do anything that looks in this direction, my comrades; but you certainly will if you go about hiring yourself, influenced by no higher motive than how you can get the most wages.

In choosing a life-work, the Salvationist will not be guided merely by what appears agreeable. He does not live to please himself; and, while it may not only be allowable, but wise and desirable, to follow the natural tendency of the children's minds, or of his own, in the choice of an employment, still, the higher motive of usefulness… must be supreme.[2]

**Lord, my prayer this day is for those who are setting out on life's way; those choosing study courses or career options. Please speak to them; may your Spirit guide and influence their decision-making. Amen.**

1 1 Corinthians 2:2 *KJV*
2 From *Religion for Every Day.*

# JULY 16TH

IT IS GOD WHO WORKS IN YOU TO WILL AND TO ACT IN ORDER TO FULFIL HIS GOOD PURPOSE

**(Philippians 2:13 *NIV*)**

Holy souls are saved from sin. You all know what sin is. And it is important that you should, and that you should be able to define it at a moment's notice to whomsoever may enquire. John says: "All unrighteousness is sin" [1 John 5:17 *KJV*] That is, everything that a man sees to be actually wrong, that to him is sin. Whether the wrong be an outward act, or an inward thought, or a secret purpose, does not affect its character. If the act, or thought, or purpose is wrong to that particular soul, it is sin. Whether the wrong be done in public and blazoned abroad before the world as such, or whether it be committed in darkness and secrecy, where no human eye can follow it, it matters not; it is sin. To be holy, I say, is to be delivered from the commission of sin. Is not that blessed?

To be holy is to be delivered from the penalty of sin: "the wages of sin is death…"[1] Holy men are fully and freely forgiven. One of the evidences of the possession of holiness is the full assurance of that deliverance. Salvation from doubt as to this. Is not that blessed? Holiness includes deliverance from the guilt of sin. Sin has a retributive power. At the moment of commission it implants a sting in the conscience which, in the impenitent man, lights a flame which, without the application of the precious blood, is never extinguished. In holiness the sting is extracted, and the fire is quenched. Is not that blessed?

Holiness supposes deliverance from sin. Sin pollutes the imagination, defiles the memory, and is a filth-creating leaven which, unless purged away, ultimately corrupts and rots the whole being. In holiness all the filth is cleansed away. The soul is washed in the blood of the Lamb. This is the reason for so much being said in the Bible, and in the experience of entirely sanctified people, about purity of heart. Is not that blessed? Holiness means complete deliverance from the bondage of sin… Is not that blessed?[2]

**Father, you are a God who loves to bless. Likewise, your blessings are generous. May your work in my life be thorough, lest I miss any part of a blessing. Amen.**

1 Romans 6:23 *KJV*
2 From *The Seven Spirits*.

# July 17th

God said, "Let us make man in our image, after our likeness"
(Genesis 1:26 *ESV*)

"A Tramp" says: "I've been in most Casual Wards in London; was in the one in Macklin Street, Drury Lane,[1] last week. They keep you two nights and a day, and more than that if they recognize you. You have to break 10 cwt of stone, or pick four pounds of oakum. Both are hard. About thirty a night go to Macklin Street. The food is 1 pint gruel and 6 oz bread for breakfast; 8 oz bread and 1½ oz cheese for dinner; tea same as breakfast. No supper. It is not enough to do the work on. Then you are obliged to bathe, of course; sometimes three will bathe in one water, and if you complain they turn nasty, and ask if you are come to a palace. Mitcham Workhouse[2] I've been in; grub is good; 1½ pint gruel and 8 oz bread for breakfast, and same for supper.

F. K. W.; baker. Been board-carrying today, earned one shilling, hours 9 till 5. I've been on this kind of life for six years. Used to work in a bakery, but had congestion of the brain, and couldn't stand the heat. I've been in about every Casual Ward in England. They treat men too harshly. Have to work very hard, too. Had to work whilst really unfit. At Peckham (known as Camberwell) Union,[3] was quite unable to do it through weakness, and appealed to the doctor who, taking the part of the other officials, as usual, refused to allow him to forgo the work. Cheeked the doctor, telling him he didn't understand his work; result, got three days' imprisonment. Before going to a Casual Ward at all, I spent seven consecutive nights on the Embankment, and at last went to the ward.

The result of the deliberate policy of making the night refuge for the unemployed labourer as disagreeable as policy, and of placing as many obstacles as possible in the way of finding work the following day is, no doubt, to minimize the number of Casuals, and without question succeeds... It seems to me that such a mode of coping with distress does not so much meet the difficulty as evade it.[4]

**Lord of love, it is sad and wrong that anyone is treated as a part of a social project, however well-meant. May your Church deliberately avoid schemes that inadvertently deny anyone of their God-given individuality and personal dignity. Help us always to prioritize people over plans. Amen.**

1 London. Named after Charles Macklin, an actor at the Theatre Royal, Drury Lane.
2 London.
3 Workhouse Unions were in place to build up more, and bigger, workhouses.
4 From *In Darkest England and the Way Out.*

# July 18th

When one of you says, "I am a follower of Paul," and another says, "I follow Apollos," aren't you acting just like people of the world?

(1 Corinthians 3:4 *NLT*)

There's Jim Grumbleton; he's a very decent fellow. He earns pretty good money, and I must say he's always ready with a trifle for the good cause; but he's not much of a hand in a prayer meeting, you know; and he's never at a loss for doing a bit of fault-finding. Now, Jim, he works down at our place, and I tumbled over him as I went to the factory a morning or two after the meeting.

"Well, Sergeant-Major," says he, "that new captain of ours is a decent fellow, I fancy, and means well; but I can't see," says he, "how a lad like him's going to mend things much. What does he know; and what can he do? Why, bless my soul, he's not much older than I am. Now, if you could get the General or the Commissioner to come this way and have 'a big go', and get the Mayor into the chair, and rouse the town; or if the Chief of the Staff[1] would come to Darkington, and hold one of those wonderful meetings of his, and show us locals how we could raise the corps, and fill the hall, and get the money without us having to be at any trouble, that would be something like. "Anyhow," says he,… "I'm not going to put myself about over the corps for some time to come; I've tried before to mend things. There was that waxwork affair with the limelight, when Captain Swellum was here; it cost me about fifty shillings, from first to last, but nothing came of it."

"Sergeant Grumbleton," I says… "I am ashamed to hear you talk in that way; if we had the General here… he could only do the corps any real good by stirring up us locals and soldiers and getting us to repent of our coldness, and go to work praying for ourselves, and visiting and weeping over the poor sinners, and doing the open-airs, and that sort of thing; and can't we do that without the General?[2]

**Lord of the Church, forgive us when we favour one leader over another, especially if that hinders the progress of your work. Grant your people grace and wisdom to work together and to actively avoid division. Amen.**

1 Second-in-command to the General.
2 From *Sergeant-Major Do-Your-Best.*

# July 19[th]

### Who can forgive sins but God alone?

(Mark 2:7 *NIV*)

You ask – "What must I do to be pure?" and in reply I say that there is certainly something to be done, and something that you will have to do yourselves. To understand what that something is, you must keep well before your minds the fact that there are two forces or powers that have to unite in the purification of the heart. The first is the divine – that is, God. The second is the human – that is, man, which means yourself.

God and man are partners in the transaction. This is nothing new; it is the same in the affairs of your everyday life. You use the natural abilities God has given you to buy and sell, and plough and plant; and, as the result, God gives you food and raiment. This was the case when you were converted; you repented and believed, and God saved your soul. It will be the same when you are sanctified. The great work of cleansing your heart, and keeping it clean, will be performed by God himself; but there will be some conditions which you will have to fulfil on your part.

From first to last it is "God that saves". Fix your mind well on that truth. If ever you have a pure heart, it will come from God's own hand. When Jonah arrived definitely at the belief that salvation was of the Lord, and trusted him for it, his deliverance was nigh; for we read that immediately the Lord spake unto the fish, and it vomited him on to the dry land.[1] Only God can take out of your heart the bad temper, pride, malice, revenge, love of the world, and all the other evil things that have taken possession of it, and fill it with holy love and peace. To God you must look; to God you must go. This is the work of the Holy Ghost; he is the purifying fire; he is the cleansing flame; he only can sprinkle you with the water that purges the dross and takes away the sin; he only can make and keep you clean.[2]

**Dear God, I praise you because you can do what willpower cannot do. I praise you because you can do what human determination cannot do. Remind me to turn to you for my every need, including my need of a clean heart. Please, Lord, take away the rubbish day by day. Thank you, Lord. Amen.**

1 Jonah 2:10
2 From *Purity of Heart.*

# July 20[th]

## Show us your mighty power

(Psalm 80:2 *NLT*)

You have a God who is not only so mighty, but so willing to save!…

But… there is something to be done on your side, and the chief part of that something is the exercise of faith… God purifies the heart by faith. That is to say, when the soul comes to God, and offers itself to him for the doing of all his sacred will, and believes that for the sake of Jesus Christ, he does then and there cleanse it from all sin, that moment the Spirit answers to the faith, the work of purity is done…

This purification is not effected by any human power. No priest or officer can by his own force cleanse your heart. We can help one another by our example, by our testimony, by our exhortations, by our advice. There is not a soldier here who, if he will yield himself up to God, and trust him for full deliverance, will not at once receive power to bless and save those around him as never before. But no comrade has the power to reach into the heart of a comrade, and cleanse it from the evil he finds there; that is the work of Jesus Christ alone.

He can touch you this very moment… and say, "I will; be thou clean",[1] and the work will be done. You will not get a pure heart from your fellow-creatures; if ever the treasure is yours, you will get it from God, and you will get it by faith. Purification will not be effected by any ceremonials, meetings, kneeling at the mercy seat, singing of songs, or the like, apart from the Spirit of God. These forms and observances can wonderfully help you. Oh, what a marvellous influence goes out from soul to soul when comrades kneel together, and join heart and hand to seek God's sanctifying grace! But such gatherings will be a curse, rather than a blessing, unless they carry you on to that simple faith in God himself which claims and receives the sanctifying power.[2]

**Almighty God, if I have placed my trust in anything except you alone, please forgive me. Receive my worship when I sing, and my adoration when I share in ceremonial events, but remind me that these do not constitute my salvation or my sanctification; that is your gift to me, your work within me, and yours alone, to your glory. Amen.**

1 Mark 1:41 *KJV*
2 From *Purity of Heart.*

# July 21st

## Godly sorrow brings repentance that leads to salvation

(2 Corinthians 7:10 *NIV*)

[A] sign of sincere repentance will be the immediate alliance of the penitent with the people whose society and influence are most likely to keep his feet in the way of righteousness.[1] I often say when I am speaking to penitents, "Unite yourselves with the people from whom you will be likely to get the most good, and through whom you will be likely to do the most good, and who will be most likely to keep you from falling into those sinful habits from which you have been delivered." Is not that sound advice?...

The continuance of the spirit of repentance is another proof of its genuineness. Regrets and confessions, and tears and pledges, which only last for an hour, are void and useless, however impressive they may appear, and can be of no service unless they result in the determined and permanent consecration of every power to the holy and abiding serving of the Living God...

The putting forth of earnest efforts to bring wrongdoers to abandon their evil ways, and turn to God, is another proof of genuine repentance. To care for the salvation of father and mother, husband or wife, children and friends, follows naturally in the heart and life of the man or woman who has experienced the grace of true repentance. Nothing will so convincingly prove the genuineness of repentance in the eyes of comrades and neighbours, or be so likely to increase its power and ensure its continuance as open and straightforward efforts to promote the grace of repentance in the hearts of others...

A bold acknowledgment of the wrong of past evil conduct and the resolution to renounce it for ever constitutes a fruit meet for repentance.[2] This is a course expected by everyone who has any acquaintance with the evil-doer. When I was labouring in Cornwall, fifty years ago, it was a common thing for converts to shout their farewell to the drinking saloons as they passed them from the meetings to their homes, whether by night or by day; and no one who heard them felt there was anything incongruous in their conduct.[3]

**Father, I realize that weeping is useless, unless my tears indicate a permanent change of heart. Help me to keep short accounts with you, so that my repentance is whole and sincere. Thank you for the gracious way in which you convict and chastise, in love. Amen.**

1 Psalm 37:23
2 Matthew 3:8
3 From *The Founder's Messages to Soldiers.*

# July 22nd

## Better is the end of a thing than its beginning

(Ecclesiastes 7:8 *ESV*)

Every man has some ruling, controlling object in life. That is, there is something which forms the chief attraction of his existence, and influences him most in all he feels and says and does in his everyday life. Perhaps he does not realize the presence or power of this force, or the influence it exerts over him, but it is there all the same.

That object constitutes his ideal. All the great things done by men are, in the first instance, simply ideals; that is, pictures in the mind of what they would like to accomplish. And their realization of these things usually comes about in something like the following fashion: they see the thing in imagination, they see that it ought to be done, they see how it might be done, they yearn after its being done and they give themselves up to the doing of it. They say, "It shall be done, and I will do it, if it be possible." To illustrate what I mean, take one or two of the achievements of human genius: the Suez Canal, the Alpine Tunnels. In the first place, the idea was conceived. The ways in which the idea might be accomplished were formulated. The undertaking was resolved upon. The work was embarked upon. The task had to be persevered in. Finally, but not until each of the other stages had been reached, the thing was triumphantly completed.

Now the real object for which The Salvation Army exists is known to us all. It is to save men; not merely to civilize them. That will follow. Salvation is the shortest and surest cut to civilization. The Army's real object is not to educate them. That will follow also; and if it does not, men and women had better live good lives, and get into Heaven at last, than, with heads full of learning, whether secular or religious, finish up in Hell. The Army's real object is not merely to feed them; that is good, very good, so far as it goes… but it is only a step forward towards the purpose we wish to accomplish.[1]

**Sometimes, Father, you call us to the long haul, whereas we might be tempted to prefer short-term fixes. Give your people sticking power, I pray, that every objective might be achieved, and half-measures rejected. Strengthen those whose strength has failed as their labours increase; give them grace as their burdens grow greater. Amen.**

1 From *The Founder Speaks Again.*

# July 23rd

His mother was his counsellor in doing wickedly
(2 Chronicles 22:3 *ESV*)

A good example is of untold value, because it impresses the minds of children with the importance and necessity of a life of godliness… You will always be in sight, and they can read you by night and by day all the year round. Be sure, therefore, that your example truly explains to them what the nature of true religion is.

The great infidelity of the present age, and perhaps of all past ages, is not so much, it seems to us, scepticism with regard to the existence of God, as it is unbelief in the existence of godly people. But if children see before their eyes their own parents acting from godly motives and divine consolations, revelations, and joys, such unbelief to such children is at once and for ever made impossible. When tempted by books, atheists, and devils in after days to doubt and question the reality of supernatural and divine things, the sainted form of such a departed parent will rise before them, and the exclamation will unconsciously rise to their lips, "The example of my glorified father, or sainted mother, utterly forbids." We solemnly believe in the impossibility of anyone who has ever been closely brought into association with a truly godly man or woman ever being at heart an infidel. How much more impossible will this infidelity be if the example has been that of a father or a mother!

What shall we say of the reverse of this? How shall we describe the disastrous effects flowing from the example of parents whose daily lives contradict all that God affirms or good men believe about truth and holiness, Heaven and hell? Such examples stand like an impassable wall between the little ones and salvation, a wall not only too high for them to climb, but difficult for anyone else to drag them over. The example of a holy father or mother makes it easy for the children to be saved and almost impossible for them to be damned, while a worldly, Godless parent smooths the way down to perdition, and makes the road to Heaven all but inaccessible…[1]

**Great Father, as I pray, please bring to mind the names and faces of any children for whom I might have any spiritual responsibility. I lift them before you now. There are hundreds and thousands, millions of children, yet you know every one, and their names are written on your memory. Save them, I pray, and bring them to a safe eternity. Amen.**

1 From *The Training of Children.*

# July 24th

I am afraid that as the serpent deceived Eve by his cunning, your thoughts will be led astray from a sincere and pure devotion to Christ

(2 Corinthians 11:3 *ESV*)

I am not aware that there is a larger proportion of those saved in the Army who fall away than is the case in other great awakenings. At the same time I should not be surprised if it were so, considering the terrible ordeal of trial and difficulty and persecution our people have to suffer, oft-times through the influence of the very people who bring the charge against us.

But enough. There is the fact. As in the days of the Saviour, many fall back. Of these no doubt many return; many wander away into other parts of the world to be restored through other agencies; and at every barracks are a number like moths at a candle, who are constantly hovering around, to be ultimately caught again in the holy flame; while many who have grown weary in well-doing throng the haunts of sin, or sleep idly on the banks of the course on [which] a while ago they were contending for an everlasting crown.

What can we do for them? They proclaim our weakness as saviours of men, and throw constant discredit upon the power of God to save and to keep. They are a standing disgrace to us, and to the Kingdom of God. They are in continual danger of the damnation of Hell. We will not enter into a theological dispute with any who may deny the possibility of those who have once been truly saved being everlastingly lost. There can be no dispute about the fact – alas! alas! Too patent to all – that in this land there are tens of thousands of men and women who at one time or other professed to be children of God, and walked in the joy of his salvation, who are now confessedly outcasts from his favour, and who are as weak [and] godless as other men. These backsliders die every year, every month, every day. These men die in their sins, and therefore cannot go where God is. They die without the knowledge of God, in their wickedness; and consequently, if the Bible is true, they are driven away to Hell.[1, 2]

**Heavenly Father, as you are faithful to me, please grant me a faithful heart, even in difficult and trying times. I visualize those who were once comrades and whose Christian fellowship I enjoyed, but have now slipped away. I do not judge them, Lord; I simply pray for their safe return. Bring them home. Amen.**

1 The Salvation Army adopts a theology based in part upon Arminianism, from the theological ideas of the Dutch theologian Jacobus Arminius. The Salvation Army does not believe, or teach, that someone is "once saved, always saved". Salvationist Doctrine No. 9 states: "We believe that continuance in a state of salvation depends upon continued obedient faith in Christ."

2 From *The General's Letters*.

# July 25th

### Your word is a lamp for my feet, a light on my path

(Psalm 119:105 *NIV*)

Comrades and friends, the British and Foreign Bible Society, which is an association existing for the spread of the Bible all over the world, recently celebrated its 100th anniversary, at a great meeting in the Royal Albert Hall, London. On that occasion the society did The Salvation Army the honour of inviting your General, along with a number of bishops and other religious celebrities, to deliver an address. There was a magnificent gathering. In that speech, among other things, I said something like the following:

"The Bible is one of God's greatest gifts to man. It contains not only the announcement of the sacrifice of his dear Son, but a revelation of his will as to the manner of life he wants men to live."

The Bible has already worked saving wonders of great magnitude, and is now closely associated with almost every important advance for the betterment of mankind which the human race has experienced. The extent of the world's indebtedness to that sacred book for the privileges it enjoys will never be known either in this life or the next. What marvellous works of healing, alike to body, mind, and soul we Salvationists have witnessed through its wonderful words! Still, we expect to see the Holy Spirit accomplish far greater miracles by means of the blessed book.

To effect these wonders can we not do something more than we are doing to secure for the Bible a wider circulation? There ought not to be a house in the wide, wide world without a Bible, nor a man, woman, or child ignorant of its promises, or uninstructed in the value of its counsels and commands. If I entertained the notions of some millionaires with respect to the Bible and had the money at my disposal, I would place a copy of the Scriptures in every home in the civilized world, with explanations that would bring its most important truths within the comprehension of every occupant…

I know that with many, the sacred book is regularly read in a formal manner; but I want to see it more carefully and thoughtfully studied.[1]

**Lord of the word, I pray that your gracious Spirit would hover over my every reading of the Bible, shining light on its great truths, and showing me line upon line of love in its pages. Amen.**

1 From *The Founder's Messages to Soldiers.*

# July 26th

**And Miriam the prophetess, the sister of Aaron, took a timbrel in her hand; and all the women went out after her with timbrels and with dances**

(Exodus 15:20 *KJV*)

Miriam was one of the chosen ambassadors who came direct from the divine presence with the sacred message on her lips, "Thus saith the Lord!" And, thank God, he has not left himself without ambassadors, apostles, ministers, and prophets, known by whatever name these officers may be, in our time, and he has prophetesses, Miriams, also. When the prophetesses disappear you may look out and tremble, for the prophets will be in great danger as well. But God, by the mouth of his servant the prophet Joel, said, in this very dispensation, our daughters should prophesy, and Peter confirmed the prophecy by declaring its fulfilment;[1] and, indeed, and of a truth, we are the people whose own eyes have seen, and whose own ears have heard the full verification of the same.

We see them with our eyes, hear the word at their lips, and God confirms it as the word of the Lord with signs and wonders following. We accept the gift, open wide the door for its fullest exercise, and bless the Giver.

In those days the prophetesses led the people in open-air processions. Miriam did, and no doubt it was quite a common thing for her to do so. On this occasion the people were evidently in good practice, falling in at the word of command, and all ready for the time, and the tune, and the song. Our prophetesses do the same. Why not? If processions are right, and lawful, and scriptural, and useful – as who in their senses can truthfully deny – then why not the prophetesses to the front? People have objected, and do object but, then, what is there that they won't object to, specially in practical godliness of any shape or form? They will let women sell in public, sing in public, dance in public – anything in public, out door or in, save and except, in a straightforward manner, discharge the divine mission of a prophetess, and carry the message of mercy from the lips of Jehovah to dying men, or lead the Lord's elect to battle and victory.[2]

**Father, you occasionally raise up those with the gift of prophetic leadership. Help your Church, I pray, not to suffer gender-prejudice, but to welcome such leaders with respect. I pray this day for women who hold leadership positions, and I ask you to affirm them in their ministries. Amen.**

1 Joel 2:28 and Acts 2:17
2 From *Salvation Soldiery.*

# July 27th

## I will counsel you

(Psalm 32:8 *ESV*)

There are many occupations in which it will be very difficult, if not impossible, to keep a good conscience. I need not counsel you to leave these severely alone. Your own conscience will tell you what you ought to do…

What is a Salvationist to do, who is employed in the homes or about the persons of people whom he knows to be ungodly? As, for instance, what is a carpenter to do who finds himself building a house, or a compositor printing a book, or a housemaid waiting at the table, for individuals openly opposed to the word and work of God? They must remain at their posts and do their duty and thereby seek to win those whom they serve to Christ, unless plainly called by God elsewhere. To get entirely away from the service of wicked people, or from having any connection with their doings, is utterly impossible, circumstanced as we are at present. To do so, we should have to go out of the world altogether.

I remember once hearing a celebrated doctor say that a certain wealthy brewer had written him asking his advice concerning a particular malady from which he was suffering, and which was likely to prove fatal. My friend, who was an ardent Temperance man, said to me that he had no doubt he could help him, and perhaps save his life, but the question with which he was occupied was whether it was his duty to assist in keeping a man alive whose business was so palpably opposed to the best interests of mankind.

Now many servants might reason after this fashion with regard to their masters and mistresses, and even with the members of their own families, but it does not appear to me possible or desirable to act upon such a rule. God does not do so himself. He allows the wicked to live and to prosper. He sends his rain, and makes his sun to shine with almost equal benefit on the evil and on the good, seeking, no doubt, by the bestowment of these mercies to lead the transgressors to repentance.[1, 2]

**Lord, my prayer today is for those who find themselves in this kind of dilemma. Please guide them by your Spirit, and open doors of opportunity if you wish them to move from one place to another. Let them know your leading and confirmation. Amen.**

1 Matthew 5:45
2 From *Religion for Every Day.*

# July 28th

I do not box as one beating the air

(1 Corinthians 9:26 *ESV*)

Fighting is the common experience of men in this life… Fighting is the order of the day in the present world. Whichever way you look, you will find that nothing is obtained without strife of one kind or another… The whole life of man is little but a conflict.

There is the fight to get into the world. There is the fight to keep living in it when you are in it. Look at it; a least 100 millions of people have to fight to obtain food barely sufficient to keep body and soul together. Even then there are millions – 40 millions in India alone – who are seldom free from the sensation of hunger. What a fight is theirs! Look at the fight of still millions more with the diseases that wait to slay them at every turn. To them – indeed, in one sense, to us all – life is one long struggle with death. Look at the fight men make for money. How they resist the claims of health and home, and fight against their own flesh and blood for gold! Look at the fight men make for fame. See how they will sacrifice time, health, friends, nay, life itself, to get what they call a name. How they will glory in dying, as they term it, in the arms of victory. Look at the fight men make for the governments they prefer.

When you come to religion you will find this principle of conflict still more manifest. Here man will get nothing without a fight. There are any number who will get nothing evil without fighting for it. For instance, a man cannot commit sin, mock God, trample on the blood, resist the Holy Ghost, put out the eyes of his own conscience, and die in despair, without fighting, and a good deal of hard fighting too. And if this applies to evil things, how much more to good things? The moment a man starts to save his soul, difficulties of all kinds spring up before him. [1]

**Lord, help me this day to pick my battles well; not to fight over the small stuff that doesn't matter, but to contend for truth. Strengthen me and surround me. Amen.**

1 From *The Seven Spirits.*

### ALL THE PEOPLE CAME TOGETHER AS ONE IN THE SQUARE

(Nehemiah 8:1 *NIV*)

We met at the hall, at seven o'clock. There was a nice lot of us; you see, some was there that I never expected would come out for such a job, I assure you… After a good time at prayer, the captain said a few words. "Comrades," says he, "we're going on a rather difficult undertaking tonight. I've been through the fair already, and I find the devil is there in strong force. You men had better button up your coats, put the sisters in the middle of the march, and cast yourselves on God for guidance, and courage, and patience, and love. Keep as calm as you can; look well about you; hold together; don't get separated. Sing with all your might. Let those who speak, shout it out. Keep believing, and God will give us the victory."

And then away we went. But just as we were coming to the outskirts of the fairground, and the mixed noise of the music, and shouting, and hooters, and drumming, was being pretty plainly heard in a little pause of the singing, who should we meet but Deacon Propriety! Now, the deacon is a great man, and a good man, too, at the fine church as has a steeple just above the hall. He stopped as he came along, and made straight for the captain, and began lecturing him, so that we could all hear him quite plain.

"What mad thing are you after tonight?" says he. "We're going to the fair," the captain said, quite calmly. "What!" says the deacon. "Are you going amongst that drunken, devilish mob, and taking these young people with you, too" – looking at some of the Corps Cadets,[1] who just looked like angels, flushed as they were with a little excitement – "to hear all that horrid language, and see all the fighting and things that are going on? Besides, is not the whole thing a dragging of our holy religion in the mire, and degrading it in the sight of the world? What can justify such a spectacle? How can you expect the blessing of God on it?" [2]

**Father, I pray your blessing upon all who uphold the name of Jesus in public; open-air preachers, beach evangelists, Salvation Army bands, and the like. Anoint them with holy courage, wisdom, and the right words. Open the lives of those who hear them, or receive gospel literature from them. Amen.**

Cont/…

1 Young people in a Salvation Army corps who undertake weekly lessons in Scripture, Salvation Army procedures, and evangelism.

2 From *Sergeant-Major Do-Your-Best.*

# July 30th

**There will be more rejoicing in heaven over one sinner who repents than over ninety-nine righteous persons who do not need to repent**

**(Luke 15:7 *NIV*)**

Cont/…

Now, the captain was just waiting for him to finish, and getting a nice and proper answer ready, when Sarah, who stood by, was unable to hold herself quiet any longer, and she burst in:

"Deacon Propriety," says she (she did not forget to give him his title, you see, although her blood was up to boiling point), "Deacon," says she, "if your boy or your girl was in a burning building, and the flames was all around them, and they were just going to perish, would you not be thankful if anybody went in to try and save them, even if there was a cursing, vulgar lot of people all about, and even if they might get their faces blackened, and their clothes spoiled, and run a little danger of getting themselves burnt into the bargain? Deacon," says she, and her eyes flashed again, and she clenched her little fists, "somebody's boys and girls are in that fire of debauchery, and drink, and Hell, and if God will help me, I'm going to get one of 'em out tonight; and if God don't help me, I'm going to do the best I can by myself."

That was a very foolish speech of Sarah's, was it not? A very foolish speech! But I don't know that I ever felt so proud of the little woman before, and it was rather excusable, wasn't it? As she was excited by the cold-bloodedness of the deacon, who reckons he is the principal shining light of what he calls the most intellectual church in Darkington…

Didn't we get rolled about, and no mistake; but we sang, and we preached, and we prayed; and they offered us gallons of drink, and when we would not have it, they threw it over us. Didn't they mess up my new uniform, as Sarah has been saving up for for three months… However, everybody was good-natured, and even the publicans said that we were the only religious folks in town who practised what we preached; and, best of all, we got one poor prodigal down at the drum.[1, 2]

**Gracious God, I pray for those whose Christian witness is met with hostility, and whose work irritates the devil. Grant them grace to persevere with holy belligerence. Amen.**

1 It was the practice in Salvation Army open-air meetings for the big bass drum to be laid flat on the pavement, or in the middle of the meeting, with an invitation for "prodigals" to come and kneel at it for prayer and counsel.

2 From *Sergeant-Major Do-Your-Best.*

# July 31st

God so loved the world that he gave his one and only Son, that whoever believes in him shall not perish but have eternal life

(John 3:16 *NIV*)

Gave him? Yes. To whom? The world – all men: "… unto us a child is born."[1] That means me, you, everybody. What have you done with the gift? The angels sang about it. Have you? That is, have you made real melody in your heart about it? – been inwardly merry and glad? The wise men of the East travelled a long, long journey to adore him. If he came again in the same way and the same place, I suppose you would want to do a pilgrimage to Bethlehem to worship him, and I suppose you would want to take some present with you to lay at his feet. Do you worship him here in the very town and house where you live? And what sort of a present are you going to lay at his feet?…

Mary cherished him! I suppose no heart can imagine what a joy that child, that holy child, was to her… First, he meant love. She loved him as he has been seldom loved since. She at least loved him with all her heart. Is it so with you? Secondly, he meant also, as he always means, sorrow to her, as to thousands more, he came, not to bring peace, but a sword[2] – a sword that pierced her heart with unutterable anguish. From the stable to the cross she followed, and followed closely in his track of anguish and blood. Are you following him in the cross-bearing way? Thirdly, he meant to Mary service, consecration. She desired nothing higher. Her joy and life and rapture was to wait upon and cherish and serve him. Are you his servant? Fourthly, to his mother he brought joy and honour and glory. The sorrow of his lifetime and the agony of his cross were followed by the joy of resurrection and the glory of the Baptism of Fire.

And, oh! Brother, sister, comrade, has Christ brought to your heart not only the Bethlehem and Gethsemene and Calvary, but resurrection and Pentecost and the glory of having a share in the gathering of a world to his feet?[3]

**Thank you, Lord Jesus, for a full salvation. Amen.**

1 Isaiah 9:6 *KJV*
2 Matthew 10:34
3 From *Salvation Soldiery.*

# August 1st

### Seek, and you will find

(Luke 11:9 *ESV*)

You can do for your children what you wish had been done for you…

Few questions of greater importance can arise in the hearts of parents than that which asks, "What shall we do with the children? How are they to earn their livelihood? What employment shall we choose for them?"…

Do not choose for them any work which will make it difficult for them to live a truly godly life. When any form of industry is proposed, your first enquiry respecting it should be – "Is this business, to which I am about to consign my child, such a one as can be followed by him with honour and truth and righteousness? Is it an employment that is favourable to his keeping a clear conscience and exhibiting the character of Jesus Christ? Is it one upon which he will look back with satisfaction in the world to come? Is it one that will permit him to put forth a fair share of effort for the salvation of souls and the glory of his Saviour?"

Now, if it is not, I beseech you to let no prospects of wages, or position, the pleasing of friends, the wishes of the child himself, or anything else, lead you to consign him to it. No earthly allurement must be strong enough to induce you to give your child to an employment that must be, more or less, one of conflict with his conscience all through his life, and which may involve the ultimate loss of his soul.

Do not consign your children to those kinds of employment, where the surroundings will be likely to lead them from God. There is a great difference in the class of temptations that have to be averted, and the companions that have to be resisted, in the various trades around you. Some are, indeed, and of a truth, a broad way leading straight down to destruction. Any other destiny for those whose feet are placed thereon seems all but impossible. By all and every honest means keep your children away from these downhill roads to Hell.[1]

**Caring Father, I lift to you in prayer parents who are anxious regarding their children. I pray too for careers officers and those who will offer advice and suggestions. Bless them all with your guidance and goodwill. Amen.**

1 From *Religion for Every Day.*

# August 2nd

When I called, you answered me; you greatly emboldened me

(Psalm 138:3 *NIV*)

Fighting has always been a necessity when anything out of the common course in the way of the salvation of men has been sought after. Read history. It would do some of you much more good than the half-penny papers. Go to the prophets! What a fight Moses had! – Jeremiah – Jesus Christ – the apostles – the martyrs – the reformers. My heart has ached many a time beyond description when I have read the biographies of the beautiful spirits who have wept, and fought, and laid themselves down to die without seeing the things accomplished for which they have suffered.

Fighting has ever been my own experience. From the beginning I have had to contend with earth or Hell, and sometimes with both, for every success God has been pleased to give me. Fighting has been your experience. The day may come when the salvation ship will glide along the stream of time, laden with souls bound for the Gloryland, without any pulling of the oars, or firing up of the furnaces, without any look-out for stormy breakers ahead. But that time is not yet. Stop rowing, and you will see. Stop feeding the furnace. Stop fighting. You know what the result will be.

If you are saviours of men, you must fight. Make up your minds that it is so, and that nothing on earth or in Heaven, human or divine, can change it. The devil has got possession of the world anyway, of the people that dwell in it, and if you want them for Christ and holiness and Heaven, you will have to take your stand, and hold your post, and close with your enemy, and fight for their rescue; and you may be sure he won't loosen his grip without inflicting all the damage he can upon those who dare to attack him and his prey. This law is not of my making. I am not responsible for it. I found it in my Bible when I first started to save myself and those around me, and it has been my experience ever since. It is God's plan and God's plan for us.[1]

**Almighty God, we own no person as enemy; sin is our challenged foe. Arm your people with the mind of Christ, I pray, wherever your invading forces march. Amen.**

1 From *The Seven Spirits*.

# August 3rd

WHILE PETER WAS IN PRISON, THE CHURCH PRAYED VERY EARNESTLY FOR HIM

(Acts 12:5 *NLT*)

Society professes to attempt the reclamation of the lost… by the rough, rude surgery of the gaol. Upon this a whole treatise might be written, but when it was finished it would be nothing more than a demonstration that our prison system has practically missed aiming at that which should be the first essential of every system of punishment. It is not reformatory, it is not worked as if it were intended to be reformatory. It is punitive, and only punitive. The whole administration needs to be reformed from top to bottom in accordance with this fundamental principle, viz, that while every prisoner should be subjected to that measure of punishment which shall mark a due sense of his crime both to himself and society, the main object should be to rouse in his mind the desire to lead an honest life; and to effect that change in his disposition and character which will send him forth to put that desire into practice.

At present, every prisoner is more or less a training school for crime, an introduction to the society of criminals, the petrifaction of any lingering human feeling and a very Bastille of despair. The prison brand is stamped upon those who go in, and that so deeply, that it seems as if it clung to them for life. To enter prison once means in many cases an almost certain return there at an early date.

All this has to be changed, and will be, when once the work of prison reform is taken in hand by men who understand the subject, who believe in the reformation of human nature in every form which its depravity can assume, and who are in full sympathy with the class for whose benefit they labour; and when those charged directly with the care of criminals seek to work out their regeneration in the same spirit. The question of prison reform is all the more important because it is only by the agency of the gaol that society attempts to deal with its hopeless cases.[1]

**Lord, have mercy on those who are in prison. Justice must be seen to be done, but please let those who hand down sentences, and run prisons, be kind and helpful, as well as just. Bless those whose relatives and loved ones are incarcerated; draw near to them. Amen.**

1 From *In Darkest England and the Way Out.*

# August 4th

Jesus wept
(John 11:35 *NIV*)

If a woman, driven mad with shame, flings herself into the river, and is fished out alive, we clap her into prison on a charge of attempted suicide. If a man, despairing of work and gaunt with hunger, helps himself to food, it is to the same reformatory agency that he is forthwith subjected. The rough and ready surgery with which we deal with our social patients recalls the simple method of the early physicians. The tradition still lingers among old people of doctors who prescribed bleeding for every ailment, and of keepers of asylums whose one idea of ministering to a mind diseased was to put the body into a strait waistcoat. Modern science laughs to scorn these simple "remedies" of an unscientific age, and declares that they were, in most cases, the most efficacious means of aggravating the disease they professed to cure. But in social maladies we are still in the age of the blood-letter and the strait waistcoat.

The goal is our specific for despair. When all else fails, society will always undertake to feed, clothe, warm, and house a man, if only he will commit a crime. It will do it also in such a fashion as to render it no temporary help, but a permanent necessity. Society says to the individual: "To qualify for free board and lodging, you must commit a crime. But if you do you must pay the price. You must allow me to ruin your character, and doom you for the rest of your life to destitution, modified by the occasional successes of criminality. You shall become the child of the State, on condition that we doom you to a temporal perdition, out of which you will never be permitted to escape, and in which you will always be a charge upon our resources and a constant source of anxiety and inconvenience to the authorities. I will feed you, certainly, but in return you must allow me to damn you." That surely ought not to be the last word of civilized society.

There still remains this great and appalling mass of human misery.[1]

**Lord, it must hurt you when you witness man's inhumanity to man; be with those who cry out to you in despair, whose circumstances go from bad to worse. Whether they are literally in prison, or imprisoned by misery, or the choices of others, please touch their lives. Amen.**

1 From *In Darkest England and the Way Out.*

# August 5th

### Are you still maintaining your integrity?

(Job 2:9 *NIV*)

Not a 100th part of the time of a military soldier, whether officer or private, is occupied with the excitement of battle, even in wartime. All his other time and energies are taken up with doing uninteresting, monotonous, out-of-sight work. There is the drill. What an uninteresting set of repetitions that usually is! The guard – the watch, by day and by night. The long, weary marching, or the endless journeys by rail or ship; the carrying to and fro of ammunition; the preparation of the food: rough and ready as it often is, both officer and soldier are frequently glad if they can get any to prepare; the clothes to be kept whole; the cleaning of the weapons; the reporting of every movement of the enemy and of his own force; the doing of all these things must be very uninteresting, but none of them can be dispensed with.

Think of the unceasing night-and-day work necessary to keep a railway running. Think of the monotonous work necessary to keep the doors of a big bank open, to construct a railway, make a tunnel, or a dock, or to conduct any similar operation. Work, work, work, is the order, the necessity of these and all similar transactions. They cannot be carried on without work.

This has applied to my own warfare. It is very easy to make a mistake here. You see me on the platform, you hear me talking to the thousands, etc. You say, "Ah, the General has a rare old time of it. He is sustained by the whirl of holy excitement. Bless him! Let us give him another volley![1] How different is his lot from mine!" but behind the scenes, out of sight, my body, and heart, and brain have to grind on night and day, and that with as little cessation as is the lot of any officer in this hall. I have not had a furlough for fifteen years. I have just decided to take a month on a motor car, but I am going to hold three meetings a day![2, 3]

**How tempting it is, Father, to imagine that living for Jesus involves exciting daily activity. Help me, I pray, to be faithful and diligent when my warfare is carried out in secluded ways, on manoeuvres that are repetitive. On such days, help me to grit my teeth en route to Glory. Amen.**

1 In Salvation Army meetings, the loud exclamation of encouraging Bible verses by members of the congregation was known as "firing volleys".

2 Booth adopted the idea of motorcades whereby he would travel through a town or a district by car, stopping to stand and preach from the vehicle once a crowd had been attracted. Sometimes, cars were adorned with Army flags or flags carrying Army slogans.

3 From *The Seven Spirits*.

# August 6th

## He has inspired him to teach

(Exodus 35:34 *ESV*)

Think of the work some battles have involved. The monstrous toil of thousands of men for months, nay, years, in preparing for it. It is said that the Japanese had been preparing for the struggle with Russia for ten years…[1] The officer must do this kind of work, in order to prepare his soldiers to fight. That is, he must deal with them as soldiers. He must train them. One great difference between an officer and a soldier is the amount of training that has been received.[2] Not merely as bearers, supporters, contributors, collectors, admirers, but as soldiers…

Every officer ought to be encouraged by the consideration of the wonderful things this monotonous kind of work has already established. It is true that the public aggressive warfare has been largely instrumental in securing the remarkable success with which we have been favoured, but the steady out-of-sight labour has greatly assisted, not only in making that public fighting effective, but in conserving and consolidating the results. Take, as a definitive illustration of my meaning, the work that has been involved in one branch of Army effort – the creation of our 18,000 bandsmen. An immense amount of toil has been entailed in: Getting them saved. Watching over them. Selecting them. Teaching them. Keeping them faithful. Then look at the work they have had to do themselves in learning: How to make the sounds. How to read the notes. How to keep the time. The Italian and French words. I heard of a drummer who used to take the drum to bed with him, and practise in the small hours of the morning.

Now let me take the aggressive side of a Salvation Army officer's life and warfare; and by that I mean the unflinching and fearless attack upon wrongdoing and wrongdoers. He must fight evil wherever and whenever he finds it. He must not leave it alone. Tempted, though he will be, to say, "Let us have peace in our time, O Lord", he must unsparingly attack it. He must bring to that attack a determined mind, and a bold and loving heart.[3]

**Father, whether they be Salvation Army officers, Salvation Army bandmasters, or anyone else involved in teaching others the rudiments of Christian warfare, I lift those people to you today. Thank you for those who are willing to pass on their expertise. Teach us all to fight, whatever our role in your Church. Amen.**

1 Russo-Japanese War, 1904–1905.

2 Salvation Army officers receive residential training prior to being commissioned. Soldiers do not.

3 From *The Seven Spirits*.

# August 7th

## Do to others as you would have them do to you

(Luke 6:31 *NIV*)

[Some say] "Emigration is the true specific. The waste lands of the world are crying aloud for the application of surplus labour. Emigration is the panacea."

I have no objection to emigration. Only a criminal lunatic could seriously object to the transference of hungry Jack from an overcrowded shanty – where he cannot even obtain enough bad potatoes to dull the ache behind his waistcoat, and is tempted to let his child die for the sake of the insurance money – to a land flowing with milk and honey, where he can eat meat three times a day and where a man's children are his wealth. But you might as well lay a new-born child naked in the middle of a new-sown field in March, and expect it to live and thrive, as expect emigration to produce successful results on the lines which some lay down. The child, no doubt, has within it latent capacities which, when years and training have done their work, will enable him to reap a harvest from a fertile soil, and the new-sown field will be covered with golden grain in August.

But these facts will not enable the infant to still its hunger with the clods of the earth in the cold spring time. It is simply criminal to take a multitude of untrained men and women and land them penniless and helpless on the fringe of some new continent. The result of such proceedings we see in the American cities, in the degradation of their slums, and in the hopeless demoralization of thousands who, in their own country, were living decent, industrious lives…

Emigration, by all means. But whom are you to emigrate? The girls who do not know how to bake? The lads who never handled a spade? And where are you to emigrate them? Are you going to make the colonies the dumping ground of your human refuse? On that the colonists will have something decisive to say, where there are colonists; and where there are not, how are you to feed, clothe, and employ your emigrants in the uninhabited wilderness?[1]

**Lord of all humanity, help me always to regard everyone I meet with respect. Send your people to situations where human beings made in your image are treated as commodities, to speak words of love and dignity. I pray for those who are trafficked; those who are refugees; those no one wants. Amen.**

1 From *In Darkest England and the Way Out.*

## THE LOWLY HE SETS ON HIGH

(Job 5:11 *NIV*)

The prevalent rage for what are considered to be more "respectable" methods of earning a livelihood, is working very injuriously amongst the labouring parts of the community. Everywhere parents who have themselves brought up families by hard, manual toil, are carried away with the desire to put their children into positions by which they shall be able to earn their bread by what they have the vain conceit to imagine is an easier and more reputable way than that which served them so well.

They think that if they can make them clerks or teachers, get them behind counters, or train them for some profession which will not soil their hands, it will be preferable to domestic service, or to the mining or mechanical or other laborious trades followed by themselves. Hence, all round the world, those branches of industry which are regarded as being genteel are overcrowded; the wages paid in them being often insufficient to purchase the necessities of life for the workers and the families. So that when they get the opportunity of marriage, a respectable semi-starvation is frequently the result of what they had thought would be a change for the better.

Now I want you to realize that the work of the servant in the kitchen, or the artisan in the workshop, or the labourer in the field, is as respectable, before God, as that of the master in the counting-house, or the mistress in the drawing room. The employment of the stoker in the fire-hole of the steamer is just as honourable as that of the engineer who superintends the machinery; of the doctor who prescribes for the sicknesses of the passengers; or the captain who directs the course of the vessel.

Other considerations, no doubt, enter into this question, some of which I may refer to another time. But what I now beg of you is not to be led off by any stupid notions as to hard, manual, common work being in itself degrading, or anything of the kind. No true honourable labour on the face of the earth, which works no ill to one's neighbour, is to be despised.[1]

**Thank you, Lord, for the skills and gifts you distribute to your children, leading us into all kinds of employment. Thank you that you place us where you most need us to be; in a factory, at the wheel of a lorry, in a classroom, or in public office. Let your pleasure be our only motivation, not status or the opinions of others. Amen.**

1 From *Religion for Every Day.*

# August 9th

Since we have been justified through faith, we have peace with God through our Lord Jesus Christ

(Romans 5:1 *NIV*)

Jesus does save his people from their sins... But what are we to understand by holiness?

All unsaved men are totally unholy. We all know that we are born into the world and grow up in it with a sinful nature. At any rate, we all hold that when man reaches the age of accountability, grace finds him with a heart completely and thoroughly depraved[1] – deprived of grace, without God, and under the power and domination of his selfish and sinful appetites. This condition is thorough – entire. In his flesh there "dwelleth no good thing".[2] We need not quote Scripture; we know that its testimony, no less than our experience and observation, describes and demonstrates the fact that man in his natural state is totally gone away from God, and that from the crown of the head to the sole of the foot, he is all wounds and bruises and putrefying sores.

I want to remark that holiness, in its broad signification, means separation from all unrighteousness and consecration to God. Nay, it means that the soul is brought into a state in which it has both the liberty and the ability to serve God as he desires, and that it constantly does so. I remark that in the early stages of Christian experience this deliverance is only partial. That is, although the soul is delivered from the domination and power of sin, and is no longer the slave of sin, still there are the remains of the carnal mind as roots of bitterness left in the heart, which springing up, trouble the soul, often lead it into sin, and which, if not continually fought against and kept under, grow up, attain their old power, and bring the soul again into bondage. Nevertheless, in this state the soul, when faithful, has peace with God, the guidance, energy, and witness of the Holy Spirit, which together create in the soul a blessed certainty of salvation, and a joy which is unspeakable and full of glory. All this is, however, perfectly compatible with the conscious existence of sin in the soul.[3]

**Thank you, Lord, for those you have gifted to teach on matters such as holiness and our relationship with you; thank you for the understanding they impart. Please, today, bless and use theologians, lecturers, writers, and Bible teachers, that their work would encourage, help, and inspire. Amen.**

1 Salvation Army Doctrine No. 5: "We believe that our first parents were created in a state of innocency, but by their disobedience they lost their purity and happiness, and that in consequence of their fall all men have become sinners, totally depraved, and as such as justly exposed to the wrath of God."

2 Romans 7:18 *KJV*

3 From *Salvation Soldiery*.

# August 10th

The grass withereth, the flower fadeth: but the word of our God shall stand for ever

(Isaiah 40:8 *KJV*)

I know that with many, the sacred book [the Bible] is regularly read in a formal manner; but I want to see it more carefully and thoughtfully studied, and I want to make sure that all who read it understand its true meaning.

I am afraid that many of those Christians who profess to rest their every hope for earth and Heaven upon the Bible, and who make the loudest boast of its importance, only very imperfectly act out the practical principles it contains, and that only where such obedience is agreeable to their feelings. We want the Bible not only to be read and committed to memory, and repeated at all manner of times, and in all kinds of places, but to be really understood. For example, what strange mistakes are made with respect to its teaching. Only think of the error so commonly made in imagining that the favour of God can be enjoyed without obedience to his commands.

There are plenty of arguments designed to lessen the importance of the sacrifice of Jesus Christ, or to explain away its merit altogether, although the spirit of that sacrifice, and the blessings it brings, are the glory of the Bible. There is plenty of interpretation of the Bible which vainly attempts to explain away the punishment of the wicked, so clearly announced in its pages. Take away these things, and the Bible becomes not only an ordinary, but an uninteresting book, to be neither feared nor cared for.

We want the Bible to be studied with a view to practical godliness. You must read the book, my comrades, in order to learn how better to obey its commands and realize the blessings it offers. It is only in this way that you can discover the height, and length, and depth, and breadth of the religion of purity, and peace, and divine communion, which are described and revealed in its pages.[1] I want my people to read the Bible with an eye on their obligation to follow Jesus Christ in that life of self-denying service which he led to seek and save the souls of men.[2]

**Thank you, Lord, for your gift of this extraordinary book. It is nothing short of a miracle that you have communicated with humankind through the pages of the Bible, and I praise you for doing so. Amen.**

1 Ephesians 3:18 *NIV*
2 From *The Founder's Messages to Soldiers.*

# August 11th

Rejoice in the Lord always. I will say it again: rejoice!

**(Philippians 4:4 *NIV*)**

Let us make 1885 a memorable year for the restoration of our lost comrades. Let us survey the field – find the lost tribes. If we sought them when they were yet sinners[1] – strangers to us, before we had clasped their hands and looked into their eyes – how much more ought we to love and seek and suffer for them now? We shouted, and laughed, and rejoiced when we first got them to the mercy seat. Get them there again. They are our prodigals. They have gone away from the barracks, which was their Father's house. Some may have gone into a far country, but multitudes are nigh at hand. They companion with the enemies of God and man. They are feeding on husks and tending swine.[2] They hunger and thirst, and no man has power to give unto them that which will satisfy their hunger or quench their thirst. They are dying of this hunger. And having known the sprinkled blood, and had the Holy Ghost, and calculated upon heaven, they are dying in their sins,[3] and being damned for ever.

My comrades, something must be done. Something shall be done. In recent Officers' Meetings I have been pleading for a special campaign in favour of the backsliders, and the officers have promised me and promised God that they will go back to their corps for some circumstances that they fancy will be more favourable. You must beat them out of all this. Make them see that their backsliding is the result of their wickedness, not their misfortune; that a fuller consecration will bring more power. Drive them up to trying again.

Happy enthusiasm is often very powerful with backsliders. The happiness of saints reminds them of happy days gone by, brings back the memory of the blessedness they once enjoyed. They see what they have lost, and long for it to be restored… I have found in multitudes of instances, at the tail-end of meetings, when all the saints have been rejoicing over the sinners that have been saved, that backsliders have… given up and come out, broken down, to the mercy seat.[4]

**Father, let me never underestimate the value of joy; my happiness might speak to someone else, without me ever realizing it. Keep me alert to the fact that someone might be watching me, and that my disposition might help them back to God. Amen.**

1 Romans 5:8
2 Luke 15:11–32
3 John 8:24
4 From *The General's Letters.*

# August 12th

## Do not be discouraged

(Joshua 1:9 *NIV*)

It is well known that crabs and small shellfish of the same class walk after what the children would call a "sideways" fashion. Once upon a time this, it is said, greatly disgusted the fishes, and after due consideration they resolved to teach these mistaken fellow-inhabitants of the great deep the proper mode of locomotion, namely, to go forward.

Accordingly they started a Sunday school and collected all the little crabs of the neighbourhood to receive instruction. At the close of the first day it is reported that the teachers were delighted at the progress made, and dismissed the scholars after obtaining the promise that they would come again the following Sunday… When the day came they were all in their places but, to the great surprise of the fishes, their pupils were all going "sideways", as before. However, not disheartened, they set to work with a will to do the business over again, and by the end of the day not only was the error rectified, but the teachers were filled with hope that their scholars were established in the habit of "going forward", and so they dismissed them a second time.

Sunday came round again, and the crabs were once more in their places but, to the utter dismay and disappointment of the benevolently disposed fishes, the crabs were all going "sideways" as badly as ever. There was a complete return to their former bad habits… A teachers' meeting was immediately called to consider what was best to be done, and to enquire into the cause of this backsliding.

The problem was soon solved and the reason of their failure readily explained by an elderly fish, who made a short speech to this effect:

"You see, my brothers and sisters, that we have these crabs under our control for one day only, whereas they return and watch their fathers and mothers the other six days, and the influence of their example in the wrong direction in the six days more than destroys any good we may be able to effect in the right direction in only one."[1]

**Father, I pray for parents, teachers, and Sunday school teachers who must sometimes feel exasperated. If they feel like giving in, Lord, encourage them with ideas that might stand a better chance of success; grant them fresh inspiration. I pray for a Church with flexible tactics. Amen.**

1 From *The Training of Children*.

# AUGUST 13TH

BEING FOUND IN APPEARANCE AS A MAN, HE HUMBLED HIMSELF BY BECOMING OBEDIENT TO DEATH – EVEN DEATH ON A CROSS!

**(Philippians 2:8 *NIV*)**

The Spirit of Devotion, with the crimson cross inscribed upon his shoulders, who comes to us from the Throne of God, asks for our full consecration… For this consecration certain things are necessary.

We need the knowledge of its nature. Many of you, I have no doubt, offered yourselves for a soul-saving life years ago. You knelt down, as I did, on the day you were converted – perhaps in the very act of being converted, and said, "Lord, help me to live for the salvation of those around me." But you have had much experience since then. You see what it means in the way of tears, of toils, of disappointments, of conflicts, really to follow the Lamb that was slain. What is asked from you by the Spirit from the Throne is that with this knowledge and actual experience you should give yourself up to it again.

This consecration also implies a definite, intelligent offer of yourself to this object without reservation. This must be done in the face of all the possibilities before you, with all you really have and are, for better or for worse, and that for all your days. This consecration involves the giving up of the pleasures and satisfactions that come from the world around you; for instance, the love of money, pleasure, and admiration. The spirit, rather than the possession, of these things is the snare of the officer. This consecration involves also a life of self-denial and toil. There is no other way.

Now, for the offering of ourselves to live and suffer for the salvation of the world after this fashion, we have the consecration of Jesus Christ as an example. Look for a moment at what was involved in the suffering he made for us. He foresaw all the humiliation, sorrow, suffering and mockeries that would have to be undergone, and the cruel death that crowned it all. And yet he voluntarily and deliberately and gladly gave himself to the task. It was voluntary. It was made without regard to success or failure. It was actuated by a motive which made it acceptable to God.[1]

**Thank you, Father, for the astonishing consecration of your Son, Jesus Christ, whereby I might be saved. At the name of Jesus, every knee shall bow – including mine. Amen.**

1 From *The Founder Speaks Again.*

# August 14th

How good and pleasant it is when God's people live together in unity!

(Psalm 133:1 *NIV*)

The poor drunkard we captured has turned out a capital case. I thought he would. Sergeant Look-'em-up took him home with him the same night, gave him a dose of strong tea, some good advice, had a good pray with him, and then saw him to his own place. That was good and, oh, my word, wasn't his wife glad to hear the news! The poor little woman has been half-starved, and the children – well, there's better times before them all, now, I hope.

But what do you think? This man turns out to be a sort of foreman in Deacon Propriety's mill, and one of the best workmen he has. The deacon has a lot of patience with him, and threatened to discharge him ever so many times on account of his drunken goings-on. He says he has borne with him on account of his wife and children; but I suspect that his being such a clever fellow with the machinery, and such a good hand with the men, has had something to do with it.

Anyhow, the deacon called on the captain the next morning, to say how glad he was to hear the news about Will Boozham – for that is his name – and that he is sorry he said anything against our going to the fair; and that Sarah's speech had troubled him all night; and as how as Boozham's case had quite altered his opinions about the Army; that he didn't understand us before.

And, then, he asked the captain to pray for a son he has somewhere in Australia who, he says, is a bit unsteady, and left a sovereign to pay for repairing the drum that he had heard was broken in the scrimmage; and then told the captain that when he was hard-up to… give him a call.

Now, that did please Sarah when the captain told us about it at night. "Sergeant-Major," says she, when we got home, "isn't that just what I've always been telling you – that the way to make friends and get money for the corps is to go and get the poor lost creatures saved?"[1]

**Thank you, Lord, for the value of reconciliation; its healing power. Help me never to be slow to apologize when I am wrong, and to make amends as best I can. Amen.**

1 From *Sergeant-Major Do-Your-Best.*

# August 15th

## Abram called on the name of the Lord

(Genesis 13:4 *NIV*)

Abraham made a great profession of religion, as any man will do who has any to profess. But Abraham was extraordinarily religious, and he used to say as much. He said he loved God with all his heart, that he had the most boundless confidence in the divine direction, that all he had was on the altar, that wife, family, good life were all given up to the service of God. He used to argue that it was just as sensible and reasonable for him to do everything that God told him in that country where he lived, as it would be when he came to live in Paradise. And he even went so far as to say that no matter what might happen he would be faithful, and that anywhere and everywhere God might reckon on his doing his will as the angels did it in Heaven.

This great profession of Abraham's made a great stir. It was talked about in all directions. Some, the open enemies of God, mocked and made sport of it; they said every man had his price, and that somewhere there was a temptation for every man, which if brought face to face with him would be sure to pull him down. In short, they said, let Abraham only be tried in a tender place, and he will go over, like anyone else.

Others of those who professed to be the friends of God, but who did not believe in extremes, said such faithfulness was impossible; they held that sin – that is, disobedience – was a necessity. No man could reckon on persevering in unswerving loyalty and faithfulness to the end; it was good for people to fall now and then, and it was calculated to deepen their humility to expect it. Moreover, this class specially doubted about Abraham because there were "shadows" on his past life. He had made several ugly slips that had been, might be, nay "they felt certain" would be, again; therefore they reckoned Abraham's confidence as little short of presumption. Moreover, God himself seems to have been in some uncertainty concerning Abraham.[1, 2]

**God of Abraham, your people live in a world where faith is often mocked; where trust in God is regarded as something anachronistic and pointless. Satan revels in pointing out past failures and stirring up doubt. Oh, Lord, pour out strong faith today, on those who need it most this hour! Amen.**

Cont/…

1 Genesis 11–25
2 From *Salvation Soldiery.*

# August 16th

God tested Abraham. He said to him, "Abraham!" "Here I am," he replied. Then God said, "Take your son, your only son, whom you love – Isaac – and go to the region of Moriah. Sacrifice him there as a burnt offering on a mountain I will show you"

(Genesis 22:1–2 NIV)

Cont/...

He [God] does seem to have felt some doubt whether there might not be some stress of temptation before which Abraham's supreme affection for him would give way. So Jehovah resolved to settle this controversy for ever – Abraham should be tested. He would himself "tempt" – that is, try – him, and in such a manner that there should be neither room nor reason for further discussion while the world stood. God effected this by giving Abraham the remarkable command quoted... How Abraham received the message, rose up, made the necessary preparations for the journey, and went off the nearest way, pausing not until he reached the place appointed for this sacred tragedy, is not only recorded in the Bible, but is known throughout the whole world. It is also known that in doing this, Abraham gave to us one of the most wonderful and effective illustrations of obedience to God recorded on the pages of history... This obedience is only another word for the active side of religion; and a very important side it is, and unless it is well understood, and better still, well practised, all the other sides of religion will soon disappear...

Abraham was a man subject to and possessed of like passions with ourselves. That is, he was a man after the fashion of ordinary men, with the same feelings as a father, husband, and so forth, and that we are not to regard this noble action as the outcome of some altogether exceptional spirit, some iron will or superhuman power possessed by him; but that, being just such a one as ourselves, we may naturally hope to be able, under similar circumstances, to do the same...

God is no respecter of persons in the bestowment of divine power. Therefore that any man may lay claim, and actually receive unto himself, as much divine grace and power as will enable him to acquit himself as manfully before God and man as did Abraham...

In this incident we have set forth the very essence of divine obedience.[1]

**Empowering God, Abraham's obedience to your voice was quite staggering. May I respond obediently to whatever it is you ask of me today. I pray for those called to obedience that is frightening and sacrificial; equip their hearts as you did Abraham's. Amen.**

1 From *Salvation Soldiery.*

# August 17th

THEIR WORK WILL BE SHOWN FOR WHAT IT IS, BECAUSE THE DAY WILL BRING IT TO LIGHT. IT WILL BE REVEALED WITH FIRE, AND THE FIRE WILL TEST THE QUALITY OF EACH PERSON'S WORK

**(1 Corinthians 3:13 *NIV*)**

The Master's providence, everybody knows, is, not only to choose the work of his servants, but to get it done, if possible, to his satisfaction. He has appointed me to do my work. He has arranged that I should direct the movements of this great Army, preach salvation, write letters for you to read, save as many sinners as I can, and strive to get my soldiers safely landed on the Celestial Shore. Before all else, I must do this work, as nearly as I can, to satisfy my Lord – and nothing short of the best work I can produce will accomplish that.

As with me, so with you. He has chosen your work, if you have put your life into his hands, just as truly as he has chosen mine, although it may be of a different kind. I am writing this letter in the train. I am a poor writer at best. When I was a child, my schoolmaster neglected to teach me to hold my pen properly. In this respect he did not do good work, and I have had to suffer for it ever since. Still, I am doing my work as well as I can, in order that it may profit you and please my Lord...

Is not this the distinct command of our Lord, given through the apostle Paul to the Salvationists at Ephesus, the most of whom would probably be slaves? They were to do their work, "Not with eyeservice, as menpleasers; but as the servants of Christ, doing the will of God from the heart; With good will doing service, as to the Lord, and not to men: Knowing that whatsoever good thing any man doeth, the same shall he receive of the Lord, whether he be bond or free."[1]

Now, that passage contains the Divine Orders and Regulations for these Ephesian soldiers,[2] with regard to their daily work; and if it means anything at all, it signifies that whether bond or free, treated well or treated badly, we are to do our work to please God.[3]

**All my work is for the Master; let that be my heart's desire. Amen.**

1 Ephesians 6:6–8 *KJV*
2 The Salvation Army publishes *Orders and Regulations for Soldiers.*
3 From *Religion for Every Day.*

# AUGUST 18TH

THE ADVANTAGE OF KNOWLEDGE IS THAT WISDOM PRESERVES THE LIFE OF HIM WHO HAS IT

(Ecclesiastes 7:12 *ESV*)

No one but a fool would say a word against school teaching. By all means let us have our children educated. But when we have passed them through the Board School Mill we have enough experience to see that they do not emerge the renovated and regenerated beings whose advent was expected by those who passed the Education Act.[1] The "scuttlers"[2] who knife inoffensive persons in Lancashire, the fighting gangs of the west of London, belong to the generation that has enjoyed the advantage of compulsory education.

Education, book-learning and schooling will not solve the difficulty. It helps, no doubt. But in some ways it aggravates it. The common school to which the children of thieves and harlots are driven, to sit side by side with your little ones, is often by no means a temple of all the virtues. It is sometimes a university of all the vices. The bad infect the good, and your boy or girl come back reeking with the contamination of base associates, and familiar with the coarsest obscenity of the slum.

Another great evil is the extent to which our education tends to overstock the labour market with material for quill-drivers and shopmen, and gives our youth a distaste for sturdy labour. Many of the hopeless cases in our shelters are men of considerable education. Our schools help to enable a starving man to tell his story in more grammatical language than that which his father could have employed, but they do not feed him, or teach him where to go to get fed. So far from doing this they increase the tendency to drift into those channels where food is least secure, because employment is most uncertain, and the market most overstocked. The developing in a man of all his latent capabilities for improvement may cure anything and everything. But the education of which men speak when they use the term, is mere schooling.[3]

**Father, I thank you for good systems of education, and for all those who work hard to educate. Schools and colleges are a great privilege. However, may we never prize intelligence over compassion, or book-learning over heart-learning. Guide me, I pray, in all that I study, that my learning may include a combination of truth and intellect. Amen.**

1 Elementary Education Act 1870
2 Neighbourhood-based armed youth gangs.
3 From *In Darkest England and the Way Out.*

# August 19th

I appeal to you, brothers and sisters, in the name of our Lord Jesus Christ, that all of you agree with one another in what you say and that there be no divisions among you, but that you be perfectly united in mind and thought

(1 Corinthians 1:10 *NIV*)

"Try Trades Unionism," say some, and their advice is being widely followed. There are many and great advantages in Trades Unionism. The fable of the bundle of sticks is good for all time. The more the working people can be banded together in voluntary organizations, created and administered by themselves for the protection of their own interests, the better – at any rate, for this world – and not only for their own interests, but for those of every other section of the community.

But can we rely upon this agency as a means of solving the problems which confront us? Trades Unionism has had the field to itself for a generation. It is twenty years since it was set free from all the legal disabilities under which it laboured. But it has not covered the land. It has not organized all skilled labour. Unskilled labour is almost untouched. At the Congress in Liverpool only 1½ million workmen were represented. Women are almost entirely outside the pale. Trades Unions not only represent a fraction of the labouring classes, but they are, by their constitution, unable to deal with those who do not belong to their body. What ground can there be, then, for hoping that Trades Unionism will by itself solve the difficulty?

The most experienced Trades Unionists will be the first to admit that any scheme which could deal adequately with the Out-of-Works and others who hang on to their skirts and form the recruiting ground of blacklegs and embarrass them in every way, would be, of all others… most beneficial to Trades Unionism.

The same may be said about cooperation. Personally, I am a strong believer in cooperation, but it must be cooperation based on the spirit of benevolence. I don't see how any pacific readjustment of the social and economic relations between classes in this country can be effected except by the gradual substitution of cooperative associations for the present wages system… I look to cooperation as one of the chief elements of hope in the future. But we have not to deal with the ultimate future, but with the immediate present.[1, 2]

**Lord, let our work for you be altruistic, benevolent, and done in cooperation. Amen.**

1 A cooperative is an autonomous association of persons who voluntarily cooperate for their mutual social, economic, and cultural benefit.

2 From *In Darkest England and the Way Out.*

# August 20th

## There will be showers of blessing

(Ezekiel 34:26 *NIV*)

Purifying faith is the faith that has some definite knowledge of the nature of the blessing desired, and the means by which it is attained. That knowledge may be very imperfect, but it is enough to apprehend the nature of the purity sought for. This faith sees that purity is not merely a passing wave of feeling or a deliverance from temptation. It perceives that it is not a condition of uninterrupted happiness, but a state of holiness in which the servant of God ceases to grieve the Holy Spirit, obeys the call of duty, and loves him with all the power he possesses.

Purifying faith fixes its eye on the blessing, and says, "I want a pure heart, I need it; it is the will of God that I should have it. Christ bought it for me when he died on the cross. O God, let it be mine." Has your faith got as far as that, my comrades? Do you see what purity means? If so, that is a gratifying attainment. Hold it fast until God bestows the greater treasure upon you.

Purifying faith sets the soul longing after the possession of this treasure. Looking at a thing which you consider valuable and possible will certainly awaken the desire for its possession. If I am informed of some site of land, or some piece of property, which I see would be of great service to the Army, the more I think about it, the longer I look at it, the more strongly shall I desire its possession. It is so with holiness, my comrades. If you believe it to be the precious thing it really is, you will consider it, keep it before your mind, turn it round and round, and the more you do so the more you will desire it. Does your faith compel your attention? Does it make you think, "O Lord, increase our faith"? If you will only keep on looking at it you will come to long after it with earnest desire.

Purifying faith is the faith that leads the soul to choose the blessing.[1]

**Lord, I pray for showers of blessing – upon me, upon your Church, upon your people. Disturb us with dissatisfaction so that we turn to you for more blessing – not for our own sakes, but so that more of your will may be complete in our lives. Amen.**

1 From *Purity of Heart*.

# AUGUST 21ST

AS YOUR DAYS, SO SHALL YOUR STRENGTH BE

(Deuteronomy 33:25 *ESV*)

Constituted as human nature is, even saved human nature, there will always be some trouble or some evil to be faced by every real commanding officer and lover of souls.

The officer must help his people in their fight with their own personal trials, temptations, and sins. He should make them feel that he is a real stand-by in their difficulties. Many of them are sorely tried. Look at their depressions! How many of them go down into low spirits and despondency, and feel like giving up the struggle as hopeless. The officer must fight that depression; he must encourage them, show them the bright side of the cloud, have patience with them. The balance of many a battle has been turned by one kind word, and thousands have been strengthened in the conflict with this kind of trial by the feeling that their leaders would cheer them up.

Look at the afflictions of the people! How few homes there are without sickness, and how few hearts without [sorrow]. Disappointment and loss and separation seem to be the common rule of the great mass. Look at the trials of parents in their children, and the trials of children in their parents. Remember the loneliness and separation of some wives and some husbands. And how many of our people all over the world are set alone in families and households far from their own loved ones. Now an officer's duty is to help them in these trials. He is to get to know them, and give such advice as is helpful to them; stand firm as a rock by the side of those who are suffering, so that they may lean on him. In short, he must help them to fight their trials.

Look at the temptations of our people!… Remnants of old habits, and fiery temptations which come by old companionships, calling them back to evil… Living in families opposed to goodness… The constant butt of sarcasm and ridicule… It is the officer's business to help them fight these evils.[1]

**Without question, Lord, the pathway of duty is sometimes thorny, or stony – yet, it is the way the Master trod. Help me, today, to follow in his footsteps. Bless those church leaders who carry the burdens of many. Bless, too, those whose pathway is particularly difficult, or painful, to navigate this day. Grant them extra strength and grace. Amen.**

1 From *The Seven Spirits*.

# August 22nd

Don't let this upset you; the sword devours one as well as another. Press the attack against the city and destroy it

(2 Samuel 11:25 *NIV*)

Look at the spiritual foes of our people. Their weak natures. Do they not require help? It is no use blaming them. There they are, poor, wobbling, feeble creatures, many of them so by birth. Look at their wicked natures. It is no use disguising the fact. Many hearts seem unfavourable to the work of God's grace – stony, selfish natures. Twisted, awkward creatures, who go all through life taking everything and everybody awry. What a foe to man's soul such a nature must be! Devils. Do we sufficiently realize that devils are told to destroy, and trip up, and overthrow? Every officer here has some people under his care who are, this very day, being dogged, and pestered, and watched, and followed, with sleuth-like tenacity, by the fiends of Hell who are seeking to get hold of them.

Now I say you are to fight these difficulties. You have not been saved and washed, and sanctified and called, and set apart and promoted, merely to record them, or to moan over them. All this has been done for you, that you may fight them with your own hands, and with your own hearts, and with your own strength of mind and soul. You must grapple with these evils. How can you better do this than you have done it in the past? That is the question. How can you more really conform to the command of the spirit of war than hitherto?…

Believe that victory is possible… Never let go your faith in the possibility of God's final triumph in any soul you have to deal with. Say to yourself in the face of every weakness and disappointment, and say to them: "God can; God is able." Keep a smiling face. Many a battle has been won by the confident look of the General's countenance. Many a poor soul has been plucked from despair and damnation by the smiling face of his captain in the hour of difficulty.

Do not let temporary defeats discourage them, or prevent them trying again. Forget the things which are behind… Do not show the white feather.[1]

**Father, here is the secret of holding on when Satan's arrows wound and pierce. Help me, I pray, to hold on in the warfare, and then, in faith, to keep holding on. Amen.**

1 From *The Seven Spirits*.

# AUGUST 23RD

WE KNOW THAT IN ALL THINGS GOD WORKS FOR THE GOOD OF THOSE WHO LOVE HIM

(Romans 8:28 *NIV*)

Now, there's one thing that I do think our Sarah is a trifle too anxious about, and that is over making the children into officers. I am a Salvationist myself, and my salvation is of the "Blood-and-Fire" sort, or else I should not do for the sergeant-major of the first corps of the important town of Darkington. Still, you can carry even important things a little too far, for Sarah, you see, will not be content with the children being saved and getting to Heaven; she wants them all to be officers, and that is rather a high target to aim at.

She says to me: "Why not, Sergeant-Major? Can anybody tell me why they shouldn't be? They are all healthy and strong, and have got the perfect use of their faculties. Is there anything half so important they can do in the world? They belong to Jesus Christ; I have heard you say so yourself, and the General says officers of the right sort are the great need of the Army; and why should not my children be the right sort? And why shouldn't they go on to help the dear Lord? And they shall, if I can rule; and I am going to rule, if I can!" And then she gets excited about it, and really does harass me not a little on the subject every now and then.

You see, the first three came into the world in a bit of a hurry, and grew up to be pretty big children, and did mostly as they liked – worse luck! – before their father and mother were converted; and Tom, the eldest, when he was about fourteen, went off to America with a neighbour, who took a great fancy to him, and promised to look after him, and nothing else would satisfy the boy; and though his mother was dead set against it, he teased me until I consented; and off he went; and then Sarah so abused me about it that I repented, and had a week's drinking over it, which ended, strange to say, in my getting beautifully saved. Bless the Lord for that! My Heavenly Father knows how to bring good out of evil.[1]

**Father, how often we plan our course in life, setting our sails in one specific direction. Sometimes we are right, and sometimes we are wrong. What a comfort it is to know that you watch over us, and that even when matters don't turn out as planned, you are there, to graciously bring positives from negatives. Thank you, Lord. Amen.**

1 From *Sergeant-Major Do-Your-Best.*

# August 24th

Repent, then, and turn to God, so that your sins may be wiped out, that times of refreshing may come from the Lord

(Acts 3:19 *NIV*)

In dealing with [backsliders] you must always remember what vast numbers there are who pass for backsliders, but who have never been regenerated – never really known the power and joy of a real salvation. Find this out on your first attack. If they have never been properly saved, you have a mighty plea to urge on them. You can then show them that they fell because they were trying to keep the holy laws of God with unholy hearts, and show them that if they get properly saved they will have a power they never had before to fight the world, overcome the flesh, and resist the devil.

Backsliders are often open to feel the importance of the example they are setting to those about them. I have often broken a father's heart by showing him that he has been leading his children direct to Hell. A mother who has once loved God and loved souls can be pierced to the quick with the thought, urged lovingly and forcibly upon her, that she is making a straight track for her children's feet down to perdition. Set before a man who knows that he has been reckoned a saint in his neighbourhood that he is now influencing those same people against Christ and in favour of their damnation, and I don't see how he can ever be happy any more till he gets converted and comes out before them in his old character. Drive this in upon backsliders.

You can always assume that backsliders know all you say to be God Almighty's solemn truth. Never argue or quibble with them. Never hear a backslider bring his infidel arguments out. If he begins to spread them before you, tell him plainly to his face that he knows they are all rubbish and twaddle, and that there is nobody in his parish who knows it better than he does. Infidelity – with backsliders at any rate – is a thing of the head rather than the heart.[1]

**Gracious God, your mercy persists with those who wander away from you – thank you. Hear my prayer today for those you are calling back to yourself; may they take that crucial step to Jesus. Amen.**

1 From *The General's Letters*.

# August 25th

### When I preach the gospel, I cannot boast, since I am compelled to preach

(1 Corinthians 9:16 *NIV*)

Open-air work – This we regarded at the outset, and consider still, our special sphere. It was the throngs in the great thoroughfares, romancing about on the Lord's Day, thoroughly indifferent to spiritual and eternal things, that first woke up our sympathies. It was these that God laid on our hearts. On coming [in]to closer contact with them, we found that though the aversion of the working classes to churches and chapels was as strong as could readily be conceived, yet would they eagerly listen to any speaker who, with ordinary ability, in an earnest and loving manner, could set before them the truths of the Bible in the open air.

At any season of the year, in nearly all kinds of weather, at any hour of the day, and almost any hour of the night, we could obtain congregations. As a rule, too, there was but little interruption. Occasionally a sneering infidel or a bitter papist would ask a question, or an intoxicated man, stimulated from some neighbouring gin palace, would try to divert attention; but, met with a little tact and good humour, they were easily silenced, and we have usually found the crowd take sides with the speaker.

Of this facility to obtain an audience we tried to take advantage to the very uttermost, and thus reached with the glad tidings of mercy multitudes who could not in any other way be brought under the word. At the same time, our experience taught us that every outdoor meeting should, if possible, be connected with an indoor meeting, where, free from those dissipating influences which more or less always accompany outdoor preaching, especially in the streets of London, the gospel could with greater clearness be set forth, further appeals could be made in favour of an immediate closing with Christ, earnest prayer could be offered, and an opportunity secured for personal conversation with the people. Acting on this opinion, thousands have accompanied us from our open-air stands to our halls, rooms, and chapels, and there many have been led at once to the Saviour. In this actual closing with Christ consists the only or chief ground of hope we have for sinners.[1]

**Lord of love and salvation, I pray for those engaged in preaching the gospel, whether that be indoors or in the open air. Grant them a fresh anointing, I pray. Inspire their messages, so that some may be saved. Amen.**

1 From *The Founder Speaks Again.*

# August 26th

Listen, my son, to your father's instruction and do not forsake your mother's teaching. They are a garland to grace your head and a chain to adorn your neck

(Proverbs 1:8–9 *NIV*)

"Do as I say, but not as I do" was the poor piece of counsel some minister once gave to his flock, a member of which had been complaining that his life did not square with what he taught from the pulpit. It was a very useless piece of advice for a minister to give to his people, but it would be still more useless and less likely to be followed if given by a parent to his children for, far more than grown-up people, they tend to work to pattern and write from copy.

Good and holy example lives for ever in the memory of the child. How is it possible that the beloved face and form, the sayings, and doings, and plans, and purposes of father and mother should ever be forgotten? True, in the first rush and whirl of man and womanhood life, there may be some sort of waning of interest in the home of childhood and the memory of those who filled the largest measure of space in it. New scenes and associations and employments for a time create new interests, which occupy and absorb the attention. But as the journey of life goes forward, memory reasserts itself, and the influence of the holy example of good and godly parents is felt again with perhaps greater power than ever, giving additional meaning and force and feeling to the operations of the Divine Spirit, and in a majority of cases having a particularly powerful influence in the great work of personal salvation.

We have heard hundreds of people, from youth to hoary age, when publicly narrating the means by which they were led to the Saviour, connect their conversion with the recollections of a sainted mother or father. Consequently it seems to us that no means or agencies employed by God are of equal force, or can be calculated upon with such certainty for accomplishing the salvation of the children as the example of godly parents. Father, mother, mind how you live! You see, parents are everything to their children. The father and mother of a little child are like God and king.[1]

**How important it is, Father, for Christian parents to establish a lasting example; one that will carry through the years. It is no easy task, and I pray for families who are entrusted with that responsibility. Bless those parents and those children. Amen.**

1 From *The Training of Children.*

# August 27th

## Rightly handling the word of truth

(2 Timothy 2:15 *ESV*)

The Bible should be more widely circulated… No one has more profound respect for it, or wishes to circulate it more widely than the Army does… The Bible should be more carefully read and understood. Let us never lose a chance of getting the right interpretation of its precious words… The Bible should be more truly believed. Holy and enthusiastic Salvationists will greatly help the attainment of that result… The Bible should be more fully obeyed, both in the spirit and the letter. We had God in man 2,000 years ago; now we need the Bible in man.

To do something towards supplying this great need, every Salvationist should be a living, walking, fighting Bible, which can be seen, and read, and felt by every soul about him. The apostle John says that "The Word was made flesh, and dwelt among us".[1] Now, as you know, words are used to express our thoughts and feelings to those about us. So Jesus Christ, the divine Word, became a man in order to make us know by his speech, action, suffering, and death what the thoughts and feelings of God really are towards us.

So we want the words of the holy book to be made flesh in our day. That is, we want the truths and doctrines of the Bible to so take possession of the souls of men that they shall live and act them out before the people around them, and show them by living pictures what the Bible teaches. The men and women that are moved and actuated by the Bible will explain the goodness and love of God by being good and loving themselves. They will teach the evil of sin by trampling it underfoot themselves. They will teach the beauty of holiness by living true, honest, industrious, kindly, pure lives themselves. They will teach the sacrificing compassion of Jesus Christ by themselves pitying the lost, and seeking to save the souls of men…

Notwithstanding all that has been said and done, men everywhere are woefully ignorant of the all-important things revealed in the Bible.[2]

**Thank you, Father God, for sending Jesus into the world as the incarnate Word. Thank you, too, for the wealth of Bible study resources that are easily available free of charge. Inspire your people to dig deep into the Bible, not only to find treasure, but to share treasure too. Amen.**

1 John 1:14 *KJV*
2 From *The Founder's Messages to Soldiers.*

# August 28th

The Lord was gracious to Hannah; she gave birth to three sons and two daughters. Meanwhile, the boy Samuel grew up in the presence of the Lord

(1 Samuel 2:21 *NIV*)

It seems as how [my son] Tom has got into bad company, does a little betting, and takes nips of brandy, and cocktails, and such things. Now, I don't know what cocktails are, except it is that they stir the spirits they drink with feathers of some sort. Anyway, from the latest accounts, poor Tom is going down the broad road, and that at a pretty round pace.

Now, when I had read the last letter over to Sarah, and when she was crying over it fit to break her heart, I felt I must say something to comfort her, and so I says: "Sarah, ought we to be surprised at this? Isn't this all through my example? What did he see in his father – and, as far as that goes, in his other, as well – to lead to anything different?" – for we both lived very far away from God. "What else could we expect?"

And you should have seen her! All at once she wiped her tears away with her apron. She always has a nice clean apron on, no matter what work she is doing. Well, she wiped her tears away, and her eyes flashed fire, and she turned on me furious-like, and she says: "What can I expect, Sergeant-Major? Why, I'll tell you what I expect – I expect that God is going to convert the boy. That is what I expect. Nothing else will do for his mother, whether it does for his father or not. Haven't I repented for him, and cried myself to sleep nights without number, and prayed for his salvation every day since God converted my poor soul? And does not our captain say that if we believe with all our hearts God will give us the things for which we ask? And if that comes true of strangers in the hall, won't it come true of our own flesh and blood?"

Yes, I believe that God is going to convert Tom, and make an officer of him. Of course I do. I can't be happy in England now, with Tom serving the devil in America; and how could I be happy in Heaven with my poor Tom in Hell?[1]

**Father, hear my prayers today for those I love who are not saved. However far away from me they might be, in terms of geography, I believe they are never far at all from your heart, and your interest. Reach them with saving power, for Jesus' sake. Amen.**

1 From *Sergeant-Major Do-Your-Best.*

# August 29th

### He purified their hearts by faith

(Acts 15:9 *NIV*)

Purifying faith goes further than merely admiring and talking, and longing and praying: it elects to make the experience its own. It says, "Now, Lord, this great deliverance shall be mine. I choose it. If it is to be attained, I'll have it!"

We all know how the sinners around us pain our hearts by the way they trifle with salvation. They say, "Oh, yes, it is good, and it's very kind of Jesus Christ to make it possible for us to be saved. We must have salvation. We must not be lost. But we won't seek it now." Even so, I am afraid many soldiers trifle with holiness. They say, "I ought to be holy; I wish I were holy. O Lord, make me holy – but not now." It says, "I'll begin to seek now with all my heart – and I'll seek until I find."[1]

Purifying faith compels the surrender of everything that stands in the way of the possession of holiness. It is willing to pay the price. Oh, how cheerfully people give up pleasant things in order to gain those which they believe to be still more desirable. So here, when men really do see and believe in the worth of purity, they will be ready to abandon everything which seems likely to hinder them obtaining it. Oh, my comrades, have you got thus far? Does your faith duly value the treasure we are talking about? If not, it cannot be said to be purifying faith…

Now, my dear comrades, has your faith got as far as this? I am afraid many come close up to this point, and then grow afraid. They shrink from the full consecration, and give up the holy strife. They will say, "If I place myself in the hands of God, for him to do just as he likes with me, who can tell where he may send me, or what he may want me to do?" For instance, I fancy some of my soldiers [hang] back from the fear that God should say to them: You will have to put on the uniform.[2]

**Father, if faith of any kind is your gift to impart, then it follows that my part in the deal is to welcome and receive that gift. If there is anything in my heart that would hinder purifying faith, please show me, so that I can address the issue and receive fully from your generous hand. Amen.**

1 Matthew 7:8
2 From *Purity of Heart.*

# August 30th

He has delivered us from the domain of darkness and transferred us to the kingdom of his beloved Son

(Colossians 1:13 *ESV*)

You see the fiends of Hell, devouring the happiness and lives and souls of the people by thousands. I believe many of you do. I would to God you all did! You can see the devil going about like a roaring lion.[1] Are you willing to let those fiends feed on the bodies and souls of the people in peace? No! Then you must fight.

Again, you see around you the giant fiends of earth doing the same deadly work. Fouler fiends, I was going to say, are these fiends of earth than the fiends of Hell. There is pride; there is malice; there is worldliness in its unnumbered forms; selfishness; covetousness; drunkenness and the drunkard-makers; harlotry and the harlot-makers; war and the war-makers. What will you do with them? What is the will of God that you should do with them? What does the message you have received from the Throne of God… say that you should do with them? You must fight them.

You must fight for the absolute rescue of these poor and deluded victims. Helping them is very good in many ways; but I am not quite sure of its advantages, if you leave them still gripped fast in the clutches of the devil. Anyway, you must not be content with: 1) Merely ameliorating their temporal miseries, or of delivering them from them. 2) Instructing them. 3) Changing their outward habits. 4) Attaching them to your corps, or making them helpers in your work. You must not stop short of actually rescuing them from their sins, and changing their hearts, and making them into soldiers of Jesus Christ…

You must do this by making people know the truth. As regards God. Bring him home to them. Make them realize that he is, and that his nature is love, justice, purity. By making them realize the truth as regards sin… Make them feel something of what he feels about their sinning against him. By making them feel the truth as regards judgment, Heaven, and Hell.[2]

**Thank you, Lord, for this reminder of what the Church is about – rescuing people from darkness and presenting the light and love of God to them. Touch your Church with a new awareness of this reality, so that it may colour everything we do. Amen.**

1 1 Peter 5:8

2 From *The Seven Spirits.*

# August 31st

When they arrived at the place where God had told him to go, Abraham built an altar and arranged the wood on it. Then he tied his son, Isaac, and laid him on the altar on top of the wood. And Abraham picked up the knife to kill his son as a sacrifice

**(Genesis 22:9–10 *NLT*)**

God said to Abraham, "Do this," [sacrifice Isaac] and although it seemed like giving up all the light and joy of existence, yet he did it. This was the kind of obedience Abraham gave Jehovah. His was none of your cheap, easy, self-considerate kind of service that cost him little, consisting mostly of form and ceremony and talk – service which was great in sentiment and profession of what it would do, but which edged off all the commandments and duties which meant hardship and suffering and loss.

Oh, listen to this, all ye people, who talk about all the hard things you have to do for God. Come along, my comrades, with the stories of the sacrifices, and presentations, and mobbings, and fightings, and temptations you have to endure in following Jesus Christ. Look at this old patriarch. Journey with him. Enter into his feelings. Share his anguish. And then stand prepared for the same path of consecration that he trod. God asks the same spirit from every one of his servants. There is no other way.

To obey God then, as now, meant often, if not always, to disobey men. To please God meant then, as now, to displease yourself and your neighbours and the devil, and to make things very unpleasant all round in a general sort of way. To keep right with God by doing his will was, as now, to get wrong and keep wrong with kindred and friends and fellow-workmen, and many others with whom it is far more pleasant to keep right. Many people spend a lifetime trying to harmonize the service of God and man, and to please at the same time God and the devil. But it is impossible, my comrades. There are not two standards of service – one a painful one for Abraham, and the other an easy one for you. To obey God you must follow Abraham, and with an obedience that shrinks from no sacrifice. God desires to be obeyed… with him "to obey is better than sacrifice, and to hearken than the fat of rams".[1, 2]

**O Lord, this is a tough one! I want to obey you, but I also want to be on good terms with people – so please show me how to walk that particular tightrope for Jesus! Amen.**

1 1 Samuel 15:22 *KJV*
2 From *Salvation Soldiery.*

# September 1st

We hear that some among you are idle... They are not busy

(2 Thessalonians 3:11 *NIV*)

My dear comrades, having dealt with the question of the quality of our work, let me now proceed to consider the question of the quantity. Is the amount of work a man does a matter of choice with him? Or if he can manage to get along without any work at all, is he at liberty to do so?

To this question I reply that, in my judgment, a man ought not only to earnestly strive to do good work, but to definitely seek to do as much of it as he possible can. A notion very generally prevails that, instead of doing all the work of which you are capable, you should do as little as possible, and certainly no more than you are paid for. This, I admit, will be the wisest course to take, if you have work to do which is injurious to your fellow-creatures. In that case, as I have said before, I say again – that whether you get paid for it or not, you had better not do it at all.

But, if you can do anything that will be of any service to the people round about you, I recommend that you get at it; by all means, and do as much of it as possible, irrespective of the benefits you may reap from it, or indeed, whether you reap any benefit or not.

For instance, take the crowd of able-bodied men that you can see every day hanging about the public houses, or at the corners of the streets, for hours together, with their hands in their pockets, waiting for a gossip, or a drink, or a job, which the devil, as is the custom with idle hands, will not be slow to furnish. Would it not be better for them to be helping their wives with the washing, or lending a hand at cleaning up the house, or digging in somebody's garden, or mending the road, or doing anything else from the bare love of doing work that would be beneficial to their fellow men? I think it would – nay, I am sure of it.[1]

**Lord, give me wisdom to distinguish between rest and laziness. I would much rather wear away than rust away, so I ask you for plenty to do, and plenty that is useful. Amen.**

1 From *Religion for Every Day*.

# September 2nd

Children should not have to save up for their parents, but parents for their children

(2 Corinthians 12:14 *NIV*)

Thrift is a great virtue, no doubt. But how is thrift to benefit those who have nothing? What is the use of the gospel of thrift to a man who had nothing to eat yesterday, and has not threepence today to pay for his lodging tonight? To live on nothing a day is difficult enough, but to save on it would beat the cleverest political economist that ever lived. I admit without hesitation that any scheme which weakened the incentive to thrift would do harm. But it is a mistake to imagine that social damnation is an incentive to thrift. It operates least where its force ought to be most felt. There is no fear that any scheme that we can devise will appreciably diminish the deterrent influences which dispose a man to save.

Thrift is a great virtue, the inculcation of which must be constantly kept in view by all those who are attempting to educate and save the people. It is not in any sense a specific for the salvation of the lapsed and the lost. Even among the most wretched of the very poor, a poor man must have an object and a hope before he will save a half-penny. "… let us eat and drink; for to morrow we [die]"[1] sums up the philosophy of those who have no hope. In the thriftiness of the French peasant we see that the temptation of eating and drinking is capable of being resolutely subordinated to the superior claims of the accumulation of a dowry for the daughter, or for the acquisition of a little more land for the son.

Of the schemes of those who propose to bring in a new Heaven and a new earth by a more scientific distribution of the pieces of gold and silver in the trouser pockets of mankind, I need not say anything here. They may be good or they may not. I say nothing against any short cut to the Millennium that is compatible with the Ten Commandments.[2]

**Father, some have nothing, and cannot hope to save; they need all the help they can get. For those of us who are able to save, be it a little or a lot, bless us with wisdom and let us not forget charity. Amen.**

1 Ecclesiastes 8:15 *KJV*
2 From *In Darkest England and the Way Out.*

# September 3rd

Are not five sparrows sold for two pennies? Yet not one of them is forgotten by God

(Luke 12:6 *NIV*)

The dark and dismal jungle of pauperism, vice, and despair is the inheritance to which we have succeeded from the generations and centuries past, during which wars, insurrections, and internal trouble left our forefathers small leisure to attend to the well-being of the sunken tenth.[1] Now that we have happened upon more fortunate times, let us recognize that we are our brother's keepers, and set to work, regardless of party distinctions and religious differences, to make this world of ours a little bit more like home for those whom we call our brethren.

The problem, it must be admitted, is by no means a simple one; nor can anyone accuse me… of having minimized the difficulties which heredity, habit, and surroundings place in the way of its solution, but unless we are prepared to fold our arms in selfish ease and say that nothing can be done, and thereby doom those lost millions to remediless perdition in this world, to say nothing of the next, the problem must be solved in some way. But in what way? This is the question. It may tend, perhaps, to the crystallization of opinion on this subject if I lay down, with such precision as I can command, what must be the essential elements of any scheme likely to command success.

The first essential that must be borne in mind as governing every scheme that may be put forward is that it must change the man when it is his character and conduct which constitute the reasons for his failure in the battle of life. No change in circumstances, no revolution in social conditions, can possibly transform the nature of man. Some of the worst men and women in the world, whose names are chronicled by history with a shudder of horror, were those who had all the advantages that wealth, education, and station could confer, or ambition could attain.

The supreme test of any scheme for benefiting humanity lies in the answer to the question, "What does it make of the individual? Does it quicken his conscience, does it soften his heart?"[2]

**Father, if my daily activity and witness makes little difference to the individuals I meet in the street, in the supermarket, on the other end of the telephone, then something is probably amiss. Grant me grace to prize and highly value the individual, so that my life may make a positive difference in theirs. Amen.**

1 "If Mr Booth has not inaugurated remedial work among the submerged tenth, he has certainly set the fashion of writing and talking about them." (Newspaper paragraph, 13 October 1891; newspaper unknown.)

2 From *In Darkest England and the Way Out.*

# September 4th

"For my thoughts are not your thoughts, neither are your ways my ways," declares the Lord

(Isaiah 55:8 *NIV*)

Ever so many things have happened at Darkington Corps... and, bless the Lord! The best of all is that the good work of soul-saving... has been going on ever since. It is true, we only get our captures, as the captain very properly calls them, by one here and one there; but I cannot help thinking that this may, after all, be one of God's intended plans, although Sergeant Splashem was complaining about it the other night as we walked home. "Sergeant-Major," says he, "why don't we have great sweeps of conversions like what we read of in the apostles' days[1] – such as the General gets in those great demonstrations they tell us about week after week in *The War Cry*? Why don't we have wonderful things like them done at Darkington? That is what I want to know."

"Well, Sergeant," says I, "that is a difficult question you put to me; but the way I look at the subject is like this. You see, when the General goes along, there is a great fight, and half the officers of a division go up to help him; and it would be a pity if something extraordinary didn't happen at any place with such a lot of hands on the job.

"It was like that at Jerusalem, I suppose, on the day of Pentecost. All the officers in the country were at work that day, and they were all fully of the Holy Spirit into the bargain, and they rushed all over the place like mad people, preaching and praying, and inviting people to be saved. If only we could get as many officers, and locals [local officers], and soldiers at Darkington all as red-hot as those men and women were on that wonderful day, something out of the common would happen here, I can tell you.

"But, then," says I, "look here, Sergeant. Don't you think that this slow way of doing things, as you find fault with, may, after all, be as much God's plan as the great sweeps that you admire so much?"[2]

**Lord of the harvest, sometimes we long for more and more people to be saved, and to join our churches. Help us to trust you with those who make their way to faith one by one. We don't pretend to understand your ways and methods, but we do trust in your unfailing love and mercy towards the lost. I pray for my church to see converts. Amen.**

1 Acts 2
2 From *Sergeant-Major Do-Your-Best.*

# September 5th

Give to the one who asks you

(Matthew 5:42 *NIV*)

Comrades and friends, I want to say something upon a subject which is often brought before you; though not always, I fear, in the most welcome manner; and that is, begging. The begging to which I refer is: Begging for money to help the poor and suffering. Begging for the cost of the salvation war; for saving the souls of men. Begging for the maintenance and extension of the Kingdom of God upon earth.

Some people do not like being begged from, and that for various reasons. With some it is heartlessness. They do not care what becomes of either the bodies or the souls of others. With others it is meanness. They do not like to give anything to anyone, for any purpose whatever.

Some people do not like the duty of begging from others. I must say there is some begging I do not like myself. For instance, I do not like begging that hinders more important work. Nor do I like begging that is promoted by objectionable means, such as falsehood or raffles, or other worldly methods. But when I come to the genuine thing, that is, begging for a right object, and at the right time, in a religious spirit and in a lawful manner, I confess to having no objection to begging.

I am a beggar by trade. I was apprenticed to it at fifteen years of age; that is, on the day I got converted. I have been begging ever since, and shall be begging, I expect – or, at least, I hope – till I go to the grave, and possibly for ever afterwards. I have had a measure of success in my calling; having, by the grace of God, been enabled to collect directly and indirectly as much money for the cause of Christ, for the salvation of souls, and the relief of human suffering, as any man living or, perhaps, as any man who ever did live.

The Spirit of the Living God goes about the world begging. He begs by his holy word. He begs by his servants. He is begging all the time.[1]

**Father, deliver us from the evils of heartlessness and meanness. When we meet beggars, prompt us to buy them a pie and a hot drink, even if we feel it unwise to give them cash. When we meet with charity collectors in the street or on the doorstep, inspire generosity if we agree with the aims of their collection. Amen.**

1 From *The Founder's Messages to Soldiers*.

# September 6th

He looked up and saw the rich putting their gifts into the treasury, and He saw also a certain poor widow putting in two mites. So He said, "Truly I say to you that this poor widow has put in more than all; for all these out of their abundance have put in offerings for God, but she out of her poverty put in all the livelihood that she had"

(Luke 21:1–4 *NKJV*)

As a beggar, I have my Heavenly Father for a pattern and example. He is the greatest beggar in the universe. Nearly all the love and service he gets from men is got by begging for it. He begs for possession of the hearts of men. As soon as I could understand anything, God sent his Son knocking with his wounded hands at the door of my soul, begging me to give him my heart. The Holy Spirit begs men to help him in the discharge of his difficult task. He wants them to cooperate with him in saving the world from sin, suffering, and Hell. He begs for the money of men. God knows that his work cannot be carried on without money.

Now, my comrades, you must follow the example of your Heavenly Father. You must go on begging for the poor. You cannot leave them to perish for the want of a piece of bread. You cannot leave the wretched drunkards, or the daughters of shame, or the criminals, to die in their wickedness, when a little help will deliver them. You must beg for money to pay for the expenses connected with your citadels, and to generally extend the holy war. You must beg for the support of your missions to the poor heathen, who are ignorant of the blessings provided for them.

You must beg with a holy boldness. Hold up your heads, and push your claims. You have no need to blush or tremble in the discharge of his duty. If you were begging for yourselves you might be ashamed, and stammer out your request, but you are not. You must beg without growing weary. Whether you succeed or fail, whether you are blessed or cursed, you must never tire. You must beg from the rich. Remind them that what they give may bring a blessing down upon what they still enjoy. You must beg from the poor. Why should the poor of our time be denied the privilege and thereby the same blessed commendation of Jesus Christ which fell to the widow for giving her two mites, nearly 2,000 years ago?[1]

**Father, if I'm honest, asking for money doesn't always come easy; it is not something I enjoy doing. I pray, therefore, for holy courage to support your works as best I can by collecting and fundraising to the best of my ability, when there is a need. Amen.**

1 From *The Founder's Messages to Soldiers.*

# September 7th

Each of you must show great respect for your mother and father

(Leviticus 19:3 *NLT*)

Is family government an important matter? Yes, most important. If the good government of a nation is essential to the welfare of the people – if their happiness physically, socially, and politically, and – we were going to say – religiously, to some extent, rises and falls with the character of its government (which it most certainly does), how much more intimately must every interest of children, earthly and heavenly, depend upon the good government of the home in which they live?…

Firmness is essential to a good family government. Indeed, government of any sort without it is an impossibility; and children, as well as everybody else in the home, if things are to go with any degree of smoothness, regularity, and order, must be made to feel that there is a strong directing will at the head of affairs.

Children are usually full of life, vigour, and spirit, and must in their first years be made to do things, not only because they are right, or because they ought to do them, but because they must. Children, during the early part of their lives, are little better than mere animals; influenced by their instincts and feelings, rather than by their reason. So to manage them easily – indeed to manage them at all, they must thoroughly know and understand that they are "under authority".

A good family government must mean, therefore, that there is a head to whom all look up. Nominally that head is the father, but between father and mother there should be such union of spirit, aim, and will, that both shall be felt to be as one. The expressed will of the one will then be taken as that of the other, and the children will know no difference in power and authority between the one and the other. This is the order of God, who puts both parents conjointly over their children…

We would say to parents, ponder this well over. How much depends upon the presentation of this unity in front of the children, it is not very easy to describe.[1]

**My prayer today is for parents who have not yet mastered the art of a united front, and whose homes are sometimes in disarray. Help them, Lord, for the sake of their children. Lead them to people who can advise them well, so that harmony might prevail. Amen.**

1 From *The Training of Children*.

# September 8th

Prepare for war!

(Joel 3:9 *NIV*)

What a remarkable example is being set before our Army in connection with the history of this country! There it is, written in big letters in every newspaper, more or less throughout the civilized world; so that indeed he who runs may read it.

I mean the war business which is raging in the Sudan, where bloody battles are being fought, all manner of hardships are being endured, and all manner of sacrifices are being made. Nay, not only is this war raging, for surely it is being waged at fever heat in the minds and hearts of the people in the City of London, and in all the principal cities and towns and villages of this land – notwithstanding its loud and often repeated boast that it is under the dominion and government of the Prince of Peace.[1] But it is the prince of war that rules just now – with a vengeance. For in all the clubs and public houses and parks and village greens, and at firesides, and even in churches and chapels, men talk and pray about the strife. Nay, it may be said that in the hearts of multitudes of men cannon are being fired and rifles shouldered, and that their very thoughts and wishes breathe threatenings and fire.

"Khartoum is fallen!" "Is Gordon dead or alive?" "If dead, let him be avenged!" "If alive, let him be rescued!" These are the questions and answers that come and go unbidden to men's lips. "Why does not the army march to Khartoum – march on Metammeh – march on Berber – march everywhere?"[2] Why? Something must be done – quick – that will strike terror into the enemy. Mighty issues are at stake, and so the authority goes out to those in command to do the work thoroughly, no matter what it costs or what suffering it inflicts. "Push the war!" "Send out men!" "Never mind the money!" "Retreat is impossible; we are in for victory!"

Now we say that in this mode of waging war, the children of this world are wiser, and more thorough-going and, it seems to us, more self-sacrificing than the professed children of light.[3]

**Lord, may your Church ever be gracious enough, and humble enough, to learn from others, so that pride never stands in the way of progress and success. Amen.**

1 Isaiah 9:6

2 The Battle of Khartoum, Siege of Khartoum or Fall of Khartoum (1884–85) was the conquest of British-held Khartoum by the Mahdist forces led by Muhammad Ahmad. Major-General Charles George Gordon, British Army officer and administrator, was killed in the conflict.

3 From *The General's Letters*.

# September 9th

If the trumpet does not sound a clear call, who will get ready for battle?

**(1 Corinthians 14:8 *NIV*)**

We Salvationists are always glorying in the death of Jesus Christ, and testifying to the benefits that have flown from it to mankind. Perhaps no text is more frequently quoted than the words of John, "the blood of Jesus Christ [God's] Son cleanseth us from all sin".[1]... Not only do we glory in the sacrifice of Jesus Christ as something that happened 2,000 years ago, and wear the sign of it on our uniform, but we glory in the belief that unnumbered multitudes of our fellow-creatures have been washed in the fountain that was opened for sin and uncleanness when he died upon the cross. Nay, we go further than this, and triumph in the fact that his shed blood has brought salvation to our own hearts, lives, and homes...

This personal experience of salvation has much to do with the desire of the true Salvationist, that the benefits brought to us by the sacrifice of the cross may swell and spread until the knowledge of the Lord covers the earth as well as the waters of the sea.[2] It lays on our hearts the obligation to proclaim to the sons and daughters of men, so far as we have opportunity, the virtue and value of Christ's blood. It makes us feel like the man who said, "Were the highest hills my platform, and had I a voice as loud as the trumpet of doom, I would sound throughout Jehovah's boundless empire the glorious truth, that Jesus shed his blood for all mankind."

Now, this doctrine, which is one of the foundation truths of The Salvation Army is, I fear, only faintly understood and feebly grasped, and therefore imperfectly proclaimed at the present day. On this subject, however, the trumpets of many of the leaders of God's professed people are, I fear, giving a very uncertain sound. The blood of Christ is not too often mentioned by them; and, when it is, only in a questioning spirit, and with bated breath. Others, supposed to be sound in the faith, have, of late, taken an open stand against the doctrine of the atonement.[3]

**Saviour, in my daily striving, may this message be heard. So help me, God. Amen.**

1 1 John 1:7 *KJV*
2 Habakkuk 2:14
3 From *The Founder's Messages to Soldiers.*

# September 10th

### Go out into the world uncorrupted, a breath of fresh air in this squalid and polluted society

**(Philippians 2:15 *The Message*)**

There are multitudes, myriads, of men and women, who are floundering in the horrible quagmire beneath the burden of a load too heavy for them to bear; every plunge they take forward lands them deeper; some have ceased even to struggle, and lie prone in the filthy bog, slowly suffocating, with their manhood and womanhood all but perished. It is no use standing on the firm bank of the quaking morass and anathematizing these poor wretches; if you are to do them any good, you must give them another chance to get on their feet, you must give them the firm foothold upon which they can once more stand upright, and you must build stepping stones across the bog to enable them safely to reach the other side.

Favourable circumstances will not change a man's heart or transform his nature, but unpropitious circumstances may render it absolutely impossible for him to escape, no matter how he may desire to extricate himself. The first step with these helpless, sunken creatures is to create the desire to escape, and then provide the means for doing so. In other words, give the man another chance…

Any remedy worthy of consideration must be on a scale commensurate with the evil with which it proposes to deal. It is no use trying to bail out the ocean with a pint pot. This evil is one whose victims are counted by the million. The army of the lost in our midst exceeds the numbers of that multitudinous host which Xerxes led from Asia to attempt the conquest of Greece.[1] Pass in parade those who make up the submerged tenth, count the paupers indoor and outdoor, the homeless, the starving, the criminals, the lunatics, the drunkards, and the harlots – and yet do not give way to despair! Even to attempt to save a tithe of this host requires that we should put much more force and fire into our work than has hitherto been exhibited by anyone. There must be no philanthropic tinkering, as if this vast sea of human misery were contained in the limits of a garden pond.[2]

**Lord, you send your people to the rescue, with a gospel of grace. Where would you have me go today?**

1 The Persian army was alleged by the ancient sources to have numbered over 1 million but is today considered to have been much smaller (various figures are given by scholars ranging between about 100,000 and 150,000).

2 From *In Darkest England and the Way Out.*

# September 11th

A crown of beauty instead of ashes, the oil of joy instead of mourning, and a garment of praise instead of a spirit of despair

(Isaiah 61:3 *NIV*)

Difficult as the task may be, it is not one we can neglect. When Napoleon was compelled to retreat under circumstances which rendered it impossible for him to carry off his sick and wounded, he ordered his doctors to poison every man in the hospital. A general has before now massacred his prisoners rather than allow them to escape. These lost ones are prisoners of society; they are the sick and wounded in our hospitals. What a shriek would arise from the civilized world if it were proposed to administer tonight to every one of these millions such a dose of morphine that they would sleep to wake no more. But so far as they are concerned, would it not be much less cruel thus to end their life than to allow them to drag on day after day, year after year, in misery, anguish, and despair, driven into vice and hunted into crime, until at last disease harries them into the grave?…

The triumphs of science deal so much with the utilization of waste material that I do not despair of something effectual being accomplished in the utilization of this waste human product. The refuse which was a drug and a curse to our manufacturers, when treated under the hands of the chemist, has been the means of supplying us with dyes rivalling in loveliness and variety the hues of the rainbow. If the alchemy of science can extract beautiful colours from coal tar, cannot divine alchemy enable us to evolve gladness and brightness out of the agonized hearts and dark, dreary, loveless lives of these doomed myriads? Is it too much to hope that in God's world God's children may be able to do something, if they set to work with a will, to carry out a plan of campaign against these great evils which are the nightmare of our existence?

The remedy, it may be, is simpler than some imagine. The key to the enigma may lie closer to our hands than we have any idea of… it is only stubborn, reckless perseverance that can hope to succeed.[1]

**God of transformation, you alone have great power to change lives, change circumstances, and change hearts. I praise you that no situation is beyond the reach of your healing touch. I bring to you today those issues known to me that appear to be hopeless. Bless your Church with a perseverance based on faith. Amen.**

1 From *In Darkest England and the Way Out.*

# September 12th

God said, "Take your son, your only son, whom you love – Isaac – and go to the region of Moriah. Sacrifice him there as a burnt offering on a mountain I will show you." Early the next morning Abraham got up and loaded his donkey. He took with him two of his servants and his son Isaac

(Genesis 22:2–3 *NIV*)

Abraham's obedience was of the kind that went forward independent of all human encouragement. He does not seem to have had a solitary heart to confide in, or to lean upon. It is very improbable that he should have breathed a word to Sarah. He spared her tender soul. It would have possibly been more than a mother's feelings could have endured. And all alone he received the message; all alone he carried the burden of that [weight] upon his heart. Not a word could he whisper to the servant; not a word, above all, could he breathe to Isaac. What a three days in the wilderness it must have been! What an opportunity for the devil. Seldom equalled. Oh, it must have been a terrible ordeal for the grand old patriarch!

Oh, man's is a clinging nature, always feeling about for other hearts of kindred mould to lean upon. And sympathy, human sympathy, is a very tower of strength. The hurrahs of the bystanders, the cheers of comrades, have carried men many a time through deeds of daring and suffering and sacrifice, far beyond ordinary human strength and endurance. All this was denied Abraham. Still on he went. He walked the ocean of this agony all alone.

So, more or less, every true man of God has to stand alone. There are sorrows and questionings, and sometimes very demons in his own breast, and oft-times outside of it, with which a man has to fight, with no human heart or hand to help him.

Abraham exhibited the true spirit of obedience in obeying God straight away. I don't know when he received the message, probably during the night, and the next morning he was away to fulfil the command. Here was no waiting – no begging for time to make preparation. It would have taken some people I know a long, long time to get ready for such a terrible business. But not so with Abraham; he only needed to know that God wanted his son; and although it was a dreadfully painful trouble to him, he rose early in the morning to obey.[1]

**Lord, if and when I am called to serve you privately, in unseen ways, help me to do so. I praise you because your Spirit is my unfailing Counsellor and confidant. Amen.**

1 From *Salvation Soldiery.*

# September 13th

O Lord my God; light up my eyes, lest I sleep the sleep of death

(Psalm 13:3 *ESV*)

Men sleep on the very verge of Hell. You must fight to awaken them. They walk about in their sleep, and live as in a dream. Their business, their pleasure, their sorrows, their miseries, hold them fast in a slumber nearly as deep as death itself – nay, they are dead while they are alive.

You must awaken them, you know how to waken people ordinarily who are asleep. You rush in upon them. You make them feel, hear, see something. You startle them, you change the current of their thoughts, you inflict a passing pain, or do something entirely unexpected. So here with these sleeping souls. You must do something. You must come in upon them in their business, and amidst their amusements. You must shake them in their sorrows, and in their bitter miseries. Startle them out of the fatal stupor in which they stand all unheeding on the brink of a burning Hell. Fight the sleeping sickness.

You must fight to make men repent. Not merely to listen to you and wish they were better, but to be sorry, angry with themselves, broken-hearted because they have been so wicked and so bad as to lift themselves up against God. He willeth not the death of a sinner, but that all men should repent.[1] Your business is to fight for their repentance. You must do all this – amongst other means, by your own talking and appeals. Especially will this apply to your meetings. A satisfactory meeting, in my opinion, has always meant a real fight – a regular struggle to get something done [for] somebody for their good in time and in eternity. This applies no matter how large or small the meeting may be.

You must make men feel and see that there is a Heaven, that there is a Hell, and that there will certainly be a great Judgment Bar, before which they must stand. You must make them know the truth as regards the sacrifice of Jesus Christ and its sufficiency. Publish abroad the efficacy of the precious blood, and all the blessings that flow from salvation.[2]

**God of life, I think of all the meetings and services taking place in my church this week, this month, this year; graciously pour your Holy Spirit upon them so that they may be spiritual arenas of conflict and victory. May many awake to a bright new dawn in Christ. Amen.**

1 2 Peter 3:9
2 From *The Seven Spirits.*

# September 14th

Take a lesson from the ants, you lazybones. Learn from their ways and become wise!

(Proverbs 6:6 *NLT*)

At a railway junction where I had to wait the other day for a train, I saw about twenty navvies[1] sitting or standing alongside the line, some of them smoking, but otherwise doing nothing. It was a very cold, raw morning, with an east wind blowing up the gully in which the station stood, that seemed to pierce your very bones.

For a time I could not understand why these men should be shivering alongside their work, without striking a stroke, while I could see, with half an eye, that if they had been picking and shovelling, they would have been warm, and comfortable, while the work would have gone forward into the bargain. A little reflection, however, showed me that it was the breakfast hour, and that having concluded their meal, they were simply waiting for the allotted time to elapse before they started afresh.

This method of doing things appeared to me to be wrong, both in principle and practice – anyway, wrong for a Salvationist, who looks at his life from the standpoint of the Bible, which teaches him the duty of doing as much good work for his fellow men as possible. Instead of standing there, shivering, waiting for the clock to strike, it would, I imagine, have been better for these navvies to have resumed their task as soon after the meal was concluded as they reasonably could, and I see several advantages that would have resulted from their doing so…

They would have been more comfortable at work than they were standing idle. The improvement they were effecting on the railway… would have been forwarded. Their employers would have been pleased with the disinterested manner in which they pushed their business forward, and would have been likely to have given them some extra payment… They would have done this, had they been working for themselves… They would have allowed no reasonable thing to prevent them getting on with their task if they had been doing it for their Heavenly Master, and had been influenced by the desire to please him.[2]

**Father, a decent break for a well-earned breakfast is one thing, but loafing around doing nothing is pointless. Preserve your Church from pointlessness! Amen.**

1 Navvy, a shorter form of navigator (UK) or navigational engineer (US), is particularly applied to describe the manual labourers working on major civil engineering.

2 From *Religion for Every Day*.

# September 15th

## He gave him the plans of all that the Spirit had put in his mind
(1 Chronicles 28:12 *NIV*)

I propose to devote the bulk of this volume to setting forth what can practically be done with one of the most pressing parts of the problem, namely, that relating to those who are out of work, and who, as the result, are more or less destitute. I have many ideas of what might be done with those who are at present cared for in some measure by the State, but I will leave those ideas for the present.

It is not urgent that I should explain how our Poor Law system could be reformed, or what I should like to see done for the lunatics in asylums, or the criminals in gaols. The persons who are provided for by the State, we will, therefore, for the moment, leave out of the count. The indoor paupers, the convicts, the inmates of the lunatic asylums are cared for, in a fashion, already. But, over and above all these, there exists some hundreds of thousands who are not quartered on the State, but who are living on the verge of despair, and who at any moment, under circumstances of misfortune, might be compelled to demand relief or support in one shape or another. I will confine myself, therefore, for the present to those who have no helper.

It is possible, I think probable, if the proposals which I am now putting forward are carried out successfully in relation to the lost, homeless, and helpless of the population, that many of those who are at the present moment in somewhat better circumstances will demand that they also shall be allowed to partake in the benefits of the scheme [Booth's "Darkest England" project]. But upon this, also, I remain silent.

I merely remark that we have, in the recognition of the importance of discipline and organization, what may be called regimented cooperation, a principle that will be found valuable for solving many social problems other than that of destitution. Of these plans, which are at present being brooded over with a view to their realization when the time is propitious and the opportunity occurs, I shall have something to say.[1]

**Father, it is gracious of you to share your plans with us, and to instruct us in your ways. Thank you, Lord, that you do not leave us ignorant or expect us to manage without knowing what it is you require of us. Amen.**

1 From *In Darkest England and the Way Out.*

# SEPTEMBER 16TH

"THE SPIRIT OF THE LORD IS ON ME, BECAUSE HE HAS ANOINTED ME TO PROCLAIM GOOD NEWS TO THE POOR. HE HAS SENT ME TO PROCLAIM FREEDOM FOR THE PRISONERS AND RECOVERY OF SIGHT FOR THE BLIND, TO SET THE OPPRESSED FREE"

(Luke 4:18 *NIV*)

Men perish in ignorance. You are sent to instruct them in the things that belong to their peace.[1] Men are blind. You must make them see. This is your duty. You must make them see the evils of sin. You must make them see the dangers of damnation. They go over the precipice because they don't see it. They don't see the preciousness of the divine favour. You must show it to them. They don't see the beauty of believing. You must prove it to them.

Men are deaf. You must make them hear the voice of God calling them to his arms, imploring them to come and help. Men are insensible to the charms of salvation. You must make them feel. This is your business.

[To] do this effectively you must be true yourselves. You must trust yourselves to know the meaning, and important, and reason of the truths you proclaim to others. All over the world the cry is for more secular knowledge. Voices can be heard in all directions crying: "Give us more scientific knowledge, give us more technical knowledge, give us more knowledge about commerce and trade, give us more mechanical knowledge, give us more military knowledge." The cry is being attended to, and everywhere men and women and children are hard at work with the prevalent answer to it. Men are learning how to make machinery, explore the mazes of science, make fortunes, etc.

There is no denying the fact that twenty years ago the Russians would have swept the Japanese off both sea and land in a very short time. What has made the difference? Knowledge. The Japanese now know as much, man for man, as the Russians, if not more. All that is necessary to be believed in order [for] your own salvation and the salvation of those about you with whom you have to deal, is already revealed. You do not need to study in order to discover the foundation principles that have to do with the salvation of the world. There they are, revealed and unalterable, for you to examine, receive, believe, and obey.[2]

**I praise you, Lord, because you have provided all that needs to be known for salvation. Thank you for the day that knowledge came into my life. I give you the glory. Amen.**

1 Luke 19:42
2 From *The Seven Spirits.*

# September 17th

I WILL HURRY, WITHOUT DELAY, TO OBEY YOUR COMMANDS

(Psalm 119:60 *NLT*)

Let us have obedience, whether sightless or seeing. There is plenty of obedience blind enough to human laws and regulations. Earthly lords, and commanders, and masters exact it with all rigour and strictness, and but for it in soldiers, and sailors, and workers, and children, in short, in men generally, this world would soon come to a standstill. And yet, in dealing with God, there are multitudes whose attitude seems to say, "I want to know what I shall gain in this, or why should I inconvenience myself by doing that? Until I can understand the atonement and the resurrection and the judgment, I decline to trouble myself to do as God wants me," and, quibbling and waiting for the Almighty to enable them to comprehend the infinite, they stand out against the divine requirements, and perish.

With Abraham there was no quibbling, or cavilling, about the rightness or wrongness of the command. There is nothing in the narrative to lead us to imagine that he lost any time in arguing the matter over with the Lord. He does not seem to have regarded the matter as being peculiarly mysterious, or waited until Jehovah gave such explanations as satisfied him about the wisdom and profitableness of the course he wished him on this occasion to take. He did not understand the why and wherefore of the matter, of that we may be assured; one thing, and I should think that was the only thing he did understand about the matter, was that God wanted him to offer Isaac for a burnt offering on Moriah.

He only needed to know that God wanted his son; and although it was a dreadfully painful trouble to him, he rose early in the morning to obey. Now, my comrades, that is the way to do the will of God; no hanging back, and begging for time, and then being driven to it with all the reluctance that an ox goes to the slaughter. "Straight away!" is the word, whether you like the business or not. Does God want you to do it? Then hurry up! Make haste to do his will![1]

**Father, if I need to do something for you today, help me to overcome any feelings of fear, reluctance, or procrastination. Thank you, Lord, for your presence when difficult challenges arise. Amen.**

1 From *Salvation Soldiery.*

# September 18th

The Lord God took the man and put him in the Garden of Eden to work it and take care of it

(Genesis 2:15 *NIV*)

In describing the illness of her husband the other day, and her own part in nursing him, a woman informed me that she had not taken her clothes off for her ordinary rest for seventeen days and nights. She did not complain of this hardship; on the contrary, she was pleased at having been favoured with an opportunity of proving her love for her partner. Her affection was the mainspring of her sacrifice. Now, love for his earthly master and his Heavenly Lord should be the ruling principle with every Salvationist in his daily toil; and when this is the case, his strength and the claims of other duties will alone limit the amount of work he will do…

In settling how much work he will do, a man must have due regard to the claims of his own health. If he rushes at his work without due discretion, and does more than his strength will reasonably allow, he will probably break down, and so prevent his working altogether, or for a season, at least. Whereas, if he exhausts no more energy than he can recover by sleep and food and rest, at the time, he can go steadily forward, and by doing so, accomplish a great deal more in the long run than he would by temporary extravagant exertion.

When speaking on this subject, I sometimes say that I use my body as I should a horse, if I had one – that is, I should not seek to get the most labour out of him for a week, regardless of the future, but I should feed and manage him with a view to getting the most I could get out of him all the year round. That is doubtless the way a man should use his body, and to do this he should take as much time for his food and daily rest as is necessary to replace the energies he has used up by his work.

My dear comrades, it is the duty of every Salvationist to do as much good work as is reasonably possible.[1]

**I thank you, Lord, for the privilege of work, and for all its benefits. Likewise, I thank you for rest and relaxation. Thank you, Creator God, for your loving awareness of our every need, and all that enables us to function well. Amen.**

1 From *Religion for Every Day.*

# September 19th

I HAVE HEARD THAT YOU ARE ABLE TO GIVE INTERPRETATIONS AND TO SOLVE DIFFICULT PROBLEMS

(Daniel 5:16 *NIV*)

What is the outward and visible form of the problem of the unemployed? Alas! We are all too familiar with it for any lengthy description to be necessary. The social problem presents itself before us whenever a hungry, dirty, and ragged man stands at our door asking if we can give him a crust or a job. That is the social question. What are you to do with that man? He has no money in his pocket, all the he can pawn he has pawned long ago, his stomach is as empty as his purse, and the whole of the clothes upon his back, even if sold on the best terms, would not fetch a shilling.

There he stands, your brother, with sixpennyworth of rags to cover his nakedness from his fellow men and not sixpennyworth of victuals within his reach. He asks for work, which he will set to even on an empty stomach and in his ragged uniform, if so be that you will give him something for it, but his hands are idle, for no one employs him. What are you to do with that man? That is the great note of interrogation that confronts society today. Not only in overcrowded England, but in newer countries beyond the sea, where society has not yet provided a means by which the men can be put upon the land and the land be made to feed the men. To deal with this man is the problem of the unemployed.

To deal with him effectively you must deal with him immediately; you must provide him in some way or other at once with food, and shelter, and warmth. Next you must find him something to do that will test the reality of his desire to work. This test must be more or less temporary, and should be of such a nature as to prepare him for making a permanent livelihood. Then, having trained him, you must provide him wherewithal to start life afresh.

What we have to do in the philanthropic sphere is to find something analogous to the engineers' parallel bars.[1]

**Thank you, Father, for those you gift with the ability to solve problems; thank you for the gift of practical wisdom. I pray for those who will grapple this day with complex social issues and matters of human welfare. Bless and direct their decision-making. Bless your Church as it seeks ways to alleviate suffering. Amen.**

1 From *In Darkest England and the Way Out.*

# September 20th

SOLOMON'S PROVISION FOR ONE DAY WAS THIRTY MEASURES OF FINE FLOUR, AND THREESCORE MEASURES OF MEAL, TEN FAT OXEN, AND TWENTY OXEN OUT OF THE PASTURES, AND AN HUNDRED SHEEP, BESIDE HARTS, AND ROEBUCKS, AND FALLOWDEER, AND FATTED FOWL

(1 Kings 4:22–23 *KJV*)

As I rode through Canada and the United States some three years ago, I was greatly impressed with the superabundance of food which I saw at every turn. Oh, how I longed that the poor starving people, and the hungry children of the east of London and of other centres of our destitute populations should come into the midst of this abundance, but as it appeared impossible for me to take them to it, I secretly resolved that I would endeavour to bring some of it to them. I am thankful to say that I have already been able to do so on a small scale, and hope to accomplish it ere long on a much vaster one.

With this view, the first Cheap Food Depot was opened in the east of London[1] two and a half years ago. This has been followed by others, and we now have three establishments; others are being arranged for. Since the commencement in 1888, we have supplied over 3½ million meals. Some idea can be formed to the extent to which these Food and Shelter Depots have already struck their roots into the strata of society which it is proposed to benefit, by the following figures, which give the quantities of food sold during the year at our Food Depots.

Food sold in Depots and Shelters during 1889:

Soup 116,400 gallons. Bread 192.5 tons (106,946 4lb loaves). Tea 2.5 tons (46,980 gallons). Coffee 15 cwt (12,949 gallons). Cocoa 6 tons (29,229 gallons. Sugar 25 tons (300 bags). Potatoes 140 tons (2,800 bags). Flour 18 tons (180 sacks). Peaflour 28.5 tons (288 sacks). Oatmeal 3.5 tons (36 sacks). Rice 12 tons (120 sacks). Beans 12 tons (240 sacks). Onions and parsnips 12 tons (240 sacks). Jam 9 tons (2,880 jars). Marmalade 6 tons (1,920 jars). Meat 15 tons. Milk 14,300 quarts.

This includes returns from the Food Depots and five Shelters. I propose to multiply their number, to develop their usefulness… those who have visited our Depots will understand exactly what this means.[2]

**Father, these statistics are tremendous. I praise you for the work of The Salvation Army in feeding the hungry. I pray your providential blessing on every similar agency. Amen.**

1 Limehouse.
2 From *In Darkest England and the Way Out.*

# September 21st

"You shall open wide your hand to your brother, to the needy and to the poor, in your land"

(Deuteronomy 15:11 *ESV*)

At each of our Depots, which can be seen by anybody that cares to take the time to visit them, there are two departments, one dealing with food, the other with shelter. Of these both are worked together and minister to the same individuals. Many come for food who do not come for shelter, although most of those who come for shelter also come for food, which is sold on terms to cover, as nearly as possible, the cost price and working expenses of the establishment. In this our Food Depots differ from the ordinary soup kitchens. There is no gratuitous distribution of victuals. The following is our Price List:

For a child: Soup per basin 1/4d. Soup with bread 1/2d. Coffee or cocoa per cup 1/4d. Coffee or cocoa with bread and jam 1/2d.

For adults. Soup per basin 1/2d. Soup with bread 1d. Potatoes 1/2d. Cabbage 1/2d. Haricot beans 1/2d. Boiled jam pudding 1/2d. Boiled plum pudding 1d. Rice 1/2d. Baked plum 1/2d. Baked jam roll 1/2d. Meat pudding and potatoes 3d. Corned beef 2d. Corned mutton 2d. Coffee per cup 1/2d; per mug 1d. Cocoa per cup 1/2d; per mug 1d. Tea per cup 1/2d; per mug 1d. Bread and butter, jam, or marmalade per slice 1/2d. Soup in own jugs 1d per quart.[1]

Ready at 10 a.m.

A certain discretionary power is invested in officers in charge of the Depot, and they can in very urgent cases give relief, but the rule is for the food to be paid for, and the financial results show that working expenses are just about covered. These cheap Food Depots I have no doubt have been and are of great service to numbers of hungry, starving men, women, and children, at the prices just named, which must be within the reach of all, except the absolutely penniless; but it is the Shelter that I regard as the most useful feature in this part of our undertaking, for if anything is to be done to get hold of those who use the Depot, some more favourable opportunity must be afforded than is offered by the mere coming into the food store to get, perhaps, only a basin of soup.[2]

**Father, in a world that is all too often dominated by profit or greed, it is refreshing to read of an enterprise that was, so far as economically possible, charitable and altruistic. I pray your blessing on every such enterprise, where kindness is the currency. Amen.**

1 Penny (pre-decimal) = 1d (0.5 pence, strictly 1/240 of £1).
2 From *In Darkest England and the Way Out.*

# SEPTEMBER 22ND

[DO] NOT GIVING UP MEETING TOGETHER, AS SOME ARE IN THE HABIT OF DOING

(Hebrews 10:25 *NIV*)

Nothing, for a long time, has made a greater stir in our corps than what happened at one of our holiness meetings. You see, we had got into such an unbelieving way about it that nobody ever expected anything particular to come out of this kind of meeting, and it was done unto us according to our unbelief. I am ashamed to say that I never expected anything myself; and as to Sarah, why, she gave up going altogether; and when I said to her that she ought to make a try to be there sometimes, she up and says to me: "No, Sergeant-Major, Saturday is a very hard day for me. There's the extra clearing-up and the cooking of something a bit nice ready for Sunday – and there's mending the children's clothes – and there's getting them scrubbed a bit extra – and ever so many things that men can't be expected to know anything about, so that I'm pretty well played out when night comes round. Then, you see, I'm getting older, as you know, and I'm so tired on Sunday morning that except there is something at the hall to go for, why, then, I feel I can rest myself a little extra. Besides, it gives me a good chance of writing a bit of a letter to one of the children."

"But," says I, "Sarah, don't you think that being, as you are, the wife of the Sergeant-Major of the corps, you ought to attend an important service as the holiness meeting?"

"Well," says she, "I don't count your holiness meeting so very important, after all. It don't seem to me to be much better than a Free and Easy,[1] and not so good as some of them that I have seen; indeed, I can't see any difference. If I was the captain – which I could never have expected to be, but which, thank God, Jack is, and my Polly will be – I would not call such a meeting a holiness meeting at all."

Now, that was rather uncharitable of Sarah, wasn't it? And I told her so. But she said: "Sergeant-Major, don't you know that they say that you ought to 'call a spade a spade'?"[2]

**Father, I pray for those who lead worship services and who plan meetings for worship; bless them, Lord, for theirs is no easy job. It's unlikely they will ever please all the people all the time. May our worship always give priority to substance over style. Amen.**

1 Marked by informality and lack of constraint.
2 From *Sergeant-Major Do-Your-Best.*

# September 23rd

I pray that the sharing of your faith may become effective
(Philemon 1:6 *ESV*)

We do not require any new revelation as to the being of God, his nature and attributes, and the purpose he has in view in his dealings with men. Perhaps Enoch, and Moses, and John knew all that we know, and all that can be known down here. We do not require any new revelation respecting the person of Jesus Christ, his compassion, his miracles, his sacrifice, his resurrection and ascension, together with the virtue of his precious blood. We do not require any new revelation respecting the Holy Ghost. His ability to purify and inspire the soul of man with the fire of burning love for a dying world is manifested. We do not require any new revelation about salvation itself, or the conditions on which it may be won, in order to share in the enjoyment of all its benefits. We do not require any new revelation about the consequences of the acceptance or rejection of God's mercy. We may have yet more light spread upon these joys and sorrows, but the great unalterable facts are there to accept or reject.

But while we do not require any new revelation about salvation, or its author or character, there is room, nay, an absolute necessity, for definite improvement in the methods employed for its promulgation. The corn and oil carried from one part of the world to another are neither better nor worse than those precious commodities were in the Saviour's days. But there is a great improvement in the means of transit. I guess it would take Jacob's sons a longer period to traverse those couple of hundred miles between Canaan and the city of the Pharaohs[1] than it now takes to bring corn to England from the western prairies of the United States or the north-western portions of Canada, a distance of 5,000 miles or more.

Suppose there had been anything like an equivalent advance in the method of spreading abroad the Bread of life to that which has been made in the natural stuff of existence, the whole world would have been filled long ago with the song: "Glory to God in the highest".[2, 3]

**Lord, I have a calling to serve the present age. Please equip me to fulfil my mission in my generation. I know that you will – thank you. Amen.**

1 Genesis 46 – 47
2 Luke 2:14 *KJV*
3 From *The Seven Spirits.*

# September 24th

## Who is my neighbour?

(Luke 10:29 *NIV*)

I am continually haunted by the curiosity which seeks an answer to the questions: Does anyone read what I write? And reading, do they understand what I say? And understanding, do they agree with what is said? But what is most important of all: Is anybody the better for what I have written? However, without waiting for the answers to these questions, I suppose I must practise what I preach, and go on writing my letters as well as I possibly can. At the risk of being tedious, I propose again to mention some of the things for which I have contended, and to add one or two more arguments in their favour.

My contention, then, is that whether in the shop or on the ship, in the parlour or in the kitchen, in the factory or in the field, on the salvation platform or in the coal mine, whether officers or soldiers, we are all alike, as servants of God, under the obligation to do all we possibly can in the service of men; and to do it with the holy motive of pleasing our Heavenly Father. Here let me review my warrant for requiring from you the kind of loving labour that I advocate.

The Bible enjoins it… "Not with eyeservice, as menpleasers; but as the servants of Christ, doing the will of God from the heart; With good will doing service, as to the Lord, and not to men".[1] That is all I ask for. It is enjoined by the doctrine of brotherly love. I cannot understand how anyone can suppose, for a moment, that he is living a life acceptable to God unless he is striving, with all his might, to fulfil the divine command, "Thou shalt love thy neighbour as thyself."[2] Your master, or whoever has a claim upon your service, must be included in the term "neighbour"; and to comply with the command of the Saviour, you must work for that master, or mistress, as the case may be, from the voluntary principle of love rather than the earthly and selfish principle of gain.[3]

**Father, help me to see everyone as my neighbour, not just people who live in my neighbourhood, and not just those with whom I have plenty in common. Pour your love into my heart today, so that I may serve those I meet. Amen.**

1 Ephesians 6:6 *KJV*
2 Mark 12:31 *KJV*
3 From *Religion for Every Day.*

# September 25[th]

By this you know the Spirit of God: every spirit that confesses that Jesus Christ has come in the flesh is from God

(1 John 4:2 *ESV*)

The holiness meeting at Darkington Corps had got down about as low as it very well could; and one of the first things our captain made up his mind to was to raise it; and this is how he set about the work. He announced that on the next Sunday, instead of our regular holiness meeting, he was going to have a confessional meeting. And he made out that it was going to be a most important affair.

Now this announcement made quite a little stir, and a great deal of talk. Some of our people said the captain was going to bring in the Roman Catholics; and some said one thing, and some said another. But all said: "We must go and see what happens!"

Well, all that week the captain went round making the soldiers promise to attend, and pray hard that God might come on us all, and make the gathering a mighty time; and he was so earnest about it that nobody could very well refuse him. He got round Sarah and her difficulties very easily. I think he gave her a hint as to what he was after; for, after a little talk, she says: "Well, Captain, though I do get dreadfully tired by Saturday night – and since these east winds have begun to blow I do begin to have twinges of my old enemy, the rheumatics – still, if you are really going to try and do something fresh, I'll be there, and my little lot will all be there as well."

So, when Sunday morning came, we had quite a good company – at least three times as many as usual. Of course, we were mostly soldiers; but still, there was a sprinkling of our old friends the ex-soldiers, and those regular attendants whom you can't make anything of, but who seem to come because they can't stay away. The captain, God bless him, began the meeting in a serious sort of manner with the song, "Come, Saviour Jesus, from Above!"[1] "Comrades," he says, as he gave it out, "let us sing this song for ourselves, and think about it while we sing."[2]

**Lord, I am aware of two points in this story – the fact that the captain prayed that God might come to the people, and the fact that the people sang for Jesus to come amongst them. This reminds me of your Incarnation, Lord Jesus, when you came to earth in great humility, to show us the love of God. I praise you for doing so, and for reaching my heart by this; wonderful love, coming to me from Heaven above. Amen.**

1 Charles Wesley (1788–1851), "Come, Saviour Jesus, from Above!", Song No. 480, *The Salvation Army Song Book* (1986).

2 From *Sergeant-Major Do-Your-Best.*

# September 26th

When they reached the place God had told him about, Abraham built an altar there and arranged the wood on it. He bound his son Isaac and laid him on the altar, on top of the wood. Then he reached out his hand and took the knife to slay his son. But the angel of the Lord called out to him from heaven, "Abraham! Abraham!" "Here I am," he replied. "Do not lay a hand on the boy," he said. "Do not do anything to him. Now I know that you fear God, because you have not withheld from me your son, your only son."

(Genesis 22:9–12 *NIV*)

If, my comrades, you are not satisfied as to the call of Jehovah – not sure what he wants you to do in the matter – go and deliberate, consider, enquire, pray, but when the light has come, and you see clearly the divine will and the guiding hand, cease enquiring – the time for asking questions has gone by, and the hour of action has arrived. Away to your post. If you are bid to Moriah, go there, by the nearest path, and God help you, as he will help you, all the way and, when you arrive, there may be for you what there was for Abraham, an equally agreeable surprise.

The obedience that Abraham manifested here was thorough. Having put his hand to the plough – painful, and bloody, and agonizing as it was, and bid fair to continue to be – he looked not behind him.[1] Having begun the business, he went through with it, step by step, day by day. The nearer he came to Moriah, the firmer his resolution became. At last, the mount was reached, and the hour came, and the terrible act had to be performed, and now every feeling in his nature rises up against his compliance.

Some people imagine, or seem to imagine, that by some sort of conjuring or spiritual magic, all that was painful was extracted from the sacrifices and losses these old worthies endured in obeying God, that although the fire burnt sharp, it did not hurt. It is all a mistake – a foolish mistake. It was just as sorrowful and painful for Abraham to do this that we have been describing, as it would have been for any father who reads this, and just as difficult. But God said it must be done, and now that the moment has come, we may well enquire, will he flinch? Will he go through with it? Oh, yes! His heart is as strong as ever, and he holds not back his sword from blood. Isaac is offered! God saw it, stayed the descending arm and the gleaming knife, and accepted the will for the deed. Isaac was offered, and yet Isaac was saved.[2]

**Lord, grant me obedient, unflinching faith. May I too be found as one who fears – and loves – God. Amen.**

1 Luke 9:62
2 From *Salvation Soldiery.*

# September 27th

Jesus... said, "Go home to your own people and tell them how much the Lord has done for you, and how he has had mercy on you"

(Mark 5:19 *NIV*)

Two or three hundred men in the men's Shelter, or as many women in the women's Shelter, are collected together, most of them strange to each other, in a large room. They are all wretchedly poor – what are you to do with them?...

We hold a rousing salvation meeting. The officer in charge of the Depot, assisted by detachments from the Training Homes, conducts a jovial Free and Easy social evening. The girls have their banjos and their tambourines, and for a couple of hours you have as lively a meeting as you will find in London. There is prayer, short and to the point; there are addresses, some delivered by the leaders of the meeting, but most of them the testimonies of those who have been saved at previous meetings, and who, rising in their seats, tell their companions their experiences. Strange experiences they often are of those who have been down in the very bottomless depths of sin and vice and misery, but who have found at last firm footing on which to stand, and who are, as they say in all sincerity, "as happy as the day is long".

There is a joviality and a genuine good feeling at some of these meetings which is refreshing to the soul. There are all sorts and conditions of men; casuals, gaol-birds, Out-of-Works, who have come there for the first time, and who find men who last week or last month were even as they themselves are now – still poor but rejoicing in a sense of brotherhood and a consciousness of their being no longer outcasts and forlorn in this wide world. There are men who have at last seen revive before them a hope of escaping from that dreadful vortex into which their sins and misfortunes had drawn them, and being restored to those comforts that they had feared so long were gone for ever; nay, of rising to live a true and godly life.

These tell their mates how this has come about, and urge all who hear them to try for themselves and see whether it is a good and happy thing to be soundly saved.[1]

**Lord, today I pray courage for new converts, as they each begin to witness to their families, friends, workmates, and neighbours. The devil is sure to target them, so I pray that you will send angels to fend off every attack. May others be influenced by good words of testimony. Amen.**

1 From *In Darkest England and the Way Out.*

# SEPTEMBER 28TH

### DAYS ARE LIKE A FLEETING SHADOW

(Psalm 144:4 *NIV*)

If I could go back to the days of my youth…

I would take more care of my health. Many of you have heard me speak about health, and tried earnestly and successfully to forget, at the earliest opportunity, the common-sense counsels I gave you on those occasions. Others, I have reason to know, profited by them; but alas! They are only the exceptions. I am able to speak to you experimentally. I have had difficulties on this matter all my life. But until a serious attack of fever when I was sixteen, I scarcely knew what a day's sickness was. As far as my own feelings went, I did not know that I had any digestive organs until then. I went on raging and tearing, outdoors and in, night after night, with long business hours, day after day, and long walks to preaching engagements on a Sunday. Then the breakdown came, and I have suffered in consequence ever since. Nevertheless, I am still in the same work. I am now going to say "follow my example". I have no revelation, but my experience is an object-lesson which should, I think, be studied.

I would cultivate the habit of observation as a means of obtaining information. Not lazily allowing things to pass before my gaze without looking into them and asking myself, "How far can I profit by them?" But carefully studying men and women and children of all classes and conditions with a view of learning something from their badness and their goodness, their joys and their sorrows. I would ask questions as I went along when I saw things that I did not understand. And not let everything pass as a matter of course unworthy of my thought and understanding. I would seek to strengthen my power of thought. Thinking is one great want of the Salvation Army at the present day. Officers do not sufficiently say to themselves, "Is there no way of doing this work more effectively? How can I improve on this plan? How can I better understand this truth?"[1]

**Lord of my days, I have no idea at all how long I will live! That is entirely up to you. Today, I thank you for my life thus far, for granting me the sheer privilege of being alive. Teach me to count my days well, and to value time as a precious commodity, making the most of each moment, for I do not know which day will be my last. Amen.**

1 From *The Seven Spirits*.

# September 29th

THE HEART OF THE DISCERNING ACQUIRES KNOWLEDGE, FOR THE EARS OF THE WISE SEEK IT OUT

(Proverbs 18:15 *NIV*)

Now, my comrades, we must have more skill. Oh, what folly to talk against new measures. Let us have new and more ingenious inventions of every kind. Soldiers, rack your brains. Bring forth plans new as well as old – specially new. Not to keep those with – or rather, for – whom we fight off us, but how to bring them near. How to get at them. To bring them down to the Saviour's feet, conquered by love and won for the King.

Plenty of mistakes and blunders there doubtless will be in this campaign; mistakes with ships and boats and ammunition and weapons and food – and I know not what; mistakes in telegrams and letters and messages and everything else. Still it must be a wonderful display of system to be able to equip and send forth those thousands of men right into the heart of that African desert, and a still more wonderful thing it must be to supply them with food and water, and all the necessities of war when they are there.[1] One word explains the whole business, and that word is "system".

My comrades, we must have more of this science. It means finding out how to do things in the best way, and then keeping on doing them. Let us all join hands at this. It means that somebody gives the order how things are to be done, and then everybody concerned goes quietly to work to obey. Soldiers, mark that! Do you want to see the war waged with greater vigour and rushed forward to mightier results? Bear this in mind: every man to his post, and let every man do his duty when he is there.

We must learn better to sacrifice and to endure. There have been some deserters, perhaps; some who fled at the sight of the enemy, or who fell out of the march in the heat of the sun when not compelled to do so; or there may have been someone who has gone over to the foe. But we have not heard of such cowardice or treachery. They have been true to their oath.[2]

**By your grace, Lord, I'll be true. Enable me to be ever-learning, and ever-willing to adapt, in order that my faithfulness may be matched with skill. For those who fall, gracious Father, grant forgiveness and restoration. This, all for your glory in the battle. Amen.**

1 The Mahdist War/Sudan Campaign, 1885.
2 From *The General's Letters*.

# September 30th

This is what the Lord of Heaven's Armies says: Look at what's happening to you!

(Haggai 1:7 *NLT*)

"Comrades," says he, [the captain] "you've had a good many professing meetings in the blessed Sunday mornings that are gone. You've professed to be on 'the Lord's side'; you have said out plain that you were converted; you've professed that you loved the dear Saviour, and that you were going to live and die in his service – all of which I know is the honest truth, and I am glad that you know it too. You would be of no use to either God or man in this fight if you didn't.

"You've talked about the wonderful things you've done for Jesus Christ, and for the souls of your neighbours; and I'm proud of it…

"But now," says he, "I want us all – myself among the number – to look at some of the things we haven't done, which we ought to have done; and at some of the things we have done that we ought not to have done. We have had a lots of 'professional' meetings – now we'll have a 'confessional' meeting."… Then he went on to tell us how he had not lived as a Salvation Army officer ought to live in his corps, in his family, and before the world; and then he told us what agony he had suffered, because he was afraid he had not done all his duty in warning the people, outdoors and in, of their dreadful danger. And then he said he was afraid that he had been content with the smiles of the people, and with good meetings, and hadn't prayed and wrestled and toiled until he had won the souls of the people he ought to have done…

"Friends, I have wept over it all, as I've told you, at my Saviour's feet, and again given myself over to live and die for my Lord; and he has forgiven the past, and cleansed my heart, and baptized me with the Holy Ghost for the sanctification of Darkington soldiers and the salvation of Darkington sinners."

He said a lot more that I can't remember; and then he sat down.[1]

**Father, I give time today for healthy spiritual introspection. I know that with you there is no condemnation, but I want to know if there is anything I am doing that I shouldn't be doing, or anything I am not doing that you would like me to do. Holy Spirit, grant me insight as I lay my ways before you. Amen.**

1 From *Sergeant-Major Do-Your-Best.*

# OCTOBER 1ST

## WHOEVER GETS SENSE LOVES HIS OWN SOUL

(Proverbs 19:8 *ESV*)

A paragraph went the round of the newspaper world, a little while back, describing how an American millionaire had decided to spend the rest of his days on a leper island in the Pacific Ocean,[1] in order to labour for the amelioration of the miseries of its unfortunate inhabitants. Wonder and admiration everywhere greeted the announcement.

Shall we go back on all this spirit of self-sacrifice? Shall this kind of thing die out, or only have an existence in poetry books, platform quotations, or anecdote collections? Shall we change over to the "pound-of-flesh" principle, and hire out the work of our hands, the thoughts of our minds, and the burning passions of our souls, for the largest amount of filthy lucre,[2] and the greatest measure of earthly comfort that we can obtain for them; so justifying the lying libel on humanity, long since spoken, and still often sneeringly quoted, that every man has his price? Or shall we say that love – the love of God and man – is the highest and divinest motive of labour – a motive possible not only to the sons and daughters of genius, but accessible to the plainest, humblest man or woman who suffers and toils on the lowest round of the ladder of life.

I argue in favour of this doctrine on the ground of its profitableness for the worker. My readers will probably have asked long before this, how far do these propositions harmonize with the interests of the servant? Ought he not to take his own well-being into account? Certainly. He must have just as true a regard for his own welfare and the welfare of those dependent upon him, as he has for that of others. The command, "Thou shalt love thy neighbour as thyself"[3] can only be rightly interpreted by another, like unto it, which read: "Whatsoever ye would that men should do to you, do ye even so to them."[4] Therefore, he must ask that others should do unto him as he would do unto them, supposing they occupied changed positions. This must mean that while righteously concerned for the interests of others, he must be reasonably concerned for his own.[5]

**Thank you, Lord, for this reminder of the responsibility I have to cater for my own well-being as well as that of others. Guard me from unwise extremes in either direction, I pray. Amen.**

1 Possibly Molokai, Hawaii.
2 Titus 1:7
3 Matthew 19:19 *KJV*
4 Matthew 7:12 *KJV*
5 From *Religion for Every Day.*

# October 2[nd]

### My flesh and my heart may fail

(Psalm 73:26 *NIV*)

We want now to consider the secret of Abraham's ability to obey. How came it about, this blood and iron kind of service – this unflinching and unswerving discharge of duty? It is much admired everywhere. Oh, we do love the faithful spirit – the "die-at-your-post men and women" – but, alas! How scarce they are, and what a pity they are so, seeing they are so much wanted. People who have no capacity for the hour of danger, no backbone, no capacity for standing alone, who dare not suffer, are of little or no use in this world.

Soldiers who yield and run when the balls are flying, and their comrades are wounded, are no good; sailors who tremble and hide when the hurricane sweeps, and the masts snap, and the vessel leaks, are no good; and saints who have no courage for the hour of danger, who fly when the enemy comes in sight, are no good either. We want people who can go through with things, no matter who, or what, comes in the way, who can literally offer up the love of father and mother, and house and land, and ease, ay!, and life itself, who can put all on the altar, and stay and see it burn to ashes, if it comes between them and duty.

Oh! My comrades, come and meditate here. Do you see here the image of your own character? Is this your method of consecration and service? Is this the kind of obedience you make manifest in your daily lives?… Is this the way you offer up your love of ease, and society, and gain, and pleasure, things allowable, and things forbidden? And having been once convinced as to what the Lord requires, in spite of the pleadings of nature and family, and respectability, and friendship, and everything else, do you go through with it?

Or are you among those… who are always coming to Moriah, who seem to spend the larger part of their lifetime in taking Isaac there, and bringing him [home] again?… Their hearts fail them.[1]

**Lord, by your grace, preserve me from heart failure in the line of duty. Amen.**

1 From *Salvation Soldiery.*

# October 3rd

He led me to a place of safety
(2 Samuel 22:20 *NLT*)

Our sleeping arrangements [in Shelters] are somewhat primitive; we do not provide feather beds, and each of them forms a cubicle. There is a mattress laid on the floor, and over the mattress a leather apron, which is all the bedclothes that we find it possible to provide. The men undress, each by the side of his packing box, and go to sleep under their leather covering. The dormitory is warmed with hot water pipes to a temperature of 60 degrees, and there has never been any complaint of lack of warmth on the part of those who use the Shelter. The leather can be kept perfectly clean, and the mattresses, covered with American cloth, are carefully inspected every day, so that no stray specimen of vermin may be left in the place. The men turn in about ten o'clock and sleep until six.

We never have any disturbances of any kind in the Shelters. We have provided accommodation now for several thousand of the most helplessly broken-down men in London, criminals many of them, mendicants, tramps, those who are among the filth and offscouring of all things; but such is the influence that is established by the meeting and the moral ascendency of our officers themselves, that we have never had a fight on the premises, and very seldom do we ever hear an oath or an obscene word. Sometimes there has been trouble outside the Shelter, when men insisted upon coming in drunk or were otherwise violent; but once let them come to the Shelter, and get into the swing of the concern, and we have no trouble with them.

In the morning they get up and have their breakfast and, after a short service, go off their various ways. We find that we can do this, that is to say, we can provide coffee and bread for breakfast and for supper, and a shake-down on the floor in the packing-boxes I have described in a warm dormitory for fourpence a head. I propose to develop these Shelters, so as to afford every man a locker, in which he could store any little valuables that he may possess.[1]

**Loving God, you offer the shelter of your love to those who trust in you; you do not ever promise to remove your children from life's storms, but you offer steadfast love throughout. Today, I pray for those in need of shelter – both literally and metaphorically; emotionally, or spiritually. Please spread your wings over them. Thank you. Amen.**

1 From *In Darkest England and the Way Out.*

# October 4th

HE WILL BE LIKE A REFINER'S FIRE OR A LAUNDERER'S SOAP
(Malachi 3:2 *NIV*)

In Trafalgar Square, in 1887, there were few things that scandalized the public more than the spectacle of the poor people camped in the square, washing their shirts in the early morning at the fountains. If you talk to any men who have been on the road for a lengthy period they will tell you that nothing hurts their self-respect more or stands more fatally in the way of their getting a job than the impossibility of getting their little things done up and clean. I would allow… the use of a boiler in the washhouse with a hot drying oven, so that he could wash his shirt overnight and have it returned to him dry in the morning.

In our poor man's "home" everyone could at least keep himself clean and have a clean shirt to his back, in a plain way, no doubt; but still not less effective than if he were to be put up at one of the West End hotels, and would be able to secure anyway the necessities of life while being passed on to something far better. This is the first step. Only those who have had practical experience of the difficulty of seeking for work in London can appreciate the advantages of the opportunity to get your shirt washed.

We had at one of our Shelters the captain of an ocean steamer, who had sunk to the depths of destitution through strong drink. He came in there one night utterly desperate and was taken in hand by our people… he regained his position in the merchant service, and twelve months afterwards astonished us all by appearing in the uniform of a captain of a large ocean steamer, to testify to those who were there how low he had been, how utterly he had lost all hold on society and all hope of the future, when, fortunately led to the Shelter, he found friends, counsel, and salvation, and from that time had never rested until he had regained the position which he had forfeited by his intemperance.[1]

**Father, bless today those who minister to people who have lost all grip on reality by gently handling their filthy, flea-ridden clothing, and doing so for Jesus. Thank you for those whose gracious service for the Kingdom involves work that many of us would resist. For clean shirts and clean souls, I praise you. Amen.**

1 From *In Darkest England and the Way Out.*

# October 5th

His word is in my heart like a fire, a fire shut up in my bones. I am weary of holding it in; indeed, I cannot

(Jeremiah 20:9 *NIV*)

The officer in The Salvation Army who does not see the grandeur of the opportunity he possesses of speaking to men about God and eternity, and who does not earnestly desire to qualify himself for the effective discharge of the duty, must be altogether unworthy of his post.

God has given me some ability as a public speaker. I have already referred to the tens of thousands I have been permitted to see kneeling broken-hearted at the mercy seat. These thousands of souls all impressed, nay, deeply convicted and saved, bear witness to the power I possess as a salvation preacher. The Salvation Army itself is, to some extent, an evidence of my ability to talk to the hearts of men. Am I glorifying in myself? God forbid. I say these things for your sake, to justify me in advising you in listening to my counsel.

Now how did I acquire this ability to talk? Beyond question I possess some natural gifts – they came into this world with me. But for the encouragement of every young officer here today, I want to say that the bulk of my little ability as a public speaker has come by way of industrious, persistent, self-denying cultivation. My soul was drawn out in desire after the power to speak of the things of God to the hearts of men in the earliest hours of my first love. I yearned after it with an unutterable yearning, and that long before I had any reason to believe that this gift would ever be mine.

I made up my mind to seek it before I had been saved twelve months, and at once set myself to the task. I have fought hard in this pursuit. Few officers here have had more disappointments, and depressions, and temptations in their talking than I have myself. But I have persevered, and I am still following on as earnestly as ever in the pursuit. But I never expect to reach satisfaction with my attainment in this respect, and so shall still fight on to gain greater ability to persuade men to abandon the path of evil and seek God.[1]

**Father God, I lift before you those who are struggling to identify their gifts in your service. I pray that you would give them passionate clarity of thought, strong determination to cultivate their abilities, and solid protection against every discouragement. Help them to discover their unique role in the Church. Amen.**

1 From *The Seven Spirits.*

# October 6th

Truly he is my rock and my salvation; he is my fortress, I shall not be shaken

(Psalm 62:6 *NIV*)

Our captain is quite different to Captain Do-it-all, God bless him, what used to give us such exalted discourses about things we did not understand or care very much about either. But then they were very clever and, though none of us were any the better for them that I know of, they brought us good congregations and collections; and then, you see, he used to make some real beautiful prayers.

Why, bless him, he did almost all the work of the corps himself, and a lot of us had little to do but sit by and look on. And when he went away, and another captain came, all the people who used to come to hear Captain Do-it-all went away too, and we felt quite lost, because, you see, we not only lost the captain, but the congregation too.

Now, Captain Faithful is quite different to this. He is everlastingly starting some scheme or other that brings somebody fresh to the front, and so he has us all up and doing by turns. His last move is to stir up the locals [local officers]. We know he was going to do something in this line, because he came along and had a long talk with both me and Sarah. He always likes to rope Sarah in, and have her opinion on things, specially when he has a fresh game on the board. He has a great opinion of Sarah, and so have I, bless her!

"The locals," says the captain, "are not very active in Darkington. Are they, Mrs Do-your-best?" "Active!" says Sarah. "No, I should think not. They are a heap better than they was, but they are a long way short of what they should be. The fact of the matter is, most of them are real lazy, and I am afraid they are too well off ever to be anything else." "Don't say that, Sarah," says I. "How is it with you and me? Things are better with us, as far as this world goes, than they used to be. Aren't they?"[1]

**Unchanging God, how reluctant we can be, sometimes, to accept change! I pray, Lord, that if I am "roped in" to help with new ideas, I would do so with enthusiasm and effort, for Jesus' sake. Amen.**

1 From *Sergeant-Major Do-Your-Best.*

# October 7th

## The well is deep

(John 4:11 *NIV*)

I am coming to the opinion that every man must learn for himself how to talk, if ever he learns at all. However, I will give you a few hints. And I will do so by describing the things which, taken together, are likely to make a successful Salvation Army talker.

He must be actuated by right, God-pleasing motive; almost everything will depend on the character of the motives which carry him to the people. His aim must be above all self-seeking – vain, man-pleasing feelings. If he is after the praises of men, or the rewards of this world, he cannot expect the Holy Ghost to second his efforts. His motive must be beyond the mere desire to preach the truth or explain the Bible, or remind his hearers of what they already know. In these things there is no practical application of truth to the present need of those before him. His aim must be to bless them by saving them in some form or other from sin, and leading them on to a more earnest, self-denying life for God and the salvation of others.

Having this aim, much will depend upon preparation for the right discharge of the duty. There are different views on the subject of preparation for the platform. I will tell you mine. Some think that no preparation is needed; that it is wrong to pray and study as to the message you are to deliver. "Open your mouth wide," they say, "and God will fill it."[1] That is not my view, and it has never been my practice. To those who entertain these notions I would say: If you are on such good terms with the Blessed Spirit that he will fill your pitcher with the living water without any trouble to yourself, very good. I have always had to draw mine out of the well, and very deep I have often found that well to be; and very hard pumping it has usually been to get out what I wanted… I have had to work my brain, search my Bible, look over my experience.[2]

**Lord, the richness of your blessings is marvellous – thank you. It is always worth digging deep to discover more about your love and your great truths. Make me a digger; someone who is not content with shallow excavations. Amen.**

1 Psalm 81:10
2 From *The Seven Spirits.*

# October 8th

Love... is not self-seeking

(1 Corinthians 13:4–5 *NIV*)

What does love care for gain in its calculations of service? The husband who loves his wife as Christ loved the Church does not stop to consider the claims of duty, or the advantages following its discharge in toiling for her welfare. He will be willing to die for her, as Christ died for the Church.[1]

He does not say, "I will toil for my delicate wife, and deny myself pleasant things, in order to obtain for her the necessaries and comforts she requires, because she would do the same for me, if I were in her place and she in mine." Nothing of the kind! The wife I spoke of, who told me the other day that she had not had her clothes off for seventeen days and nights in nursing her husband, did not make it appear that she thought she was doing anything extraordinary, or that she rendered this service to her companion in life because she felt sure that had he been the wife and she the husband, he would have gladly done the same for her...

Supposing, however, that we come down to the low level of self-interest, we insist then that those who work from the motive of love, rather than the motive of gain, will not necessarily be sufferers in consequence, so far as this world goes. But it may be asked, "Will not unprincipled masters or mistresses be likely to take advantage of this docile and unselfish spirit?" Perhaps, nay, doubtless, in many cases, they will. The Salvation Army has been taken advantage of all through its past history, and so have all the true saints of God, because they have submitted to wrong, and have not fought the injustice and false representations and persecutions inflicted upon them from the beginning. It will possibly be so to the end, but that does not affect the principle for which I argue, which is, that we must do good work, and as much of it as we can, regardless of what the world may give us in return.[2]

**Thank you for Jesus, whose love was beautifully demonstrated in utterly selfless sacrifice. Thank you that he gave his life without thought of return or even respect; just because of love. Amen.**

1 Ephesians 5:25

2 From *Religion for Every Day.*

# OCTOBER 9TH

EVEN HEREUNTO WERE YE CALLED: BECAUSE CHRIST ALSO SUFFERED FOR US, LEAVING US AN EXAMPLE, THAT YE SHOULD FOLLOW HIS STEPS

(1 Peter 2:21 *KJV*)

Our model warrior was the Lord Jesus. His life and teaching, taken together, constitute the pattern and teach the only true method in which our campaign for the deliverance of man from sin and devils is to be carried on. This was declared by Peter, a celebrated General, who fought gloriously in the early history of this war, when he said, "Even hereunto were ye called" – that is, enlisted – "because Christ also suffered for you, leaving an example that you should follow his steps." If the Holy Ghost commanded the early Salvationists to fight after the pattern of their Master, surely the same obligation is binding on us.

We must follow him. Nothing that he has done for you in the past, or that he is able to do for you in the future can relieve you from this obligation or excuse you neglecting to discharge it. How can we have any share in the merits of his sacrifice without fighting under his standard? If we secure his favour kneeling at his feet, can we retain it without following where those feet shall lead? My comrades, I say, "Impossible!" He will be the author of eternal salvation to all those who obey him – and to them only.

What is following Christ? It isn't difficult to discover. Here, anyway, a child can be on a level with a learned divine. It simply means keeping his words and copying his example. It is to the latter that I want specially to refer you. Following means imitating. The children of Israel followed the pillar of cloud; that is, they moved after it. They went in the same direction in which it went. They stopped when it stopped.[1]

Now many make a common mistake with regard to following Christ, and I think it a most disastrous one. They think it signifies following him to Heaven, and that in the most comfortable way possible. Whereas the true idea – the idea which was taught by his example and explained a thousand times over by his words – shows that following Christ means following him from Heaven into a world of sin.[2]

**Lord, you are a God who leads and guides. I thank you that I can totally rely upon your gentle guidance this day, and for the reassurance this provides. I invite you afresh to guide my thoughts and my footsteps. Amen.**

1 Exodus 13:21; Numbers 9:21–23

2 From *The General's Letters.*

# October 10th

## He gave his life to free us from every kind of sin

(Titus 2:14 *NLT*)

We are all under the rule of Jehovah, our Sovereign Lord. And just as earthly governors impose laws upon their people for the maintenance of order and the promotion of the general good, so God rules his subjects by specific laws and regulations. To maintain respect for these laws, and secure obedience to them, certain penalties are imposed upon those who break them. Laws that had no punishment connected with their transgression would be no laws at all. They would be neither more nor less than so much good advice, and consequently little or no notice would be taken of them by those for whose benefit they were made.

As you will know, men have broken these laws, and thereby exposed themselves to the penalty imposed by God upon their transgression. That penalty is everlasting punishment.

Now, the object God had before him in giving his only Son to die for the world was – to save men from this terrible punishment to which they exposed themselves by the transgression of his laws. Having forgiven their sins, and saved them from the consequences of their transgression, God seeks to induce them to live good, obedient, and useful lives on earth. God further planned to prepare them for a life of everlasting purity, joy, and worship in Heaven.

By the sacrifice of Jesus Christ, each of the three following objects was gained: 1) On the one hand, God showed to all the inhabitants of Heaven, and earth, and Hell, the importance of his laws, and the awful results consequent on their transgression. 2) While maintaining the importance and value of these laws God was enabled to pardon, sanctify, and take to his bosom all who repented of their sins, returned to obedience, and accepted his mercy, and believed on his Son. 3) And, further, by opening this wonderful way of salvation, God revealed, as he could not possibly have done in any other way, the depth of the pity and love of his heart towards sinful men. The sacrifice offered by Jesus Christ on the cross made it possible for God to deliver every man from the guilt, power, and consequences of his sins.[1]

**What a wonderful plan of redemption you have provided, Father – thorough, compassionate, merciful, yet in keeping with the Law. I praise you for this comprehensive, perfect arrangement. Amen.**

1 From *The Founder's Messages to Soldiers.*

# October 11th

Rescue the perishing; don't hesitate to step in and help

(Proverbs 24:11 *The Message*)

I was led out into a train of thought respecting the conditions of the multitudes around me living regardless of all that concerned their eternal welfare, and in the most open and shameless rebellion against God. I looked out upon the millions of people around me given up to their drink and their pleasure, their dancing and their music, their business and their anxieties, their politics and their troubles, and thousands of other things; ignorant – wilfully ignorant, in many cases – in other instances knowing all about it; but all of them sweeping on and up, in their blasphemies and devilries, to the Throne of God. While thus musing I had a vision.

I saw a dark and stormy ocean. Over it the black clouds hung heavily; through them every now and then the vivid lightnings flashed and loud thunders rolled, while the winds moaned, and the waves rose and foamed and fretted and broke and rose to foam and fret and break again. In that ocean I thought I saw myriads of poor human beings plunging and floating, shouting and shrieking, cursing and struggling and drowning; and as they cursed and shrieked, they rose and shrieked again, and then sank to rise no more.

And out of this dark angry ocean I saw a mighty rock that rose up with its summit towering high about the black clouds that overhung the stormy sea; and all around the base of this rock I saw a vast platform; and on to this platform I saw with delight a number of the poor, struggling, drowning wretches continually climbing out of the angry ocean; and I saw that a number of those who were already safe on the platform were helping the poor creatures still in the angry waters to reach the same place of safety.

On looking more closely I found a number of those who had been rescued scheming and contriving by ladders and ropes and boats and other expedients more effectually to deliver the poor strugglers out of this sea. Here and there were some who actually jumped into the water, regardless of all consequences, in their eagerness to "rescue the perishing".[1]

**What a vision this was, Father! Would you enlarge my vision today? Help me to see things as you see them. Make me a visionary for the Kingdom. Amen.**

1 From *The Founder Speaks Again.*

# October 12th

Behold, I made him a witness to the peoples, a leader and commander for the peoples

(Isaiah 55:4 *ESV*)

The captain started the meeting off with a short earnest prayer. Bless him, I do like to hear him pray. He always makes me want to be a better man. Then he went on to say that he was glad of the opportunity for a friendly little talk on the affairs of the corps, saying that he intended, when possible, to meet us every week, and let us know how things were going on. Says he: "I want to have your hearts with me, and then I shall have everything else you have. You know," says he, "that I am sent here by the General, who holds me responsible for the welfare of this corps. It is my affair. I must make it a success, and have sinners saved, and soldiers on fire, or it will break my heart. I have made up my mind to do it. It has to be done, and done it shall be, if I can manage it.

"But," says he, "the prosperity of this corps is your concern also. A Salvation Army corps is a real cooperative society, or it ought to be. We are all in the same boat; indeed," says he, "this is more your affair than mine; so I want us all to pull together; and if we do, we shall come out somewhere near the landing stage.

"Now," he said, "there are two things that are a great trouble to me just now, and that both night and day… I find we are £17 in debt… the cartridges and the offerings on week-nights and in the open-air have gone sadly down… the debt is there, and I feel it is a disgrace… Then," says he, "there is another matter that I am distressed about… and that is the state of things in the open-air… with nearly 250 soldiers on the roll, there are often not more than twenty, besides the band, in the Market Place on a Sunday morning."[1]

**Father, here is a church leader who carries the concerns of his church with him. Bless all who do, and support them. Give them answers to their prayers as they seek to lead. I pray for my leaders today. Amen.**

1 From *Sergeant-Major Do-Your-Best.*

# October 13th

"Not by might nor by power, but by my Spirit," says the Lord Almighty

(Zechariah 4:6 *NIV*)

A great writer has said, "Every Christian family ought to be, as it were, a little Christian church, consecrated to Christ and wholly influenced and governed by his rules."[1] We endorse this sentiment, only making it a little plainer to the bulk of those into whose hands this book will fall, by saying that every salvation soldier's family ought to be a little corps, trained up and governed by the laws of Jesus Christ, as understood and represented by The Salvation Army.

Where this is carried out, the family will be governed for God – as much for him in the parlour, kitchen, or nursery, or anywhere else, as in the barracks or church. The house where the family dwells will be as much the house of God as the place where the family meet their comrades for religious meetings on [the] Sabbath or the week-night.

It follows also in families where this view is entertained and carried out that everything will be done in the power and Spirit of God; not two spirits, one a spirit of self-sacrifice and solemnity in what is called a "sacred edifice", and another consisting of the service of self in its various forms of mammon worship, pleasure-seeking, vanity, and self-indulgence, constituting the worship of the flesh. There will be one spirit, the spirit of benevolence, and truth, and worship, and self-sacrificing goodwill. In short, there will be the Spirit of the Lord Jesus Christ, and whether the members of that family eat or drink, rise up or sit down, all will be done to the glory of God.

A godly family government will be characterized by justice. That is, the spirit of rightness and justice will influence the dealings of the parents with the children and with everybody else, and they will see and feel this. If the children know that their father deals unjustly in his business, if they hear things that are tricky and contrary to strict uprightness talked over at the table and approved in any degree, no matter what zeal that father may display in teaching his children to be good, it will all be in vain.[2]

**Holy Spirit, come today and reign in my heart. Amen.**

1 Jonathan Edwards, American theologian and puritan; quoted from a sermon and subsequently reproduced in several journals and books.

2 From *The Training of Children*.

# October 14[th]

Faith cometh by hearing, and hearing by the word of God

(Romans 10:17 *KJV*)

There are a great many people on earth, and a growing number in Heaven, who have been converted through some personal word spoken by the lovers of Jesus at unexpected times and in unusual places.

The opportunities for this kind of usefulness are so numerous that they cannot be counted. They come to us every day, and to most of us many times a day. But, alas! How often they come and go unnoted and unimproved! This should not be. I want to ask you to take advantage of them… Of course, opportunities will ever be occurring to you to speak to the members of your own family about their spiritual interests. But it is not these opportunities to which, at this moment, I refer, important as they may be. Neither am I asking you to avail yourselves of every chance of speaking to your comrades on these subjects. I am asking for something more than this. I am urging you to seize every opportunity of putting in your word for salvation with the ungodly people around you.

I am not now asking you to visit them in their homes, on their sick beds, in the drinking saloons, in the workshops or elsewhere, although that is important – very important – and multitudes of your comrades all over the world have been successful in such efforts. But I am asking you to drop a word or have a little conversation with the people you meet in the train or on the tram; that when you buy or sell, when you are at the mill, when you meet friends or strangers by the way, you should be ready to speak a word for God and salvation.

Now some of you will say, "I cannot do that sort of thing. I never could. I do not like it." Perhaps not. But… I recommend you to make up your mind to speak about God's will to the first stranger that crosses your path after reading this message. Do not think it absolutely necessary to decide beforehand what you shall say. The Holy Spirit will supply you with words, and bless you in speaking.[1]

**This is quite some challenge, Father! Can you show me how? With your help and inspiration, I'd like to do this today. Just where you need me, Lord, place me. Amen.**

1 From *The Founder Speaks Again.*

# October 15th

The harvest is plentiful but the workers are few

(Matthew 9:37 *NIV*)

I want to remark that although many of our people experience difficulty and reluctance in testifying for Christ, we are no whit behind any other section of Christ's people. On the contrary, as is well known, no section of the community makes a bolder or more public confession of faith than does The Salvation Army. Ours is a peculiarly "house-top religion". Still, there is room for an immense advance even with Salvationists in the discharge of this duty. Let us therefore enlist a body of soldiers who will accept it as a special obligation before God.

But now I want to ask, why this unwillingness to speak upon a subject of such thrilling and infinite importance, after the fashion I have described? Well, the first reason may be traced to custom. Religious people do not generally discuss their religion in public; anyway, they do not very often describe their own experience. God and his services are, they consider, only to be referred to on particular occasions, and in what are called sacred places. To speak of the love of Christ, the value of the soul, the forgiveness of sins, and the hope of Heaven, in a railway carriage, or a goods store, or by the roadside, or at the tea-table, would be regarded by many professing Christian people as being bad form, if not next door to profanity.

Now, many Salvationists have, no doubt, been influenced by the professing Christians around them, and have fallen into some of their customs. But when customs are bad we must break away from them. We, at any rate, cannot allow the crowds at our doors to transgress the laws of God, to trample underfoot his mercy, and to perish without a word of warning. To speak to them as I have advocated is one method of warning them; and, however others may regard it, this duty must be discharged…

Many soldiers do not see it to be their duty to personally warn their friends and neighbours, or to invite them to the cross. Many soldiers, I am sorry to say, do not see it to be their duty to save sinners at all![1]

**Oh, Lord, banish all reluctance from my heart. Thrill me again with the message of the gospel, so that witnessing for Jesus becomes not only a duty, but a joy and a privilege. Amen.**

1 From *The Founder's Messages to Soldiers.*

# October 16th

## Work hard to show the results of your salvation

(Philippians 2:12 *NLT*)

Some people are always complaining. Nothing is right with them. The weather is wrong, trade is wrong, their employers are wrong, their family is wrong – everything is wrong about them. Reader, do you belong to this class? If so, we can find out the reason. Instead of the trade and the family and the neighbours and other people and things that you complain of so much as being wrong, perhaps after all it is yourself.

It is true that sinners' hearts are very hard, and that is the reason they are not converted; and some of your comrades are cold, and that is the reason why you don't get better meetings; and your officers may not be so clever and devoted as they might be, and that is the reason why you don't get more sinners into the barracks, and therefore things are not so bright and prosperous at your corps as they might be.

But is there not another reason, which you have not mentioned, for your discomfort and the want of success in your corps, namely, that you are not right yourself? May there not be something terribly wanting in your own personal religion? Let me talk to you about it. Deal faithfully with your own soul. Tell the truth about your own heart to your own self, as fully as you would of anybody else's…

Are you satisfied with your own religion? Other people can only make guesses about you. No matter how frequently they may be with you, they can still only infer what you really are from what you do. When people talk to you about your soul, about your state from the platform, or in the holiness meeting, you can put them off, tell them that you are right. I have no doubt you hope you will be when death or judgment finds you.

Tell the truth now. Are you really and truly satisfied with your state?… Are you satisfied with what you realize of God in your own heart?… Are you satisfied with what you personally know of the cleansing blood of Jesus Christ?[1]

**Thank you, Lord, that you love your children too much to leave us as we are. Your loving plan for us is that we should continually explore our spiritual experience in order to grow in our faith and come ever closer to you. Amen.**

1 From *The General's Letters.*

May you have the power to understand, as all God's people should, how wide, how long, how high, and how deep his love is

(Ephesians 3:18 *NLT*)

Of the practical results which have followed our methods of dealing with the outcasts who take shelter with us we have many striking examples. Here are a few, each of them a transcript of a life experience relating to men who are now active, industrious members of the community upon which but for the agency of these Depots they would have been preying to this day.

A. S. – Born in Glasgow, 1825. Saved at Clerkenwell, 19 May 1889. Poor parents, raised in a Glasgow slum. Was thrown on the streets at seven years of age, became the companion and associate of thieves, and drifted into crime. The following are his terms of imprisonment: fourteen days, thirty days, thirty days, sixty days, sixty days (three times in succession), four months, six months (twice), nine months, eighteen months, two years, six years, seven years (twice), fourteen years; forty years three months and six days in the aggregate. Was flogged for violent conduct in gaol eight times.

W. M. "Buff" – Born in Deptford, 1864, saved at Clerkenwell, 31 March 1889… Mother was a disreputable, drunken slattern; a curse and disgrace to husband and family. The home was broken up, and little Buff was given over to the evil influences of his depraved mother. His seventh birthday present from his admiring parent was a "quarter o'gin".

He got some education at the One Tun Alley Ragged School,[1] but when nine years old was caught apple stealing, and sent to the industrial school at Ilford for seven years. Discharged at the end of his time, he drifted to the streets, the Casual Wards, and metropolitan gaols, every one of whose interiors he is familiar with. He became a ringleader of a gang that infested London; a thorough mendicant and ne'er do well; a pest to society. Naturally he is… one of those spirits that command a following; consequently, when he got salvation, the major part of his following came after him to the Shelter, and eventually to God. His character since conversion has been altogether satisfactory, and he is now an orderly at Whitechapel, and to all appearances a "true lad".[2]

**So great is your love, Father, to reach down into the human condition and illuminate deepest darkness with saving grace. May your Church ever go for souls, and go for the worst. Thank you, Lord, for the staggering dimensions of your love. Amen.**

1 The One Tun public house, London, converted into a Ragged School (a charitable institution dedicated to the free education of destitute children).

2 From *In Darkest England and the Way Out.*

# October 18[TH]

Masters, treat your servants considerately. Be fair with them. Don't forget for a minute that you, too, serve a Master – God in heaven

(Colossians 4:1 *The Message*)

The duty of masters to servants.

The servant is to do his work, not only for the benefit of his master, but for the love of it, for the esteem of his fellow man, and for the satisfaction of his Father in heaven.

Now, I have no doubt that many masters and mistresses will agree with the wisdom and desirability of such conduct on the part of the servants. They will say, "That is just what we wanted our servants to do. That will be good for us, and it will be good for them. Let every servant do his duty."

I come now to say, and that as plainly as I possibly can, that it is the duty of the master to deal with his servants on the same principles, and from the same motives, that he expects his servants to deal with him – that is, he must promote the welfare of his servants to the utmost of his ability. The servants are placed under his charge, by God, for this very purpose, and he is under an obligation to make them, as far as he can, happy, holy, and useful. And that obligation is, to a certain extent, as binding upon him as if the servants were his own children. For [as] masters and mistresses are not the parents of their servants, they are at least their guardians, and will have to give an account to God of the way in which they discharge their stewardship.

The obligation of the master to seek the interests of the servant is based upon the same authority as that which binds the servant to seek the interests of his master. He is to do unto others as he would that others should do unto him.

Here I want to remark that there is nothing menial or degrading in the position of a servant. Neither is there anything in that relation in which a servant stands to a master that signifies the sacrifice, in any degree, of his natural rights.[1]

**I praise you, Lord, that the Master came in the form of a servant, not to be served, but to serve. Thank you for such amazing grace and humility – this is my God! Amen.**

1 From *Religion for Every Day.*

# October 19th

### Come to me, all you who are weary and burdened

(Matthew 11:28 *NIV*)

I remember hearing a gentleman relate the following incident in a large meeting: "Some time back," he said, "I was passing through the streets of Liverpool. It was a cold, raw, wintry day. The streets were ankle-deep in an unpleasant mixture of mud and ice, and battling through it all, there came along a little procession of ragged, haggard, hungry-looking boys. Splash, splash, on they went, through the freezing slush, at every step making the onlookers shudder as they stood by it in their warm, comfortable coats and furs. In the front rank was a little fellow who was scarcely more than a bag of bones, half-naked, barefooted, his whole frame shivering every time he put his foot down on the melting snow.

"All at once, a big boy came forward, and stooping down, bade the lad put his arms around his neck and, lifting him up on his back, took his perished feet one in each hand and jogged along with his burden.

"I was moved," said the speaker, "at the sight; and going up to the boy, commended him for his kindness. In his Lancashire brogue the lad replied, 'Aye, aye, sir; two feet in the cold slush are not so bad as four.' After a while," said the speaker, "I offered to carry the little chap myself, but the honest fellow shook his head, and said, 'Nay, nay, Mister; I winna part with him. I can carry him; and he's a-warming 'o my back.'"

And so, if seeking the good of others may not bring as much worldly gain as a selfish course of action, it does ensure that joyful warmth of heart which all loving service brings, and which is among the most valuable of all the treasures of earth or Heaven. Every man who acts on this principle is adding to the general sum of human happiness. If… the reward does not come in the form of money, or houses, or lands, there will be gain in that which is far more valuable than money and houses and lands, and which money and houses and lands cannot buy.[1]

**Father, you are a burden-bearing God, and I praise you. I can leave my burdens with you in prayer, and you offer to carry them for me. Teach me, Lord, not to keep my burdens to myself, but to drop them at the Throne of Grace. Amen.**

1 From *Religion for Every Day.*

# OCTOBER 20TH

HE ASKED THEM, "WHAT IS YOUR ADVICE?... "

(2 Chronicles 10:9 *NIV*)

Were I dying before your eyes in this very hall I should call on you, by all that was sacred on earth and in Heaven, to improve yourself. With many officers there is unquestionably great advance. The commissioners are improved, and so are the staff generally. They are certainly dressed better, and from appearance I should judge they weigh much heavier. The field officers are improved; they do not appear to weigh any less. But there are other directions in which I think there is room for great improvement...

It is true that in nature every now and then you will have a good crop in your garden for which little or no preparation has been made; but is that any rule why you should give up cultivating altogether? Just so with [public] talking. Do you ask me how I would advise an officer to go about giving an address?...

Choose your subject. Your subject should in some way be – a) Applicable to the present need of the people who will hear you. Very much alike. b) Practical – something that can be turned to the present account. c) Interesting, if possible. Something that will catch the ear, and move the curiosity at once. d) Within your ability to handle. e) One on which you can ask God's endorsement and blessing.

Having chosen your subject, consider the form in which you can best present it. Explain the truth you present in the simplest language you can find. The common error is of talking over people's heads. Use your own language; such words, that is, as you are accustomed to employ when expressing yourself in the affairs of everyday life. Make certain that you are understood by the most ignorant of your hearers; illustrate freely. The simpler your illustrations are, the better. Illustrations that need explanation are next to useless. Support what you have to say, so far as you can, by facts. Nevertheless, don't drag yourself in more than advisable. Apply the truth preached as you go along. Appeal for action corresponding to what you have been urging on your hearers there and then: "now is the accepted time".[1, 2]

**Equipping Lord, may I always be someone who receives advice and tuition with gratitude, grace, and humility, so that I may serve you to the very best of my ability. Amen.**

1 2 Corinthians 6:2 *KJV*
2 From *The Seven Spirits.*

# October 21st

### Whoever loves God is known by God

(1 Corinthians 8:3 *NIV*)

Abraham believed in God. God was a reality to him, not a name, or a principle, or a good influence somewhere, but a living, almighty person, who spoke, and acted, and lived all about him, and had real power, and real love, and real hatred; a positive actual God. Abraham said so, thought so, was sure of it. That God was his Creator, Proprietor, Redeemer, and Judge, and if God really was the maker of Isaac, if he owned and sustained him, then, surely, he had a right to his own, and when God told him to take him to Moriah, he took him there.

What a hypocrite he would have been to have been pretending all this, professing, and singing, and praying about being a fully consecrated man, two or three times a week, and not really believing it all the time; or what a rebel he would have been if, believing it all, he had refused to obey, just because it was an unpleasant and painful duty on which God set him.

But he believed in God – all he said – all the time. God had realized himself in Abraham's soul, and given his own Spirit to dwell there, making Abraham sure of the fact; and once assured of God, and such a God, this obedience became easy and natural. People are awfully down on men who say they are atheists with their lips, while any number can be practical atheists, anywhere and everywhere, without rebuke, so that they don't make any talk about it.

Go and get sure about God, and then you will have no difficulty in obeying him – while you are in doubt concerning such a being, no wonder that you are too weak to run in the way of his commandments. Talk about being frightened into obedience by punishments, by the fear of Hell; only get a proper idea of God, and you will be frightened enough of disobeying so great, and powerful, and holy a being…

The secret of Abraham's obedience is found in the fact that he loved God.[1]

**Lord God, there is a sequence at work; first to know you, then to love you, then to serve you, then to see you. Thank you that you dwell in the hearts of those who receive you, and that you teach us how to love you better, day by day. You are gracious indeed. Amen.**

1 From *Salvation Soldiery.*

# October 22nd

The Lord God took the man and put him in the Garden of Eden to work it and take care of it

(Genesis 2:15 *NIV*)

Work for the Out-of-Works.

What if you are confronted with a crowd of hungry, desperate wretches, without even a penny in their pouch, demanding food and shelter? This objection is natural enough, and has been duly considered from the first.

I propose to establish in connection with every Food and Shelter Depot a Workshop or Labour Yard, in which any person who comes destitute and starving will be supplied with sufficient work to enable him to earn the fourpence needed for his bed and board. This is a fundamental feature of the scheme, and one which I think will commend it to all those who are anxious to benefit the poor by enabling them to help themselves without the demoralizing intervention of charitable relief.

Let us take our stand for a moment at the door of one of our relief Shelters. There comes along a grimy, ragged, footsore tramp, his feet bursting out from the sides of his shoes, his clothes all rags, with filthy shirt and tousled hair. He has been, he tells you, on the tramp for the last three weeks, seeking work and finding none, slept last night on the Embankment, and wants to know if you can give him a bite and a sup, and shelter for the night. Has he any money? Not he; he probably spent the last penny he begged or earned in a pipe of tobacco, with which to dull the cravings of his empty stomach. What are you to do with this man?

Remember this is no fancy sketch – it is a typical case. There are hundreds and thousands of such applicants. Anyone who is at all familiar with life in London and our other large towns will recognize that gaunt figure standing there asking for bread and shelter or work by which he can obtain both. What can we do with him? Before him society stands paralyzed, quieting its conscience every now and then by an occasional dole of bread and soup, varied with the semi-criminal treatment of the Casual Ward, until the manhood is crushed out of the man.[1]

**Lord, this account speaks of compassion, care, and dignity. May I, today, approach everyone I encounter with those Christ-like qualities, absolutely regardless of status, for that will do me good and will bring pleasure to your heart. Amen.**

1 From *In Darkest England and the Way Out.*

# October 23rd

In all their distress he too was distressed... In his love and mercy he redeemed them; he lifted them up

(Isaiah 63:9 *NIV*)

You have in your hands a reckless, despairing, spirit-broken creature, with not even an aspiration to rise above his miserable circumstances, covered with vermin and filth, sinking ever lower and lower...

I propose to take that man, put a strong arm around him, and extricate him from the mire in which he is all but suffocated. As a first step we will say to him, "You are hungry, here is food; you are homeless, here is a shelter for your head; but remember you must work for your rations. This is not charity; it is work for the workless, help for those who cannot help themselves. There is the labour shed, go and earn your fourpence, and then come in out of the cold and the wet into the warm shelter; here is your mug of coffee and your great chunk of bread, and after you have finished there is a meeting going on in full swing with its joyful music and hearty human intercourse.

"There are those who pray for you and with you, and will make you feel yourself a brother among men. There is your shake-down on the floor, where you will have your warm, quiet bed, undisturbed by the ribaldry and the curses with which you have been familiar too long. There is the wash-house, where you can have a thorough wash-up at last, after all these days of unwashedness. There is plenty of soap and warm water and clean towels; there too you can wash your shirt and have it dried while you sleep. In the morning when you get up there will be breakfast for you, and your shirt will be dry and clean. Then when you are washed and rested, and no longer faint with hunger, you can go and seek a job, or go back to the Labour Shop until something turns up"...

I do not wish to have any hand in establishing a new centre of demoralization. I do not want my customers to be pauperized by being treated to anything which they do not earn.[1]

**Father, your heart overflows with compassion. You are a God of tremendous mercy. May your heart beat in me, as it did in Booth. Amen.**

1 From *In Darkest England and the Way Out.*

# October 24th

Come near to God and he will come near to you

(James 4:8 *NIV*)

Well, Captain Faithful… he's just won the hearts of our soldiers right off; although how he came to do it so sudden it would puzzle me to tell. You see, he made a good start by attacking the devil on his own ground as he did that night at the fair; and then the confessional meeting… made a great impression. It did on Sarah, anyway, for she's been quite a different woman ever since. But it is not these things only that has set us up with him.

So far as I can make out, it has come about very much through his straight dealing with us all; for he is a faithful captain, and no mistake. When he talks, he don't stop to ask whether it will please or displease anybody. He just seems to be trying to show us where we are weak or wrong, or where we come short of our duty, and that not merely to find fault so as to make us wretched, and nothing more – like Captain Searchem, God bless him! – seemed to be always after; but he just wants to point out where we are wrong, in order that he may help us to get right, and to keep right. Long life to him!

When I hear our captain, I never think about his abilities, nor his looks, nor his voice, nor his fine talk, nor his Bible knowledge, nor anything else about him; but my thoughts always go to where I come short, and what I ought to feel and do, and how I ought to pray for the poor sinners round about me, and suchlike things.

Still, after all, the confessional meeting was a wonderful affair, and no mistake; and there was a rare lot of talk about it in the corps afterwards. The old folks said it was the very best they had ever been in, in all their lives… it was a precious time; but I think Friday night's holiness meeting that followed was more useful still.[1]

**Gracious God, it is a wonderful truth that when we approach you, be it in a formal meeting or service, or individually, you come to meet us. Thank you for your grace in doing so. May we, in every meeting and every service, always come to you in faith, knowing that you long to bless us. Grant us that holy confidence and trust, so that we come to church with high expectations. Amen.**

1 From *Sergeant-Major Do-Your-Best.*

# October 25th

When he had finished speaking with Abraham, God went up from him

(Genesis 17:22 *NIV*)

The revelation Abraham had was a very imperfect one in many respects; very imperfect compared with ours; that is, so far as books go. He knew but little of the history of God's dealing with other souls, compared with what we do; but God had so sufficiently and directly revealed himself to Abraham as to create in his soul a very passion of affection for him. He had shown himself so good, and wise, and loving a being, that all Abraham's heart went out after him – he loved God.

Do you want to gauge Abraham's love? Come along! Bring your measuring line. Now, then, measure his love for Isaac, and Sarah, and home, and earthly greatness. Measure all, and when you have taken it all in, then remember that Abraham offered, without hesitation, all this to please Jehovah. Oh! How he loved him!

What will love not do? It was painful but easy for Abraham to give all up. He loved God so much, that he gave him all his other loves, only loving them in him.

Another secret of Abraham's was that he knew that he was obeying God. He had the command direct from him. He heard his voice; it was not a thing done in any haphazard, speculative sort of way – all in the darkness of spiritual uncertainty, sometimes thinking he was acting in obedience to the voice of man, and sometimes his own voice. He knew God had spoken, and this made it comparatively easy for him to obey. How, when, and where he heard this voice, I don't know; perhaps it was an angel brought the message, or it might have been some hieroglyphic written communication, or it might have been a vision – God appearing, as was his wont in those days, in some earthly form, and speaking to him as a man does to his friends. Or it might have been in the depths of his inmost soul that God made him feel the command.[1]

**How gracious you are, Father, to communicate with your children – to talk to us. How wonderful it is to talk with God! Let me never take this privilege for granted, but always speak to you about everything that concerns me, and to do so with thanksgiving. Bless you, Lord, for the marvellous, mysterious way in which you speak to our hearts. Amen.**

1 From *Salvation Soldiery.*

# October 26th

Without faith it is impossible to please God, because anyone who comes to him must believe that he exists and that he rewards those who earnestly seek him

(Hebrews 11:6 *NIV*)

How desolate we should all be without faith, no matter what else we possessed, either of this world or any other. It is only by means of faith that we can obtain any satisfactory assurance of the existence of God. To be without faith, then, is to be without God. That is, "without hope and without God in the world".[1] It is true that there are voices in nature and voices in providence, and voices within us, and voices that come from the good and true around us that are ever saying, "There is a God;" but unless we believed their testimony all would be in vain. Anyway, they would do little more than land us in the desolate swamps of uncertainty on this all-important question.

But, while accepting the fact of the being of God, it is only by faith that we know that he has spoken to man. Therefore, to be without faith would be equivalent to being without a Bible. What that loss would be it is difficult to conceive. Suppose we woke up tomorrow morning, and found that every Bible at present in existence had been taken out of the world? Or suppose – which would amount to the same thing – that all at once we discovered that every page in our Bibles had become blank paper? What a mourning and lamentation there would be, and justly so. People who had never thought it worth the trouble to read their Bibles would wail. People who had read, and disbelieved, would mourn. Even people who had read and disobeyed would feel they had lost what could not be replaced.

And yet, to have the Bible without a living faith in its revelations, and a positive obedience to its precepts, is really worse than having none at all. For he that reads his Maker's will, and believes it not, is not likely to obey; and to know and not to do is to be visited with the greater condemnation.

It is only by faith we can obtain any assurance of an existence beyond the grave. To be without faith is, therefore, equal to being without immortality.[2]

**Lord, the gift of faith is arguably the most important gift you can impart, for without it we are unable to know you or anything about you. I praise you for imparting belief, from which our experience of your love grows and deepens. Thank you, Father. Amen.**

1 Ephesians 2:12 *NIV*
2 From *The Seven Spirits*.

# October 27th

Six days you shall labour, but on the seventh day you shall rest

(Exodus 34:21 *NIV*)

Let me introduce you to our Labour Yard. Here is no pretence of charity beyond the charity which gives a man remunerative labour. It is not our business to pay men wages. What we propose is to enable those, male or female, who are destitute to earn their rations and do enough work to pay for their lodging until they are able to go out into the world and earn wages for themselves. There is no compulsion upon anyone to resort to our shelter, but if a penniless man wants food he must, as a rule, do work sufficient to pay for what he has of that and of other accommodation. I say as a rule because, of course, our officers will be allowed to make exceptions in extreme cases, but the rule will be first work then eat. And that amount of work will be exacted rigorously. It is that which distinguishes this scheme from mere charitable relief... So much coffee, so much bread, so much shelter, so much warmth and light from me, but so much labour in return from him.

What is labour? It is asked. For answer to this question I would like to take you down to our Industrial Workshops in Whitechapel. There you will see the scheme in experimental operation. What we are doing there we propose to do everywhere up to the extent of the necessity, and there is no reason why we should fail elsewhere if we can succeed there.

Our Industrial Factory at Whitechapel[1] was established this spring. We opened it on a very small scale. It has developed until we have nearly ninety men at work. Some of these are skilled workmen who are engaged in carpentry. The particular job they have now in hand is the making of benches for The Salvation Army. Others are engaged in mat-making, some are cobblers, others painters, and so forth. This trial effort has, so far, answered admirably. No one who is taken on comes for a permanency. So long as he is willing to work for his rations he is supplied with materials and provided with skilled superintendents.[2]

**Lord, I pray today for the modern equivalents of Industrial Factories, wherever your people offer shelter, food, and the opportunity of honest labour to those who might otherwise be destitute. Bless such places, Lord, whatever the differences between Booth's day and ours. Essentially, the needs remain the same, and people need your love as much as ever. Amen.**

1 London.
2 From *In Darkest England and the Way Out.*

# October 28th

## God is not a God of disorder

(1 Corinthians 14:33 *NIV*)

City Industrial Workshops. Objects: These workshops are open for the relief of the unemployed and destitute, the object being to make it unnecessary for the homeless or workless to be compelled to go to the workhouse or Casual Ward, food and shelter being provided for them in exchange for work being done by them, until they can procure work for themselves, or it can be found for them elsewhere.

Plant of operation: All those applying for assistance will be placed in what is termed the first class. They must be willing to do any kind of work allotted to them. While they remain in the first class, they shall be entitled to three meals a day, and shelter for the night, and will be expected in return to cheerfully perform the work allotted to them. Promotions will be made from this first class to the second class of all those considered eligible by the Labour Directors. They will, in addition to the food and shelter above mentioned, receive sums of money up to 5s at the end of the week, for the purpose of assisting them to provide themselves with tools to get work outside.

Regulations: No smoking, drinking, bad language, or conduct calculated to demoralize will be permitted on the Factory premises. No one under the influence of drink will be admitted. Anyone refusing to work, or guilty of bad conduct, will be required to leave the premises.

Hours of work: 7 a.m. to 8:30 a.m.; 9 a.m. to 1 p.m.; 2 p.m. to 5:30 p.m. Doors will be closed five minutes after 7, 9, and 2 p.m. Food Checks will be given to all as they pass out each meal time. Meals and shelter provided at 272, Whitechapel Road.

Our practical experience shows that we can provide work by which a man can earn his rations. We shall be careful not to sell the goods so manufactured at less than the market prices. In firewood, for instance, we have endeavoured to be rather above the average than below it… we are firmly opposed to inuring one class of workmen while helping another.[1]

**These are well-made plans, Lord. The benefits of this sort of organization are obvious. Help me, in my relationship with you, to apply good structure and routine – in my prayer life, for example, and Bible reading – so that I may gain maximum benefit. Amen.**

1 From *In Darkest England and the Way Out.*

# October 29th

## The Master you are serving is Christ

(Colossians 3:24 *NLT*)

Suppose that we have here a master named Brown, who lives in the City of London. He has a son who is the servant of a man named Smith, a Salvationist, who resides in the country. Brown loves his son and, as a father, naturally desires his welfare. He is, therefore, anxious that Smith, while grinding a reasonable amount of work out of his boy, should at the same time care for his happiness and welfare. He would like him also to have an eye on his companions, and the way he spends his money and his leisure. At the same time, he thinks it quite reasonable to expect that Smith, being a Salvationist, will also care for the welfare of his soul.

Now, if this is what Brown would desire and expect from Smith, has not Smith an equal right to claim from Brown an equivalent amount of consideration and attention? For instance, is it not quite reasonable that Mr Smith should say, "Come now, Mr Brown, I want you to do for my son, who is in your employ, just precisely the same as I have done for your son, for 'one good turn', you are aware, 'deserves another'." That is, therefore, an equivalent or an expectation – I contend it is one which all fathers and mothers have a right to hold, respecting the treatment their sons and daughters should receive from their employers. It is an expectation which the servants themselves have a right to entertain. It is a duty enjoined by the Master himself…

Men used to think and publish abroad that a slave had no legal claim for anything beyond what his master thought proper to give him, and that seldom extended beyond the supply of the barest necessaries of life. To be allowed even to live and toil for the benefit of his master was by many looked upon as a favour. To treat his slave as a servant, or having a just claim for wages or any worldly comforts, was, with few exceptions, unknown.[1]

**Stir in me, Lord, that high ambition to have no ambition other than that of serving Christ. Amen.**

1 From *Religion for Every Day.*

# October 30th

## The Lord... gives supernatural guidance

(Isaiah 28:29 *NET*)

Now, my brethren, do you hear the voice of God in some form or other? Does he speak to you, so that you know it is he calling you forward in the path of duty and sacrifice, consecration and service? That it is a divine commission you have. If you are in any doubt as to whether God is positively directing, and leading, and guiding you, no wonder you are so much at sea with regard to the things you try to do for him. If all the authority you have in your soul for obedience is man-made, or is drawn from what you know other souls have rendered to him, or from the lips of those who speak to you in his name, or even from that holy book itself, no wonder your sense of responsibility should be weak, and the driving wheel of your will should drag heavily in the direction of service and sacrifice. You will never go beyond the merely human, unless you have the supernatural in command.

Your soul must hear, and know it hears, the voice of God himself saying, "Thus saith the Lord"; and then your soul shall shake itself free from all the fears, fashions, and doubts which have possessed it and, in the face of all possible difficulties and devils, offer a service as mighty as that which Abraham offered. Men – were they priests or anything else – might have thundered in his ears till doomsday, "Offer up Isaac!" They might have assured him till they were blue in the face that they had a message from God that it was to be done, but they would have urged and exhorted in vain. God himself must speak in Abraham's soul, and then Abraham rises up in a hurry to obey...

In Abraham's soul there was divine power. It was not enough for God to express his wishes to Abraham, but he must actually and positively, by his own Spirit, impart to Abraham's soul the power to trample on the human within him, and to obey this command.[1]

**What a wonderful privilege you provide, Lord; sharing some of the counsel of Heaven with your people. Grant me that sensitivity of soul, I pray, so that I may discern – and hold fast to – your voice above all others, that I may know your will. Amen.**

1 From *Salvation Soldiery.*

# October 31st

A good measure, pressed down, shaken together and running over, will be poured into your lap

(Luke 6:39 *NIV*)

It is only by means of faith that we can obtain any satisfying assurance of the favour of God. Without faith there can be no real peace amidst the trials, conflicts, and agonies of life. All the attempts of philosophy to manufacture consolation in such circumstances have proved a dead failure. They have been tried. They are a mockery, a delusion, and a snare.

To be without faith is to be without any ground of hope for the future. It is only by faith that we can have any reasonable ground for expecting any happier state of things in the new world than we have in the present. To be without faith is to have no Calvary, no Saviour, no forgiveness. We only know that Jesus died for our sins, and lives again to save us from them, through believing in God. Indeed, without faith in him life must be a dismal wilderness, and the future a dark starless blank.

Not only is faith the only medium by which we can come to know and realize spiritual things, but the measure of our faith will generally be the measure of that realization. In other words, the religious life of an officer will be governed by his faith. Salvation is commenced by means of faith, maintained by faith, and brought to a triumphant issue by faith. 1) Your conversion was by faith. 2) Your assurance of it has been received by faith. 3) Your peace and gladness have been according to your faith. 4) Your usefulness in honouring God and saving men has been, and will be, according to your faith. 5) Your triumph on your dying bed will be according to your faith. 6) Your crown, happiness, honour, and reward in Heaven will depend upon the extent to which the Spirit of faith has led you, and enabled you to do all the holy will of God.

1. If you have a little faith, a half-starved, neither-hot-nor-cold affair, you will only have a little salvation.

2. If you have a bigger, bolder, stronger faith, you will have a bigger, grander, more glorious salvation.[1]

**Father, I like this description of faith, and I ask you to bless me today with a measure of faith that is rich and wholesome. Thank you, Lord. Amen.**

1 From *The Seven Spirits.*

# November 1st

Look to the right and see: there is none who takes notice of me; no refuge remains to me; no one cares for my soul

(Psalm 142:4 *ESV*)

"Captain," I say, "the way to increase our attendances is to make the meetings more interesting. Nothing draws like hot and happy meetings; they fetch the people."

Well, as I have said, we had a nice little crowd, and there was a lively beginning; and then the captain, he set the ball a-rolling. "Comrades," he said, "last week we had a confessional meeting, and a blessed time it was. I got a great lift myself. I have been walking closer to God, and feeling more about eternal things all the past week than I think I have ever done before. God helped me that night to acknowledge where I saw that I had come short, and to give myself up afresh for the doing of his blessed will, and – to his honour and glory I say it – he has kept me faithful to my promise."

And then he went on: "Comrades," says he, "how has it been with you? Last Sunday, you, too, confessed your shortcomings and neglects, and the different ways in which you had grieved the Holy Spirit. But you will be no forrarder for that unless you do different in the future. Indeed," says he, "that meeting will rise against you in black condemnation at the Judgment Day unless you do better.

"You complain of the Catholics confessing their sins, and then going and doing the same again, just as if nothing had happened. Now, aren't you in danger of acting very much after the same fashion? And if you do, what better will you be for it all? Think a bit," says he. "It's not only confession of sin that you want; it's salvation from sinning.

"And then," he went on, growing more solemn every moment, "some of you," he said, "confessed last Sunday morning that you hadn't done your duty by the souls of your relations – and well you might. I have been reckoning with my own heart on that very score myself. But I'm going to do better, God helping me, and I want you to do the same."[1]

**Lord, this day, touch my heart with a love for the lost and a great concern for souls. Amen.**

1 From *Sergeant-Major Do-Your-Best.*

# November 2nd

Jesus answered, "It is written: 'Man shall not live on bread alone, but on every word that comes from the mouth of God'"

(Matthew 4:4 *NIV*)

A master, while seeking his own welfare and comfort, shall at the same time take the welfare and comfort of his servants into consideration… James the coachman, Mary the housemaid, or Jones the shoemaker, cannot live by bread alone; and I have said, and say again, that every employer is responsible before God for supplying his servants… with these things.

In conversing with a gentleman some time ago, I remember his saying to me, "When I came to this estate, I found a large portion of it under the cultivation of the plough, but I laid it all down for grazing, with the exception of a few acres. As such, it had given me infinitely less trouble than it would have done under the old system, and while not requiring more than a third of the number of men to work it, it pays me just as well, if not better, than before." That is to say, with much less anxiety on the landlord's part, the estate yielded him as much profit.

But what had become of the men, who for years had earned a livelihood on the land, as their fathers had done before them, he did not say. They had to move off, I suppose, to the city, drifting down probably to the slums, or even lower still. Now this gentleman was a downright, kind-hearted man, and a Christian of loud profession; but he did not see, as he should have done, I think, that when planning for the easier management of his farm, he ought, at the same time, to have considered the welfare of his workmen.

In pleading the servant's cause, and trying to show the duty of the master or mistress, I do not think I have asked for anything impossible or unreasonable. Neither have I had money, or the supply of things that money will buy, exclusively in my mind. In addition to the supply of the bare necessities of existence, I have been thinking of the care and the sympathy, the counsel, and the thousand other things indispensable to the servant's well-being, for which the master ought to feel some reasonable concern.[1]

**Lord, I lift employers to you today, asking that you would prompt them to care for their employees; not just in the provision of a salary, but with kindness too, and an interest in their personal welfare. Bless the bosses. Amen.**

1 From *Religion for Every Day.*

# November 3rd

David gave orders to assemble the foreigners residing in Israel, and from among them he appointed stonecutters to prepare

(1 Chronicles 22:2 *NIV*)

We are endeavouring to raise the standard of labour…

But, it will be asked, how do these Out-of-Works conduct themselves when you get them into the Factory? Upon this point I have a very satisfactory report to render. Many, no doubt, are below par, under-fed, and suffering from ill health, or the consequence of their intemperance. Many also are old men, who have been crowded out of the labour market by [the] younger generation. But, without making too many allowances on these grounds, I may fairly say that these men have shown themselves not only anxious and willing, but able to work. Our Factory superintendent reports:

Of loss of time there has practically been none since the opening… Each man during his stay, with hardly an exception, has presented himself punctually at opening time and worked more or less assiduously the whole of the labour hours. The morals of the men have been good; in not more than three instances has there been an overt act of disobedience, insubordination, or mischief. The men, as a whole, are uniformly civil, willing, and satisfied; they are all fairly industrious; some, and that not a few, are assiduous and energetic. The foremen have had no serious complaints to make or delinquencies to report…

I had a return made of the names and trades and mode of employment of the men at work. Of the forty in the shops at that moment, eight were carpenters, twelve labourers, two tailors, two sailors, three clerks, two engineers, while among the rest was a shoemaker, two grocers, a cooper, a sailmaker, a musician, a painter, and a stonemason. Nineteen of these were employed in sawing, cutting, and tying up firewood, six were making mats, seven making sacks, and the rest were employed in various odd jobs. Among them was a Russian carpenter who could not speak a word of English. The whole place is a hive of industry which fills the hearts of those who go to see it with hope that something is about to be done to solve the difficulty of the unemployed.[1]

**Loving Lord, please reach out today to those who even in these times can't find work. I think of the Russian man in the story, and pray your blessing upon economic migrants who find themselves in strange lands. May your love touch them all. Amen.**

1 From *In Darkest England and the Way Out.*

# November 4th

If a countryman of yours becomes so poor with regard to you that he sells himself to you, you shall not subject him to a slave's service. He shall be with you as a hired man, as if he were a sojourner

(Leviticus 25:39–40 *NASB*)

Although our factories will be permanent institutions, they will not be anything more than temporary resting places to those who avail themselves of their advantages. They are harbours of refuge into which the storm-tossed workman may run and re-fit, so that he may again push out to the ordinary sea of labour and earn his living. The establishment of these Industrial Factories seems to be one of the most obvious duties of those who would effectively deal with the social problem. They are as indispensable a link in the chain of deliverance as the Shelters, but they are only a link and not a stopping-place. And we do not propose that they should be regarded as anything but stepping stones to better things.

These shops will also be of service for men and women temporarily unemployed who have families, and who possess some sort of a home. In numerous instances, if by any means these unfortunates could find bread and rent for a few weeks, they would tide over their difficulties, and an untold amount of misery would be averted. In such cases, work would be supplied at their own homes where preferred, especially for women and children, and such remuneration would be aimed at as would supply the immediate necessities of the hour. To those who have rent to pay and families to support, something beyond rations would be indispensable.

The Labour Shops will enable us to work out our Anti-Sweating experiments. For instance, we propose at once to commence manufacturing matchboxes, for which we shall aim at giving nearly treble the amount at present paid to the poor starving creatures engaged in this work.[1] In all these establishments our success will depend upon the extent to which we are able to establish and maintain in the minds of workers sound moral sentiments and to cultivate a spirit of hopefulness and aspiration. We shall continually seek to impress upon them the fact that while we desire to feed the hungry, and clothe the naked, and provide shelter for the shelterless, we are still more anxious to bring about that regeneration of heart and life which is essential to their future happiness.[2]

**Lord, regard the prayer of the destitute, and heed their supplication. Amen.**

1 In 1891, Booth opened a match factory in Old Ford, London, aiming at vast improvements in the conditions of match makers. Workers (young girls) in this industry frequently suffered from fatal necrosis, or "phossy jaw", a dreadful bone cancer caused by the poison used in match heads. Booth introduced safety matches, the manufacture of which was nowhere near as harmful. His first match works was fitted with large windows and washbasins, almost unheard of in such times.

2 From *In Darkest England and the Way Out.*

# November 5th

**Sluggards do not plough in season; so at harvest time they look but find nothing**

**(Proverbs 20:4 *NIV*)**

One more element in [Abraham's] obedience was that he obeyed sharp – that is, he went straight off and did it. That was, in all human probability, his only chance. If he had tarried, and argued, and postponed, and conferred with flesh and blood, the probability is that he would have been worsted and defeated – some excuses would have been found, and Isaac would never have been offered. But no! He went off promptly to obey. He did not wait for pleasant feelings, as many do; he just went off with his heart torn and bleeding as it was, to do just as he was told.

He did not wait to consult any wise, religious people, anyone specially advanced and experienced. We have no reason to suppose that he mentioned the matter to a soul. The probability is that had he done so, he would have been persuaded off it. Had he felt led to lay the matter before some body of elders, or before a committee of management; or had he sought the advice and blessing of some church meeting, he would have had such a revelation of the difficulties connected with the course proposed that he would never have gone to Moriah at all. No! He knew the mind of God on the matter, and that was enough for him.

Just so with you, my comrades, and everyone else, as far as that goes; if you want to do it right, on pleasant or unpleasant lines, go straight at it; get satisfied as to what you ought to do, and then give up deliberating. Cease weighing the matter over, getting the advice of good, timid people, and at once commit yourself, in the most emphatic and public manner possible, to the doing of the thing. This is your only chance, and if you don't act in this way, ten to one if you act in the right way at all.

Oh! What hosts of people there are who [are] continually coming up to sacrifice, and consecration, and service, and they know what the great God wants from them, and they don't go any further.[1]

**What shall I do for you today, Lord? Tell me, please, and then quicken my heart – not to make another cup of tea, not to read the paper and then get on with it, not to watch television for another half an hour, but to set to, like Abraham. Amen.**

1 From *Salvation Soldiery.*

# November 6th

Anyone who does not provide for their relatives, and especially for their own household, has denied the faith

(1 Timothy 5:8 *NIV*)

"I am ashamed to know that there are Salvation soldiers who have fathers and mothers who are unsaved – fathers and mothers who nursed them in infancy, and fed and cared for them in after years – fathers and mothers who are not far from the grave, not far from Hell."

As the captain said these words, a shudder went through the meeting. "Oh!" he went on. "Think of having a father or a mother wandering about the caverns of despair – a father or a mother who is a lost soul!"...

There are Salvationists who have sons and daughters living in sin, under its mastery, in ignorance of the fact that it may carry them to lives of shame in the streets, to lives of ignominy in prison, to fill a drunkard's grave in a cemetery, or – lower still – to lie down among the damned in Hell.

"There are Salvationists – alas! alas! Where are they not? – who have brothers and sisters, or other relations, who are travelling to destruction. What is to be done for them?

"Now," said the captain, "I don't know you nor your families as I hope to do... but I have no doubt that what I have said applies to some – perhaps a great many – who are here. There is someone in your home circle for whose salvation God has in some special manner made you responsible, and I want to ask you a question about them." Here the captain made quite a long pause, and then he asked his question: "If your father, mother, wife, or children were in a house on fire, would you not feel a special responsibility to get them out? If they were sick and ready to die, would you let them go to the grave without having done what you could to save them? Now, is it not true that some of your relations are in their sins, going down to destruction, and will be cast into the fires of Hell... unless they are got to the Saviour's feet? Have you done what in you lies to save them?"[1]

**Lord of life and death, this is not easy reading. Stay with me as I ponder these words, and weigh their importance. Form my response as you see fit, I pray, for Jesus' sake. Amen.**

1 From *Sergeant-Major Do-Your-Best.*

# November 7th

**Blessed be the Lord God of Israel; for he hath visited and redeemed his people**

(Luke 1:68 *KJV*)

I met a young man, one day, in the north, who said to me, "I have been thinking and talking about the blessing of holiness for a long time, and have been going to consecrate myself fully to the Lord, but yesterday afternoon, at three o'clock, I went upstairs and did it."

There are doubtless many here who have been considering the subject of this entire consecration for a long time; I hope this morning you have come… to do it. If you do nothing more than consider and hear, you will go away very little, if any, forwarder than when you came… I want to see, this morning, if there is not something said in the Bible about holiness of heart as definitely as we Salvationists say it, although in somewhat different phraseology. The prophecy I am going to read [Luke 1:68 ff.] was descriptive of the work our Lord Jesus Christ was to accomplish in the hearts and lives of his own people. It not only referred to him, describing him, but specially referred to and described what he should do for those who received him – what he should do for and in them, not in the Glory Land up yonder, but down here on the earth.

Now, let us go down and speak in supplication to our hearts, and beg of them to receive all the blessedness which Jesus Christ died to procure for us, for which he is now interceding with the Father, and for the accomplishment of which he has sent the Holy Ghost, this very morning, to persuade us to accept.

It seems to me that our position should not be so much that of knocking at the door of Heaven to ask God to come and do something for us, as that of knocking at the door of our own hearts to beseech them to put away all their stupid prejudices and all their obstinate unbelief – to put away that unbelief which when beaten away from one hiding place does not give in and give up the controversy and own itself defeated.[1]

**I praise you because you are a redeeming God; you redeem your people, you redeem our hearts and our ways, you redeem our lives. What a great redemption. Amen.**

1 From *Salvation Soldiery.*

# November 8th

"Whenever you receive a message from me, warn people immediately"

(Ezekiel 3:17 *NLT*)

It is often a great mistake to suppose that testimony on the subject of religion is disagreeable; in many instances it would be most welcome, especially from the lips of a Salvationist…

They think this is the work of their officers; that is, of those who are set apart and paid for the performance of the task. They do not feel any responsibility for the souls of their workmates or the strangers about them, but seem willing to let them go, quietly and comfortably, down to Hell, so far as they are concerned. Much less would they run the risk of sacrificing their good opinion, or incurring their displeasure, by speaking to them in an omnibus, on the deck of a steamer, or in the roadway. What an awful blindness this is! May God open the eyes of all such ignorant, shrinking souls…

Oh, how I have mourned on my own account over chances of this description lost for want of thought. "Why," I have said to myself, "did it not occur to me to speak? That chance I can never have again, and I may never have another." Sometimes the reason may be traced to a spurious kindness. There is a fear of hurting other people's feelings. I am afraid that this fear often shuts the mouths of those who ought to utter words of solemn warning, and for this reason many a poor sinner is left to die in the dark… Alas! There is occasionally another reason, which is a very unhappy one. The Salvationist is troubled with doubts and fears about his own safety; and, not being certain about his own salvation, is, consequently, unwilling to speak to others on the subject.

Only too often his voice is silent because he is not too sure about his own standing with God, and the rightness of his own life. It is true that the stranger by his side may know nothing of his inconsistency; but that friend, whose name is Conscience, who resides within him, knows how matters stand between him and God.[1]

**Soften my heart, Lord, for souls. When I speak to someone – anyone – prompt me to remember my high calling of evangelism. May the words I speak dovetail with the work of grace you are already doing in that person's life. Amen.**

1 From *The Founder's Messages to Soldiers*.

# November 9th

And when he comes, he will convict the world of its sin
(John 16:8 *NLT*)

The captain said, "Now, what are we to do? There are two courses open to us:

"First, we can go on just as we have been going, in which case we cannot expect anything different in the future from what we have had in the past, and can therefore reckon on the members of our own families, our own flesh and blood, going on in their sins and being lost.

"The second course for us to take is to set to work with all our might to get them saved. So I want you to go down before God and tell him –

"That you will start afresh from tonight to pray for them.

"That you will make desperate efforts to get them to the meetings.

"That you will begin anew to plead with them personally."

We spent a few minutes on our knees in silence, broken only by sobs and groans, and then the meeting closed. We walked a good part of the way home – that is, Sarah and I – before a word was spoken; and then I said, "Well, wife, what do you think of that for a holiness meeting?" "What do I think about that meeting, Sergeant-Major?" said she. "I will tell you what I think about that meeting. I think that that man has been sent by God to show me my sins, in neglecting to seek the salvation of my own flesh and blood; and when I looked at them tonight as I sat in that hall, I felt condemned for my neglect, and that I deserved to be sent to Hell right away."

Now, this was awful, was it not? – and I said: "Sarah, Sarah, you always was too hard on yourself; and what you're saying now is too dreadful to think about; for," says I, "aren't you my wife? And aren't you a good woman? And aren't you converted? Yes, Sarah, you are. I never shall forget the night when we knelt together at that blessed penitent form. And then, Sarah," I says, "I believe you are sanctified as well."[1]

**Gracious Spirit, you come to convict us of our sins, and I thank you for your ministry, for if I don't know what's wrong, I can't hope to put it right. Thank you that you not only convict, but help to repair too. Amen.**

1 From *Sergeant-Major Do-Your-Best.*

# November 10th

## Syria did business with you because of your abundant goods

(Ezekiel 27:16 *ESV*)

Some… who read this will, doubtless, be engaged in trade, either as shopkeepers, masters, mechanics, farmers, or some other business which will devolve upon them the duty of buying or selling good of various descriptions. I feel, therefore, that I cannot pass by a subject so intimately connected with their lives. The counsels I propose to give you shall, as we sometimes say with respect to our speeches, be "short and to the point"…

Have nothing to do with any form of trade on which you cannot ask the blessing of your Heavenly Father. That will shut you out from all business involving injustice, or falsehood, or which cannot be followed without trespassing upon the welfare of your fellow men. God is just, true, and benevolent. You cannot, therefore, expect him to give his approval on any trade or profession that is unjust in its character, which violates truth in its maintenance, or which can only succeed by inflicting injury upon others. You might as well expect him to bless and prosper the work of the devil as anything of that kind.

When, therefore, you are considering a business for yourself, or for your children, ask the question, "Can I buy or sell in this shop, or engage in this profession, as truly in the spirit of love and faith, as I can take my place in the open-air, or stand up and give my testimony in the salvation meeting? If not, I will have nothing to do with it." I know that such a resolution, or the acting upon it, will, as I have already said, close the door to many trades or professions…

A gentleman said to me a little time back: "I have had considerable experience of business… and exceptional opportunities for judging the character of the methods that prevail… and I have come to the conclusion that there is no trade or profession that is not, more or less, dependent for its prosperity on fraud and falsehood"… I think his opinion must have been an exaggeration.[1]

**Father, whether William Booth was right, or the businessman was cynical, I pray for Christians engaged in commerce today; protect them, Father, from any temptations of dishonesty or underhand dealing, and use them, in a competitive world, to set a shining example of trustworthiness that will speak volumes. Amen.**

1 From *Religion for Every Day.*

# November 11th

I will build my church, and the gates of Hades will not overcome it

(Matthew 16:18 *NIV*)

Faith will have to do with the measure of your success; indeed, that success will be largely determined by the measure of your faith. Other qualities and gifts will certainly be required. For instance... natural gifts and conditions, such as:

Good health. Pleasant appearance... An agreeable voice. Fluency in talking. Intelligence. Special gifts. But all these put together will be of little service without faith. Indeed such gifts, without faith, are often a hindrance rather than a help. For, with a simple earnest faith, an officer may do a thousand times more for God and souls without these advantages than he will do with them all, if he has no faith.

For, consider:

An officer's success will largely depend upon his faith in himself. This will apply to his personal realization of the experience he urges on others. If he is uncertain as to whether he himself possesses the salvation he pushes on his hearers, his trumpet cannot be expected to do any other than give an uncertain sound.[1] To be doubting and fearing about himself while he is talking will mean weakness and failure in all he says. His success will depend upon his faith in the consistency of his life with the standard he holds up before others.

The faith of an officer in the Army will have much to do with his success. It is so with me. You all know how I feel about the Army. You all know that I believe in it, and that faith helps me to study, and write, and travel, and pray, and talk, and govern. I feel that it is worth all the effort I can make. That faith cheers me in success, and comforts me in disappointments and defeat. I say to myself of a particular effort or special meeting, "If this is not as effective as I desire, it cannot prevent the onward march." For instance: If you only know and believe in the Army's history, I am sure you will fight for it. Ditto, its principles. Ditto, its system and future.[2]

**Father, while it is true that denominations are man-made, it is also true that you place us where you can best use us. I praise you because your people can worship you and serve you in a variety of ways; thank you for that diversity. I pray for my denomination today, and I ask you to bless my Christian brothers and sisters of all traditions. Amen.**

1 1 Corinthians 14:8
2 From *The Seven Spirits*.

# November 12th

Remember the Lord your God, for it is he who gives you the ability to produce wealth

(Deuteronomy 8:18 *NIV*)

When we have got the homeless, penniless tramp washed, and housed, and fed at the Shelter, and have secured him the means of earning his fourpence[1] by chopping firewood, or making mats or cobbling the shoes of his fellow-labourers at the Factory, we have next to seriously address ourselves to the problem of how to help him get back into the regular ranks of industry. The Shelter and the Factory are but stepping stones, which have this advantage – they give us time to look round and to see what there is in a man and what we can make of him.

The first and most obvious thing to do is to ascertain whether there is any demand in the regular market for the labour which is thus thrown upon our hands. In order to ascertain this I have already established a Labour Bureau,[2] the operations of which I shall at once largely extend, at which employers can register their needs, and workmen can register their names and the kind of work they can do.

At present there is no labour exchange in existence in this country. The columns of the daily newspaper are the only substitute for this much-needed register. It is one of the many painful consequences arising from the overgrowth of cities. If a farmer wants a couple of extra men for mowing or some more women for binding at harvest-time, he runs over in his mind the names of every available person in the parish. Even in a small town there is little difficulty in knowing who wants employment. But in the cities this knowledge is not available; hence we constantly hear of persons who would be very glad to employ labour for odd jobs in an occasional stress of work, while at the same time hundreds of persons are starving for want of work at another end of town.

To meet this evil, the laws of supply and demand have created the Sweating Middlemen, who farm out the unfortunates and charge so heavy a commission for their share that the poor wretches who do the work receive hardly enough to keep body and soul together.[3]

**Lord, this was a brilliant scheme, and I give you all the glory for inspiring the idea. May we see similar inventiveness at work today, on behalf of those needing work. Amen.**

1 Some of the payments to workers were in the form of specially minted tokens – stamped "The Salvation Army Social Wing 4d" – which could only be spent at certain places. This was aimed at preventing wages being spent on alcohol.

2 The Central Labour Bureau was located in the Army's City Colony and Social Headquarters at 272 (later renumbered 20–22), Whitechapel Road, London.

3 From *In Darkest England and the Way Out.*

# November 13th

The servant of God may be thoroughly equipped for every good work

(2 Timothy 3:17 *NIV*)

It is obvious that the moment you begin to find work for the unemployed labour of the community, no matter what you do by way of the registration and bringing together of those who want work and those who want workers, there will still remain a vast residuum of unemployed, and it will be the duty of those who undertake to deal with the question to devise means for securing them employment.

Many things are possible when there is a directing intelligence at headquarters and discipline in the rank and file, which would be utterly impossible when everyone is left to go as he pleases, when ten men are running for one man's job, and when no one can be depended upon to be in the way at the time he is wanted.

When my scheme is carried out, there will be in every populous centre a captain of industry, an officer specially charged with the regimentation of unorganized labour, who would be continually on the alert, thinking how best to utilize the waste human material in his district. It is contrary to all previous experience to suppose that the addition of so much trained intelligence will not operate beneficially in securing the disposal of a commodity which is at present a drug in the market.

Robertson of Brighton[1] used frequently to remark that every truth was built up of two apparent contradictory propositions. In the same way I may say that the solution of every social difficulty is to be found in the discovery of two corresponding difficulties. It is like the puzzle maps of children. When you are putting one together, you suddenly come upon some awkward piece that will not fit in anywhere, but you do not in disgust and despair break your piece into fragments or throw it away. On the contrary, you keep it by you, knowing that before long you will discover a number of other pieces which it will be impossible to fit in until you fix you unmanageable, unshapely piece in the centre.[2]

**Lord, for those who devote their time and intelligence to solving the problems of humankind, with the intention of making life better for some, I thank you. Bless those who hold positions of influence, to whom you have given strategic skills, whatever their specific field. Use them today to bring relief to others. Amen.**

1 Frederick William Robertson (1816–53), known as Robertson of Brighton, was an English divine/preacher.

2 From *In Darkest England and the Way Out.*

# November 14th

### Salvation from our enemies and from the hand of all who hate us

(Luke 1:71 *NIV*)

Jesus Christ has come to you and to me, to deliver us from sin. No one would want to localize this purpose, or contract it, by saying he was intended to save a man from getting drunk, from telling lies, or swearing, or thieving – that is, to take the outworks, while the very citadel, the heart, is left infected with pride, selfishness, envy, hatred, revenge, bad temper, and everything that is bad, rotten, devilish, and unlike God. Surely, to deliver him, he must not only break the neck of the open and outward foes who have domineered over him, but he must destroy those inward enemies, and save us out of the hands of all that is devilish in our own secret passions, tempers, and dispositions.

Now, I think I hear you say, "How far can I be saved in this direction? Is there such a thing as an uttermost salvation? I am wonderfully saved already. I do now enjoy a wonderful salvation. A wonderful change has been wrought within me. I am not what I used to be by any comparison, but still I am conscious that there is sin within me – sin of which I alone am conscious," for every man has, so to speak, two characters. He has a character with which the outer world is conversant, and an inward character which is only known to him and his Maker.

Of this inner character, many may say, there are in it blots and blurs, much that is selfish, much that is devilish, much of which they would be ashamed to have the record transcribed on paper and read out before their fellow men, but there they are, evils springing up, roots of bitterness continually grieving them, pricking them and bringing them into bondage; and the cry often goes up to Heaven from such hearts, "Can I be saved from these inward sins?"

I answer... He came to save you out of the hand of your enemies, that is, out of their grip – make you free from their power – so deliver you that they shall have no hold upon you.[1]

**You are a great God – mighty, magnificent, and merciful. Amen.**

1 From *Salvation Soldiery.*

# November 15th

If you are pure and upright, even now he will rouse himself on your behalf and restore you to your prosperous state

(Job 8:6 *NIV*)

Be upright in all your transactions. Be straight. Be truthful; that is, be as good as your word. If people can rely upon your representations about the things you sell, they will be pleased to be your customers. If they find that you are upright, and do not cheat and deceive them in the work you do, they will be glad to employ you. If they find that you are honourable, and do not take advantage of their ignorance, they will be pleased to deal with you, and will recommend their neighbours and friends to do the same. Honesty, in both word and deed, has usually been found to be the best policy in the long run; and if it does not pay as well in this world, God will see that it pays far better in the next.

What I have said... about doing good work, I recommend to the consideration of all who may be either engaged in business or contemplate entering upon it... Do the right thing in your business transactions, whether it is profitable or otherwise, and always do it. Do right if the heavens fall. If you do right, you shall prosper. If you refuse to do right, though all the inhabitants of earth and Hell swear to the contrary, you will perish.

If people ask whether your dress-prints will keep their colour in washing, and you know they will not, tell them so. If they are buying eatables, or medicines, thinking they are pure, when you know they are not, tell them that the articles are adulterated. If you are selling a horse that has a blemish, point it out to your customer. You are not under any obligation to sell the animal, but you are under an obligation to do right and keep from sin, and John tells us that "All unrighteousness is sin".[1]

What does missing the sale of your horse matter, because you will not lie about it, compared with laying your head upon your pillow with that sin upon your conscience?[2]

**Thank you, Lord, that your Kingdom is about righteousness and integrity, more than it is about profit and gain. In a greedy society, plant your values ever-deeper into my heart. Thank you, Lord, for this refreshing perspective. Amen.**

1 1 John 5:17 *KJV*
2 From *Religion for Every Day.*

# November 16th

Now may the Lord value my life, even as I have valued yours today

(1 Samuel 26:24 *NLT*)

You cannot succeed without hard, self-denying, cross-bearing work. And whether you do that work heartily or not will largely depend on the estimate you set on the value of the men and women for whom you fight...

She was a Salvation Army lass, and her lot was a hard one. Working from seven in the morning till six o'clock at night, weaving hair-cloth, was dull and poorly paid work, but in addition she had to bear the constant and thoughtless gibes of her fellow-workers. One autumn morning a spark from a bonfire on some adjoining allotment gardens entered an open window, alighted on a heap of loose hair, and the next minute the place was ablaze. A rush for safety of the work-girls followed. "Is everybody down?" asked the foreman. His question was answered by one of the weavers who, holding up a key, shrieked, "My God! I locked Lizzie Summers in the piece shed for a joke not a minute ago!" The piece shed was a room to be reached only through the burning building, through which it seemed impossible to make way. Girls and men were standing aghast and helpless, when two figures stumbled through the smoke which poured from the weaving-room. One was seen to be Lizzie Summers; the other was, for the time being, unrecognizable. It was the Salvation Army lass. She had stayed behind, burnt, blistered, and half-suffocated, to batter down the door in order to liberate and save the life of her coarsest-tongued tormentor.

If you don't think that the people are of any great worth you won't be likely to face either fire or water to save them. But if you believe –

1. that they are immortal, that they will live for ever
2. that their souls are of indescribable worth
3. that God loves them, and wants to get them into Heaven
4. that Christ thought them of sufficient value to lay down his life for them
5. that they are every hour in peril of the wrath of God and the damnation of Hell... you will work, and weep, and pray, and fight to save them.[1]

**Father, as a jeweller values gems, and as a merchant values gold, may I value the souls of those around me; never-dying, and of inestimable worth. I praise you because you sent Jesus to pay the colossal price of sin. Amen.**

1 From *The Seven Spirits.*

# November 17th

I LOOKED, AND THERE BEFORE ME WAS A WHITE HORSE! ITS RIDER HELD A BOW, AND HE WAS GIVEN A CROWN, AND HE RODE OUT AS A CONQUEROR

**(Revelation 6:2 *NIV*)**

I am not afraid of being damned. Some of these people behind me [on the platform] used to be afraid of it, but they are saved from fear now, for the Lord has raised up a Conqueror, and his name is called Jesus, because he should save his people, not only from the consequences of their sins, but from the sins themselves.

I wish people were as anxious to be saved from sin as they are to be saved from the penalty. What should we think of the man who said, "I don't care so much about a bit of thieving. I don't see any particular harm in it, but the evil I see is being caught and put in prison. That is what I object to"? There are some people who say there is no harm in doing wrong except you are found out. Now, what should we say of people who talked in that fashion?

Oh, Hell is a calamity, looked at in one sense, in the same way as our prisons are; but our prisons are a necessity, and Hell is a necessity, and if men will sin, then men must suffer. If men will be thieves, we must have a prison for them, and if men will sin, then God must have a prison to put sinners in.

I thank God, he came to save me from its burning, and my wife, and children, and this great multitude of people; and by his grace, I am going to do what I can, as long as he lets me live, to get other people saved. I have laid myself, and my family, my good, and my hours, on the altar, and I will try and get others to do the same.

But the Conqueror... came not only that he might save us from the punishment of sin, but from sin itself. You never need sin any more. He is a Saviour for you. Do you hear? You need never sin any more. Here's the Conqueror. He is coming this way.[1]

**Jesus has conquered! Evil shall perish, and righteousness shall reign. Amen.**

1 From *Salvation Soldiery.*

# NOVEMBER 18TH

I KNOW A MAN IN CHRIST WHO FOURTEEN YEARS AGO WAS CAUGHT UP TO THE THIRD HEAVEN. WHETHER IT WAS IN THE BODY OR OUT OF THE BODY I DO NOT KNOW – GOD KNOWS

(2 Corinthians 12:2 *NIV*)

There have been seasons and days in your memory, that is, they have been to you as the days of Heaven on the earth, and you said, "Oh, if they could but have lasted!" Thank God! You can have them over again, and they may last.

There is a deliverance – a deliverance from all sin – that can last all the days of your life, if you live to be as old as Methuselah; and if you get properly saved, I shall be very sorry for you to die at all. May the Lord save you properly, and then people will be sorry when they hear about your funeral.

People say this is applicable to Heaven; they believe in holiness in Heaven; they would all be sad if I were to come and announce, "Mary Jones, I have had information from Paradise that you will go into a bad temper when you get up there." "Then," I think Mary Jones would say, "I don't want to go there."

There are very few of you who would care to go to Heaven if you expected you were going to carry in with you the peevishnesses, the devilishnesses, and selfishnesses which mar and spoil your peace on earth. "Oh," you would say, "if Heaven is not going to be a holy place, all the joy, and glitter, and spangle about it has gone for me. I want to go where I shall be holy; to go away from my evil self."

There is only one place where you can get away from your evil self, and that is in the fountain of Christ's blood. There is no other place. If you went to Heaven as you are… this morning, you would wake up in Heaven much as… you were in your home yesterday. But, oh! If this morning, you, my comrades, my brethren, my friends, if we could all help one another, if the Holy Ghost would help us to get our hearts into the river… we should get away from our heart plagues.[1]

**Your presence, Lord, creates Heaven on earth. Thank you for those glimpses of the life to come – and thank you for the eternal perfection of that life. I praise you. Amen.**

1 From *Salvation Soldiery.*

# November 19th

### Speak thou the things which become sound doctrine

(Titus 2:1 *KJV*)

Richard Cecil,[1] one of the great soul-winners of bygone days, in words which produced a great effect on my own heart, says: "Faith is the master spring of the minister. Hell is before more and thousands of souls shut up there in everlasting agonies; Jesus Christ stands forth to save men from rushing into this bottomless abyss; he sends me to proclaim his ability and his love. I want no fourth idea! Every fourth idea is contemptible! Every fourth idea is a grand impertinence!!"

Faith will determine what you are and what you do. The success of an officer will be largely influenced by his faith in the means he employs to ensure that success. For example: His faith in the doctrines he preaches will have to do with his success. If he does not really believe in them, they will have little effect on his own heart, and consequently little effect on the heart of anyone else. But if he has received them into his own soul, if they are realities to him, they will move him and, moved by them, he will move the people he talks to. Especially if his faith is "mixed with faith in them that hear" his message. For instance: if he sincerely believes –

1. that there is a glorious heaven
2. that there is an awful Hell
3. that there is going to be a Judgment Day
4. that Jesus Christ came down and died for men
5. that the miseries of the people before and around him can be cleared away by the power of God, his own soul will be so moved.

His faith that the truths he proclaims apply to the persons to whom he proclaims them. If he believes that the truth of the doctrines he preaches will take hold of the very people present at that particular time, he will be likely to pour out the truth. If he is quite sure that what he has to say about conscience, and death, and judgment, and Hell will shake the souls of the sinners who sit before him… he will be likely to talk effectually.[2]

**We have such a great gospel, Lord – thank you for its life-changing power. Whatever our slight differences of doctrine, bless your people with an anointing fit for the gospel, that truth will be preached with conviction and authority. Bless preachers. Amen.**

1 Richard Cecil (1748–1810) was a leading Evangelical Anglican clergyman of the eighteenth and nineteenth centuries.

2 From *The Seven Spirits.*

# November 20th

## You shall not covet

(Exodus 20:17 *NIV*)

Beware of covetousness. By that I mean not only the desiring of other people's possessions for which you have no lawful claim, but the longing after wealth, or houses, or lands, or trade, or any other worldly thing, for its own sake. It cannot be wrong to desire what are known as the necessaries of life, either for ourselves, or for those depending on us. Neither can it be wrong to desire money or position, so that we may be the better able to help those whose miseries constitute their only claim upon our assistance. And we are equally sure that it is right and commendable to desire, with all our strength, the graces of God's Holy Spirit. For this have the authority of the apostle, who tells us to "covet earnestly the best gifts".[1]

But to have food and raiment, and yet to be everlastingly yearning after more of the world's treasures, great or small, is evil, and only evil, and evil continually. The children exhibit this vice before they have learned to distinguish good from ill. Give the babe in its mother's arms one of the two apples that lie upon the table, which is as much as its little hand will carry, and it will want the other. It cares little that its sister desires and has a right to it. That is covetousness in the child, although the desire may not be sinful in itself, seeing the child has not, as yet, acquired the knowledge of good and evil; but when we come to its grown-up brothers and sisters, we find the same passion in a much more hateful and injurious degree.

Their knowledge of right and wrong, in fact, has now made it actually sinful. Although possessed of the one apple, they desire the other also, although they know, which the child does not, that their brothers and sisters will suffer, nay, perhaps die, for the want of it.

Beware of covetousness! God forbids it... It is the fruitful source of heart-burnings, strife, starvations, seductions, adulteries, suicides, murders, and almost every other form of human wickedness.[2]

**Thank you, Father, for all that you have graciously provided for me; food and drink, and clothes to wear, somewhere to live. I am grateful to you for giving me all I need. Amen.**

1 1 Corinthians 12:31 *KJV*
2 From *Religion for Every Day.*

# November 21st

The land allotted to the tribe of Judah, according to its clans, extended down to the territory of Edom, to the Desert of Zin in the extreme south. Their southern boundary started from the bay at the southern end of the Dead Sea, crossed south of Scorpion Pass, continued on to Zin and went over to the south of Kadesh Barnea. Then it ran past Hezron up to Addar and curved around to Karka. It then passed along to Azmon and joined the Wadi of Egypt, ending at the Mediterranean Sea. This is their southern boundary

(Joshua 15:1–4 *NIV*)

In the work of piecing together the fragments which lie scattered around the base of our social system we must not despair because we have in the unorganized, untrained labourers that which seems hopelessly out of fit with everything around. There must be something corresponding to it which is equally useless until he can be brought to bear upon it. In other words, having got one difficulty in the case of the Out-of-Works, we must cast about to find another difficulty to pair off against it, and then out of two difficulties will arise the solution to the problem. We shall not have to seek far before we discover in every town and in every country the corresponding element to our unemployed labourer. We have waste labour on the one hand; we have waste commodities on the other… Herein we have a means of immediately employing a large number of men under conditions which will enable us to permanently provide for many of those whose hard lot we are now considering.

I propose to establish in every large town what I may call a "Household Salvage Brigade", a civil force of organized collectors who will patrol the whole town as regularly as the policeman, who will have their appointed beats, and each of whom will be trusted with the task of collecting the waste of the houses in their circuit. In small towns and villages this is already done, and it will be noticed that most of the suggestions which I have put forth in this book are based upon the central principle, which is that of restoring to the overgrown and, therefore, uninformed masses of population in our towns the same intelligence and cooperation as to the mutual wants of each and all, that prevails in your small town or village. The latter is the manageable unit, because its dimensions and its needs have not outgrown the range of individual intelligence and ability of those who dwell therein. Our troubles in large towns arise chiefly from the fact that the massing of population has caused the physical bulk of society to outgrow its intelligence.[1]

**I like this strategic approach, Lord, and the concept of salvaging waste. Food for thought!**

1 From *In Darkest England and the Way Out.*

# November 22nd

THEY KEPT THE MAN IN CUSTODY UNTIL THE LORD'S WILL IN THE MATTER SHOULD BECOME CLEAR TO THEM

(Leviticus 24:12 *NLT*)

Mother Boozham was in such distress about her son, Tom. It seems he had enlisted in the Navy, and soon after had written to say that he had been converted and joined The Salvation Army. But before the old woman had well taken in the joyful news, by some means or other she learned that he had committed a serious offence, for which he had been sent to Blankland Prison. Well, I promised to see the captain, and get him to enquire at headquarters if they could find out anything about the prodigal...

Well, by and by, the information came, and the captain had a letter from headquarters. I will give you a piece of it:

> *"Dear Captain, After enquiry, we find that Tom Boozham enlisted in the Navy some time ago, and for a while led a very rackety life... Being passionate and impulsive, he was always getting into rows, and having to suffer the consequences. But meeting with some Salvationist Blue Jackets,*[1] *he was tackled by them, got on his knees, and was properly converted... His ship was ordered into the Mediterranean, and he was soon known as the most earnest Leaguer on the Station. But, unfortunately, some officer on the vessel persecuted him with great bitterness on account of his religion. Tom bore it bravely for a while, then gave way, went back in his soul, lost his temper, kicked the officer, and was sentenced to ten years' penal servitude for the offence.*
>
> *"In Blankland Prison he again sought God, found forgiveness, and was restored to the favour of his Heavenly Father, and is now getting his fellow-prisoners saved. A little time back I paid him a visit, and instead of being taken to the edge of the cage to see him... I had leave to see him in a private room with only one Warder, who allowed us to have a prayer meeting. I had a Blue Jacket for an escort, and you may depend upon it we had a good time."*[2]

**Thank you, Lord, that you redeem things when we mess up; not in a superficial way, to "spin" circumstances, but in a gracious way that produces good fruit from our sins and errors, if we seek you afresh. Thank you for this grace. Amen.**

1 Possibly, wearers of the first formalized style of Salvation Army uniform, featuring dark blue jackets, as opposed to early collections of military-style outfits in different colours.

2 From *Sergeant-Major Do-Your-Best.*

# November 23[rd]

Through your offspring all peoples on earth will be blessed

(Acts 3:25 *NIV*)

One of the first notions about the Saviour of men taught in every professedly Christian home is that he, their example – although the King of Heaven – was "meek and lowly in heart".[1] And at family prayer, and in church and chapel, children have read to them from their Bibles such exhortations as the following: "Let this mind be in you, which was also in Christ Jesus: Who, being in the form of God, thought it not robbery to be equal with God: But made himself of no reputation, and took upon him the form of a servant, and was made in the likeness of men: And being found in fashion as a man, he humbled himself, and became obedient unto death, even the death of the cross. [Philippians 2:] 5–8 [*KJV*]. And the first line of poetry generally taught the little ones is, "Gentle Jesus, meek and mild".[2]

What a farce it is for parents to teach such sentiments, and to be asking God to make their children Christians, which really means to be like Jesus Christ, when all the time the whole spirit and bearing of the home is just as far from it as Hell is from Heaven! Yet this sort of thing is as common as can very well be imagined…

True religion is love. Christianity is love in action. It will be seen at a glance, therefore, that no matter how wisely parents or other teachers of children may endeavour to impress the hearts and minds of children with Christian notions and feelings, or how persistently they may endeavour to lead them into the practice of a Christ-like life, their labour will be very largely thrown away, if mother and father and everybody around them are living to please themselves.

When the supreme concern of the entire family is to seek their own pleasure or profit or honour or something else that seems essential to their interests, how can the children be trained to a life-long supreme seeking of the things that are Jesus Christ's?[3]

**These are strong words, Father, but they speak of the value of consistency. With your help, may my witness for Christ be consistent, today and every day. Thank you, Lord. Amen.**

1 Matthew 11:29 *KJV*.
2 Charles Wesley, 1707–78, "Gentle Jesus, Meek and Mild".
3 From *The Training of Children.*

# November 24th

## Give me your heart

(Proverbs 23:26 *NIV*)

"Whatsover thy hand findeth to do, do it with thy might".[1] Do it, and do it at once. Your life is uncertain; your days are numbered, and at the longest, in view of what you have to do, they are very few; therefore take the work that God has by his Spirit and providence made evident to be your work, and do it at once, with all the energy you possess of body and soul. Do it with thy might.

We have a conviction that this might-work is the great want in the Christianity of the present day. Men take up religion with the tips of their fingers, as a matter of little or no importance; worthy of being considered and attended to, but only in its place – and that mainly on the Sabbath, and always in subordination to considerations of reputation and pleasure and gain. No wonder that such persons make no progress and have no strength, and find no inward peace and gladness in the Saviour's cause.

The great God, whose first claim is the heart, and who will go no further with any man under any circumstances until that claim is complied with, spurns such [a] worshipper and disowns such disciples. "The kingdom of heaven suffereth violence, and the violent take it by force."[2]

Dear brethren in a crucified and risen Saviour, fellow soldiers in the army of Immanuel, we urge upon you this exhortation that whatever the master requires, you should gird up the loins of your mind and, trusting only in him for strength, go forth and do it with your might.

Separate yourselves from all evil. You are called to a separate life from the worldling: "… come out from among them, and be ye separate."[3] Renounce the pomps of the world and the works of the devil in reality. Put away from you all known sin, of whatever kind and whatever degree. Have no communion with the unfruitful works of darkness. Touch not the unclean thing; that is, whatever God by his Spirit or word makes you feel to be unclean, touch it not.[4]

**Lord of my heart, I give that heart back to you; that which is yours, I return. I renounce ownership, and gladly surrender its rights. Amen.**

1 Ecclesiastes 9:10 *KJV*
2 Matthew 11:12 *KJV*
3 2 Corinthians 6:17 *KJV*
4 From *The Founder Speaks Again.*

# November 25th

About the gifts of the Spirit, brothers and sisters, I do not want you to be uninformed

(1 Corinthians 12:1 *NIV*)

Attention is being given just now to what are known as the extraordinary "gifts of the Spirit"; that is, the ability to do something which is beyond the power of man to do without the direct operation of God. Such gifts as these were, without doubt, possessed by the apostles both before and after the death of our Lord. They had the gift of tongues; that is, they received, suddenly, the power to speak languages which they had never learned. They had the gift of healing; that is, they cured the sick, opened the eyes of the blind, unstopped the ears of the deaf, and restored the dead to life instantaneously without the use of ordinary means. They wrought miracles; they caused events to happen that were contrary to the usual course of nature. These were very remarkable gifts, proving that God was with them, because no man could do these things unless God was operating directly through him.

These gifts were useful, inasmuch as they called attention to those who possessed them, declared that the mission of these officers was divine, and justified men everywhere in believing what they had to say. For this reason they were important to the world, and their possession today might be a great blessing to mankind. There is not a word in the Bible which proves that we may not have them at the present time, and there is nothing in experience to show that they would not be as useful today as in any previous period of the Church's history.

No man, therefore, can be condemned for desiring them, and the recent remarkable signs and wonders wrought amongst us not only demand but shall have our most profound and sympathetic consideration. But it has occurred to me that while desiring these extraordinary gifts, some of us may be neglecting forces and powers already existing within and amongst us that are equal to – perhaps greater in value than – those thus coveted. The apostle Paul exhorts the early saints to "stir up the gifts that were in them."[1] These gifts were imparted by God… but they lay dormant, and therefore useless.[2]

**Lord, I would hate to miss out on any gift you wanted to impart. Please, therefore, grant me that spiritual balance whereby I might covet the extraordinary gifts so far as you are pleased to dispense them to me, while at the same time nurturing the gifts I already possess. Thank you, Lord. Amen.**

1 See 2 Timothy 1:6
2 From *The General's Letters*.

# November 26th

EACH OF YOU SHOULD USE WHATEVER GIFT YOU HAVE RECEIVED TO SERVE OTHERS, AS FAITHFUL STEWARDS OF GOD'S GRACE IN ITS VARIOUS FORMS

(1 Peter 4:10 *NIV*)

By all means let us aspire after higher gifts, but by all means let us use those we already possess. How true it is that to him that hath – that is, who uses what he has – shall be given; and from him that hath not – that is, who uses not what he possesses – that which he already has shall be taken away! Neglect the ability you have for glorifying God and saving men, and that ability will shrivel up, degenerate, and waste away.

It must never be forgotten that all real healing, whether of body or soul, whether accomplished in a moment or in a year of time, whether done apparently without means or through the use of means, is alike affected by the direct operation of the power of God; it is God who saves.

And it must ever be remembered that all gifts – ordinary or extraordinary – alike come from God; and that there is a danger of straining after those that seem to be extraordinary, while those already possessed lie unused and therefore useless. For instance, a man may be longing after the "gift of tongues" and neglecting the tongue he already has; thinking how much good he could do if he could suddenly speak the German language, while all the time he is comparatively neglecting the use of English, which he can speak. Does anyone say, "What a wonderful thing it would be if I could suddenly speak in a foreign tongue!" Let such a one stop and think what a wonderful thing it is that he can speak at all.

Think, my comrade, if you had never possessed the power of speech, and were to have it suddenly bestowed, what a remarkable miracle it would appear. Suppose you knew something about it before; how you would desire it! How you would promise God to use it for his glory and the salvation of souls if he would give it to you!... And yet in reality it would not be a whit more a gift, or more remarkable, than is the ability to talk that you possess today.[1]

**Thank you, Lord, for this helpful sense of perspective. I do not want there to be anything useless about my life with you. Please enhance whatever gifts you wish me to use, always for your glory, and for Jesus' sake. Amen.**

1 From *The General's Letters.*

# November 27th

Well then, if you teach others, why don't you teach yourself?
(Romans 2:21 *NLT*)

The early Friends – Quakers, they were called[1] – made a great name, and piles of money into the bargain, by selling only superior articles. At one time – and that not very long ago, either – if you wanted clothes, or silks, or linens, or other things of first-class quality, you were sure of finding them at establishments kept by members of the Society of Friends. It is true you had to pay for the article, but you got the quality for your money – and there are those who still maintain that good things are always the cheapest, even if a high price has to be paid for them. Anyway, the Quakers found the plan paid handsomely.

Acting on this advice will, I have no doubt, often be found a little difficult. To such extraordinary lengths has the practice of adulteration been carried, that not only buyers are very much in the dark as to what they buy, but sellers also as to what they sell. Anyway, so far as you can, be frank with your customers. If the articles are not likely to last for ever and a day, you can, at least, be sure that their value is in proportion to the prices charged for them – that is, that the purchasers have their money's worth.

Look after your own business. If you want a thing done well, do it yourself. I think that is a proverb; if not, it ought to be. In my [affairs], I am sure I have ever found it to be a safe rule of action. No matter what trade a man may embark in, he should himself understand it, as far as possible, in all its various details. If not, he will be left to the judgment of other people, and they may not always guide him aright. Therefore, if you do not buy your own goods, serve your own customers, keep your own books, manage your own stocktaking, and do the whole round of business yourself, see that you understand how it ought to be done, otherwise you will certainly be unable efficiently to direct those you employ to do it on your behalf.[2]

**Father, in minding my own business, may I always aspire for quality; help me to accept responsibility but, also, to avoid leaning on my own understanding. Amen.**

1 During and after the English Civil War, many dissenting Christian groups emerged. A young man named George Fox was dissatisfied by the teachings of the Church of England and non-conformists. He had a revelation that *there is one, even, Christ Jesus, who can speak to thy condition*, and became convinced that it was possible to have a direct experience of Christ without the aid of an ordained clergy. Fox was brought before magistrates on a charge of blasphemy. According to Fox's autobiography, Bennet (one of the magistrates) "was the first person that called us Quakers, because I bade them tremble at the word of the Lord". It is thought that George Fox was referring to Isaiah 66:2.

2 From *Religion for Every Day*.

# NOVEMBER 28TH

WHEN THEY HAD ALL HAD ENOUGH TO EAT, HE SAID TO HIS DISCIPLES, "GATHER THE PIECES THAT ARE LEFT OVER. LET NOTHING BE WASTED"

(John 6:12 *NIV*)

When I was a boy one of the most familiar figures in the streets of a country town was the man who, with his small barrow or donkey-cart, made a regular patrol through the streets once a week, collecting rags, bones, and all other waste materials, buying the same from the juveniles who collected them in specie, not of Her Majesty's current coin, but of common sweetmeats, known as "claggum" or "taffy". When the tootling of his familiar horn was heard, the children would bring out their stores, and trade as best they could with the itinerant merchant, with the result that the closets which in our towns today have become the receptacles of all kinds of disused lumber were then kept swept and garnished.

Now, what I want to know is why we cannot establish on a scale commensurate with our extended needs the rag-and-bone industry in all our great towns? That there is sufficient to pay for the collection is, I think, indisputable. If it paid in a small north-country town or a Midland village, why would it not pay much better in an area where the houses stand more closely together, and where luxurious living and thriftless habits have so increased that there must be proportionately far more breakage, more waste and, therefore, more collectable matter than in the rural districts?...

It has occurred to me that in the debris of our households there is sufficient food, if utilized, to feed many of the starving poor, and to employ some thousands of them in its collection... What I would propose would be to go to work on something like the following plan:

London would be divided into districts, beginning with that portion of it most likely to furnish the largest supplies of what would be worth collection. Two men, or a man and a boy, would be told of for this purpose to this district. Households would be requested to allow a receptacle to be placed in some convenient spot in which the servants could deposit the waste food, and a sack of some description would also be supplied for the paper, rags, & c.[1]

**Lord, I stand amazed at the genius of William Booth, whose plans were years ahead of their time; I praise you for inspiring such genius. Thank you, Lord, that recycling speaks of care and restoration, and touches on the heart of the gospel, that no one is worthless in your sight, but all are worthy of reclamation. Amen.**

1 From *In Darkest England and the Way Out.*

# November 29th

The father said to his servants, "Quick! Bring the best robe and put it on him. Put a ring on his finger and sandals on his feet"

(Luke 15:22 *NIV*)

Of the immense extent to which food is wasted, few people have any notion except those who have made actual experiments. Some years ago, Lady Wolesley [*sic*][1] established a system of collection from house to house in Mayfair, in order to secure the materials for a charitable kitchen which, in concert with Baroness Burdett-Coutts,[2] she had started at Westminster. The amount of food which she gathered was enormous. Sometimes legs of mutton from which only one or two slices had been cut were thrown into the tub, where they waited for the arrival of the cart on its rounds. It is by no means an excessive estimate to assume that the waste of the kitchens of the West End [of London] would provide a sufficient sustenance for all the Out-of-Works who will be employed in our labour sheds at the industrial centres. All that it needs is collection, prompt, systematic, by disciplined men who can be relied upon to discharge their task with punctuality and civility, and whose failure in this duty can be directly brought to the attention of the controlling authority...

Much of the food collected by the Household Salvage Brigade would not be available for human consumption. In this the greatest care would be exercised... But food is only one of the materials which we should handle. At our Whitechapel Factory there is one shoemaker whom we picked off the streets destitute and miserable. He is now saved, and happy, and cobbles away at the shoe leather of his mates. That shoemaker, I foresee, is but a pioneer of a whole army of shoemakers constantly at work in repairing the cast-off boots and shoes of London.

Already in some provincial towns a great business is done by the conversion of old shoes into new. They call the men so employed translators. Boots and shoes, as every wearer of them knows, do not go to pieces all at once, or in all parts at once. The sole often wears out utterly, while the upper leather is quite good, or the upper leather bursts while the sole remains practically in a salvable condition.[3]

**Father, these works are entirely in keeping with your heart of compassion. I praise you because you are a God who will stoop to salvage, as you did when you sent your Son. Amen.**

1 Possibly Louisa, wife of Field Marshal Garnet Joseph Wolseley, 1st Viscount Wolseley.

2 Baroness Angela Georgina Burdett-Coutts (1814–1906), a nineteenth-century philanthropist and at one time the richest heiress in England.

3 From *In Darkest England and the Way Out.*

# NOVEMBER 30TH

I BELONG TO MY BELOVED

(Song of Songs 7:10 *NIV*)

"Prayer," he [the captain] said, "is a wonderful thing. God answers prayer." And then he talked a bit on that passage [Matthew 18:19 *KJV*]– "if two of you shall agree on earth as touching any thing that they shall ask, it shall be done for them of my Father which is in heaven."... "I want those who have unsaved relations for whom they desire our prayers to signify it by standing up before God and before us. And first," he said, "let those husbands who have unconverted wives, for whom they desire our prayers, stand up on their feet." At once I should think a dozen sprang up. With one or two, I observed a little hesitation. Jim Grumbleton was one of those who hung back. He has just married that worldly girl... and gone and done it with his eyes open. She was not there; and perhaps he thought she would not like him to make her unconverted state known to the corps – as if every one of us did not know it already! – and think he was very foolish for having done as he has done...

"If you have wives whom you have reason to think are on the way to Heaven, sit still.

"If you have unsaved wives, who are on the way to Hell, and you think standing up and saying so will hinder rather than help you to get them put right, sit still.

"If you have unsaved wives, and don't want our prayers, sit still.

"But if you have unsaved wives, and want our prayers for them, stand up."

Here Jim Grumbleton, who at the bottom is a true fellow, struggled to his feet. It was a melancholy confession to make, but he made it.

Then the captain went through much the same form of things with the other classes. First he called for the wives to stand up who had unsaved husbands. There were nearly twenty of them. My heart did ache as I looked... As to Sarah, she must have had that "fountain of waters" in her head that night that Jeremiah prayed about,[1] for she cried all the time.[2]

**Today, Lord, I pray for marriages, and for married people known to me. I thank you and praise you for the gift of marriage. I pray for rocky marriages, that you will step in. I pray your blessing upon those who come to mind as I pray. Amen.**

1 See Jeremiah 9:1

2 From *Sergeant-Major Do-Your-Best.*

# December 1st

Pray that you will not fall into temptation

(Luke 22:40 *NIV*)

You must confess the fact that God has cleansed your heart, and that by his Spirit he enables you to live day by day without grieving him. It may be, at times it will be, a cross. But you must take it up, and in doing so you will become a light and a power and a joy to your comrades and friends. To retain the blessing you must strive to live in the same spirit of submission, obedience, and consecration to God as that which you entered into its enjoyment. Your everyday experience must be that which we often sing:

*Here then to thee thy own I leave;*
*Mould as thou wilt the passive clay;*
*But let me all thy stamp receive,*
*And let me all they words obey,*
*Serve with a single heart and eye,*
*And to thy glory live and die.*[1]

To keep this experience you must continue in the same spirit of trust that first brought the blessing into your heart. You did not receive the gift of purity by feelings or knowledge or works; no, nor by desire nor by prayer. You believed and you were saved. If you had said, "I won't or I can't believe that Jesus cleanses, unless I feel the work to be done in my heart," you could not have rejoiced in its possession. You trusted and the work was done. You must go forward in that spirit. There will be hours when all will seem to be hard and dark and desolate. Those will be the hours when you will have to fight the fight of faith, and to cling to the beginning of your confidence, whether you feel pleasant or unpleasant, whether you heart seems hard or tender, that the blood cleanses. Hold it fast! To keep a clean heart you must resist temptation.

*What though a thousand host engage*
*A thousand worlds, my soul to shake?*
*I have a shield shall quell their rage,*
*And drive the alien armies back:*
*Portrayed it bears a bleeding Lamb*
*I dare believe in Jesus' name.*[2, 3]

**So help me, God.**

1 Charles Wesley, 1707–78, "Behold the Servant of the Lord".
2 John Wesley, 1703–1791 and Charles Wesley, 1707–78, "Surrounded by a Host of Foes".
3 From *Purity of Heart.*

# December 2nd

He who testifies to these things says, "Yes, I am coming soon."
Amen. Come, Lord Jesus

(Revelation 22:20 *NIV*)

"I have seen what real religion is as I have never seen it before. It is not only singing, and talking, and praying, and giving… but it is love. But if so be as we don't love the souls of our own flesh and blood, and care for them as well, how can we pretend to have the love of Christ in us? But, bless the dear Lord, I have got a little love for my dear old father, and I mean to have him saved, if I can manage it; and, to get it done, I shall give him no rest, and I shall give myself no rest, and – I say it with all the respect which a poor woman like me should feel – I shall give my Heavenly Father no rest until the work is done."

When we got into the house, she [Sarah] poked up the fire, and got me out the bread, and then she says: "Sergeant-Major, you can just boil the milk yourself, and when you've had your supper I recommend you to kneel down there," pointing to the chair in the corner, "and pray for your poor backslidden brother, who'll be at the left hand of the Judgment Bar soon if somebody don't care about him; and who should that somebody be but his own brother?"

Then I says, "Sarah, what are you going to do? It is past ten o'clock, and you must be faint."

"Yes," she says, "I know the time, but I feel that I can't either eat or sleep until I have done something for my poor father's soul; and I am going to write him a letter this very night before I see my bed." And then she broke out weeping again, and as she left me I could hear her saying, "O God, spare my poor father until I get him into the fountain!"

I can tell you I did not want any supper after this. I just went down alongside my old chair, as Sarah had recommended me to do, and began to cry to God to save my brother Jim.[1]

**Lord Jesus, I pray that you would "come soon" into the hearts and lives of my family members who do not follow you. Bless them with your presence as I name them before you in prayer. Have mercy, Lord. Amen.**

1 From *Sergeant-Major Do-Your-Best.*

# December 3rd

To him who is able to do immeasurably more than all we ask or imagine, according to his power that is at work within us, to him be glory in the church

(Ephesians 3:20–21 *NIV*)

I call your attention to the great truth which lies at the foundation of all real service for the Master; admitted by almost every professed follower of his, and yet so commonly forgotten and neglected in practice, viz, that every gift we possess – ordinary or extraordinary – of body or mind or soul, comes directly from God,[1] belongs to him, and is only entrusted to us that we might therewith promote his glory and the accomplishment of his purposes towards mankind.

People go to religious meetings and talk about all they have belonging to God, and of being under the most solemn obligation to use it in his interests, and then go straight to their shops and warehouses and homes, and think and act in the most opposite manner. They reckon in their hearts and say by their conduct, "My time, my abilities, my good are my own, to do with as I like, to use as seems most likely to promote my own gratification."

Now this is in direct opposition to the principle we have just observed. You are a steward, and your gifts belong to your Master, and you are to use them as he wishes, and if you do not, he will reckon with you at last. But you, my comrades, honestly want to do this. Let me help you; and here I note:

You must know you have a gift before you can use it. Every man is a genius in some direction. There is some speciality in which he excels those around him. There is a pearl of great price in his soul somewhere.[2] But he must find it out, or it will be in danger of dying with him. No doubt the Army has helped thousands to discover and employ gifts for the Master which they never dreamt they possessed. At the same time I am afraid it fails with thousands of others; they live and die with abilities which, had they been discovered, might have been the means of saving multitudes.

My comrades, examine yourselves. Shake the napkins at every corner. Pray about it.[3]

**Thank you, Father, that your faith in me is sometimes greater than my faith in you! Forgive me for those moments when I feel I have little or nothing to offer, when in reality your provision is always granted according to my need. Help me to lean on you. Amen.**

1 James 1:17
2 Matthew 13:45–46
3 From *The General's Letters*.

# December 4th

## Strengthened with all power according to his glorious might

(Colossians 1:11 *NIV*)

You must pray with all your might. That does not mean saying your prayers, or sitting gazing about in church or chapel, with eyes wide open, while someone else says them for you. It means fervent, effectual, untiring wrestling with God. It means that grappling with Omnipotence, that clinging to him, following him about, so to speak, day and night, as the widow did the unjust judge,[1] with agonizing pleadings and entreaties, until the answer comes and the end is gained.

This kind of prayer be sure the devil and the world and your own indolent, unbelieving nature will oppose. They will pour water on this flame. They will ply you with suggestions and difficulties. They will ask you how you can expect that the plans and purposes and feelings of God can be altered by your prayers. They will talk about impossibilities and predict failures; but, if you mean to succeed, you must shut your ears and eyes to all but what God has said, and hold him to his own word: and you cannot do this in any sleepy mood; you cannot be a prevailing Israel unless you wrestle as Jacob wrestled,[2] regardless of time or aught else, save obtaining the blessing sought – that is, you must pray with your might.

Go about pleading with men and women for their souls, but do it with your might. Visit them from house to house, but not for mere chit-chat. Much house-to-house visitation, we fear, amounts to little more than gossip. Merely talking about the gospel and giving good advice will not go far. A few kind words are useful to introduce you; then introduce your Master, and sit down if you can, but only preparatory to kneeling down. Be sure and deal faithfully with every soul with whom God gives you opportunity.

Visit the open shops on the Lord's Day; plead with the people who are on the way to Hell, wherever you meet them, and do it with your might. Oh, my brethren, what a blessing this might-work has brought with it in the past! What wonderful things are recorded of it![3]

**Lord, I praise you today because I can rely upon your might to enable me in all that you ever ask me to do for you. By myself, I am weak, but with your help, I can do mighty things – all to your glory. Amen.**

1 Luke 18:1–8
2 Genesis 32:23–32
3 From *The Founder Speaks Again.*

# December 5th

### You will receive power when the Holy Spirit comes on you
(Acts 1:8 *NIV*)

When you see your chance, take up your cross boldly,[1] and go straight for the discharge of your duty. Listen to no arguments in favour of silence from your own heart. Do not be hindered by what people may think or say about you. If you see the opportunity of warning a soul from the way of death, seize it there and then.

Beware of the dangerous notion that we are not to speak for Christ unless moved thereto by a divine impulse. John Wesley tells us that he was at one time so far influenced by this doctrine that he resolved to give it a fair trial. Accordingly, he says he rode from York to Barnet without being moved to speak to a single soul. Then he threw this notion overboard, and began again to speak to all with whom he came in contact, whether he felt led to do so or not. The opportunity for this or any other kind of usefulness is the divine call.

At the onset, always throw yourselves on God for his guidance and blessing on what you say and do. I have already said this, but I say it again. Reckon on the conscience of every individual to whom you speak being on your side. For, however worldly they appear, or with whatever scorn or indifference they may at first receive your words, everyone has a conscience, although perhaps dormant, but which may be quickened by the Holy Spirit using some word you may say.

Study how you can perform your task in the most effective manner. Treat all to whom you speak with kindness and reasonable respect. With a heart full of love, practice will bring the chief qualification for this kind of work: and that is courage. Practice, plenty of practice, still more practice, will ultimately make you perfect.

In The Salvation Army, you will hear the exhortation ringing out on every hand, "Do your duty." God expects the Salvationist to do his duty; your General, your officers, your comrades, and even the wicked world around you, expect it of you.[2]

**Gracious Father, with your Spirit living within me, I am always equipped to share a word of witness. Help me not to delay, but to quickly call for inspiration, and then to trust that what I say will be from you. Amen.**

1 Matthew 16:24–26
2 From *The Founder's Messages to Soldiers.*

# December 6th

The Spirit of truth who goes out from the Father – he will testify about me

(John 15:26 *NIV*)

God is as much concerned about the character and life of children as he is of grown-up people. You will teach them to say every day of their lives, "Thy will be done," and you will desire that prayer to be answered in them, otherwise it will be useless for you to teach them to offer it. But how can your children do the will of God unless they are made to know what that will is? You must, therefore, teach them the exact truth about these important things as carefully as you seek to make them understand about earthly things – and even more so. Even when they have learned the truth about spiritual matters, you must lead them on to seek power to act in accordance with it; and then the Spirit will set them free,[1] and make them fit to go and help to set other children free.

But are children capable of understanding spiritual truths?

They will be if you teach them in a suitable way. Of course, your teaching must be fitted to their intelligence and capacity. So soon as the heart of the child can form any idea of God as a Supreme being, the Holy Spirit will enable you to impress it with a sense of fear and love. So soon as the child is capable of understanding that God has an authority over him, the Spirit will enable you to implant in him a feeling of respect for that authority. As soon as the child is able to understand what it is to sin, or offend against that authority, the Spirit will enable you to produce conviction and a sense of sorrow for that offence,[2] and to lead the child to seek forgiveness from God.

In teaching children, it must never be forgotten that we have the divine assurance that a measure of the Holy Spirit is given to every human being,[3] and that the Holy Spirit so given will cooperate with you in planting spiritual ideas, creating spiritual inspirations, and securing a real consecration of all that the child has to the service of the King.[4]

**I praise you, Lord, because you back up my efforts to witness for you; you do not leave me to work in isolation. However faltering my attempts may be today, Lord, please apply your Holy Spirit's power to turn them into something effective – for Jesus' sake. Amen.**

1 2 Corinthians 3:17
2 John 16:8
3 John 1:9
4 From *The Training of Children.*

# December 7th

The land that was desolate shall be tilled, instead of being the desolation that it was in the sight of all who passed by

(Ezekiel 36:34 *ESV*)

I have already described how I propose to deal, in the first case, with the mass of surplus labour which will infallibly accumulate on our hands… I fully recognize that when all has been done that can be done in the direction of disposing of unhired men and women of the town, there will still remain many whom you can neither employ in the Household Salvage brigade, nor for whom employers, be they registered ever so carefully, can be found. What, then, must be done with them? The answer to that question seems to me obvious. They must go upon the land!

The land is the source of all food; only by the application of labour can the land be made fully productive. There is any amount of waste land in the world, not far away in distant continents, next door to the North Pole, but here at our very doors. Have you ever calculated, for instance, the square miles of unused land which fringe the sides of all our railroads? No doubt some embankments are of material that would baffle the cultivating skill of a Chinese or the careful husbandry of a Swiss mountaineer; but these are exceptions. When other people talk of reclaiming Salisbury Plain, or of cultivating the bare moorlands of the bleak north, I think of the hundreds of square miles of lands that lie in long ribbons on the side of each of our railways, upon which, without any cost for cartage, innumerable tons of city manure could be shot down, and the crops of which could be carried at once to the nearest market without any but the initial cost of heaping into convenient trucks.

These railway embankments constitute a vast estate, capable of growing fruit enough to supply all the jam that Crosse & Blackwell[1] ever boiled. In almost every county in England are vacant farms and, in still greater numbers, farms but a quarter cultivated, which only need the application of an industrious population working with due incentive to produce twice, thrice, and four times as much as they yield today.[2]

**Father, in your Kingdom, there is no wastage. By your grace, you make the very most of everything – and everyone – laid at your disposal. I praise you because you are a God who looks for every opportunity to salvage and reclaim. Amen.**

1 Crosse & Blackwell is a food production company which has been in existence since 1706.
2 From *In Darkest England and the Way Out.*

# December 8th

Nathanael said to him, "Can anything good come out of Nazareth?"

Philip said to him, "Come and see."

(John 1:46 *NKJV*)

"What?" it will be said. "Do you think that you can create agricultural pioneers out of the scum of Cockneydom?" Let us look for a moment at the ingredients which make up what you call "the scum of Cockneydom". After careful examination and close cross-questioning of the Out-of-Works, whom we have already registered at our Labour Bureau, we find that at least 60 per cent are country folk, men, women, boys, and girls, who have left their homes in the counties to come up to town in the hope of bettering themselves. They are in no sense of the word Cockneys, and they represent not the dregs of the country but rather its brighter and more adventurous spirits who have boldly tried to make their way in new and uncongenial spheres and have terribly come to grief.

Of thirty cases, selected haphazard, in the various Shelters during the week ending 5 July 1890, twenty-two were country-born, sixteen were men who had come up a long time ago, but did not ever seem to have settled to regular employ, and four were old military men. Of sixty cases examined into at the Bureau and Shelters during the fortnight ending 2 August, forty-two were country people; twenty-six men who had been in London for various periods, ranging from six months to four years; nine were lads under eighteen, who had run away from home and come up to town; while four were ex-military.

Of eighty-five cases of dossers who were spoken to at night when they slept in the streets, sixty-three were country people. A very small proportion of the genuine homeless Out-of-Works are Londoners born and bred. There is another element in the matter, the existence of which will be news to most people, and that is the large proportion of ex-military men who are among the helpless, hopeless destitute. Mr Arnold White,[1] after spending many months in the streets of London interrogating more than 4,000 men [sleeping rough]… returns it as his conviction that at least 20 per cent are Army Reserve. Twenty per cent![2]

**How easy it is, Lord, to write someone off simply because of what we perceive to be their cultural origin or background! Thankfully, you ignore such things and concentrate instead on each person's true worth and potential. Help me to do the same. Amen.**

1 Arnold Henry White (1848–1925): English journalist, political activist, and essayist.

2 From *In Darkest England and the Way Out.*

# December 9th

Your beauty should not come from outward adornment, such as elaborate hairstyles and the wearing of gold jewellery or fine clothes. Rather, it should be that of your inner self, the unfading beauty of a gentle and quiet spirit, which is of great worth in God's sight

(1 Peter 3:3–4 *NIV*)

Man has been described by someone as "a clothes-wearing animal". It could not be intended, by that expression, that he is the only animal that wears clothes, for there are few creatures that walk the earth around him, or dwell in the sea beneath him, that are not as usefully and as becomingly clad as he is – most of them much more so. Still, he is the only creature on this planet who has any choice in the character of his outer covering, or in the manner of putting it on and taking it off, which things I suppose, taken together, do constitute a clothes-wearer in the sense that animals generally are not. Clothes may, from their all but universal use, be considered an absolute necessity to our race. There are few people, even of those nations counted most barbarous, that do not affect some kind of apparel, however simple and crude it may be…

Clothes may be regarded as a mark of civilization. The fact is that any tribe, of any race, found in any part of the globe not wearing clothes is considered to be a proof of their savage state, pure and simple. One of the first things by which converts to civilization express the change that has transpired, whether in the forests of Africa, the jungles of India, or elsewhere, is to get into some form or other of dress. Indeed, many of these Aborigines [*sic*] measure the height to which they have risen in the scale of civilization by the quantity and costliness, to say nothing of the ridiculous fashion, of the clothes they are able to carry about with them.

Something of the same kind often follows the salvation of the lowest and most vicious outcasts. One of the immediate results of their coming to Christ is their appearance in decent clothing; and it is wonderful too, how the most degraded can and do fix themselves up within a few hours. Literally, they are soon found, like the man in the gospel, "sitting at the feet of Jesus, clothed, and in [their] right mind."[1, 2]

**It's something of a strange prayer, Father, but if my appearance puts people off following Christ, then keep me sensitive to that priority. If how I dress is a form of witnessing, then guide me in those choices. Amen.**

1 Luke 8:35 *KJV*
2 From *Religion for Every Day.*

# DECEMBER 10TH

### ALEXANDER THE METALWORKER DID ME A GREAT DEAL OF HARM

(2 Timothy 4:14 *NIV*)

In the early days of the Army we used to sing a song…

*Don't get weary,*
*Don't get weary,*
*Fighting for your Lord…*[1]

The advice given by the song was excellent, and it has been brought afresh to my mind by some words of Scripture to which I want to call your attention today. You will find them in Galatians, 6th chapter, and the 9th verse, and they read, "let us not be weary in well doing: for in due season we shall reap, if we faint not" [*KJV*]. Now, both the song and the text were very applicable to us at the time of which I speak, for alas! Growing weary was no uncommon experience in those days. Many earnest souls, on whose cooperation I had built fond hopes for the future, drew away from my side, and left me to struggle on as best I could without them; and others, on the strength of whose promises of undying faithfulness I had undertaken large responsibilities, turned to be my enemies, and fought against me.

I say sometimes that, had every officer and soldier who has at one time or another vowed to live and fight and die under our flag remained faithful to their pledges, The Salvation Army would, indeed, have been a mighty force today. It would have been sufficiently powerful to shake the world… I am speaking of those who simply grow weary in the struggle for the salvation of their fellows, and withdraw from the contest. Alas! They ever constitute a numerous and heart-wounding crowd…

I have little doubt that some listening to this message will belong to this class. Others are probably taking a little extra rest on their beds, or having a gentle walk to improve their health, or have gone for a "day in the country". Others, having discovered that a little more educational teaching in their religion is required by themselves and their families, have removed to some more respectable church or chapel in the neighbourhood, where they think there is a reasonable chance of the needed enlightenment being found.[2]

**Father, keep me faithful. Amen.**

1 Source unknown.
2 From *The Founder's Messages to Soldiers*.

# December 11th

I ALSO WILL ANSWER WITH MY SHARE; I ALSO WILL DECLARE MY OPINION
(Job 32:17 *ESV*)

Now I understand that the humble opinions I have expressed… have given offence to some of my old captains, and I am downright sorry for that, because it is one of my particular rules to stand up for my officers and support their authority. I have always done it, and always shall do it while I am sergeant-major of this corps.

And now, here is Captain Windy, God bless him!, writing to our secretary and saying that he is real offended, and will never come near our corps again if he can help it. Now, that seems to me to be a great pity for Captain Windy's own sake…

And, now, here is Miss Pinkem, who was brought up at a boarding school, and got married to our baker; she told our Sarah the other day that her husband, who is a deacon of a sect they call "The Superior People", wanted to hear Captain Windy again, as he thought that his oratory style would just suit their taste; and now the captain says he won't come near us again, and so he will lose this chance. However, if people will stand in their own light, it is not for such humble folks as I am to go against them.

Then Captain Gentleton told our lieutenant, at the Officers' Meeting last week, that I had no business to have opinions about other people, and that all the opinions belonged to the filed officers. But, then, how can I help having opinions? You see, they come up whether you will or no. And, now, here is Captain Swellum writing to say that if I did have such opinions, I ought to keep them to myself, that nobody wants to hear them, and he says in the letter that I am a pessimist![1]

**Lord, how often matters of church life are influenced by personal opinions! Guide your people by your Holy Spirit, that we may not be reluctant to speak our minds, but only ever subject to your will and way; may that be our guiding principle, for the Kingdom's sake. Amen.**

1 From *Sergeant-Major Do-Your-Best.*

# DECEMBER 12TH

THEIR EYES WERE OPENED, AND THEY SUDDENLY FELT SHAME AT THEIR NAKEDNESS. SO THEY SEWED FIG LEAVES TOGETHER TO COVER THEMSELVES

(Genesis 3:7 *NLT*)

Salvationists are clothes-wearers. We are great at clothes – indeed, we have a style of dress that we call uniform, which, in style and appearance, is all our own. We reckon that this dress saves us from certain serious evils, and serves several very useful purposes.

Uniform is a public witness to our Lord, and avowal of our devotion to his cause, and of our willingness that all the world should know the fact.

It is an open declaration of the renunciation of evil, and of our determination to be out-and-out for God, and to live and die for the salvation of men.

Uniform makes opportunities for usefulness. By it men can recognize the Salvationist as the servant and messenger of God, and are often led to converse with him. If the uniform does occasionally lead those who hate religion to indulge in ridicule, it will, at the same time, afford the wearer an opportunity of proclaiming to them the mercy of God through Jesus Christ.

But necessary and useful as the clothes-wearing habit may be, like other things that are good in themselves, it can be so far abused as to be the means of doing much harm. This is just what has happened; and the material, shape, and general character of clothes have become sources of temptation to a large part of the human race. Indeed, they can be counted on as among the most fruitful causes of evil with which poor human nature has to battle.

For instance, clothes may easily become the means of fostering and feeding the pride and vanity of the human heart. Introduced in consequence of the sin of our first parents, and on that account to be regarded as being really marks of disgrace, it is curious to contemplate the extent to which they have come to be gloried in by their posterity… That in the present day they should have come to foster the vanity, occupy the time, and involve the foolish expenditure of energy and money that we see around us, is one of the most convincing evidences… that man is, indeed, a fallen creature.[1]

**Thank you, Lord, for this perspective. We may not all wear Salvation Army uniform, but even in our approach to what we do wear, we can serve you. Grant us the wisdom of the wardrobe! Amen.**

1 From *Religion for Every Day.*

# December 13th

For Zion's sake I will not keep silent, for Jerusalem's sake I will not remain quiet, till her vindication shines out like the dawn, her salvation like a blazing torch

(Isaiah 62:1 *NIV*)

A widespread visitation of love is more needed by our poor undone world than all else beside. The vast majority of its inhabitants are hopelessly sinking down in slavery, debauchery, idolatry, and all manner of iniquities. These things lead to every kind of wretchedness in this life and in the life to come. Luxury, law, wealth, science, learning, and no end of other human contrivances have failed to remedy this state of affairs, and will fail. Love is the remedy. Here is the divine panacea, this is the recipe for millennium-love. Divine love. Oh, for a deluge of this blessed spirit!...

Above and beyond all else, my soul longs for a fresh and more powerful visitation of this blessed, fiery flame. In this desire I feel certain that the hunger of hundreds, nay, thousands of hearts... is in harmony with my own...

I need not say that the love of which I am going to speak is the pure, unselfish affection. I leave out of our enquiry the human sentiment often spoke of by the term "love", and which has no moral character in it. That is a mere instinct at its best, differing little from that possessed by the animal creation around us, and cannot be said to have either praise or blame attached to it. The love which would make a bear fight to the death for her cubs is of the same level with that which would make a mother die for her children. I am simply going to deal with that holy, celestial flame, which, emanating from the heart of God, unselfishly seeks the highest well-being of its subject, both for this world and the next...

There is a love that is lukewarm...There is a love that is fickle and spasmodic... Then there is the steady, earnest, burning passion which, whatever feelings may come or go, whatever advantages may promise, or whatever threatenings may frown, is ever the same overpowering principle in the soul. That is what I call "burning love".[1]

**Almighty God, set my heart on fire with love – a love for souls fuelled by a love for you. Cause me to love afresh all that you already love. Amen.**

1 From *The Seven Spirits.*

# December 14th

David said to the Philistine, "You come against me with sword and spear and javelin, but I come against you in the name of the Lord Almighty, the God of the armies of Israel, whom you have defied. This day the Lord will deliver you into my hands, and I'll strike you down and cut off your head. This very day I will give the carcasses of the Philistine army to the birds and the wild animals, and the whole world will know that there is a God in Israel

(1 Samuel 17:45–46 *NIV*)

There is in English law a curious fiction by which no man who once becomes a clergyman can ever cease to be one. If he goes into the greengrocery line he is still a clergyman, if he goes to prison he is still a clergyman, if he goes to the gallows he is still a clergyman; and, I suppose, nay, I am sure, when he goes up to the Judgment Bar he will be dealt with in the light of all the solemn responsibilities implied in such a position.

Now, although you may by cowardice, or unfaithfulness, or disobedience, or other infamous action, be deemed unworthy of your position, and drummed out of God Almighty's Army – covered with disgrace and infamy – still the memory of your position, and the responsibilities of what you might have accomplished in it, will cleave to you, and grow upon you, and haunt you, and harrow you for ever more. How important, then, for you to be faithful.

The most solemn vows ever uttered by any of the inhabitants of God's universe have been on your lips; you have boasted of what you will be, and what you will do, with boastings so loud that God and angels and devils have heard them, and I don't condemn you for so doing.

Some people are dreadfully afraid of any boasting in religion, but I say if your boasting be the outcome of true hearts, if it be the outleaping of a holy fire which must have an outlet or consume the very bones, if it is in the Lord, then let it come "housetop" fashion if you will.[1] Go and tell Goliath that you are going to cut off his head and to give his carcase to feed the birds of the air and the beasts of the earth, and come what may you are going to shout victory over him. That is if you feel true, and are going to keep on feeling true; but if not, then so much greater the pity and the infamy… We cannot go back, we cannot shunt, we must not, will not, dare not, fear.[2]

**Lord, give me something to shout about today, please – a faith objective, a note of confidence, a testimony to your power – and let it be entirely to your glory. I have little to boast of in myself, but I have a God who is worthy of all praise. Amen.**

1 See Jeremiah 20:9

2 From *Salvation Soldiery.*

# December 15th

You are enthroned as the Holy One; you are the one Israel praises
(Psalm 22:3 *NIV*)

Praise is another element of worship. The psalmist says, "Whoso offereth praise glorifieth [God]".[1] That is, makes him to be more admired and famous in the eyes of angels and men. Burning love never tires of sounding forth the praises of the object loved. It praises him, and his wonderful works, and all around. It lies before him, and speaks them in his own listening ear. The language of burning love is:

*I'll praise my Maker while I've breath,*
*and when my voice is lost in death,*
*praise shall employ my nobler powers;*
*my days of praise shall ne'er be past,*
*while life, and thought, and being last,*
*or immortality endures.*[2]

But worship means more than either realization, appreciation, gratitude, or praise; it means adoration. The highest, noblest emotion of which the soul is capable. Love worships.

Burning love will promote your resemblance to God. As I have said, love is largely made up of admiration. What the soul admires it imitates, whether intending to do so or not. This is said to be the case physically. I have heard it said that the love existing between husbands and wives leads to their resemblance of each other in bodily appearance. We see it mentally every day. We know it so morally. The company and example of good men make good men, or ought to do so. So, if you love God with this burning passion, you will, you must, grow like unto him.

Burning love promotes obedience. We have all heard it said that love is a slave, which means that the lover delights to do the will of the beloved. It does not have to punish itself, [nor] to be punished, to make it carry out the wishes of the object loved, so far as it has the ability. So, when the soul loves God, "I delight to do thy will."[3]

Burning love opens the soul to new and overflowing sources of unspeakable joy. To begin with there is the joy of loving. The chief satisfaction arising from love is found not in being loved, but in loving.[4]

**Father God, some days I simply wish to sit in your presence and adore you; not to ask anything of you except that privilege, and not to bring any petitions or requests. This is one of those days. You are always worthy. Amen.**

1 Psalm 50:23 *KJV*
2 Isaac Watts, 1674–1748/John Wesley, 1703–1791, "I'll Praise my Maker While I've Breath".
3 Psalm 40:8 *KJV*
4 From *The Seven Spirits*.

# December 16th

## Their god is their appetite

**(Philippians 3:19 *NLT*)**

Eating and drinking have so much to do with the comfort, health, and usefulness of most people, whether in youth, manhood, or old age, that I cannot pass the subject by without offering some suggestions with respect to it, however imperfect they may be.

If it is suggested that religion cannot be brought down to the doings of the table without affecting its dignity, I shall reply in the words of the apostle Paul, "Whether therefore ye eat, or drink, or whatsoever ye do, do all to the glory of God."[1] That is, every meal of which we partake should be a sacrament, and every action we perform a part of our religion. To help my readers to bring their Salvationism to bear upon such ordinary and yet necessary occupations as eating their breakfasts, dinners, teas, and the like, is my purpose in this letter. I am, I must confess, not a little doubtful as to the success that may attend my effort…

Eating and drinking are closely associated with the ability to think. Every intelligent man knows that food, unsuitable in quantity or quality, or taken at unsuitable times, has a bad effect upon his brain. It clips the wings of imagination, dulls the perception, darkens memory, depresses the spirits, and clothes the future with gloom. Many a bad speech, and many a bad bargain too, has come of what is often called a good dinner.

A man's food has much to do with the exercise of his gifts. It affects his ability to sing, to pray, to reason, to talk, or to lead. A hearty meal of the plainest fare, or a very small quantity of richer food, will often clothe my soul with torpor, make my brain feel like a log of wood, and render speaking or writing a positive torture. I have no doubt that it is so, more or less, with numbers of other speakers, some of these being either ignorant of the fact, or too fond of the knife-and-fork business to curb their appetites for the sake of the profitable discharge of their duties.[2]

**Father, it seems a little odd to think of you as the Lord of my lunch, yet that is what you are – you are either Lord of all, or not Lord at all! Help me, I pray, whether it is in regard to a bowl of soup, or a snack, or dinner in a restaurant, to grant you control of my appetite. Thank you, Father, for your gracious provision. Amen.**

1 1 Corinthians 10:31 *KJV*
2 From *Religion for Every Day.*

# December 17th

Standing behind him at his feet, weeping, she began to wet his feet with her tears

(Luke 7:38 *ESV*)

The captain says: "I ain't going to let these people die in their sins, and go to Hell, if I can stop them"...

There's Tom Hardnut; he's one of the best soldiers we have now; but he was as stupid as you could imagine before he was converted. He used to sit through the meetings, and look about him when everybody else was crying, as if he hadn't got any soul at all. But one night the captain crept up to him in the after-meeting, and began to talk to him about his sins, and Jesus Christ, and Hell; but, bless your soul! Tommy only laughed in his face. And then the captain fell on his knees, and began to pray. And he did pray. It was enough to melt a stone; and when the captain opened his eyes and saw Tom as unconcerned as ever, he burst into tears, and downright sobbed again; and then Tom began to cry himself, and rushed out to the penitent form; and I have never seen anybody seeking salvation shed such a lot of tears as Tom did that very night.

Then, there's Deborah Do-as-you-please. She's the best junior sergeant[1] we have. But wasn't she a character! She used to mock until I was afraid that some day she would die with some ridiculing of religion on her lips. Well, one night, the Divisional Officer was at the corps, and he had been talking about the Judgment Day, and the children of pious parents having to be parted from their fathers and mothers for ever and ever, and it was very affecting, and everybody felt so, even if they didn't show it. But Deborah, whose mother was a good woman, and died praying for her daughter, was joking with her companions...

The captain couldn't stand it no longer; but he just went down to her seat, and sat down beside her, and talked to her about her mother so kind and tender like that at last she gave in, and marched to the penitent form, and got thoroughly and properly saved.[2]

**Lord, when it comes to leading people to Jesus, may we never be afraid of tears, either our own, or theirs. May we regard them as beautiful if they clear the way for someone to receive sight of your mercy. Amen.**

1 Responsible for a Sunday school class.
2 From *Sergeant-Major Do-Your-Best.*

# December 18th

**The animals of the forest are mine, and I own the cattle on a thousand hills**

**(Psalm 50:10 *NLT*)**

I am aware that there are few subjects upon which there are such fierce controversies as the possibilities of making a livelihood out of smallholdings, but Irish cottiers[1] do it, and in regions infinitely worse adapted for the purpose than our Essex corn lands,[2] and possessing none of the advantages which civilization and cooperation place at the command of an intelligently directed body of husbandmen.

Go to the Swiss valleys and examine for yourself the miserable patches of land, hewed out, as it were, from the heart of the granite mountains, where the cottager grows his crops and makes a livelihood. No doubt he has his alp, where his cows pasture in summer-time, and his other occupations which enable him to supplement the scanty yield of his farm garden among the crags; but if it pays the Swiss mountaineer in the midst of the eternal snows, far removed from any market, to cultivate such miserable soil in the brief summer of the high Alps, it is impossible to believe that Englishmen, working on English soil, close to our markets and enjoying all the advantages of cooperation, cannot earn their daily bread by their daily toil. The soil of England is not unkindly, and although much is said against our climate, it is, as Mr Russell Lowell[3] observes, after a lengthened experience of many countries and many climes, "the best climate in the whole world for a labouring man". There are more days in the English year on which a man can work out-of-doors with a spade with comparative comfort than in any other country under Heaven. I do not say that men will make a fortune out of the land, nor do I pretend that we can, under the grey English skies, hope ever to vie with the productiveness of the Jersey farms; but I am prepared to maintain against all-comers that it is possible for an industrious man to grow his rations, provided he is given a spade with which to dig and land to dig in. Especially will this be the case with intelligent direction and the advantages of cooperation.[4]

**You are Lord of all creation; bless and use those who campaign for wise stewardship of all you have provided as evidence of your loving, providential care. Amen.**

1 Cottier (or cotter): a peasant renting a small plot of land from a farmer or landlord. He was free to do with it as he wished.

2 The Salvation Army Farm Colony was established in Hadleigh, Essex, England, in 1891 by General Booth. The poor were given board and lodgings in a City Colony in exchange for a day's work, then moved to a Farm Colony for training in running smallholdings before progressing to Overseas Colonies. The City Colony was set up in Whitechapel, London, in 1889 and two years later Booth put down a deposit on land in Hadleigh.

3 James Russell Lowell (1819–91): American Romantic poet, editor, critic, and diplomat. Quote from *New Zealand Herald* 24 January 1891.

4 From *In Darkest England and the Way Out.*

# DECEMBER 19TH

**THE DRIVING IS LIKE THE DRIVING OF JEHU THE SON OF NIMSHI, FOR HE DRIVES FURIOUSLY**

**(2 Kings 9:20 *ESV*)**

They say we go too fast! This accusation is brought before us in all directions. Our enemies do not like our speed. Our friends are afraid of it. What do they mean? I am a little puzzled to know.

If they had complained that we did not go fast enough, I could understand them. If our enemies had argued that if after all we say about the evils of sin, the terrors of the Judgment Day, and the damnation of Hell, we do not believe in these things ourselves, or we should risk everything and spend everything and work and toil and pray all night and all day until we spread ourselves everywhere, killing ourselves in the undertaking with our terrible earnestness, I could understand that, and feel humbled under the indictment.

If our friends came together and said, "Why don't you increase the speed? Look at the dying millions at home and abroad. You have evidently got a wonderful way of reaching the masses. You have accomplished what no other organization has. You can make them listen and repent and fight and give and suffer and win. You can adapt yourselves to all peoples and countries and climates. Why don't you push on faster – train more cadets – build more barracks – send out more officers – deal with more slums – hunt up more criminals and drunkards and fallen women? Go faster; get up more steam! We will help you. What can we do? We will give you money, publish your principles, build you barracks, and give you our children! Only go on! For God's sake, and for the sake of a dying world, go on!!"

Now, this seems to me would be the natural way of talking for both foes and friends. Anyhow, the latter describes the way I think I should have felt and acted had I been an outsider and fallen in with the Salvation Army. But no! The cry is not "Go faster!" but "You go too fast!" What do they mean? Speed is a good thing and, if combined with safety, the faster the better.[1]

**Lord, there needs to be an urgency about our service for you, for the days are short. However, there is also a need for quieter, slower reflection. Please help me to find the right combination of both, so that I am quick off the mark, yet not moving so fast I miss your directions. Thank you, Lord. Amen.**

1 From *The General's Letters.*

# December 20[TH]

A Samaritan, as he travelled, came where the man was; and when he saw him, he took pity on him. He went to him and bandaged his wounds, pouring on oil and wine. Then he put the man on his own donkey, brought him to an inn and took care of him

(Luke 10:33–34 *NIV*)

When Professor Huxley lived as a medical officer in the East of London, he acquired a knowledge of the actual condition of life of many of its populace which led him long afterwards to declare that the surroundings of the savages of New Guinea were much more conducive to the leading of a decent human existence than those in which many of the East-Enders live.[1] Alas, it is not only in London that such lairs exist in which the savages of civilization lurk and breed. All the great towns in both the Old World and the New[2] have their slums, in which huddle together, in festering and verminous filth, men, women, and children. They correspond to the lepers who thronged the lazar houses of the Middle Ages.[3]

As in those days St Francis of Assisi and the heroic band of saints who gathered under his orders were wont to go and lodge with the lepers at the city gates, so the devoted souls who have enlisted in The Salvation Army take up their quarters in the heart of the worst slums. But whereas the Friars were men, our Slum Brigade is composed of women.[4] I have a hundred of them under my orders, young women for the most part, quartered all of them outposts in the heart of the devil's country. Most of them are the children of the poor who have known hardship from their youth up. Some are ladies born and bred, who have not been afraid to exchange the comfort of a West End drawing room for service amongst the vilest of the vile, and a residence in small and fetid rooms whose walls were infested with vermin. They live the life of the Crucified for the sake of the men and women for whom he lived and died. They form one of the branches of the activity of the Army upon which I dwell with deepest sympathy. They are at the front; they are at close quarters with the enemy… they dwell in the midst of Hell… A Slum Sister is what her name implies, the Sister of the Slum.[5]

**Father of mercies, this day I lift before you those who live in awful poverty, whose living conditions breed sickness and utter despair. Lord, reach out to them, I pray. Amen.**

1 Thomas Henry Huxley (1825–95):English biologist (comparative anatomist).
2 In the context of world history, the term "Old World" includes those parts of the world which were in (indirect) cultural contact from the Bronze Age onwards.
3 Leper colonies named after Lazarus, the patron saint of lepers.
4 Slums are heavily populated areas characterized by squalor and disease. Slum Brigades were teams of Salvationists who moved in to such districts, offering practical care, medical assistance, and spiritual counsel.
5 From *In Darkest England and the Way Out.*

# December 21st

### One who is patient calms a quarrel

(Proverbs 15:18 *NIV*)

I want to say something… upon a very important and somewhat difficult subject; and that is, quarrelling. I need not stop to explain to you what I mean by quarrelling. Every child knows what it is, and most children have had some considerable experience of it in practice.

Quarrelling supposes the existence and display of differences of opinion and feeling between individuals on questions of mutual interest. This often leads to hatred, malice, and slander, and is only too commonly followed by hot words, bad language, hard blows, and other evil doings. Quarrelling is a wretched business. When strangers wrangle it is bad enough; when kindreds or friends fall out it is far worse; but when Salvationists quarrel it is worst of all.

Quarrelling is opposed to the health and happiness of those indulging in it. Who can eat, sleep, work, or do anything else in comfort when the spirit of hatred, malice, and all uncharitableness is gnawing like a canker at his heart? Quarrelling is opposed to the temporal prosperity of those carried away with it. What numbers of people I have known who have lost their situations, bankrupted their families, been ruined in their business, and become estranged from their loved ones for the rest of their days by quarrelling.

Quarrelling destroys all true religion. It is impossible for a man who hates his brother to love God.[1] Quarrelling at once arrests, and too often terminates, the usefulness of Salvationists… But, notwithstanding the hateful character of this sin, some people will quarrel. They never differ in opinion from their comrades without trying to lower them in the estimation of others, by showing up their faults. They are never happy but when they are miserable; they are never at peace but when they are at war. This kind of people always have quarrelled, and always will until the archangel blows his last trump, and proclaims that time shall be no more.

Cain quarrelled with Abel, and the difference ended in blood.[2] Joseph's brethren quarrelled with him, and it very nearly led to murder.[3, 4]

**Prince of Peace, please overshadow your Church afresh with a crucial spirit of harmony, that even in disagreement, your people may be charitable and kind. Amen.**

1 1 John 4:20
2 Genesis 4:1–16
3 Genesis 37
4 From *The Founder's Messages to Soldiers.*

# DECEMBER 22ND

WERE NOT OUR HEARTS BURNING WITHIN US...?

(Luke 24:32 *NIV*)

In the bosom of Jesus Christ there dwelt the deepest hatred of evil. And yet we read that when he beheld the multitude he had compassion on them. When, from the brow of Olivet, he beheld the men whose hearts were so mastered with evil and so bitter in their hatred of the Son of God that they resolved to murder him, he wept over them.[1,2] When he looked down upon them in his last agony on the bloody cross to which they had nailed him, he prayed for their salvation, and broke his heart on their behalf.[3]

Here is an example for us, my comrades. You and I may condemn wickedness. We must condemn it. We cannot help but condemn and hate the drunkenness, the pride, the selfishness, the lust, and a thousand other devilish things that are carried on around us. But if we are possessed of this burning love we shall feel compassionate towards the guilty doers of these hateful things.... Not only compassionate, but willing to suffer on behalf of the evildoers.

A willingness to suffer on behalf of those whom you love is inseparable from all true affection. You will find plenty of examples of this even among the creatures whose love is really only instinct, as it is in the animal creation. You will find more in man with his ordinary instinct. What wonderful things a mother's love will make her do and suffer! No hardship is counted too great. What marvels the love of the patriot will accomplish! How willingly, eagerly, the love of country has carried them to deeds of daring, suffering, and death...

But this love is better than the love of kindred, and country, and friends, which has ordinarily some selfish interest behind it. Burning love unselfishly suffers for its own enemies, and for those it knows to be the foes of God and man. It was this burning love that carried the prophets of old through hardships and suffering and death... It was this burning love that carried Jesus Christ to the cross.[4]

**Amazing love.**

1 Matthew 9:36
2 Luke 19:41
3 Luke 23:34
4 From *The Seven Spirits.*

# December 23^RD

THE MOUNTAINS AND HILLS WILL BURST INTO SONG BEFORE YOU, AND ALL THE TREES OF THE FIELD WILL CLAP THEIR HANDS

**(Isaiah 55:12 *NIV*)**

In considering religion for every day, I cannot pass by the subject of conversation… everyone will know that I mean that interchange of thought and feeling between individuals which is effected by means of speech. Conversation, in one form or another, is, we can readily imagine, a privilege common to all living creatures. We know that the great Father in Heaven holds some sort of high intercourse with the holy beings by whom he is surrounded; and we have reason to believe that he does this through the medium of some celestial language. The archangels and angels, and the seraphim and cherubim, and other inhabitants of Heaven, we are expressly informed, bow before his face, and cry, "Holy, holy, holy, is the Lord [God] Almighty"[1]

The Bible contains the record of many conversations that have taken place between God and his people on the earth, in the past. Indeed, the sacred book is full of messages from Jehovah to men, commencing with, "Thus saith the Lord", and of prayers and thanksgivings addressed to God. All such communication is the nature of conversation – God speaking to man, and man speaking to God.

Then we can be quite sure that the angels talk with each other. The sins and sorrows of our poor world, together with the unremitting and self-sacrificing efforts God is continually making for its salvation, must be a theme of unceasing interest and a topic of untiring conversation to all the inhabitants of the celestial world. And who can doubt in Hell that devils talk over their infernal schemes for the destruction of souls, and recount to each other the progress [they] make in giving them effect? Ah, my God! There is no lack of interesting matter both for reflection and conversation there! The various species of the brute creation also have, beyond question, some means of conveying the feelings they entertain towards each other, that answers to what we call conversation. Many animals have the ability to think, if not reason. The habits of the ant, the bee, the dog, the horse, the eagle, and of many other creatures, furnish ample evidence of this.[2]

**Thank you, Lord, that you deign to speak to me in ways I can understand and enjoy. I praise you because all creation communicates with you in one way or another; you are a God who loves relationship, and a God who graciously senses feelings when we cannot always find words. Guide me in my conversations this day. Amen.**

1 Isaiah 6:3 *NIV*
2 From *Religion for Every Day.*

# December 24th

## Have faith in God

(Mark 11:22 *NIV*)

Religious faith is very much the same thing as any other kind of faith. The difference consists not in the faculty that believes, nor of the use made of it in believing, but in the greatness of the object to which it is directed, and the importance of the blessings that follow its exercise. Having faith in God is, therefore, so far as the act of the mind is concerned, very much the same kind of thing as having faith in man. Now, you know what it is to have faith in your brother, for instance. In the first place, you have to believe what he says.

Well, faith in God is very much the same kind of thing as that. You receive the words spoken or written by your brother as being true. Should anyone throw any doubt upon their accuracy, you would cry out: "I believe what my brother says to be absolutely correct. Has he promised these things? If he has, then, so far as he is able, he will keep his word. What he has promised he will perform."

So you will see that faith in God implies belief in the words he has spoken. However unlikely the things they set forth may appear, or however men may deny their truthfulness, or whatever doubts human opinions or knowledge may seem to throw upon their accuracy, we are to believe that every word he has spoken is true; that every prophecy he has uttered will come to pass; and that every promise he has made will be fulfilled.

But faith is more than believing in the word of God, whether spoken or written. It signifies faith in the individual. It means confidence in the speaker, apart from his words. You will often hear this kind of faith referred to in something like the following manner. A man will say of his friend: "I know him. I know his heart, bless him! I am quite sure he will do what I want him to do, if he can, whether he says so or not. I can trust him."[1]

**Father, you are completely trustworthy, and every word you speak can be relied upon. Your words are true, and your character is without contradiction. Protect my heart this day from whispers of unbelief. I place my confidence in you afresh, giving you praise. Amen.**

1 From *The Founder's Messages to Soldiers.*

# December 25th

"Do not be afraid. I bring you good news that will cause great joy for all the people. Today in the town of David a Saviour has been born to you; he is the Messiah, the Lord. This will be a sign to you: You will find a baby wrapped in cloths and lying in a manger." Suddenly a great company of the heavenly host appeared with the angel, praising God and saying, "Glory to God in the highest heaven, and on earth peace to those on whom his favour rests"

(Luke 2:10–14 *NIV*)

It is considered in this country the correct thing to wish everybody a merry Christmas, and to get one yourself if you can. We pity those who have anything which makes them sad just now, and so it has become an annual custom to be merry, and to help make other people as merry as you possibly can… We like the word "merry", and we will have it in religion if you please. Many people think it altogether out of place there. They will let the children be merry when home for the holidays, having an extra allowance of games and cake. They will let the merchant be merry when his balance sheet has come out on the right side… but we who are always overcoming sin and driving devils, or rescuing captives, or gaining victories over the King's enemies, we soldiers of the cross must always be solemn, and melancholy, and awful, and have our hearts in our shoes, and our words must be few, antiquated, and learned out of a book…

No, we say, and say it thankfully, that we have not been taught religion after this fashion. If, when slaves find freedom, and tradesmen make fortunes, and kindred, or friends, or neighbours are delivered from some threatened calamity, it is allowable to go mad with joy, and to express it by hiring music, and beating drums, and letting off fireworks, and shouting till hoarse, and everybody says that is all right, then by the same rule, if you please, and whether you please or no, we are the slaves who have now our freedom, the people who have made our fortune; we are the men who have seen our kindred and friends and neighbours saved from damnation; and therefore we have a right to be merry… so bring out the music, new music, the merriest music…

This Christmas, let us all get into tune, and let there be heavenly correspondence between the inside "heart" instrument and the outside voice, or whatever other instrument the merry sounds may be produced upon.[1]

**Thank you, God, for your gift beyond words. Thank you for giving us Jesus. Amen.**

1 From *Salvation Soldiery.*

# DECEMBER 26TH

A MAN WILL LEAVE HIS FATHER AND MOTHER AND BE UNITED TO HIS WIFE, AND THE TWO WILL BECOME ONE FLESH. THIS IS A PROFOUND MYSTERY – BUT I AM TALKING ABOUT CHRIST AND THE CHURCH. HOWEVER, EACH ONE OF YOU ALSO MUST LOVE HIS WIFE AS HE LOVES HIMSELF, AND THE WIFE MUST RESPECT HER HUSBAND

(Ephesians 5:31–33 *NIV*)

While I have been busily occupied in working out my scheme for the registration of labour, it has occurred to me more than once, why could not something like the same plan be adopted in relation to men who want wives and women who want husbands? Marriage is with most people largely a matter of opportunity. Many a man and many a woman, who would, if they had come together, have formed a happy household, are leading at this moment miserable and solitary lives, suffering in body and in soul, in consequence of their exclusion from the natural state of matrimony.

Of course, the registration of the unmarried who wish to marry would be a matter of much greater delicacy than the registration of the joiners and stonemasons who wish to find work. But the thing is not impossible. I have repeatedly found in my experience that many a man and many a woman would only be so glad to have a friendly hint as to where they might prosecute their attentions or from which they might receive proposals.

In connection with such an agency, if it were established – for I am not engaging to undertake this task – I am only throwing out a possible suggestion as to the development in the direction of meeting a much-needed want, there might be added training homes for matrimony. My heart bleeds for many a young couple whom I see launching out into the sea of matrimony with no housewifery experience. The young girls who leave our public elementary schools and go out into factories have never been trained to home duties, and yet, when taken to wife, are unreasonably expected to fill worthily the difficult positions of the head of the household and the mother of a family. A month spent before marriage in a training home of housewifery would conduce much more to the happiness of the married life than the honeymoon which immediately follows it… I often marvel when I think of the utter helplessness of the modern woman, compared with the handiness of her grandmother. How many of our girls can even bake a loaf?[1]

**Father, at this time of year, when families join together, I pray for those who would like to be married, but are not; indeed, for everyone for whom the Christmas holidays and festivities can be tense or lonely times. Touch us all with your presence. Amen.**

1 From *In Darkest England and the Way Out.*

# December 27th

They saw the child with his mother Mary, and they bowed down and worshipped him. Then they opened their treasures and presented him with gifts of gold, frankincense and myrrh

(Matthew 2:11 *NIV*)

Children should, when old enough, and sufficiently instructed to understand, be taught to read the Bible systematically. Children should read, morning and evening and at noonday, the portion of Scripture marked for the day in the *Salvation Soldier's Guide*. Explanations and illustrations, so far as there is opportunity, should be given by parents on what is read. While children are young the facts and teachings of the Bible, with explanations adapted to their age and intelligence, should be supplied them. Any number of books of this description can be obtained, such as the *Peep of Day*,[1] and others of that class. After the Bible, we recommend for the children of Salvationists, *The Little Soldier*, *The War Cry*, and other publications of The Salvation Army,[2] together with such other books as are calculated to edify and instruct them in all that concerns a godly life. To these may be added books of history, biography, natural history, travels in foreign lands, and others of a good sound moral character…

We should distinctly forbid *Jack the Giant-killer*, *Goody Two-shoes*, *Jack and the Bean-stalk*,[3] and all the fairy-tale nonsense put together with, we are sorry to say, most of the so-called "moral and religious" stories which are usually thought proper reading for the children. It is just as wicked and as stupid, if not more so, to instil silly rubbish into the minds of children, as into the minds of men. Why it should be thought right – nay, essential – in the one case more than in the other we never could comprehend. But, as we have said elsewhere, the intelligence of children is generally underestimated and, consequently, any foolish trash is thought good enough for the little ones so that it makes them laugh and passes away the idle hours… The love of the marvellous can be met and satisfied just as easily by facts, and facts which are far stranger than fiction, of which the world is full; so that there is no need for doing this with a pack of stupid lies, which are sooner or later found out to be such by the children.[4]

**Times have changed, Father! However, in our giving of gifts, guide us to be generous, thoughtful, and wise. Cause us to remember, too, children who will receive no Christmas presents, or any love at all, and to include them in our giving. Amen.**

1 "A series of religious instruction the infant mind is capable of receiving, with illustrations" by Favell Lee Mortimer (1894).
2 *The Little Soldier* became *The Young Soldier* and exists today as *Kids Alive!* – the only weekly Christian comic for children in the United Kingdom.
3 Popular children's stories of the time.
4 From *The Training of Children*.

# December 28th

## As for me, I trust in the Lord

(Psalm 31:6 *NIV*)

Jesus Christ said to his disciples, and through them he says to you, "In the world ye shall have tribulation", "If they have persecuted me, they will also persecute you".

God has promised to support you in your trials while you walk in the light; that is, while you do his blessed will. Some of the most beautiful and precious passages to be found in the Bible describe the consolations which he promises to his soldiers while they are battling with the difficulties, persecutions, and sufferings of life…

He promises you his support. "The eternal God is thy refuge, and underneath are the everlasting arms." He promises you the comfort of his presence. "When thou passest through the waters, I will be with thee; and through the rivers, they shall not overflow thee: when thou walkest through the fire, thou shalt not be burned; neither shall the flame kindle upon thee." He promises you victory. "God is faithful, who will not suffer you to be tempted above that ye are able; but will with the temptation also make a way to escape, that ye may be able to bear it." "Nay, in all these things we are more than conquerors through him that loved us."

Tribulations are intended for your profit. "All things work together for good to them that love God." Rightly accepted, they will promote your holiness and usefulness, and help you to understand and struggle for the welfare of those around you. Paul says, "For our light affliction, which is but for a moment, worketh for us a far more exceeding and eternal weight of glory". What is more, they strengthen faith, and help the formation of that character which God desires his children to possess. And then, at the end, they add lustre to the glory of that bright inheritance, where it can, truthfully, be said of those who have fought their way through, "These are they which came out of great tribulation, and have washed their robes, and made them white in the blood of the Lamb."[1, 2]

**Father, by your grace, count me faithful in the day that tries by fire. Amen.**

1 John 16:33, John 15:20, Deuteronomy 33:27, Isaiah 43:2, 1 Corinthians 10:13, Romans 8:37, Romans 8:28, 2 Corinthians 4:17, Revelation 7:14 *KJV*

2 From *Religion for Every Day.*

# December 29th

In my devotion to the temple of my God I now give my personal treasures of gold and silver for the temple of my God, over and above everything I have provided for this holy temple

(1 Chronicles 29:3 *NIV*)

There seems to be a mistaken notion very generally abroad as to the amount of money people give for religious work. So far as I have had the opportunity of judging – and that opportunity has been rather a considerable one – there is no other object in which Christian people are interested that they treat so shabbily as the religious society with which they are associated, and there is no being whom they deal with so meanly as the God whom they profess to hold in such high regard and for whom they boast such all-absorbing love.

You will hear them sounding out in their songs and their prayers and their testimonies their willingness to suffer and sacrifice and die for him, but when you ask them to give him a little of their money that is quite another thing. If they don't refuse you point-blank, they will contrive to get out of the obligation by the presentation of the smallest coin that will appear at all decent to those around them – often, in fact, leaving you to the wretched suspicion that if it were not for the sake of appearances, they would not give anything at all!

Many reasons are given for this ungenerous treatment of the cause they reckon to hold so dear. Among others it will be said that this action may be traced to natural meanness. These people, they say, are stingy by nature, and the smallness of their contributions is only a natural expression of the narrowness of their disposition.

Some say the reason of this meanness is their unbelief. They affirm boldly that if these people really believed in God as they profess to do, they would require no entreating to give him a little of their substance, but would lay themselves and all they possess at his feet. Some attribute their contracted generosity to ingratitude. If there was any measurable realization of the extent of the indebtedness under which they are laid to their Lord, they would be the happiest and most lavish of givers. I do not for a moment question but that they would![1]

**Take my silver and my gold, Lord. As this year moves towards its conclusion, please grant me your guidance in assessing my personal giving, however that giving takes shape. May I approach the year ahead knowing that what I settle on giving is pleasing to you. Thank you, Lord. Amen.**

1 From *The Founder Speaks Again.*

# DECEMBER 30TH

WE WILL SHARE WITH YOU WHATEVER GOOD THINGS THE LORD GIVES US
(Numbers 10:32 *NIV*)

It is objected that the classes we seek to benefit are too ignorant and depraved for Christian effort, or for effort of any kind, to reach and reform. Look at the tramps, the drunks, the harlots, the criminals. How confirmed they are in their idle and vicious habits. It will be said, indeed has been already said by those with whom I have conversed, that I don't know them; which statement cannot, I think, be maintained, for if I don't know them, who does?

I admit, however, that thousands of this class are very far gone from every sentiment, principle and practice of right conduct. But I argue that these poor people cannot be much more unfavourable subjects for the work of regeneration than are many of the savages and heathen tribes, in the conversion of whom Christians universally believe; for whom they beg large sums of money, and to whom they send their best and bravest people.

These poor people are certainly embraced in the divine plan of mercy. To their class, the Saviour especially gave his attention when he was on the earth, and for them he most certainly died on the cross. Some of the best examples of Christian faith and practice, and some of the most successful workers for the benefit of mankind, have sprung from this class, of which we have instances recorded in the Bible, and any number in the history of the Church and of The Salvation Army.

It may be objected that while this scheme ["Darkest England"] would undoubtedly assist one class of the community by making steady, industrious workmen, it must thereby injure another class by introducing so many new hands into the labour market, already so seriously overstocked… If the increase of workers, which this scheme will certainly bring about, was the beginning and the end of it, it would certainly present a somewhat serious aspect. But, even on that supposition, I don't see how the skilled worker could leave his brothers to rot in their present wretchedness, though their rescue should involve the sharing of a portion of his wages.[1]

**This is a challenging principle, Father – the idea that my going without in one way or another might help someone else to enjoy a better standard of living. Yet, I gladly commit to this Christ-like standard; to live simply so that others may simply live. I do so with thanksgiving, knowing that you are no one's debtor. Thank you, Lord, for the privilege of sharing. Amen.**

1 From *In Darkest England and the Way Out.*

# December 31st

## Hitherto hath the Lord helped us

(1 Samuel 7:12 *KJV*)

I might have chosen as my life's work the housing of the poor. That, in early life, presented itself to me as a most important question, most closely identified with the morals, happiness, and religion of the poor people. I honour those who are devoting themselves to the solution of the problem. But has not The Salvation Army done something in this direction? If you look abroad, you will find hundreds and thousands up and down the world who tonight have comfortable homes through the influence of the Army; indeed, there are thousands of men, women, and children who but for its assistance would have had no homes at all. For instance, there are over 200,000 homeless men sleeping under our roofs every week.

I might have given myself up to the material benefit of the working classes. I might have drawn attention to the small rate of wages and striven to help them in that direction. But have we not done something for them? Are there not tens of thousands who, but for the Army, might have been almost starved? If we had not done much in the way of increasing income, have we not done a great deal in inculcating principles of economy and self-denial which have taught the poor a better use of their wages? Their total abstinence from drink, tobacco, gambling, and wasteful finery has made hundreds of thousands of people better off than they were before they came under our influence.

I might also have given up myself to promoting temperance reform. This is a most important business. Drunkenness seems to be the curse of every civilized nation under the sun; and I have all my life honoured the men and women who have devoted themselves to the solving of that problem. But has not The Salvation Army done something in that direction? Every Salvationist all over the world is a strict abstainer from intoxicating liquor, and the children are growing up to follow in their parents' footsteps. Tens of thousands of the most devilish and abandoned drunkards that the world has ever known have been reached and reclaimed, made into sober men and women, good fathers and mothers, good sons and daughters, and useful members of society.

I might have chosen as my life's object the physical improvement and health of the people by launching out on to a medical career. As a matter of fact, I think the medical system is capable of improvement, and if I had been a doctor I should certainly have paid more attention to diet than to drugs. I am not a great believer in drugs, and when doctors advise me to take a drug, I ask them if they have ever taken it themselves. We have done something in the way of medical aid, and possess at the present time twenty-four hospitals, while others are coming into existence, and there is no knowing to what extent the enterprise will reach in this direction. As it is, we deal with thousands of patients every year.

I might have chosen to devote my life to the interests of the criminal world. The hundreds and thousands of poor wretches who are pining in the prison cells, while we are sitting here at ease, ought to have our sympathy and our help. I heard of a man the other day who had spent fifty years of his life in prison, and the whole of his thefts did not amount to £20. He pleaded that he had never had a chance in life, but when he comes out of prison – if he does come out – the Army will give him a chance. Some 178 women prisoners have been admitted to our homes in this country during the year, and of these, 130 have proved satisfactory. We have done something for the criminal, but it is only the commencement of a mighty work the Army is destined to do for the unhappy class.

I might have carried out my consecration for the improvement of the community by devoting myself to politics. I might have turned Conservative, or I might have been a Radical, or a Home Ruler, or a Socialist, or have joined the Labour Party, or, what is more profitable, if the catastrophe had occurred, I might have formed another party. I saw something better than belonging to either party, and that by being the friend of every party I was far more likely to secure the blessing of the multitude and the end I had in view. And the object I chose all those years ago embraced every effort, contained in its heart the remedy for every form of misery and sin and wrong to be found upon the earth, and every method of reclamation needed by human nature.

And now, my comrades and friends, I must say goodbye. I am going into dry-dock for repairs, but the Army will not be allowed to suffer, either financially or spiritually, or in any other way by my absence; and in the long future I think it will be seen – I shall not be here to see, but you will – that the Army will answer every doubt and banish every fear and strangle every slander, and by its marvellous success show to the world that it is the work of God and that the General has been his servant… While women weep, as they do now, I'll fight; while little children go hungry, as they do now, I'll fight; while men go to prison, in and out, in and out, as they do now, I'll fight; while there is a drunkard left, while there is a poor lost girl upon the streets, while there remains one dark soul without the light of God, I'll fight – I'll fight to the very end![1]

**To God be the glory.**

1 Reputed to be William Booth's last public address, delivered in London's Royal Albert Hall on 9 May 1912. Booth was promoted to Glory on 20 August 1912. From *The Founder Speaks Again*.

## What will you do with Jesus?

## Asks the Founder General William Booth in his last Easter address

Jealous of the popularity of our Lord, ignorant of his divinity, hating the purity of his teaching, rebelling against the self-sacrificing character of his life, and for other reasons, the High Priest, chief dignitaries and leading citizens of Jerusalem resolved to compass his destruction. But not having the power of life and death in their tribunals, they denounced him to Pilate, the Roman governor, as a religious impostor, a stirrer-up of strife and an enemy of the government, requesting that Jesus be put to death.

Pilate received our Lord, examined the charges made against him, but not being able to prove him guilty of any offence worthy of death, proposed to release him. To the utter amazement of Pilate, with one voice the crowd called, "Release unto us Barabbas!" [see Luke 23:18 *KJV*]. Pilate tried to reason with them, but they only cried out the more, "Barabbas, Barabbas!" Rising from his throne and taking the Saviour by the hand, in order to better command their compassion, he led him forth, and asked the question, "What shall I do, then, with Jesus?"

Now, as Pilate led Jesus forth on that eventful occasion, so in spirit, with my heart full of reverence, I bring that same blessed Saviour before your attention and ask the same question, "What will you do with Jesus?" I do not say, "What shall I do?" That is a question that was settled a long time back. Sixty-seven years ago I laid myself at his feet and took him to my heart. I have never regretted that consecration. I never shall. Out of it wonderful things have grown.

It is not what shall I do with Jesus, but what will you do with him? Can I help you to the right decision?

You must do something with him. Neutrality is impossible. The possession of the opportunity for doing the right thing imposes the obligation to do it. There is no middle course possible here. You must be either for him or against him. You must either take him to your heart or reject him to your ruin. Your treatment of Jesus Christ will determine your Heavenly Father's treatment of you. In deciding how you will treat this offer, remember what it means to you. Remember that Jesus Christ brings you from his Father the free and full forgiveness for every past sin, reconciliation with himself, purity, power, happiness in life, happiness in death, and happiness forever. On your treatment of him hangs your everlasting destiny – Heaven or Hell. Your treatment of Jesus Christ will determine the salvation or damnation of men and women living around you or who will live after you. That is a very serious business. Suppose that High Priest and the Jewish crowd had accepted Jesus Christ and had crowned him the Lord of their hearts. Who can conceive the difference that decision would have made?

No man liveth to himself. No man can confine the consequences of his conduct to himself.

In view of these solemn considerations I want to ask you, what will do with the blessed Saviour, and what will you do with him now? There are several courses to you. What will you do with him? Not, what have you done? What are intending to do, in the future, when you are dying? I bring him before you and demand an answer to my question. What will you do? Shall I indicate a few courses?

You can deny his divine mission – you can say he was an impostor. There were plenty in those days who did this, and there are plenty who do the same thing in our day. Some went so far as to say he had a devil. What do you say to that? No, that does not suit you. Well, you can deny your need of any Saviour. You can say. "I have no soul, I shall have no hereafter," or you can pretend that you never sinned and say, "There'll be no Judgment. I don't need a Saviour." That is what the Sadducees said, and [there] are thousands who say the same thing in our day. There is another course. You can openly reject him. Right or wrong, you can simply say, "I won't have him." There are plenty who took this course [while] he was on earth. They were there in force that day. Instead of taking him to their hearts, they sent him to the cruel tree. Look at their bloodthirsty eyes. Listen to their maddened cries. See them pluck the hair from his blessed cheeks and spit upon his sacred face, clothe him in the mocking robes and try to call down curses from Heaven on his head. They preferred Barabbas.

You can pretend to accept him, call yourself by his name, although your heart is far from him. There were any number who adopted that course while he was on earth. He upbraided them. "Why call ye me Lord, and do not the things which I say?" [See Luke 6:46 *KJV*.] What do you say about being an empty, powerless, worldly formalist? You say, "No. If ever I do anything with religion I will have the real thing. I won't be a hypocrite."

There is another course. You can treat the whole matter with indifference. There was a crowd in Jerusalem on that day who took no notice whatever of the affair. The shops were all open. The buyers and sellers were all busy. There were marriages and feasts, parties and amusements, all in full swing while the Son of God was hanging on the cross. These people were indifferent. They did not care.

Here is one more person whose example you may follow. What do you say to being a Judas? Will you betray and sell your Lord as Judas sold him? O Backslider! You were once a soldier of the cross. Yes, you loved him, praised him, swore you would die for him, and then deserted him.

What did you leave your Lord for? How much did you get by the transaction? Judas got thirty pieces of silver.

There is one more course you can take, and I recommend it with all my heart. It has been before you many a day. I place it before you once more. It may be the last chance you will have of accepting it. Accept this blessed Jesus as your Saviour and submit to his authority. Wash every stain away in his blood, enthrone him in your heart as your King and fight for him all the rest of your days. That is what I did more than sixty years ago. Do it now![1]

1 From *The War Cry*, USA National, 5 April 1980.

# Bibliography

Barnes, C. J., *The Founder Speaks Again. A Selection of the Writings of William Booth* gathered from a variety of Salvation Army publications. St Albans, UK: The Campfield Press, 1960.

Booth, W., *Essential Measures,* letters to Territorial Commanders. Written on Christmas Day 1911. London, UK: Salvation Books, reprinted 2009.

Booth, W., *In Darkest England and the Way Out*, London: International Headquarters of The Salvation Army 1890. Reprinted Milton Keynes, UK: Lightning Source UK Ltd, 2010.

Booth, W., *Letters to Salvationists on Religion for Every Day, Volume 1* These letters were, with one or two exceptions, originally published in *The Social Gazette* and *The War Cry*, two of the weekly publications of The Salvation Army in the UK. First published 1902, reprinted New Delhi, India: Isha Books, 2013.

Booth, W., *Purity of Heart*, first published in 1902, reprinted London: Salvation Books, 2010.

Booth, W., *Salvation Soldiery by the General of The Salvation Army,* first published by The Salvation Army International Headquarters in 1899. Reprinted with permission by Salvo Publishing, The Salvation Army, Australia Southern Territory, 2012. Contains scanned pages of the 1899 edition of *Salvation Soldiery*, subtitled *A series of addresses on the requirements of Jesus Christ's service.*

Booth, W., *The Founder's Messages to Soldiers During Years 1907–8 with Preface by The General,* St Albans, UK: The Campfield Press, 1921.

Booth, W., *The Founder Speaks, extracts from the writings of William Booth, The Army's first General.* Originally published for The William Booth Centenary Call Campaign, 1928–29. London: The Salvation Army.

Booth, W., *The Salvation War, 1883. Under the Generalship of William Booth,* Salvation Army Book Depot, London, Paris, Australia, United States, India.

Booth, W., *The Seven Spirits or "What I Teach My Officers"*, outlines of a series of addresses by General Booth, delivered to officers at the International Congress, London in 1904. Salvation Army International Headquarters 1907. Reprinted Milton Keynes, UK: Lightning Source UK Ltd.

Founder, The, *The Training of Children or How to Make the Children into Saints and Soldiers of Jesus Christ,* third edition. London: Salvationist Publishing & Supplies Ltd,1927.

General of The Salvation Army, *The General's Letters, 1885. Being a reprint from* The War Cry *of letters to soldiers and friends scattered throughout the world,* London, New York, Melbourne, Toronto: The Salvation Army Publishing Department, 1986.

*Salvation Army Handbook of Doctrine, The,* London: Salvation Books, 2010.

*Song Book of The Salvation Army, The,*, St Albans, UK: The Campfield Press, 1986.

*War Cry, The,* USA National, 1980.

## Internet Sources

https://archive.org/details/sergeantmajordo00bootgoog (accessed 21.01.15) General Booth, *Sergeant-Major Do-Your-Best Of Darkington No. 1, Sketches of the Inner Life of a Salvation Army Corps,* The Salvation Army Book Department, London, Melbourne, New York, Toronto, Cape Town, 1906.

www.biblegateway.com (accessed 21.01.15) *The Message* Copyright © 1993, 1994, 1995, 1996, 2000, 2001, 2002 by Eugene H. Peterson. NKJV *New King James Version* Copyright © 1982 by Thomas Nelson, Inc.

www.biblehub.com (accessed 21.01.15) online Bible study suite regarding Bible references and translations. NIV *New International Version*, Copyright © 1973, 1978, 1984, 2011 by Biblica, Inc. NIV *New International Version* Copyright © 1973, 1978, 1984 by International Bible Society. NLT *New Living Translation*, copyright ©1996, 2004, 2007. Used by permission of Tyndale House Publishers, Inc., Carol Stream, Illinois 60188. ESV *English Standard Version* copyright © 2001 by Crossway Bibles, a publishing ministry of Good News Publishers. NASB *New American Standard Bible* Copyright © 1960, 1962, 1963, 1968, 1971, 1972, 1973, 1975, 1977, 1995 by The Lockman Foundation, La Habra, Calif. KJB *King James Bible* Text courtesy of BibleProtector.com Section Headings Courtesy INT Bible © 2012. NET *New English Translation Bible* copyright © 1996–2006 by Biblical Studies Press, L.L.C.

www.christianhistoryinstitute.org (accessed 21.01.15) regarding William Booth's theology of redemption.

www.openbible.info (accessed 21.01.15) Bible references, usually ESV.

www.wikipedia.org regarding details of Salvation Army history, persons referred to (Salvation Army and otherwise), and national and international events referred to by Booth. Likewise, regarding geographical locations mentioned by Booth.